The 1958 Balt

GREAT TEAMS IN PRO FOOTBALL HISTORY

The 1966 Green Bay Packers:
Profiles of Vince Lombardi's Super Bowl I Champions
(George Bozeka, editor, 2016)

The 1958 Baltimore Colts:
Profiles of the NFL's First Sudden Death Champions
(George Bozeka, editor, 2018)

The 1958 Baltimore Colts

Profiles of the NFL's First Sudden Death Champions

EDITED BY GEORGE BOZEKA

Associate Editors
Denis Crawford, Ron Fitch, Michael Frank,
David Krell, John Maxymuk and *Kenn Tomasch*

GREAT TEAMS IN PRO FOOTBALL HISTORY

McFarland & Company, Inc., Publishers
Jefferson, North Carolina

All photographs are courtesy of the
Indianapolis Colts, Inc., unless otherwise noted.

LIBRARY OF CONGRESS CATALOGUING-IN-PUBLICATION DATA

Library of Congress Cataloging-in-Publication Data
Names: Bozeka, George.
Title: The 1958 Baltimore Colts : profiles of the NFL's
first sudden death champions / edited by George Bozeka ;
associate editors Denis Crawford, Ron Fitch, Michael Frank,
David Krell, John Maxymuk and Kenn Tomasch.
Description: Jefferson, North Carolina : McFarland & Company, Inc.,
Publishers, 2018. | Series: Great teams in pro football history |
Includes bibliographical references and index.
Identifiers: LCCN 2018017579 | ISBN 9781476671451
(softcover : acid free paper) ∞
Subjects: LCSH: Baltimore Colts (Football team)—History. |
Football—Maryland—Baltimore—History.
Classification: LCC GV956.B3 A13 2018 | DDC 796.332/64097526—dc23
LC record available at https://lccn.loc.gov/2018017579

BRITISH LIBRARY CATALOGUING DATA ARE AVAILABLE

ISBN (print) 978-1-4766-7145-1
ISBN (ebook) 978-1-4766-3455-5

Front cover: Baltimore fullback Alan Ameche runs though a hole in the
New York Giants defense in the 1958 NFL Championship Game on December 28
in Yankee Stadium (photograph courtesy of the Indianapolis Colts)

Printed in the United States of America

*McFarland & Company, Inc., Publishers
Box 611, Jefferson, North Carolina 28640
www.mcfarlandpub.com*

Acknowledgments

George Bozeka

This book on the 1958 Baltimore Colts represents the second entry in the Professional Football Researchers Association's (PFRA) series profiling "Great Teams in Pro Football History." The first book in the series, which covered the 1966 Green Bay Packers, was published in 2016. Special thanks to Mark Durr and the PFRA board of directors for their helpful guidance and support throughout the development and completion of this project.

This book project has been a collaborative effort of the PFRA. Thanks to all our contributors for their commitment and for the many hours they spent researching, writing, and rewriting the biographies and features included in this book.

I would like to thank Jon Kendle of the Ralph Wilson, Jr., Pro Football Research and Preservation Center at the Pro Football Hall of Fame for his help in providing archived files to our contributors and photographs of John Steadman and Cameron Snyder for the book. I would also like to thank Pete Ward, the chief operating officer for the Indianapolis Colts, for his help in securing permission from the Colts organization to use photos from various Colts publications of the 1950s in the book. Thanks to Mark Palczewski for sharing a photo of Memorial Stadium from his personal archives for the book, and to Syracuse University, Stanford University, the Detroit Public Library, and the National Baseball Hall of Fame and Museum for sharing photos of Avatus Stone, Dick Horn, Ernie Harwell, Chuck Thompson, Bailey Goss, Sam Lacy, and Bob Wolff for the book.

Special thanks to David Standish and Joshua Anderson for conducting interviews of Jack Call and Leo Sanford, both surviving members of the 1958 Colts, and to Kenneth R. Crippen for his help in compiling interview contact information for the book and securing a release from the family of the late Art Donovan to use an interview Ken conducted with Art before his death for the book. Further thanks to John Vorperian for interviewing Bob Wolff for the book. John was one of the last people to interview the broadcasting legend before his death in 2017.

Thanks to Rick Schabowski for researching and compiling a newspaper article database on the 1958 Colts for our contributors.

Finally, special thanks to associate editors Denis Crawford, Ron Fitch, Michael Frank, David Krell, John Maxymuk and Kenn Tomasch for their help during the editing process.

Table of Contents

Preface

George Bozeka

The saga of the 1958 Baltimore Colts is one of redemption. The team was a lovable group of castoffs and characters, but talented. During his pregame pep talk before the 1958 NFL championship game, Weeb Ewbank famously went around the locker room and reminded his players of previous rejections and slights during their football careers. Ewbank told each player he had been unknown, unwanted or disrespected, and he didn't spare himself during his motivational speech. He reminded his players he was also an unknown of humble beginnings. Ewbank then told the 1958 Colts they could overcome that adversity by being at peace with themselves. With a victory over the New York Giants at Yankee Stadium in the title game their journey would be complete.

The 1958 title game represented a matchup of the Colts and the glamour team of the NFL, the New York Giants of Gifford, Conerly, Rote, Summerall, Huff, and Robustelli. Whereas the Colts were a group of blue collar guys in a blue collar town, in 1958 you would more than likely have found the Giants rubbing elbows with celebrities like Frank Sinatra, Jackie Gleason, Ed Sullivan, Mickey Mantle and Joe DiMaggio at Toots Shor's, P. J. Clarke's, and other legendary New York watering holes, eating dinner at 21, or taking in nightclub shows at the Copacabana and Latin Quarter. Having decisively won the NFL championship in 1956, the Giants were the talk of the Big Apple.

In contrast to the glitzy, big city atmosphere of New York, Baltimore had a friendly small town mentality and a bit of an inferiority complex, but the city absolutely loved its hard working, resilient Colts. The Colts and their fans were one.

Against this backdrop, the 1958 Colts would accept Ewbank's challenge and win the first sudden death game in NFL championship game history, defeating the Giants 23–17. Many consider the game the greatest ever played.

Nineteen fifty-eight was a simpler time for professional athletes and fans. In many ways, the Colts were the quintessential team of the 1950s. It was still a black and white world socially, politically, and athletically, but it was also a decade of flux, as the nation was slowly beginning to morph into the modern, complex society we know today.

There wasn't a huge difference between the socioeconomic status of the players and fans then, as there is today. Many of the Colts players lived in the same neighborhoods as their fans and worked in the same businesses during the off season. One Colts player even rode back to Baltimore on the same celebratory train with the fans after their compelling victory. That sense of togetherness—as a team and with their community—was at the very heart of the success the 1958 Colts experienced. Mix in the desire to prove everyone wrong and you have a team poised for greatness.

The Professional Football Researchers Association (PFRA) is a nonprofit corporation that was founded and organized in 1979 in Canton, Ohio, at the Pro Football Hall of Fame. The purposes of the organization are to foster the study of professional football as a significant cultural and athletic institution; to establish an accurate historical account of professional football; and to disseminate research information. In 2016, the PFRA began a book series on Great Teams in Pro Football History.

Following in the footsteps of our initial entry in the series on the 1966 Green Bay Packers, the life stories of the 1958 Colts players and coaches from Unitas and Berry to Marchetti and Lipscomb to Ewbank and Bridgers are inspiring, enlightening, amusing, and at times tragic.

This book offers a detailed history of the Colts' 1958 season, including coach and player biographies, game summaries and statistics, photographs, and feature essays about the city of Baltimore in the 1950s, the Colts' mercurial owner Carroll Rosenbloom, the Colts' training camp and preseason, the 1958 draft, how the team was built, Memorial Stadium, and the Baltimore Colts Marching Band. Biographies of key media personalities that covered the team complete the book.

Contributors to the project thoroughly researched the 1958 Colts by consulting newspaper articles, magazines, media guides, yearbooks, programs, Internet sites and books written by and about the team and its members. Some contributors also visited the research center at the Pro Football Hall of Fame to review materials about the team, and others conducted interviews with surviving members of the team.

The 1958 title game was a seminal moment in pro football history, laying the foundation with the American public for the ultra-popular spectacle that pro football would become, and for the marriage of the sport with television. The 1958 Colts are a deserving choice as the second entry in PFRA's Great Teams in Pro Football History book series, as we celebrate the 60th anniversary of their landmark sudden death victory over the Giants.

PART 1

The City and the Organization

Baltimore in the Fifties

Patrick Gallivan

In general, most folks have characterized the years 1950 through 1959 as a bland period marked by stability. After decades of depression and war, Americans looked forward to living the American dream. In the view of some, it may have been the best of times; marked by low divorce rates and a booming economy. In sports, baseball stood as the undisputed National Pastime and professional football hadn't yet hit its stride.

New York City ruled major league baseball. Seemingly, the sport's champions played home games at Yankee Stadium in the Bronx, Ebbets Field in Brooklyn or the Polo Grounds in Manhattan. In 1951, all three New York teams finished on top of the standings with the Yankees winning the American League pennant, and the Giants and Dodgers tied atop the National League. During the 1950s, New York teams won 14 of the 20 pennants and eight of the ten World Series. New York players won 11 of the 20 MVP awards.

Living in the shadows of and competing with cities like New York, Philadelphia, and Washington, D.C., Baltimore has always had something of an inferiority complex. "Baltimore," native son Mark Kram wrote in *Sports Illustrated*, "is an anonymous city even to those who live there, a city that draws a laugh even from Philadelphia, a sneer from Washington, with a hundred tag lines that draw neither smile nor sneer from the city: Nickel Town, Washington's Brooklyn. A Loser's Town."[1]

"Baltimore is a blue-collar, working-class town, perhaps best known for its row houses with white marble steps and painted window screens, its harbor and Chesapeake Bay crabs, its postindustrial decline and quirky charm," wrote Daniel A. Nathan in *Rooting for the Home Team*.[2]

"A sweaty city of steel mills and stevedores, Baltimore was viewed by much of the nation as a smokestack among the glistening skyscrapers of the Eastern seaboard," wrote Jon Morgan. "The post–World War II boom had brought new wealth and sophistication to New York, Philadelphia, and Washington. But Baltimore, bulked up by wartime shipyards and aircraft factories, was still strictly a blue-collar town best known for its crab houses and sleazy red-light district."[3]

Today, Baltimore bears the nickname "Charm City," but that wasn't always the case. After decades of second-class doldrums, the city convened several of the leading advertising and creative directors in a conference in 1975. Mayor William Donald Schaefer made the task sound simple enough. He wanted an advertising campaign that improved the city's image both internally and externally.

Mayor Schaefer wanted a quick fix to solve a decades old problem. New York had Broadway, Washington, the nation's capital and Philadelphia the Liberty Bell, but what did Baltimore have to offer? Some called it Washington's Brooklyn, a reference to the relationship between Manhattan and the rest of New York City. Still others saw it as just a town on the way to somewhere else. It provided the perfect place to stop and refuel on a trip from D.C. to Philadelphia.

Back in the early 1950s the loser attitude spread through the city. Its sports teams couldn't manage to win a title. For most of the 1950s, the Colts and Orioles both failed to field winning teams. Then in 1958 the football team lead by Johnny Unitas mounted success in Memorial Stadium. Baltimore did more than overcome losing records during the decade. The 1950s saw great social change throughout Baltimore. At the beginning of the decade, the restrictions of Jim Crow remained largely intact. But by 1960, most public places had opened to blacks. Movie theatres and lunch counters began to serve minorities. Schools and neighborhoods began to integrate, albeit slowly.

Today the city's Inner Harbor is a tourist destination. Back in the Colonial Days, the port provided an entry point for immigrants coming to the United States. Baltimore's location at the unofficial border between north and south made it a hub for manufacturing and trading goods. The immigrants arriving in America through Baltimore's harbor found work at the city's packing houses, railroad lines and right there on the docks. Meanwhile, factories, busy with shipbuilding and steel making, offered employment opportunities.

As immigrants of Eastern and Southern European heritage made their way to Baltimore in search of new lives and jobs, they found them in all parts of the city. Fells Point stood as the center of 18th- and 19th-century shipbuilding. Bethlehem Steel, the city's largest employer, had shipyards at Sparrows Point and along Key Highway in South Baltimore. Maryland Shipbuilding and Drydock took up the southern edge of the harbor. Glen Martin built airplanes northeast of downtown, and General Motors had a plant in Southeast Baltimore.

Immigrants stayed in Baltimore because the city provided ample job opportunities. World War II had brought jobs to Baltimore as factories geared up to produce ships and airplanes for the war effort. Flush with those wartime manufacturing jobs, Baltimore became the sixth largest city in the country according to the 1950 census. But as the war ended, some of those jobs disappeared. Even so, by the late 1950s, manufacturing provided nearly half of Baltimore's workers with employment. By the end of the century, the city fell out of America's top 20 cities by population.

During the 1950s, Baltimore had more than 1,600 manufacturing establishments where 130,000 people had jobs. In addition to steel, they produced nuclear reactors, power tools, metal cans, car and truck parts, missile warheads, and hydraulic pumps. Another 40,000 workers had jobs at the port, which handled 22 million tons of cargo annually. Only the port in New York handled more.

Much like other northeastern cities, a mix of neighborhoods and people comprised the city. Immigrants arriving in Baltimore settled where they felt most comfortable, and tended to stay in those surroundings. The Italians settled in an area on the near east side soon called Little Italy. Poles, Greeks, Germans and Slovaks divided the area surrounding Patterson Park. Many of the Polish immigrants traveled across the inner harbor to Fells Point and eventually to Highlandtown. Czech, Lithuanian, and Ukrainian districts took shape in south and east Baltimore. Jews settled in the northwest near Lombard Street while blacks occupied the west side south of Druid Hill Avenue and north of Baltimore Street. Fulton Avenue served as the city's east-west racial dividing line and formed the western border of the black settlement. To the west of Federal Hill, lay the Sharp-Leadenhill neighborhood, where African Americans lived. To many, their residences looked more like shacks than houses. Those living there could seldom afford better, and even if they could, housing laws had them boxed in.

Churches often served as the common denominator of many of these ethnic neighborhoods. St. Leo's Catholic Church sat in the center of Little Italy and adopted the customs and traditions of the inhabitants. Polish immigrants arriving in Fells Point founded the church that is known today as Holy Rosary Catholic Church. The Greek culture is evident in the neighborhood east of Highlandtown near St. Nicholas Greek Orthodox Church. The Zion Lutheran Church's service to German residents dates back to 1807. The Lloyd Street Synagogue is now the third oldest in the city in terms of continuous use. These enclaves offered the inhabitants pride in their heritage and the feeling of protection from whatever the New World threw at them.

The pockets of like individuals might have turned them into rivals. Some of the ethnic groups bore the brunt of mocking jokes and insults. Longtime Congresswoman and Senator Barbara Mikulski said the jokes were thrown in many directions, but the Polish seemed to be a frequent target of discrimination. "This is why we had to organize ourselves and form our own institutions," said Mikulski, stating it wasn't just the jokes: "We knew we were discriminated against by the downtown banks so we created our own savings and loans. We knew there was discrimination against us even in terms of getting life insurance because we worked in coalmines and factories. So that's why the Knights of Columbus had an insurance policy. That's why the Polish Women's Alliance could buy insurance, because they weren't going to give factory girls and sweatshop girls insurance."[4]

Mayor Tommy D'Alesandro, Jr., took office in the late 1940s and led the city through the 1950s. His parents came to the United States and settled in the Little Italy section of the city. Young Nancy D'Alesandro watched her mother mobilize volunteers to help elect her father mayor. Those lessons left an impression. She got married, continued in politics and became the first female Speaker of the House, Nancy Pelosi.

"When my father was mayor, the city was strictly broken up by ethnic groups," said son Tommy D'Alesandro III, who became mayor a decade after his father left city hall. "Each neighborhood was cemented by religion, by language, by ethnic background, by race. Racially there was no movement between the two. And it was based on ignorance. Survival was the first order of business, that's all. This was a generation that came though the depression and the war. It was still about jobs and putting food in front of your family. What finally happened was, as ethnic groups got stronger, their leaders began to mesh with other leaders."[5]

Over their history, Baltimore and Maryland residents had many Southern attitudes. "Americans might think of Maryland as a Northern state, but it was distinctly Southern in its attitudes toward race," wrote the editorial board of the *New York Times* recently.[6]

Maryland was a slave state when President Lincoln put it under martial law during the Civil War to avoid having the nation's capital located behind enemy lines. The state had the largest free black population of any state (75,000 in 1850), slightly less than the number of slaves (90,000).[7] The strange mix of Northern tolerance with Southern customs left the city with many questions about race relations.

In 1910, a black Yale law school graduate purchased a home in a previously all-white neighborhood. In response, the city council passed a very restrictive racial zoning law, which established block-by-block segregation. It said no black person could move onto a block where more than half the residents were white and no white person could move onto a block where more than half the residents were black. The *New York Times* called the policy "the most pronounced 'Jim Crow' measure on record."[8] The Supreme Court struck that law down in 1917; in response, some white neighborhood groups required homeowners to sign covenants barring African Americans. In short, the city has a long history of racial segregation.

Another famous Baltimore resident, future Supreme Court Justice Thurgood Marshall referred to Baltimore as "up South." He meant the city that many recognized as Northern had a distinctly Southern culture. It served as a venue for discrimination and segregation, just like in any southern state. Marshall quickly pointed out to interviewers a study conducted by the Urban League that found segregation more rigid in Baltimore than in any other city in the country. The segregation in his home city made him so angry, he promised to do something about it.

Marshall grew up in the Druid Hill neighborhood in Baltimore and attended racially segregated schools. Denied admission to the University of Maryland Law School, he attended the traditionally black Howard University. There Marshall developed a life-long relationship with Charles Hamilton Houston, dean of the law school. They worked together throughout their careers to end discrimination.

"Baltimore wasn't Selma in 1955," wrote Ron Cassie.

> It wasn't New York or Philadelphia, either. The sixth largest U.S. city at mid-century, occupied middle ground in a border state that hadn't been able to make up its mind which side to join in the Civil War.
> Baltimore had its own indecipherable tangle of prejudice. Biased by laws both written and unwritten, the city could be onerous and discriminating at one turn, accommodating the next. Forget, for a moment the big stuff, like applying for a job or buying a house. For black citizens, simply trying on clothes or shoes, seeing a movie, filling a prescription, getting a bite to eat— hell, a cup of coffee, meant navigating a labyrinth of rules that shape-shifted not just from neighborhood to neighborhood, but often store to store within a single downtown block.[9]

Unlike the Deep South, anyone could sit in any seat on streetcars and buses. But schools remained largely segregated prior to 1954. Desegregation came with the United States Supreme Court decision in the historic *Brown v. the Board of Education of Topeka* case. Oliver Brown challenged segregation in the Topeka, Kansas, public schools on behalf of his daughter, Linda Brown. That 1954 decision ended the separate but equal doctrine. Marshall represented Brown and argued the case to end segregation in schools before the Supreme Court.

Chief Justice Earl Warren delivered the unanimous decision. He said in part, "To separate the Negro children from others of a similar age and qualifications solely because of their race generates a feeling of inferiority as to their status in the community that may affect their hearts and minds in a way unlikely ever to be undone."[10]

Two weeks later, all 17 states with separate-but-equal schools were ordered to integrate them immediately. That decision touched off civil rights battles across the country, but particularly in the south. In December 1955, authorities arrested an African American woman named Rosa Parks who refused to give up her seat to a white man in Montgomery, Alabama. In response, 20 black ministers organized a bus boycott in Montgomery. Within a few days, buses ran largely empty. Martin Luther King, Jr., only 26 at the time, gave a fiery speech to thousands of bus boycotters in a church. That boycott lasted 13 months. Word of these protests spread across the country.

Earlier, in 1934, Read's Drug Store built a new store on the corner of Baltimore's Howard and Lexington Streets. Located in the downtown shopping district, this flagship store generated significant business for the drugstore chain and prompted them to open more downtown stores. Like many other businesses in the 1950s, Read's had a policy of racial segregation at its lunch counters. African American customers could purchase products from the store, but they could not eat at the lunch counter. On a frigid, windy January morning in 1955, six Morgan State College students decided to go into Read's to escape the cold and get some hot coffee.

The cold January morning made the wait for a bus seem endless. Passing buses, filled to capacity, didn't stop. "We wanted to sit down, unload our books, and get something hot to drink," recalled Helena Hicks.[11] When they got to the lunch counter, the clerks completely ignored them. Twenty minutes later, the group gave up and went back to the bus stop. Not much of a protest, but it seemed to spark what followed.

In the subsequent days similar protests cropped up at lunch counters at other Read's stores as well as those at Kresge's and McCrory's. The threat of lost business prompted a significant policy change. Several days later, an article appeared on the front page of *The Afro-American* newspaper datelined Baltimore with the headline "Now serve all." Read's, which had 39 local stores at the time, had decided to end the segregation of their lunch counters. They cited a sit-down protest at their downtown store as prompting the action. It is considered a turning point as other sit-in protests staged at other local restaurants soon forced those establishments to change their policies as well. The Baltimore protests came five years before the more nationally known lunch counter protests staged at Woolworth's lunch counter in Greensboro, North Carolina, in 1960.

During the 1950s, segregation extended across the city, even to the city's professional football team. On the field, the Colts appeared to be one unified team. Off the field was another matter entirely according to famed Colts halfback Lenny Moore. "When I came to Baltimore, we couldn't go downtown to the movies," Moore recalled. "We couldn't go to any of the eating houses. In fact, all of downtown was taboo to blacks."[12]

"I wish I could tell you I knew Johnny [Unitas] better," continued Moore. "As with the other white players on the team, we never mingled. One thing I can say about him is that I never saw him use the race card. From day one, Johnny was always consistent in the way he treated people, white or black. Another thing I liked about him: he was a true leader in every sense of the word. All he wanted to do was win ball games and he didn't care who got the ball or how it was done. He was the ultimate bottom-line competitor."[13]

Baltimore had major universities, but unlike some other major cities Baltimore didn't have a real powerhouse major college football team in the area. Navy belong to Annapolis and the city seemed indifferent to Maryland, but when the Colts came along with a marching band and cheerleaders, it had the feel of a college team. Baltimore loved the Colts. "I don't know what it was," said Art Donovan. "All I know is, Baltimore treated us like heroes from the start. We're getting beat every week and they're still coming out there. We finally win a game and they're carrying us off the field on their shoulders like we just won the championship. We got invited everywhere."[14]

Perhaps the love came from the fact that the inhabitants of Baltimore shared the inferiority complex that seemed to plague the football team as well. The Colts didn't get any respect either. The Pittsburgh Steelers cut John Unitas without even giving him an opportunity to play a game there. Raymond Berry had bad vision and one leg that was shorter than the other. "When I take an eye test, I can see that big letter E, but I can't see anything below it," he said.[15] At least, Berry could see better than Bert Rechichar, who was blind in one eye. Gino Marchetti only played college football because the coach let him tag along because he wanted Gino's brother to play on the team.

Baltimore fans admired Unitas as much for his self-effacing nature, black high-top shoes and crew cut hair style as for his comebacks on the football field. He came from the same roots as the fans. He grew up in poverty in Pittsburgh after his father's untimely death. The working class neighborhoods he encountered in Baltimore reminded him of his childhood in western Pennsylvania. And Unitas loved his fans as much as they loved him.

Unitas' crew-cut gave him the appearance of any number of men who left their homes in Locust Point or Sparrows Point to work each day. He appeared to be an ordinary working man. Folks in Baltimore saw him as a neighbor, just like the guy who worked at Bethlehem Steel. His arrival in Baltimore foreshadowed the increased popularity of the Colts.

In fact, during his rookie season he worked at Sparrows Point. Unitas felt truly at home in Baltimore. "Unitas truly loved Baltimore and its residents," observed author Lou Sahadi. "There was something about the gritty neighborhoods with its rows of gray houses that appealed to Unitas. It reminded him of the neighborhood in Pittsburgh where he grew up. More important, the people were real and that's what Unitas liked the most. The blue-collar feel was genuinely welcoming to him. It made him comfortable. 'This is a good place with good people,' he said."[16]

In the documentary film *The Band That Wouldn't Die*, director Barry Levinson captures the love affair that blue-collar Baltimore had with its professional football team. The Maryland city saw their team as a source of pride. The city seemed to put its inferiority complex on hold for a few years during the Unitas era when the Colts sat atop the NFL. Unfortunately, that down feeling all came rushing back when the Colts packed up the moving vans and left town in 1984.

Levinson, a Baltimore native, has many top films to his credit: *Diner* (1982), *The Natural* (1984), *Good Morning, Vietnam* (1987), *Rain Man* (1988), *Bugsy* (1991), and *Wag the Dog* (1997). He won the Academy Award for Best Director for his work on *Rain Man*, which also won the Academy Award for Best Picture. Levinson used his hometown as the backdrop for several of his feature films, including Diner (1982), *Tin Men* (1987), *Avalon* (1990) and *Liberty Heights* (1999).

Diner displayed Baltimore's devoted love for the Colts. The movie examined the lives of six friends who hang out at a fictional diner in Northwest Baltimore. One of the six, Eddie played by Steve Guttenberg, insists his fiancé Elyse pass a football trivia quiz as a precondition for the wedding. The quiz was not easy; his five close friends might not have passed.

The screenplay earned writer/director Levinson an Academy Award nomination and the quiz scene was one of the memorable ones. Ernie Accorsi, who worked in the Colts front office at the time, was asked to review quiz questions in the script. After checking out the questions, he appraised them as too easy. One of the original questions was "What are the Colts' colors?" Accorsi made it tougher. He revised the question to read, "What colors did the Colts wear when the franchise relocated from Miami to Baltimore in 1947?" (Elyse answers green and gray and gets credit, although the Colts' media guide listed green and silver.)

The quiz had 140 questions, but only six make it into the movie. Only the most avid football fan would get all six right. Buddy Young played for a team that no longer exists. Can you name it? The New York Yankees football team. Which current Colts player, a Heisman Trophy winner, first played in Canada? Billy Vessels (Vessels actually played for the Colts in 1956, not 1959, the year in which *Diner* was set).

The toughest question might have been the one directly related to the Colts. George Shaw was a first-round draft choice, true or false? That question sounds easy, but there is a twist to it that makes it unknowingly difficult. Shaw, the team's quarterback before Unitas, was actually drafted in the first round with a one-time "bonus pick" that the NFL allocated to each team by lottery. In 1955, the Colts got two selections in the first round of the draft: Shaw, the bonus pick, and Alan Ameche, their regular pick. Elyse answered true and was incorrect.

Queries like the tricky George Shaw question made it believable that someone could flunk the quiz. Despite her studious preparation and great desire to do well on the quiz, Elyse finished two points shy of a passing score. Eddie's father predicted he would relent and give Elyse a passing score. Instead, Eddie's first reaction is to announce, "The marriage is off." His immaturity was talking. After some deliberation, he relents and goes ahead with the ceremony.

Diner closes with the wedding between Eddie and Elyse and the Colts were nearly a third party to the marriage. The bridal colors are blue and white, which were the Colts' colors. The traditional wedding march did not signal the arrival of the bride; instead, she came down the aisle to the Colts' fight song.

Another media element put teenage life in Baltimore on display. *The Buddy Deane Show* ran on WJZ Channel 13 in Baltimore from 1957 to 1964. The show provided Baltimore's answer to Philadelphia's *American Bandstand* made famous by Dick Clark. *Bandstand*, however, aired across the country; *Buddy Deane* hit the airwaves in Baltimore.

Deane, originally from Arkansas, came to Baltimore in 1951 and soon took the city's top radio personality spot. He made the leap to television with a successful dance program that served as the basis for John Waters' film and musical *Hairspray*. The fictional story told about a successful attempt by a group of black and white teens to integrate a teen dance show called *The Corny Collins Show* in 1962.

That is where the movie differed from real life. Mr. Deane's show never successfully integrated. In a 2002 interview, Deane said the television station management wanted to integrate but felt Baltimore wouldn't accept such a bold step. "The management of the station did not realize that Baltimore was very much a southern-oriented city," Deane told the Associated Press. He said they asked each member of the show's committee of regular dancers, "what they thought about integration, and they said, 'Well, it's okay with me, but my folks won't be happy.' That was the general consensus."[17]

"'The Corny Collins Show' was entirely based on my memories and exaggerations of 'The Buddy Deane Show,'" said Waters. "In Baltimore, we were the only city in the country that didn't have Dick Clark. 'Buddy Deane' really did have 'Negro Day' once a month—it was called worse in some neighborhoods in Baltimore.... The kids on 'The Buddy Deane Show' were kids from blue-collar neighborhoods. Their parents were hardly liberal about integration in 1959 Baltimore. Even then, can you actually switch on the TV and see black and white 15-year-olds slow dancing together? Not often."[18]

The custom of the day followed the separate but equal paradigm which meant the regular dancers would be all white. Schools had started to integrate but slow dancing on television provided a completely different story. The equal aspect seemed a bit of a stretch. Black youth were invited, usually through church groups or Boys or Girls Clubs, on one Monday per month. The show called it "Special Guest Day." Most of Baltimore called it Black Monday. In *Hairspray*, it appeared as "Negro Day." On at least one of those actual occasions, Smokey Robinson and the Miracles appeared.

The 1950s comprised an era in America recalled with memories not unlike the artwork Norman Rockwell painted weekly for the front cover of *The Saturday Evening Post*. Baltimore life didn't differ all that much from the rest of the country. Kids wearing black high-top Keds chased the Good Humor ice cream truck down the street before returning home to watch Marshall Dillon catch the bad guys on television.

While kids were watching television or the movies, some of their parents liked an occasional adult beverage. Colts owner Carroll Rosenbloom encouraged his players to take jobs in the local community during the offseason. Some surmised that one trait helped cement a bond between the community and the team. That bond may have tempted some to try the beer that advertised during the baseball and football broadcasts.

Despite the fact that the beer is not brewed locally any longer, National Bohemian Beer continues to retain close ties to area sports clubs and the community. The locals fondly refer to it as "Natty Boh." Ninety percent of all Natty Boh sales come from the Baltimore area. First brewed in 1885; Jerold Hoffberger and family owned the brewery in the 19th century and grew it into one of the top 20 breweries in the country.

The one-eyed, mustachioed mascot named Mr. Boh proclaimed the beer came "from the land of pleasant living." All across Baltimore billboards displayed the mascot and big names of Baltimore, such as Edgar Allen Poe and the football Colts. Fans said they longed for "crabs, O's and Boh's."

Ultimately, Baltimore was true to its roots. Even though Marshall and Pelosi were Baltimore natives, the city's biggest hero came from the world of sports. John Unitas, who grew up in a working class household in the suburbs of Pittsburgh, came to Baltimore and said he felt right at home. He was a lunch pail quarterback who worked in a factory his first year in the city to supplement his football income. He fit in alongside those factory workers who didn't throw touchdown passes in their "other" jobs. At the end of the 1958 title game, when Unitas lead his gang of little guys from Baltimore triumphantly over the media stars in Gotham it was a memory that will live forever in the minds of the city inhabitants.

"He had an incredible, profound effect," said Barry Levinson. "Unitas happened at the time when Baltimore was just getting a football team and he rose to dominance just as football was rising to prominence…. This was Baltimore beating New York, which was a very big deal then."[19]

Notes

1. Mark Kram, "A Wink at a Homely Girl," *Sports Illustrated*, October 10, 1966.
2. Daniel A. Nathan, *Rooting for the Home Team* (Urbana: University of Illinois Press, 2013), 108–109.
3. Jon Morgan, *Glory for Sale* (Baltimore: Bancroft Press, 1997), 46.
4. Michael Olesker, *Journeys to the Heart of Baltimore* (Baltimore: Johns Hopkins University Press, 2015), 43.
5. Michael Olesker, *The Colts' Baltimore* (Baltimore: Johns Hopkins University Press, 2008), 83.
6. The Editorial Board, "How Racism Doomed Baltimore," *New York Times*, May 9, 2015.
7. Howell S. Braun, *Brown in Baltimore* (Ithaca: Cornell University Press, 2010), 20.
8. *Ibid.*

9. Ron Cassie, "And Service for All," *Baltimore Magazine*, January 2015.

10. I. F. Stone, *The Haunted Fifties*, in *The 1950s*, Stuart A. Kallen, ed. (Farmington Hills, MI: Greenhaven Press, 2000), 22.

11. Cassie, "And Service for All."

12. James Coates, Hannah Doban, and Nevon Kipperman, "Black Sport and Baltimore," in *Baltimore Sports: Stories from Charm City*, Daniel Nathan, ed. (Fayetteville: University of Arkansas Press, 2016), 185.

13. Lenny Moore with Jeffrey Jay Ellish, *All Things Being Equal* (Champagne, IL: Sports Publishing, 2005), 75–76.

14. Olesker, *The Colts' Baltimore*, 42–43.

15. *Ibid.*, 44.

16. Lou Sahadi, *Johnny Unitas: American's Quarterback* (Chicago: Triumph Books, 2004), 213.

17. "Buddy Deane, 78, TV Host and Inspiration of 'Hairspray,'" *New York Times*, July 27, 2003.

18. Chris Jones, "John Waters Narrates 'Hairspray's' Journey from Cult Movie Hoot to Broadway Hit," *Chicago Tribune*, January 18, 2004.

19. Barry Levinson, "No Athlete Meant More to Baltimore," *Los Angeles Times,* September 12, 2002.

Owner Carroll Rosenbloom

GEORGE BOZEKA

Once hailed as the NFL's first modern owner, Carroll Rosenbloom was loved by his players for his flamboyant generosity, and feared by his coaches for his demanding nature. He was a consummate businessman and power broker whose NFL teams in both Baltimore and Los Angeles had a penchant for winning and drama.

Rosenbloom was born on March 5, 1907, in Baltimore, Maryland, to Anna and Solomon Rosenbloom, the eighth of nine Rosenbloom children and the sixth and last son. Solomon immigrated from Russian Poland and began working when he was 15 years old. Eventually, he prospered manufacturing work clothing in Baltimore, allowing the Rosenblooms to live comfortably.[1] Rosenbloom stated, "I was fortunate in having a father who had worked hard and gave me something to start with."[2]

In school, Rosenbloom thrived at athletics, but concentrated very little on his academic studies. He graduated from Baltimore City College, a public high school in Baltimore, and entered the University of Pennsylvania in 1926. At Penn, he played halfback for backfield coach and future NFL commissioner Bert Bell. Rosenbloom enjoyed playing for Bell. After his sophomore season, Carroll and fellow teammate Marty Brill traveled to Notre Dame and met with legendary coach Knute Rockne. Rockne expressed an interest in both Rosenbloom and Brill. Carroll's father convinced

Carroll Rosenbloom.

him to stay at Penn, but Brill transferred. Penn line coach Lud Wray, who had been a thorn in Rosenbloom's side, got Rosenbloom benched. As a result, Carroll did not go out for the football team his senior year instead concentrating on his major studies in psychology and business.[3]

After graduating from Penn, Rosenbloom went to work for the J.G. Brill Company, a streetcar and bus manufacturing company owned by Marty Brill's family. In the midst of the Depression, his father called him home to try the family business. Carroll wanted no part of his father's business because "he and I were too much alike," but he finally gave in and returned to Baltimore.[4] Carroll's father put him to work cleaning bathrooms for a meager $3.50 a week.[5]

After toiling for nearly two years for his father, Rosenbloom got an opportunity to get out on his own. His father sent him to Roanoke, Virginia, to liquidate the Blue Ridge Overalls Company. Rosenbloom instead made a deal to purchase the business from his father with bank loans and money borrowed from his mother.[6]

Under Rosenbloom's guidance, Blue Ridge began showing a profit. Orders from the U.S. Civilian Conservation Corps and large retailers, such as Sears Roebuck, Montgomery Ward, W.T. Grant and J.C. Penney aided the turnaround. Rosenbloom realized that "if you wanted to be big, you had to be associated with large sources of distribution."[7] During the years he operated Blue Ridge, annual sales rose from $160,000 to $60 million.[8] "I always knew I'd be a millionaire," Rosenbloom stated. "I believe that anyone who wants to can make money. That's not very difficult."[9]

By 1940 business was so good that Rosenbloom was able to step away from Blue Ridge and lead the idyllic life of a gentleman farmer, raising peaches and corn at Warwick Manor on the Eastern Shore. In 1941 he married Velma Anderson. Velma had been introduced to Carroll by his friend Marty Brill.[10]

But in 1942 his father died and Rosenbloom returned to run his father's business as executor of the estate.[11] According to John Schmidt, in his 1962 *Baltimore Sun* profile of Rosenbloom, when he sold his Blue Ridge interests in 1959, they "had grown to include almost a dozen shirt and overall companies" and "the price was $7 million in cash and more than $20 million in stock."[12]

In 1953, the NFL and old friend Bert Bell came calling. Bell, now NFL commissioner, needed someone to take over the NFL's failing franchise in Dallas, the Texans. Baltimore had previously had a franchise in the All-America Football Conference (AAFC) from 1947 to 1949 called the Colts. The Colts survived the "merger" of the AAFC and NFL in December 1949, and were an NFL team during the 1950 season despite suffering through a 1–11 record and $90,000 in losses during their last AAFC season.[13]

The Colts were equally atrocious in their first NFL season again finishing with a mark of 1–11 and being outscored 462–213. As a result, Baltimore was again without a pro football team as owner Abraham "Shorty" Watner dissolved the franchise. Embittered fans in Baltimore took the news hard. Civic leaders put together a legal defense fund. Bell made overtures to Baltimore that the city could get the Colts back, but when nothing materialized, the city of Baltimore and remaining members of the Colts' board of directors filed suit against Watner and the league on November 1, 1951.[14]

On December 3, 1952, Bell announced that the city of Baltimore could inherit the Texans franchise if it could sell 15,000 season tickets. The Baltimore community responded by selling over 15,000 season tickets and depositing $300,000 in the bank.[15]

Bell needed an owner, and Rosenbloom was the man he wanted. Rosenbloom wasn't interested, but Bell kept hounding him. Arthur Godfrey, Sid Luckman, John B. Kelly (Grace Kelly's father), Bill Veeck, Jack Dempsey, and Gene Tunney were all mentioned as potential owners.[16]

In his book *America's Game*, Michael MacCambridge wrote, "Bell finally settled the impasse with his usual mix of decisiveness and gruff charm. Calling Rosenbloom on the night of January 11, 1953, Bell said, 'Carroll, you're the new owner. I just announced it.'"[17]

The terms of the sale were very favorable to Rosenbloom and his partners. Rosenbloom and his minority partners (former Directors Tom Mullan, S., William F. Hilgenberg, Zanvyl Krieger, and R. Bruce Livie) paid only $25,000 ($13,000 from Rosenbloom and $3,000 each from the others) of the $200,000 price tag up front with the remaining payments spread out over eight years without interest. Rosenbloom finally relented and agreed to assume 51 percent ownership in the team. Rosenbloom's only caveat was that Bell provide a GM to handle the day to day operations of the club. Bell tapped Don Kellett, director of operations at WFIL-TV in Philadelphia, as GM, and Keith Molesworth was named head coach for the 1953 season.[18]

"We came to town for an introductory banquet," son Steve Rosenbloom recalled, "and [local radio announcer] Bailey Goss got up and said, 'It's a good thing Carroll is in the shirt business because he is liable to lose his here.' That summed up pro football at that time. There wasn't a lot of attendance and not a lot of money in it."[19]

Initially, Rosenbloom asked Baltimore fans to give him five years to build a winner, but soon running a pro football team began to grow on the reluctant owner. "After the first year in football, I found that of all the things I've ever done, this is the thing," Rosenbloom said. "There is nothing more rewarding. You have everything wrapped up in one bundle. You meet much nicer people than you do in business. You meet the public, and you must learn to look out for them. There's no place where your word is more your bond than in sports … particularly after some of the things that have gone on in business or on Wall Street. You play a part in the lives of young men, and you help them grow. And then every Sunday you have the great pleasure of dying."[20]

John Eisenberg reported that according to his son Steve, Rosenbloom "put $1 million in the bank and privately pledged to own the team unless he lost that much, at which point he would walk away. But his timing was splendid. The NFL soon became more popular and profitable."

"And something funny happened to him, anyway," Steve recalled: "In 1953, we weren't winning, but he was impressed with how hard the players played even though they were going down to defeat. Their effort convinced him to get involved and get into it. That's when he turned the corner. I don't know if he ever looked at what was in the bank, but he became a dedicated owner."[21]

Schmidt wrote in his 1962 profile that Rosenbloom "never tried to run the Colts the way he would a business, and [said] there was no similarity between the two. Nor [did] he run it the way most professional football teams are run. In the beginning, he told the fans of Baltimore that this was their team, and he promised them a championship if they would support it."[22]

He was a very generous owner who was loved by Colts players. Rosenbloom devised incentive plans for his players, supported outside business activities by his players, favored players' unions, and helped players with loans or down payments on their homes. Before Thanksgiving each year, he had bountiful gift baskets delivered to the locker room.[23]

According to Eisenberg, "Rosenbloom advised Hall of Fame defensive end Gino Marchetti to move to Baltimore to take advantage of his popularity, and then co-signed a lease to take financial responsibility for one of the first Gino's fast food restaurants. When the chain became enormously successful, Rosenbloom helped Marchetti and his partners take the company public." Eisenberg further wrote that Marchetti stated, "He [Rosenbloom] did a hell of a lot for a lot of guys. Outside of my parents, he probably did more to influence me than anyone else in my life."[24]

The Colts finished 3–9 in Rosenbloom's first year of ownership, but he was impressed with the effort put forth by his squad, and felt an upgrade in coaching was necessary. He moved Molesworth to personnel director and hired Weeb Ewbank, then an assistant to Paul Brown in Cleveland, based on a strong recommendation by a member of the Browns' board of directors.[25]

The mix of Rosenbloom and Ewbank's leadership, professionalism and organization brought stability to the Colts. Over the next four seasons the Colts showed steady improvement culminating in the back-to-back NFL championship seasons of 1958 and 1959. However, it wasn't always a walk in the park for the coaching staff. According to Mark Bowden, in his book *The Best Game Ever*, Rosenbloom was hard on his coaches, particularly Ewbank. "He would berate Weeb mercilessly after losses."[26]

Rosenbloom was very enigmatic. Given the circumstances he could quickly morph from witty, charming, and generous to gruff and ruthless. Gene Klein, late owner of the San Diego Chargers, explained, "Carroll was one complex individual. Very smart, very tough, often very nasty. He always gave you the feeling that, if you crossed him, he was capable of slitting your throat, then donating your blood to the Red Cross blood drive."[27]

Rosenbloom was a forceful hands-on owner and leader of the Colts' organization, particularly on the business and financial side, but he was not a micromanager. Even though he could be very critical after losses he left the football decisions to Ewbank and Kellett, allowing them to do their jobs free of meddling.

"He felt you needed strong leadership at the top, and he provided that, but he also created a family environment in which everyone had a role, down to the ballboys," Steve Rosenbloom related. "He felt he could win with a family of intelligent players who had high character. It worked in Baltimore.... I have seen other owners, and worked for one, who didn't have that approach, and failed."[28]

Rosenbloom reveled in the high life. He spent most of his time in Margate, New Jersey, but he kept an office in New York, and stayed in hotels when he visited Baltimore. He dressed well and he ran in powerful circles. Joseph Kennedy, father of President John F. Kennedy, was an old friend and confidant. Rosenbloom and Kennedy met in Palm Beach in the late 1930s. When Rosenbloom was amassing his fortune, Kennedy told him: "After you get the first couple of million, you can fake the next 10."[29]

Joe Kennedy was an avid Colts fan. During his 1960 presidential campaign Jack complained that his father seemed "more interested in whether the Colts win than if I get elected." When JFK was assassinated in 1963, Rosenbloom attended the funeral and then flew to Hyannis Port to lend moral support to Joe.[30]

Rosenbloom's Colts suffered through three mediocre seasons from 1960 to 1962, hastening the exit of head coach Weeb Ewbank after the 1962 season. Rosenbloom fired Ewbank and hired Don Shula to lead the Colts. Rosenbloom called it "probably the most difficult task I've ever faced."[31]

Rosenbloom also consolidated his ownership of the Colts pressuring the minority owners to sell their shares of ownership.[32]

The Colts, under Shula's leadership returned to the NFL championship game in 1964 losing to the Browns 27–0 and again in 1968, this time defeating the Browns 34–0. This led to the Colts appearance in Super Bowl III where they famously were upset by former coach Weeb Ewbank and his New York Jets 16–7.

After the 1969 season, Shula left Baltimore to become head coach of the Miami Dolphins. The Colts hired Don McCafferty, and in 1970 he led the Colts to a Super Bowl V victory over the Cowboys 16–13. The Colts returned to the playoffs in 1971, but lost to Miami in the AFC championship game. This would prove to be Rosenbloom's last game as owner of the Colts.

Rosenbloom had grown disillusioned with Baltimore. He was feuding with the press and was being stonewalled by city leaders about the need for a new stadium. Ownership of the Rams and the Los Angeles lifestyle appealed to him. Robert Irsay purchased the Rams from the family of the late Dan Reeves for $19 million and then traded the franchise to Rosenbloom for the Colts franchise. As a result of the swap, Rosenbloom did not have to pay any capital gains. Rosenbloom assumed ownership of the Rams on July 13, 1972.[33]

Meanwhile, Rosenbloom's personal life had become a Hollywood soap opera. In 1966, he divorced his wife Velma, and shortly thereafter married his second wife Georgia. He had met Georgia, a former showgirl, at a dinner hosted by Joe Kennedy in 1957. At the time Carroll and Georgia had already had two children together.[34]

Rosenbloom continued the winning tradition he had started with the Colts with the Rams. During his ownership from 1972 until his untimely death in 1979, the Rams finished first in the Western Division seven times and made it to the Super Bowl in 1979 losing to the Steelers 31–19.

Rosenbloom died suddenly on April 2, 1979. He drowned while swimming in Golden Beach, Florida. He was 72. Though a PBS *Frontline* expose on gambling and the NFL alleged that Rosenbloom had been murdered, the Dade County Medical examiner ruled the death accidental.[35]

Gambling allegations dogged Rosenbloom throughout his life, including claims that he betted against his own team. "I know he gambled on college games over the years, but I didn't see that much when he bought the Colts.... Over the years I've heard from people doing various books and what not that they either spoke to my father or had information about specific games he bet on or said he bet on," Steve Rosenbloom said. "Whether he did or not, I can't honestly tell you. I'm not hiding anything. I'm sure if he did bet, he didn't want me involved."[36]

Over the years many have claimed that Rosenbloom ordered the Colts to go for a winning touchdown rather than a field goal in overtime of the 1958 championship game because he had a huge bet on the Colts and needed to win by more than three points to cover his wager. The allegations were never proved.[37]

Art Modell, the late owner of the Browns and Ravens, was skeptical. "It's just a wild story," Modell said. "Carroll would never have influenced a coach or anyone else, especially with Unitas as quarterback."[38]

Steve Rosenbloom agreed. "Unitas ran his own show. Half the time he didn't use the plays called in from the sideline."[39]

Over 900 people attended Rosenbloom's memorial service, including 15 NFL owners, sportscaster Howard Cosell, the entire Rams organization, and actors Warren Beatty, Kirk Douglas, Cary Grant, Jimmy Stewart, and Rod Steiger.

He was survived by his wife Georgia and children Steve, Dan, Suzanne, Chip, and Lucia.

Los Angeles Times writer Rich Roberts eloquently characterized Rosenbloom after his death: "Gamesmanship was Rosenbloom's forte. He could attack an adversary or obstructionist in subtle ways ... but it was seldom his intention to hurt anyone- unless he meant to, and then he could make his malice felt.... Carroll Rosenbloom was not the type of man who will be remembered fondly by all, but all will remember him for his presence. There will never be another quite like him."[40]

Notes

1. Robert Boyle, "The Pleasure of Dying on Sunday," *Sports Illustrated,* December 13, 1965, https://www.si.com/vault/1965/12/13/609024/the-pleasure-of-dying-on-sunday, accessed December 26, 2017.

2. John C. Schmidt, "Rosenbloom: The Man Behind the Colts," *Baltimore Sun*, October 28, 1962, Sports Section.

3. Boyle, "Pleasure of Dying on Sunday."

4. *Ibid.*

5. Schmidt, "Rosenbloom."

6. *Ibid.*

7. Boyle, "Pleasure of Dying on Sunday."

8. Schmidt, "Rosenbloom."

9. Boyle, "Pleasure of Dying on Sunday."

10. *Ibid.*

11. Schmidt, "Rosenbloom."

12. Boyle, "Pleasure of Dying on Sunday."

13. Michael MacCambridge, *America's Game: The Epic Story of How Pro Football Captured a Nation* (New York: Random House, 2004), 76.

14. Ted Patterson, *Football in Baltimore: History and Memorabilia* (Baltimore: Johns Hopkins University Press, 2000), 91.

15. John Steadman, *Football's Miracle Men* (Cleveland: Pennington Press, 1959), 83–85.

16. Patterson, *Football in Baltimore*, 97.

17. MacCambridge, *America's Game*, 79.

18. Steadman, *Football's Miracle Men*, 88–89; MacCambridge, *America's Game*, 79.

19. John Eisenberg, "Carroll Rosenbloom: Man of Mystery," Press Box Online Baltimore, www.pressboxonline.com, accessed August 1, 2017.

20. Boyle, "Pleasure of Dying on Sunday."

21. Eisenberg, "Carroll Rosenbloom."

22. Schmidt, "Rosenbloom."

23. *Ibid.*; Mark Bowden, *The Best Game Ever* (New York: Atlantic Monthly Press, 2008), 69, 122.

24. Eisenberg, "Carroll Rosenbloom."

25. John Steadman, *The Baltimore Colts: A Pictorial History* (Virginia Beach: Jordan & Company, 1978), 43.

26. Bowden, *Best Game Ever*, 69.

27. Eisenberg, "Carroll Rosenbloom."

28. *Ibid.*

29. *Ibid.*

30. Boyle, "Pleasure of Dying on Sunday."

31. "Colts Fire Ewbank, Name Shula Coach," *Ocala Star Banner*, January 8, 1963, 14.

32. John Steadman, *From Colts to Ravens* (Centreville, MD: Tidewater, 1997), 183.

33. Steadman, *From Colts to Ravens*, 183–191; Eisenberg, "Carroll Rosenbloom."

34. Richard Goldstein, "Georgia Frontiere, 80, First Female NFL Owner, Is Dead," *New York*

Times, January 19, 2008, http://www.nytimes.com/2008/01/19/obituaries/19frontiere.html, accessed December 26, 2017.

35. William Taaffe, "Unfounded Findings," *Sports Illustrated*, January 31, 1983, https://www.si.com/vault/1983/01/31/627212/unfounded-findings, accessed December 26, 2017.

36. Eisenberg, "Carroll Rosenbloom."

37. Michael E. Lomax, "Detrimental to the League: Gambling and the Governance of Professional Football, 1946–1963," *Journal of Sports History* 29, no. 2 (Summer 2002): 71.

38. Eisenberg, "Carroll Rosenbloom."

39. *Ibid.*

40. Rich Roberts, "CR," *Pro! Rams–Raiders NFL Game Program,* September 2, 1979, 67, 71.

Head Coach Weeb Ewbank

Lee Elder

Wilbur Charles Ewbank watched professional football grow up. He saw Jim Thorpe play football during the game's nascent years and as a man he stalked the sideline during three of the most important games in the sport's history. He coached two of its greatest upsets. During his final game as a coach, Ewbank watched O.J. Simpson become the first to gain more than 2,000 yards in a single season.

Football was Weeb Ewbank's life. You could argue that he brought some life to football.

Nicknamed Weeb by a sibling who could not pronounce Wilbur, Ewbank played college football with Paul Brown and served as Brown's assistant on two different teams. Then Ewbank went out on his own and coached the Baltimore Colts and New York Jets to championships, winning titles in two leagues, just like Brown did.

Ewbank was born May 6, 1907, in Richmond, Indiana, to Charles and Stella Ewbank. Charles operated a grocery store in Richmond and it was Charles who transported young Weeb to see Thorpe in 1923. Weeb had three siblings, Vernon, Helen and Myron. Weeb attended Morton High School in Richmond, where he captained the football, basketball and baseball teams.

According to Paul Zimmerman's 1974 book *The Last Season of Weeb Ewbank*, the three sport star earned some spending money during his high school and college years by playing semi-pro baseball during the summers under the name Carl (Shorty) Thomas.[1]

After his high school days ended, Ewbank attended Miami University in Oxford, Ohio, where he again played three sports. He claimed to Zimmerman in 1974 that he had a .456 batting average as a senior baseball player at Miami, and was offered opportunities to play minor league baseball but turned them down.[2]

It was while he was at Miami that Ewbank married Lucy Keller Massey. They were wed June 23, 1926, in Richmond when Weeb was 19. Lucy Ewbank was slightly

Weeb Ewbank.

older than her husband. Their marriage eventually produced three daughters, Luanne, Nancy and Jan.[3]

Ewbank played quarterback at Miami, but he seldom threw the ball. In those days, the primary offensive formations used by college football teams were the single wing and the Notre Dame box and in those offenses each man in the backfield was a potential passer. When the RedHawks needed to throw the ball, another quarterback was used because he had bigger hands and the size and shape of the football in those days made it difficult to throw for a passer with smaller hands. Miami's other quarterback was Paul Brown, the same Paul Brown who was eventually inducted into the Pro Football Hall of Fame as a coach.

"That's where Brown had it over Weeb," said Chester Pittser, who coached the two at Miami. "Weeb's hands were so small that he couldn't grip the ball well enough to pass with it. I'd play Paul when we were going to throw a lot." But, Pittser said, Ewbank started more games "because you could trust him to do exactly what you wanted. Brown was wild and unpredictable as a player. The thing that impressed you about him [Brown] was the chances he took."[4]

Pittser told Zimmerman that Ewbank was very studious and dedicated and well liked on campus. Brown, on the other hand, "was respected but he stuck to himself. A lone wolf." The two men, so different as people, worked together well as coaches. But it took something as earth-shaking as the Second World War to bring them back together after they left Miami.

After graduating from Miami, Ewbank drew his first coaching assignment at Van Wert High School in Van Wert, Ohio, where he coached for two years. In 1930, he returned to Oxford where he began a complicated working situation. He was an assistant to head coach Pittser at Miami and he coached every sport at McGuffey High School. Ewbank continued that complicated employment arrangement for 13 years.[5]

The football world got its first glimpse at what teams could accomplish with Weeb Ewbank on the sideline while he coached those McGuffey teams. In 1936, McGuffey was undefeated and unscored upon, part of a 14-game stretch in which McGuffey out-scored opponents 270–0. Ewbank's record at McGuffey was 71–21, including a 21-game win streak.[6]

As if he wasn't busy enough, Ewbank spent his summers working toward a master's of arts and teaching certificate in the supervision of health and physical education at Columbia University. He got his degree December 12, 1932.[7]

Ewbank's coaching at the high school level spanned the early years of the Great Depression and continued beyond the United States' entry into World War II. Had he continued as a high school coach in Ohio, he no doubt would have earned awards for his work at that level. That isn't what happened. In 1943, Ewbank entered the United States Navy and, waiting for him at the Great Lakes Naval Training Station was Paul Brown. Wouldn't you know it, Brown had a football team. Ewbank became Brown's assistant coach on that team. Ewbank also coached the Great Lakes basketball team.[8]

The Great Lakes football team played a schedule packed with major college teams during the war years. When the war ended, Brown and Ewbank went different directions. Brown made the decision to accept the head coaching position of the Cleveland Browns, part of the fledging All-America Football Conference, for the 1946 season.

Ewbank said, "Our families were pretty friendly at Great Lakes. I remember one night when Paul and his wife were over at our house, he told us he was going to get the

Cleveland Browns job, and he asked us to help him pick a name for the team … no matter what name we came up with, he had something against it. He had the name selected all the time. He just didn't want to tell us it was the Browns."[9]

Ewbank left Brown to his Browns and became the backfield coach at, yep, Brown University under head coach C.A. "Rip" Engle for the 1946 football season. The Bears recorded a 3–5–1 record that year. Ewbank was also the head basketball coach at Brown that year, recording an 8–12 mark. The next stop for Ewbank was Washington University in St. Louis, Missouri, where he spent his only two seasons as the head coach of a college program. Under Ewbank, the Bears were winners, going 5–3 in 1947 and 9–1 in 1948. But uneasy is the hat that sits atop the head of a football coach. Despite his success at Washington, Ewbank left the school to join Brown's staff in Cleveland in 1949 and the coaching assignment Ewbank was given may have taken a promising career and put it on the road to championships.[10]

"I'll tell you, though, one of the biggest favors he ever did me was making me the tackle coach when he first hired me at Cleveland," said Ewbank years later. "It gave me a different insight, an insight into the position I might never have gotten."[11]

At Cleveland, Ewbank's offensive tackles protected professional football's winningest quarterback, in terms of championships, Otto Graham. It was an important lesson to learn for future years when Ewbank coached John Unitas and Joe Namath.

"I've always been a strong believer in giving the passer the maximum amount of protection," Ewbank told sportswriter Arthur Daley in 1967. "It's a principle that was hammered into me when I was an assistant to Paul Brown on the Cleveland Browns. We stressed it then and I've been stressing it ever since. I guess I really got the message from Otto Graham, our quarterback."[12]

The Browns won their fourth consecutive AAFC championship in 1949 and the league folded at the end of that season. Three AAFC franchises, the Browns, 49ers and Colts, joined the National Football League for the 1950 season. The regular season opener for the Browns was one of history's most important pro games, as they were matched against the defending NFL champion Philadelphia Eagles in Philadelphia. The game produced one of the great upsets in pro football history. The Browns slammed the Eagles 35–10. The Browns went on to win the NFL title that season, besting the Los Angeles Rams 30–28 on a field goal with 28 seconds remaining in the title game. Lou Groza, a tackle, booted home the winning points.

Brown told Zimmerman years later that Ewbank's personality was something the Browns' coaching staff needed. "Weeb had a good sense of humor," Brown told the writer in 1974, during Ewbank's final year of coaching, "and he was able to get along with the players in a very natural way. I needed someone around me like that. Maybe I shouldn't say this … but Weeb was an easier-going person than me."[13]

Ewbank started getting feelers about head coaching positions when he was with the Browns. There were rumors that the University of Indiana was interested in Ewbank becoming the Hoosiers' head coach. But Brown seemed to have put a stop to Ewbank moving on from the Browns for a time. When Ewbank accepted the head coaching position with the Colts in 1954, Brown convinced the league office that Ewbank should not be allowed to leave the Browns until the college draft was completed.

"Paul liked to control everything," Ewbank said later. "I do mean everything! And that included assistant coaches. He didn't like somebody to leave until he was ready to let them go."[14]

Ewbank began preparing the Colts for the 1954 season and there was plenty to do. The Colts had struggled to a 3–9 record in 1953. But there were talented players on the team Ewbank inherited and one of them was defensive tackle Art Donovan: "Ewbank shook my hand … and then looked me up and down and said, 'I'd guess you're at 300 pounds and that's a conservative guess. If you expect to play next year you're going to have to lose a lot of that weight. You're coming into training camp at two-seventy or you can forget about coming into training camp at all.' My assessment of Ewbank's coaching ability would have to wait. But I had immediately come to one conclusion about the man: He was, indeed, a rat bastard."[15]

Donovan's weight was a point of friction with Ewbank throughout their time together with the Colts. But under Ewbank's defensive system, Donovan became a star: "When Weeb and Joe Thomas came in and introduced the keying defense—one that *depended upon* quickness and a player's ability to read offenses, man, I was in hog heaven. Weeb Ewbank made Arthur J. Donovan, Jr., a Hall of Fame football player. I loved him for that. I can honestly say that Weeb Ewbank became and remains one of the most important, cherished people in my life."[16]

Baltimore did not win right away with Ewbank. They went 3–9 in 1954. The foundation for winning came in the 1955 draft. Donovan said, "He dissected the team, realized what we needed, and in the 1955 draft went out and plucked an amazing twelve rookies who made the team, seven of whom became starters. That college draft was just about automatically responsible for turning the Colt franchise around."[17]

The Colts' record improved slightly to 5–6–1 in 1955. Ewbank was building the Colts into a winner and not just through the draft. He also made shrewd non-draft pickups of other players. There are at least two different stories about how Ewbank signed Unitas off the sandlots of minor league football and brought him to the Colts to begin his fabled Hall of Fame career but the bottom line is that Unitas got there in 1956. Once he got to Baltimore, Unitas became the Colts' starting quarterback and the team went 5–7 in 1956. In 1957, the Colts completed their first winning season, finishing third in the Western Conference with a record of 7–5.

During the 1958 championship season, the Colts led the league in scoring and allowed the second-lowest number of points.[18] Donovan credited the new, stingy nature of the Colts defense to a technique Ewbank introduced during his first season with the club, saying, "In retrospect, the keying defense appears rather academic: Where the blocking went was where the ballcarrier was coming. Read the blocking and weep for the ball carrier. But at the time I thought [Colts owner Carroll] Rosenbloom had tapped into the Albert Einstein of technique coaches. In fact, Rosenbloom took to calling Weeb, 'My crew cut IBM machine.' And that keying defense kept old Fatso in the league for eight more years."[19]

Ewbank gave a very emotional pep talk prior to the 1958 title game. The coach reminded the Colts where some of them had come from. One by one, he spoke about each player, as if to remind him that his chance to complete a long, hard journey was in front of him. Finally, the coach said, "Oh yes—Ewbank. No one knew him either—just the tackles I use[d] to work in Cleveland. Last but not least being a poor boy all my life, I didn't know any millionaires. I never heard of Carroll Rosenbloom. Yes we all have a lot to be thankful for and a lot of showing to be done. Get out there and get ready."

Ewbank was fired up himself. During the game he took a swing at Giants middle linebacker Sam Huff when a play brought Huff to the Colts' sideline. Ewbank later said he was enraged when Huff purposely kneed a Colts player when he was already downed.[20]

The 23–17 overtime victory over the favored Giants exposed Ewbank to the type of media storm that is reserved for champions. In 1958, there were fewer champions than there are today and he was very much in demand. George Usher of *Newsday* quoted Ewbank talking about the way his name was mispronounced through the years: "On St. Patrick's Day I was Mick Webbie. On radio, I've been U Weebank and at a church social I was Hebe Ubunk."

The Colts repeated as champions in 1959, beating the Giants again, 31–16, in the title game. The team was atop the football world but it couldn't stay there. A new rising power in the Green Bay Packers displaced Baltimore from the head of the Western Conference table. The Colts were 21–19 over the next three seasons, finishing above .500 just once in that span. Ewbank was fired after the 1962 season. In nine seasons he had built a field failure into a two-time champ expected to keep winning.

"No reason was given," Ewbank was quoted as saying. "Nothing was said except they felt a change was in order." He was replaced by Don Shula who, like Brown and Ewbank, was later inducted into the Hall of Fame.[21]

Colts wide receiver Raymond Berry said, "Every year, except the ones when we won the championship, you would read stories speculating about Weeb's job. I was genuinely surprised. I think the other players were, too. We didn't have all that bad a season." Cowboys general manager Tex Schramm was quoted as supposing the retirement of fullback Alan Ameche, and Ewbank's inability to replace Ameche's offensive production hurt the Colts as much as anything else.[22]

Donovan wrote, "There was nothing I could see about the team that had really changed. It was just like someone had pulled the rug out from under us.... But for all his faults, Weeb was never accused of not knowing football. And I think he was as dumbfounded as the rest of us when the victories began to slip away from us."[23]

Several NFL teams were looking for new head coaches after the 1962 season. The Colts dumped Ewbank too late for consideration for those jobs. But pro football's landscape had changed in 1960 when the American Football League opened up lots of new jobs for coaches and players. And the AFL's New York franchise, originally named the Titans but recently renamed the Jets, had a new owner who was looking for a high profile coach to take over. The franchise was not successful on the field in 1962 finishing last in the league in scoring defense and second-to-last in scoring. In three seasons, the Titans' record was 19–23.

Jets owner Sonny Werblin hired Ewbank and the coach then told New York Post columnist Milton Gross, "I've sicker cows than this get well." Gross later quoted Ewbank as saying, "My aim is to beat the record of five years it took me with the Colts."[24]

It took Ewbank six seasons to win a title with the Jets. They improved gradually. The Jets finally reached the break-even mark in 1966 when they went 6–6–2. By 1966 the Jets had their quarterback, a brash, fun-loving kid with a rifle arm named Joe Namath. For the second time, Weeb Ewbank began building a contending team around a star quarterback.

What made Weeb Ewbank a winner? He'd coached winning football teams at the high school and college levels before winning with the Colts and Jets. The sample size gave ample evidence that he could win anywhere. Experience played a role, obviously, and the willingness to put in the preparation time. His ability to reach out and find players other coaches had given up on but could still contribute was a key as well.

Coaching Namath tested Ewbank's patience. Namath's penchant for throwing interceptions, especially as a younger pro, and his well-documented nightlife would have tested any coach. But Ewbank, by then in his 60s, stayed with his long-haired star and pushed the Jets toward a championship. Ike Kuhns, a reporter for the *Newark Star-Ledger*, wrote about an occasion in 1968 when Ewbank showed a group of beat writers a thick notebook devoted exclusively to playing quarterback. "The reporters who saw the book that day began to realize that it wasn't by coincidence that John Unitas and Joe Namath, two of the greatest quarterbacks of all time, developed under the same coach." In an amazing twist of fate, those two quarterbacks would be on opposing sidelines when Ewbank coached in his most famous game, the third Super Bowl, when Ewbank's Jets faced Shula's Colts.[25]

Even as he coached the Jets the Colts were probably never far from Ewbank's mind. During the 1967 season, Ewbank got himself so worked up during a halftime talk that he forgot who he was talking to. The Jets were losing to the Boston Patriots. Ewbank tried to fire the Jets up and got emotional: "All right, all you Colts, now get out there and win this baseball game!" Trailing 24–7, the Jets came back and earned a 24–24 tie. "That's the funny thing about Weeb," Namath said. "Sometimes he may not know which team he's coaching and sometimes he may not know which game we're playing but, damn, the man gets results. It's hard to argue with results."[26]

The Jets won the 1968 AFL title, making Ewbank the only coach ever to win titles in both the NFL and AFL. On January 12, 1969, Ewbank and the Jets stunned the football world, beating the heavily-favored Colts, 16–7 in Super Bowl III. Through the years, Namath has been credited with believing the Jets would win the game, and he did. But Ewbank felt the same way and eventually the team came to believe it. The Jets used a conservative offensive game plan and forced the Colts into turnovers. The game was not as close as the score indicated.

Ewbank was again riding high and in demand. He was everywhere: awards dinners, interviews and working on administrative team matters. His work load was bigger than ever, partially because by then he was the Jets' general manager as well as the coach. He told Steve Snider of the Associated Press, "This is a lot different. At Baltimore, I was only the coach. I could accept all sorts of off-season invitations to banquets and coaching clinics and really enjoy myself. But now I'm in a spot like a man running a corporation and also coaching a football team. There isn't time for much else."[27]

The Jets reached the playoffs once more the following season, but their loss to the Kansas City Chiefs in the first round of the playoffs was Ewbank's last postseason appearance. The Jets were never again better than break-even during the regular season under Ewbank. He announced before the 1973 season that it would be his last as coach. Namath was hurt much of that season and several other players had extended contract disputes that kept them out of training camp. The 1973 Jets went 4–10.

The Jets promoted Ewbank to vice president, but he resigned from that position after a year, intending to become an assistant coach at Columbia. He then discovered that he had an odd eye problem, a weakness in his eyelids. He was diagnosed as suffering from myasthenia gravis and rather than coach at Columbia he became a spokesman for the fight against that disease. Weeb and Lucy eventually settled in Oxford, Ohio.[28]

Weeb Ewbank died in Oxford on November 17, 1998, at 91 years of age.

NOTES

1. Paul Zimmerman, *The Last Season of Weeb Ewbank* (New York: Farrar, Straus and Giroux, 1974), 23–26. The story of Ewbank watching Thorpe was related by Ewbank to *New York Times* writer Dave Anderson and appeared in a September 18, 1994, story about Ewbank. The story can be found in the Ewbank file at the Pro Football Hall of Fame in Canton, Ohio. Anderson quotes Ewbank as saying Thorpe played for the Canton Bulldogs that day, but Thorpe played for the Oorang Indians in 1923. See *Total Football II*, p. 1,344. The Indians lost at the Columbus, Ohio, Tigers 27–3 on November 25, 1923, possibly the closest game the Indians played to the Ewbank home in eastern Indiana that year. *Total Football II*, p. 1,747. If the Ewbanks did venture to Columbus to see the Tigers play the Indians, they saw Thorpe boot a 47-yard field goal. Pro-football-reference.com, accessed August 24, 2016. Thorpe did play for the Bulldogs before and after 1923.

2. *Ibid.*

3. The marriage information is available on Ancestry.com.

4. Paul Zimmerman, "The Old Coach," *New York Post,* November 23, 1968, Ewbank file, Pro Football Hall of Fame.

5. Some sources refer to McGuffey High as University High School. McGuffey was named after the man who wrote *The McGuffey Reader* but it was closed in 1956 when Ohio's Milford Township and Oxford Township consolidated three high schools into one.

6. Zimmerman, *Last Season*, 34.

7. Author's communication with Teachers College of Columbia University.

8. Ewbank file, Pro Football Hall of Fame. See the page titled "Contributors—Coaches, Administrators, Owners, Officials, Etc., Weeb Ewbank—Coach." Ewbank's complete coaching record as listed by the *Pro Football Register*.

9. Zimmerman, *Last Season*, 277.

10. Brownbears.com, accessed August 25, 2016.

11. Zimmerman, *Last Season*, 275.

12. Arthur Daley, "Sports of the Times: In the Jetstream," *New York Times*, May 22, 1967, Ewbank file, Pro Football Hall of Fame.

13. Zimmerman, *Last Season*, 277.

14. *Ibid.*, 273–276.

15. Arthur J. Donovan, Jr., and Bob Drury, *Fatso* (New York: Avon Books, 1987), 139.

16. *Ibid.*, 141.

17. *Ibid.*, 157.

18. Pro-Football-Reference.com, accessed August 24, 2016.

19. Donovan, 143.

20. The pregame notes are in the Ewbank file at the Pro Football Hall of Fame. The story about Ewbank trying to punch Sam Huff was part of the Associated Press coverage of the game. A copy of the December 29, 1958, *Des Moines Register* in the Ewbank file at the Hall of Fame has the story.

21. Gary Cartwright, "Ewbank Shocked," *Dallas Morning News*, January 10, 1963, Section 2.

22. *Ibid.*

23. Donovan, 214–215.

24. Milton Gross, "Speaking Out: Weeb Ewbank-Jet Pilot," *New York Post*, April 16, 1963, Ewbank file, Pro Football Hall of Fame.

25. "The Media Remembers Weeb…," *Pro! Jets–Bills Game Program*, December 16, 1973, 6.

26. Joe Willie Namath with Dick Schaap, *I Can't Wait Until Tomorrow Because I Get Better Looking Every Day* (New York: Random House, 1969), 177.

27. Steve Snider, "The Sports Patrol," United Press International, May 16, 1969, Ewbank file, Pro Football Hall of Fame.

28. Clyde Bolton, "When Myasthenia Gravis Hit, Ewbank Punched Back," *Birmingham* (AL) *News*, August 12, 1976, 3C.

Assistant Coaches

JOHN W. LESKO, BERT GAMBINI

Charley Winner
—*JOHN W. LESKO*

Charles Height Winner was born in Somerville, New Jersey, on July 2, 1924. The future backfield coach of the 1958 Colts, Winner was the son of a laborer who operated a street-cleaning machine. After graduating from Somerville High School in 1942, he spent his freshman year at Southeast Missouri State Teachers College. Winner spent one year at that school before fighting for the United States in World War II as a member of Army Air Forces.

Winner was a radio operator and waist gunner who flew 17 missions aboard B-17 Flying Fortress bombers over Germany. On the 17th mission in the spring of 1945, the pilot misjudged the target making a second run necessary. The plane was shot down during that second run. Winner survived but was captured by the Germans, and spent six long weeks in a prison camp.

After he was released from the service, Winner enrolled at Washington University in St. Louis and played running back during the 1947 and 1948 seasons. The team's head coach was Weeb Ewbank, Winner's future boss with the Colts. Winner graduated in 1949 and spent the next football season as the freshman coach. The following year Winner married Ewbank's daughter, Nancy.

Winner began dating Nancy while he was playing for Ewbank. Apparently, Ewbank was not particularly fond of this situation. "Weeb used to grade all the game films, and I scored pretty well until I started dating his daughter. Then my grades went down," Winner said.[1]

While Ewbank spent the next several years as an assistant on Paul Brown's staff with the Cleveland Browns, Winner was an assistant coach at the Case Institute of Technology in Cleveland. In addition to that job, he also did some scouting work for the Browns. The big break for Winner came in 1954 when Ewbank was named the head coach of the Baltimore Colts. Ewbank hired Winner to coach the team's offensive and defensive ends. In his second season with the Colts, Winner was tasked with coaching the defensive backfield.

Winner became Ewbank's right-hand man, although the head coach was tough on his son-in-law. Ewbank gave Winner tough assignments to curtail any thoughts of favoritism. "I was mean to him, really," Ewbank said. "When it'd come to Christmastime, I'd make Charley go to bowl games. I really made it tough on Nancy. But if somebody had to miss a Christmas at home, poor Charley, he was the one who had to do it."[2]

There are no indications that Ewbank's tough love had a negative effect on Winner. The Colts' pass defense became one of the league's best under Winner's tutelage. It took several years to build up the defense, but by the fifth year under Winner, the Baltimore defense had become arguably the league's best.

The Colts' pass defense received more work than any other unit during training camp. Winner's dedication to greatness in camp paid dividends during the regular season. In 1958, the Colts led the league in defensive passer rating with a mark of 35.1. The Giants finished a distant second in this category with a rating of 52.3. The zone principles implemented by Winner confused opposing passers. The Colts led the league in interceptions with 35 and fewest passing touchdowns allowed with nine. The defense allowed just 169 points for an average of only 14.1 per game. That figure doesn't include the 34 points given up by offensive turnovers and special teams play.

During the 1958 NFL championship game, Winner coached on a platform above Yankee Stadium so that he could relay information to Ewbank. Although the Colts' defense did not play a great game, the team was still victorious and Winner was very proud. "I've worked for five championship teams, but that 1958 ring is one of my most valuable possessions. I wear it a lot," Winner stated.[3]

The Colts went on to win the NFL title again in 1959. Ewbank was fired after the 1962 campaign and went to New York to coach the Jets. Winner was given the opportunity to separate himself from Ewbank and remained in Baltimore for three more seasons under new head coach Don Shula, a former Colts defensive back.

On February 10, 1966, Winner was hired as the head coach of the St. Louis Cardinals. St. Louis had a very respectable record of 35–30–5 in Winner's five seasons, but they were never able to reach the playoffs. In 1970, the Cardinals began the season with a record of 8–2–1. During a stretch of four games the team allowed a total of six points. Winner was fired after the team lost its final three contests and missed the playoffs again. He stated, "I don't think the Cardinals should've fired me. We had a ball club that was about to win a championship."[4]

Winner's next stop was in Washington where he helped mold the Redskins' defense into one of the league's best. The 1972 Redskins lost Super Bowl VII to Shula's Miami Dolphins. Winner parlayed his success in Washington into a job with the New York Jets in 1973. Ewbank planned to make his 11th season his final one as the Jets' head coach. Ewbank hired his son-in-law as an assistant in 1973 with plans for Winner to take over as head coach when Ewbank retired. Ewbank indeed retired after the 1973 season and Winner was named the new head coach of the Jets.

The only bright spot in Winner's first seven games as head coach came when the Jets defeated the Chicago Bears 23–21 in the second week of the 1974 season. The players gave the game ball to Winner. The Jets won their final six games to finish with a mark of 7–7. Winner was unable to withstand another poor start and was fired after the team started 2–7 in 1975.

Winner's coaching career ended after the 1979 season in Cincinnati where he spent four seasons as an assistant coach. Winner then moved on to a front office position in Miami where he reconnected with his old buddy Don Shula. Winner oversaw college and pro personnel work and negotiated player contracts. Winner stated, "I had to do most of the work that a general manager would do, even though I didn't have that title."[5]

Winner retired after the 1991 season even though, as he would tell it, he never really worked. "I worked for 37 years in the NFL and I never felt like I worked a day in my life."[6] The last surviving coach from the 1958 NFL championship game, he has enjoyed retirement with Nancy in Fort Myers, Florida. One of Winner's favorite leisure activities is tennis, which he continues to play into his 90s.

In addition to American hero and successful pro football coach, Winner is also a member of a Hall of Fame. In 2015, Washington University inducted him into the University's Sports Hall of Fame. Above all, he was respected and well-liked by most who knew him. Former Cardinals running back Johnny Roland said, "He's a super guy."[7]

NOTES

1. Mike Klingaman, "Catching Up with … Former Colts coach Charley Winner," *Baltimore Sun*, September 5, 2014.
2. William Gildea, *When the Colts Belonged to Baltimore* (New York: Ticknor & Fields, 1994), 130.
3. Klingaman.
4. Dave Anderson, "Charley Winner to Coach Jets in '74, Replacing Ewbank, Father-in-Law," *New York Times*, February 2, 1973.
5. Harvey Greene, "This Winner Is a True American Hero," MiamiDolphins.com, November 11, 2014, www.miamidolphins.com/news/article-1/This-Winner-Is-A-True-American-Hero/d5d 01009-1329-4bad-a923-3f071e879ab4.
6. Greg Cote, "From War Hero to Don Shula's Right-Hand Man: The Life of Charley Winner," MiamiHerald.com, May 27, 2016, www.miamiherald.com/sports/spt-columns-blogs/greg-cote/ article80355532.html.
7. Robert L. Burnes, *Big Red* (Saint Charles, MO: Piraeus, 1975), 171.

REFERENCES

Bowden, Mark. *The Best Game Ever*. New York: Atlantic Monthly Press, 2008.
"Colts Stress Pass Defense in Drills for Giants Sunday." *Baltimore Sun*, September 19, 1958.
Danyluk, Tom. *The Super '70s*. Chicago: Mad Uke, 2005.
Hummer, Steve. "Winner Knows Game Will Never Be a War." *Sun-Sentinel*, July 27, 1988.
Marecek, Greg. *The St. Louis Football Cardinals*. St. Louis: Reedy Press, 2009.
Neft, David S., and Richard M. Cohen. *The Football Encyclopedia*. New York: St. Martin's Press, 1991.
Yeatter, Bryan L. *Joe Namath, Game by Game*. Jefferson, NC: McFarland, 2012.
Washington University Sports Hall of Fame, December 9, 2014.
Zimmerman, Paul. *The Last Season of Weeb Ewbank*. New York: Farrar, Straus and Giroux, 1974.

Herman Ball

—JOHN W. LESKO

The Baltimore offensive line was coached by Herman Ball in 1958. The Elkins, West Virginia, native joined Weeb Ewbank's staff in 1956, and Ball's fine coaching helped the Colts lead the league in points scored and yards from scrimmage in 1958. Ball's charges provided excellent pass blocking for Johnny Unitas and George Shaw while also opening up lanes for the running backs.

Ball was born on May 9, 1910. He enrolled at Davis & Elkins College after graduating from Elkins High School. Ball was a running guard on the 1933 Senator squad which led the country in scoring. Ball coached at Ridgeley High School in West Virginia after graduating in 1935. He moved on to Allegany High School in Cumberland, Maryland, the following season. The Campers compiled a 56–13–1 record with three undefeated seasons during Ball's seven years of service.

Ball implemented the T-formation before the 1941 season. He was amazed at how effective the formation had been for the Chicago Bears in their 73–0 whitewashing of the Washington Redskins in the 1940 NFL championship game. In the summer of 1941, Ball attended a coaching clinic held by Clark Shaughnessy and spent some time at the Bears training camp. The other high school coaches in the area were skeptical that the T could work on the high school level, but Ball got the last laugh.

Ball secured an assistant position at the University of Maryland following the 1942 season. Although Ball's stay at Maryland was not long, it proved very valuable as he served under coaching legends Clarence "Doc" Spears, Paul "Bear" Bryant and Shaughnessy. Ball joined the Washington Redskins as a part-time scout in 1945. Ball worked for both Maryland and the Redskins through 1945. In 1946, Ball signed with the Redskins as chief scout and a full-time assistant to Glen "Turk" Edwards.

Edwards was released from his coaching duties after the 1948 campaign. His replacement was John Whelchel. Midway through the 1949 season the Redskins had a record of 3–3–1, but it was not good enough for Washington owner George Preston Marshall. Whelchel was fired due to a personality conflict with Marshall and replaced by offensive line coach Ball. The team did not fare well down the stretch and finished with a record of 4–7–1. Ball was brought back as head coach for the 1950 season, but only mustered a record of 3–9. In January of 1951, Marshall tasked Ball with finding his own replacement. Ball went to a coaches' convention in January 1951. No replacement was found, and, due in part to his popularity with the players, Ball was retained as head coach for the 1951 season.

Ball was fired as head coach after starting 0–3. Dick Todd assumed the head coaching role and went 5–4 the rest of the way. Ball's overall record of 4–16 was not impressive, but his reputation as a valuable coach kept him employed by the Redskins as an assistant coach until 1954. "[Mr. Ball] made the Redskins a more exciting team by installing the pitchouts, the wider handoffs and a semblance of a running attack on a team that had been pass-crazy to the point of spectator boredom," wrote *Washington Post* sports columnist Shirley Povich.[1]

Ball moved on to Pittsburgh in 1955. He coached one year with the Steelers before being hired by Ewbank in 1956. The Colts offensive line blossomed in 1958. When asked why that was the case, Ball replied, "We have the same personnel playing for us and we are running the same plays. I would say we are a year older and a year wiser. Both [Jim] Parker and [George] Preas apparently have benefitted from a year's experience, while [Art] Spinney is playing good ball, just like last year. [Alex] Sandusky has seemed to grow."[2]

After the Colts won the championship in 1958, there was speculation that other pro teams or colleges would try to hire Ewbank's assistants. Ball's name was mentioned in the University of Maryland's search for a head coach. He stated, "I'm very happy here. It's a good job with good money, but I would not be averse to a head coaching position."[3]

Alas, Ball stayed on with the Colts through the 1962 season. He spent a single season as the Buffalo Bills' offensive line coach. The well-liked Ball then moved on to Philadelphia. Ball's coaching career ended after the 1968 season when the Eagles finished a dismal 2–12. Ball moved off the field and into the front office in 1969 as Philadelphia's director of player personnel. He would stay in that role until 1977. Ball was a consultant for the team through the 1986 season.

Ball passed away on January 12, 1999, in Paoli, Pennsylvania, due to complications from a heart ailment. Ball was survived by his wife of 59 years, Edna Staniforth Ball, and a son, Robert L. Ball. Once described by Shaughnessy as "one of the finest T-formation coaches in the country,"[4] Ball was a likeable and quiet man who had a reputation as a top-notch football strategist.

Notes

1. "Herman Ball Dies," *Washington Post*, January 14, 1999.
2. Cameron C. Snyder, "Brito, All-Pro End, Foe of Preas Sunday," *Baltimore Sun*, October 24, 1958.
3. Cameron C. Snyder, "Colt Coaches May Advance," *Baltimore Sun*, December 12, 1958.
4. "New Redskin Coach Rated Keen Student," *Reading Eagle*, November 8, 1949.

REFERENCES

"Ball Hunts Own Successor as Coach of Redskins." *Pittsburgh Press*, January 11, 1951.
"Colt Coaches May Advance." *Baltimore Sun*, December 12, 1958.
"Herman Ball Signed by Steelers as Aide to Walt Kiesling." *Pittsburgh Press*, January 9, 1955.
"Herman Ball 'T' Student." *The News* (Frederick, MD), November 19, 1949.
https://en.wikipedia.org/wiki/Herman_Ball.
Maxymuk, John. *NFL Head Coaches*. Jefferson, NC: McFarland, 2012.
Troup, T.J. *The Birth of Football's Modern 4–3 Defense*. Lanham, MD: Rowman & Littlefield, 2014.
2014 Official NFL Record & Fact Book. New York: Time Home Entertainment, 2014.
www.profootballarchives.com/coach/ball00150coach.html.

John Bridgers
—BERT GAMBINI

Colts head coach Weeb Ewbank hired 35-year-old John Bridgers, the head football coach of Johns Hopkins University, as a Baltimore assistant in 1957. A relatively anonymous hire, Ewbank was among the first to see the promise Bridgers embodied.

The team's front office wasn't thrilled with the choice and neither were some of the players on the field. Bridgers' Baltimore contributions, however, and the subsequent unfolding of what would prove to be a brilliant career, validated Ewbank's belief in a candidate who was a previously unknown, small college commodity.

Colts owner Carroll Rosenbloom was both surprised and disappointed by Ewbank's decision to hire Bridgers. Rosenbloom felt Bridgers lacked the experience necessary for such an appointment.[1] Baltimore's future Hall of Fame lineman Art Donovan, who believed his colorful career had prepared him for all of football's possibilities, was equally shocked.

"I've had a lot of things happen to me in professional football, but the one thing I never thought would happen [was that] I would have a coach from Johns Hopkins," said Donovan.[2]

The modest Johns Hopkins Jays football program played in the non-scholarship, lower level of college football. Bridgers' 10–21–1 record with the Jays from 1953 to 1956 was as unexceptional as the division's competition. Even the *Baltimore Sun* struggled with enumerating Bridgers' football credentials when announcing his arrival on the Colts' staff, choosing instead to focus on his other gifts.

"Johnny has regaled many Baltimore sport banquets with his speaking ability which combines a penetrating wit with a soft drawl and a wonderful ability to low-rate himself, for a masterly and humorous talk," wrote Cameron C. Snyder.[3]

Yet in many ways, Bridgers' talent, or at least his presence, at the podium played a role in his hiring. Johns Hopkins sits less than two miles from the site of the Colts' former home of Memorial Stadium in Baltimore. That proximity, combined with the dynamics of an era more quaint than today, often put Bridgers and Ewbank on the same program at local sports banquets.

In fact, less than a month before Bridgers' hiring, the two were at the head table at the Annapolis Touchdown Club's annual gathering when Bridgers, unaware of his immediate future, ironically referred to himself as "the least known coach in America."[4]

He had no reason to believe that obscurity was about to change soon. Two days after the banquet, Colts assistant Frank Lauterbur signed a new contract with the team.

1958 Colts coaching staff: assistants Herman Ball, Charley Winner, Bob Shaw, John Bridgers, and head coach Weeb Ewbank.

Within weeks of that signing however, Lauterbur was unexpectedly offered a similar position at the U.S. Military Academy at West Point.

"We just couldn't stand in the way of Army's fine offer to Frank," said Ewbank.[5]

Lauterbur resigned from the Colts on March 6, 1957. Ewbank hired Bridgers the next day.

Bridgers and Ewbank met in 1948. Each of them coached at small colleges playing in the final game that year. Head coach Ewbank's Washington University (St. Louis) defeated assistant coach Bridgers' University of the South 27–6, but the future Colts head man would remember his opponent.[6] They later arrived at their respective positions in Baltimore within a year of one another, Bridgers at Johns Hopkins in 1953 and Ewbank with the Colts in 1954. The two quickly became reacquainted. Ewbank often gave Bridgers, a frequent visitor to Baltimore's practices, tickets to the Colts' home games and the two often got together to discuss football.[7]

Bridgers may have been largely unknown, but not to Ewbank.

A World War II veteran and Purple Heart recipient, Bridgers left his studies at Auburn University to enter the Army. He moved quickly through the ranks from private to captain.

He returned to Auburn following his discharge, graduated in 1947, and stayed with the school as a faculty member teaching economics and coaching football.

After Auburn, Bridgers worked as an assistant at the University of the South in Sewanee, Tennessee, from 1947 to 1951. Bridgers' time in Sewanee was interrupted by another military tour of duty. Captain Bridgers was stationed in Hokkaido, Japan during the Korean War. Bridgers served as head coach of the First Cavalry Division in 1952 before accepting the head coaching job at Johns Hopkins in 1953.

Ewbank knew Bridgers' history very well and unhesitatingly put his new hire in charge of the defensive line and offensive tackles in 1957. Bridgers analyzed film of the coming week's opponent.[8] Ewbank realigned the assignments of his assistants in 1958, making Bridgers exclusively responsible for the defensive line while Herman Ball coached the entire offensive line.[9]

Bridgers' Baltimore stint was the springboard for a career that stretched 42 years and demonstrated his abilities as a forward thinking coach and administrator.

After Baltimore, Bridgers served as head coach at Baylor University from 1959 to 1968. He helped bring the modern passing game to college football after unmooring himself from the ground-based single wing offense of his early years. He racially integrated Baylor in 1966, and featured the first African American player in the history of the Southwest Conference.

Bridgers joined the Pittsburgh Steelers' staff in 1969 and urged new head coach Chuck Noll to take Terry Bradshaw with the team's first overall pick in the college draft.[10]

Bridgers was an assistant at South Carolina from 1970 to 1972. He became Florida State University's athletic director in 1973. Bridgers hired Bobby Bowden as the team's head football coach in 1976 and rescued a financially troubled athletic program. In 1979, he left Florida State and became athletic director at the University of New Mexico, turning around a program that had previously been scandalized by NCAA infractions.

Bridgers left the Lobos in 1987. He died at the age of 84 in Albuquerque in 2006. Upon his death his son Don stated, "He had a good life. He did the thing he really, really loved, which was to coach young men and teach them how to be not just good players but good people."[11]

NOTES

1. John D. Bridgers, *What's Right with Football* (Austin: Eakin Press, 1995), 79.
2. *Ibid.*, 83.
3. Cameron C. Snyder, "Colt Tackle Coach Named," *Baltimore Sun*, March 8, 1957.
4. Edwin H. Brandt, "Little Consoles Brennan at Fete," *Baltimore Sun*, February 12, 1957.
5. "Lauterbur Quits Staff of Colts," *Baltimore Sun*, March 7, 1957.
6. Bridgers, 25–26.
7. *Ibid.*, 78.
8. Walter Taylor, "What the Colt Fans Don't See," *Baltimore Sun*, September 29, 1957.
9. Bridgers, 80.
10. Kim Gorum, *Waco Tribune-Herald*, November 26, 2006, http://www.baylorbears.com/genrel/112706aac.html.
11. *Ibid.*

Bob Shaw
—BERT GAMBINI

Baltimore Colts end coach Bob Shaw dedicated part of the week preceding the team's 1958 championship game against the New York Giants to finding the right apartment building. He wanted something that offered a view of the Harlem River, looking toward the open end of Yankee Stadium in the Bronx.

It was Shaw's second year in Baltimore as an assistant. He would leave the team in a few months and assume a similar role with the San Francisco 49ers. At this moment, he had no interest in moving his wife and six-year-old son into a new home. Instead he was on assignment to spy on the Giants in order to learn if they were working on anything new for that Sunday's game.

Shaw was a steel-nerved veteran and Bronze Star recipient who served with the Army's 104th Infantry Division,[1] but he was anxious that this sort of clandestine job might jeopardize his coaching career. Team owner Carroll Rosenbloom tried to alleviate Shaw's concerns by guaranteeing the reluctant assistant a lifetime position in one of Rosenbloom's other businesses should the plan publically unravel.[2]

It never did. Shaw's future was as a football coach. He served as an assistant for 11 years in the National Football League for five different teams and one year in the college ranks. His head coaching roles included stints with the New Mexico State Military Institute, Otterbein College, and three Canadian Football League teams, earning Coach of the Year honors in 1976 with the Hamilton Tiger-Cats.

Shaw eventually found a building that rose high above the stadium's outfield, entered through the lobby and pressed the elevator to the top floor. He climbed the access stairway to the roof and with binoculars and a notepad set about a task that revealed little save for variations on a popular Giant reverse.[3]

Shaw joined the Colts' staff in April 1957, replacing Red Cumiskey, who retired from coaching to go into business.[4]

He arrived in Baltimore after three years coaching high school teams at Washington Court House and Cuyahoga Falls in Ohio.

For the Colts, in addition to coaching the ends, Shaw prepared scouting reports on Baltimore's upcoming opponents, a task that made him well suited for other related, albeit, shadier undertakings.

If Shaw was the only member of the Colts' coaching staff with reconnaissance experience, he was also the only member of that staff with professional playing experience.[5] He played three years with the Cleveland/Los Angeles Rams (1945–46 and 1949) and one year (1950) with the Chicago Cardinals followed by another three years in Canada with the Calgary Stampeders (1951–52) and Toronto Argonauts (1953). He also spent his football off-seasons playing in the old National Basketball League for the Toledo Jeeps, Youngstown Bears and Cleveland Allmen Transfers.

A record setting end on both sides of the border, Shaw honed his craft under the guidance of head coach Paul Brown at Ohio State. He played for the university's first national championship team in 1942 while earning All-America honors.

Shaw became the first player to catch five touchdown passes in a single game during his final NFL season, an accomplishment matched only twice since by Kellen Winslow in 1981 and Jerry Rice in 1990.

He set a league scoring mark of 110 points in 1952 playing for Calgary in the Western Interprovincial Football Union (WIFU), a predecessor of the Canadian Football League. The record was broken five years later, but only after the value of a touchdown in Canadian football increased from five points to six.

Shaw spent 1947 and 1948 out of football recovering from a cracked vertebrae suffered during a 1947 exhibition game against the Boston Yanks. In August 1948 reports of his possible return to the playing field wavered from having "a clean bill of health"[6] to serious doubt about the future of his career.[7]

The end of 1948's summer appeared to mark the end of Shaw's playing days when he signed a three-year deal as an assistant football coach at Loyola University.[8]

Shaw's time at Loyola ended surprisingly. He left the team in August 1949 apparently certain his injury had sufficiently healed for him to resume playing.[9]

He returned to the game as a pioneer. Shaw was among the first to play the position later called "tight end." In 1949, Shaw still lined up next to the right tackle, while the Rams other two ends split wide under head coach Clark Shaughnessy's innovative offensive scheme.[10]

Shaw's groundbreaking contributions to the game as an early tight end also contributed to his creative thinking as a coach. Just as he had defined a new position on the field as a player he similarly helped redefine an existing position from the sideline as a coach.

"Bob Shaw came at a critical stage of my career, and those two years [he was in Baltimore] changed my entire playing career," said former Colts receiver Raymond Berry, a member of the Pro Football Hall of Fame. "His concepts of route running were something I never would have discovered if not for him being there."[11]

"He was a brilliant man," said Berry.[12]

NOTES

1. "Robert Shaw," *Columbus Dispatch*, April 13, 2011.
2. John Steadman, "1958 Colts Had Better Team—and a Big Edge," *Baltimore Sun*, December 25, 1988.
3. John F. Steadman, *From Colts to Ravens* (Centreville, MD: Tidewater, 1997), 140–141.
4. "Sports in Brief," *Los Angeles Times*, April 9, 1957.
5. John D. Bridgers, *What's Right with Football* (Austin: Eakin Press,1995), 79.
6. Braven Dyer, "Rams Pleased with Outlook for 1948," *Los Angeles Times*, August 8, 1948.
7. Braven Dyer, "Rams Mix in Crucial Tilt Wednesday," *Los Angeles Times*, August 23, 1948.
8. "Shaw Signed as Aide at Loyola of Los Angeles," *Chicago Daily Tribune*, August 24. 1948.
9. Frank Finch, "End Bob Shaw Welcomed to Ram Squad," *Los Angeles Times*, August 9, 1949.
10. Jerry Roberts, *Pass Receiving in Early Pro Football* (Jefferson, NC: McFarland, 2016), 156.
11. Rob Oller, "Shaw's Life Was the Stuff of Hollywood," *Columbus Dispatch*, April 13, 2011.
12. *Ibid.*

Building the 1958 Colts

MATTHEW KEDDIE

Just prior to the 1958 NFL championship game, coach Weeb Ewbank delivered a pep talk to the squad that highlighted their disparate origins. In a masterpiece of the "Nobody Respects Us" theme, Ewbank went from player to player, reminding almost every player that someone had rejected him as unworthy before he got to the Colts. Even top draft pick Alan Ameche was told, "The Giants say you're not as good as Jim Brown."[1] What made the talk so memorable and effective is that it was true despite the imminent greatness of the team.

Baltimore was constructed of several of the game's greatest stars: Johnny Unitas, Art Donovan, Gino Marchetti and other future Hall of Famers. Baltimore went on to repeat as NFL champions in 1959, battering the New York Giants, 31–16. This begs the question:

Were they the best team ever assembled? The talent on the 1958 squad was of the highest order. From the remarkable Johnny Unitas at quarterback to Alan Ameche, Raymond Berry, and Lenny Moore, the Colts exceeded their peers at the offensive skill positions.

On the defensive side of the ball, this team was built stoutly from the ground up. Its toughness started with the dominating front four of Gino Marchetti, Art Donovan, Gene Lipscomb, and Don Joyce, who powered through opposing lines, creating all sorts of problems for opposing quarterbacks. They were a veteran quartet that combined for 26 years of NFL experience. The man who assembled and coached this talent was Weeb Ewbank. Ewbank's first pro coaching position was under the legendary Paul Brown in Cleveland as the team's tackle coach.[2] The X's and O's were important, but Brown's teaching really set him apart.

Ewbank was well schooled in the organization of a football team. From the start, Ewbank had a vision to build a winner in Baltimore.[3] He proclaimed, "My first big goal here is to start a regime very similar to the Cleveland Browns organization," and Ewbank had the support of his boss, owner Carroll Rosenbloom.[4]

Ewbank preached that winning would not come overnight: time, patience, and the proper personnel were required. At his hiring press conference, a confident Rosenbloom beamed, "We're pledged to bring this town a league championship, and Ewbank is the man to do it." Ewbank transformed the Colts from annual losers to the pinnacle of the game's success in just five years.

Rosenbloom was a bold man, but was also a fair one. Rosenbloom believed in opportunity for his both players and coaches, and he took excellent care of his players, both on and off the field. Carroll's son, Steve, asserted, "He was about doing whatever he thought was needed to have a winning team. He really wanted to win. He demanded everything you could give and then some. The better he thought you were, the more he pushed you."[5]

Colts management displayed versatility in acquiring talent through free agent signings, the draft, and trades. The key was combining youthful talent with veteran players; the plan was to assemble the squad over several years. When the group headed by Rosenbloom acquired the failing Dallas Texans franchise that was relocated to Baltimore in 1953, a number of the Texans players also came to Baltimore. A total of three 1958 starters came via Dallas: tight end Jim Mutscheller, defensive end Gino Marchetti, and defensive tackle Art Donovan. Mutscheller did not begin his NFL career until 1954 after he completed his military obligations and the team was moved to Baltimore.[6] Punter Dick Horn was also a former Texan. The tables below list each offensive and defensive starter and how each joined the Colts, with twelve positions being filled via the draft. Seven starters on offense and five on defense were Baltimore draftees.[7]

Colts Offensive Starters[8]

Position	Player	Year	How Acquired
QB	Unitas	1956	Free Agent (Steelers)
FB	Ameche	1955	Draft, #3
LH	Dupre	1955	Draft, #27
RH	Moore	1956	Draft, #9
LE	Berry	1954	Draft, #232
LT	Parker	1957	Draft, #8
LG	Spinney	1953	Trade (Browns)
C	Nutter	1954	Free Agent (Redskins)

Position	Player	Year	How Acquired
RG	Sandusky	1954	Draft, #184
RT	Preas	1955	Draft, #51
RE	Mutscheller	1954	Dallas Texans

Table 2. Colts Defensive Starters[9]

Position	Player	Year	How Acquired
LDE	Marchetti	1953	Dallas Texans
LDT	Donovan	1953	Dallas Texans
RDT	Lipscomb	1956	Waivers (Rams)
RDE	Joyce	1954	Trade (Cardinals)
LLB	Pellington	1953	Free Agent (Undrafted)
MLB	Shinnick	1957	Draft, #20
RLB	Sanford	1958	Trade (Cardinals)
LDH	Taseff	1953	Trade (Browns)
LDH	Davis	1957	Free Agent (Lions)
LS	Nelson	1957	Draft, #126
RS, P	Brown	1958	Draft, #50
K	Myhra	1956	Draft, #139

At the skill positions, backs Alan Ameche (1955) and L.G. Dupre (1955) and receivers Lenny Moore (1956) and Raymond Berry (1954) were all drafted from the college ranks. Further, three fifths of the offensive line were draftees—tackles Jim Parker (1956), George Preas (1955), and Alex Sandusky (1954).

In contrast to the offense, the defense was more veteran laden. Linebacker Don Shinnick (1957), safety Andy Nelson (1957) and rookie safety/punter Ray Brown (1958) were acquired via the draft, as was kicker Steve Myhra (1956).

Of those taken on offense, six players were drafted in 1954 or 1955. Only two Hall of Fame players came out of those two drafts. Ironically, both played on the 1958 team: Johnny Unitas and Raymond Berry. Of all the drafts that occurred in the 1950s, 1954, 1955 and 1959 (CB Dick LeBeau), produced the fewest number of Hall of Fame players.[10]

The Ameche, Dupre, and Moore backfield trio combined for 1,779 rushing yards and 18 rushing TDs in 1958.[11] Canton-bound Moore accounted for 938 of the trio's combined 1,130 receiving yards and seven of eight combined receiving touchdowns.[12] The triumvirate teamed with players Baltimore signed away from other clubs. Of most prominence was Johnny Unitas, considered one of the greatest steals in NFL history. Drafted by Pittsburgh, he received little playing time and was released in training camp. In an effort to make ends meet, Unitas worked multiple jobs to support his family and played semi-pro football with the Bloomfield Rams at $6 per game.[13] Unitas was contacted by the Colts in 1956 and offered $7,000 to sign with Baltimore.[14] It was a near perfect fit. Unitas came in at the right time, because during the 1956 season, starting quarterback George Shaw suffered a broken leg, yielding the reigns to Unitas. Unitas led the Colts to a 4–4 mark to finish the 1956 campaign. He remained the starter in 1957 despite Shaw's return, and catapulted the Colts to a 7–5 record, the franchise's first winning season. Ewbank averred, "I'm convinced that with just one or two more replacements we will have the finest football team in the country."[15]

Not as decorated, Buzz Nutter came over from the Washington Redskins in 1953.[16] After he failed to make the Redskins, Washington cut him, and Nutter was briefly out of football. Trekking home to West Virginia, Nutter worked in the steel industry for a year, then signed on with Baltimore.[17] Nutter made the most of his opportunity by serving as a prominent lineman to protect Unitas. According to Art Donovan, "Nutter was the most outstanding offensive player on the field. He was playing like a man possessed."[18]

Donovan also had strong praise for tight end Jim Mutscheller, who joined the Colts in 1954. Mutscheller was originally drafted by the New York Yanks (who become the Texans) in 1952, but he served a two-year military tour of duty.[19] Following his service, he joined the Colts in 1954.[20] Mutscheller worked hard during camp, was almost cut by Ewbank, but saved by Gino Marchetti: "Artie [Donovan] and I voted for Jimmy. He was too valuable to let go. He was all football."[21] Mutscheller took the ball and ran with it, making the most of his time with Baltimore. Statistically speaking, his best years came between 1955 and 1959.

On defense, starting middle linebacker Bill Pellington was cut by the Browns in 1952. He signed with the Colts in 1953. Left defensive halfback Milt Davis was drafted by Detroit but served an active tour of duty with the military from 1954 to 1956.[22] Upon his return, the Lions decided to part ways with Davis, citing racial differences. Davis was told, "We don't have a black teammate for you to go on road trips, therefore you can't stay on our team."[23] Davis signed with the Colts in 1957.[24]

Some veteran leadership came through trades. The most prominent transaction came at the start of the 1953 season.[25] Baltimore engaged Cleveland in a mass exchange of players, with five Colts heading for Cleveland, and ten Browns relocating to Baltimore in the largest trade in NFL history at the time. (Dallas and Minnesota completed an 18-player deal in 1989.)[26] The two franchises were in contrasting states. Cleveland was riding a wave of success at the time, earning an NFL Title in 1950 preceded by four straight AAFC titles, while competing in seven consecutive championship games.[27] Meanwhile, the Colts were fighting to break the franchise's losing tradition in Dallas.

The Colts sent linebacker Tom Catlin, defensive tackle Don Colo, offensive tackle Mike McCormack, defensive back John Petitbon, and offensive guard Herschel Forester to the Browns, in exchange for quarterback Harry Agganis, defensive backs Bert Rechichar, Don Shula, and Carl Taseff, offensive guards Elmer Wilhoite and Art Spinney, end Gern Nagler, linebacker Ed Sharkey, and tackles Stu Sheets and Dick Batten.[28]

Most of the returns for Baltimore were gone by 1958. However, Taseff and Spinney worked their way into starting roles. Though he had been traded to the Cards and traded back, both prior to the 1958 season, Rechichar was still with the Colts and handled long distance field goals, kickoffs, and punt returns. Other Colts starters who were brought in via trade were defensive lineman Don Joyce from the Cardinals (1954) and linebacker Leo Sanford. Sanford also came to Baltimore in a deal with the Cardinals, who received linebacker Dale Meinert in return in 1958.[29]

Colts reserves were acquired in a variety of ways. Backup quarterback George Shaw was the bonus pick in the 1955 Draft. Defensive end Ordell Braase was selected in the 1954 draft (160th overall). Fullback Billy Pricer (65th) and halfback Jack Call (151st) were selected in the 1957 draft. Kick returner Lenny Lyles was selected with the 11th pick of the 1958 draft. Right defensive halfback Art DeCarlo joined Baltimore in 1957, signing as a free agent from the Redskins.[30]

Baltimore also brought in additional faces in 1958. Tackle Ray Krouse was acquired in a trade with the Lions for a third-round pick in the 1959 draft. The Colts nabbed offensive tackle and one-time draftee Cleveland Brown Sherman Plunkett from the military, and free agent punter Avatus Stone from the Canadian Football League's Montreal Alouettes. Offensive guard Fuzzy Thurston was a free agent signee cut by the Eagles.

Rounding out the Colts' reserves was defensive back Jackie Simpson, the Colts' 44th overall pick in the 1957 Draft, who finished his military service in 1958.[31]

In sum, the 1958 Colts were brought together over the course of nearly a decade, piece-by-piece. Opportunity and chance were driving forces that led the franchise to come to Baltimore, and place its keys in the hands of an ambitious owner, who hired a patient coach to break the city's curse of losing football. Patience and perseverance assembled a team of young talent and veteran leadership that boasted prowess on both sides of the ball.

Notes

1. The pregame notes are in the Weeb Ewbank file at the Pro Football Hall of Fame.
2. Paul Zimmerman, *The Last Season of Weeb Ewbank* (New York: Farrar, Straus and Giroux, 1974), 275.
3. "Baltimore Colts Select Ewbank," *Eugene* (OR) *Register-Guard*, January 15, 1954.
4. "Colts Vindicate Weeb Ewbank," *Dayton Beach* (FL) *Morning Journal*, October 31, 1958.
5. John Eisenberg, "Carroll Rosenbloom: Man of Mystery," Press Box Online Baltimore, www.pressboxonline.com, accessed August 1, 2017.
6. Mike Klingaman, "Jim Mutscheller, Colts Tight End Who Made Key Plays in 1958 Championship, Dies at 85," *Baltimore Sun*, April 10, 2015.
7. "1958 Baltimore Colts Starters, Roster & Players," Pro Football Reference, http://www.pro-football-reference.com/teams/clt/1958_roster.htm, accessed December 1, 2016.
8. *Ibid.*
9. *Ibid.*
10. "Hall of Famers by Draft Year," Pro Football Hall of Fame, http://www.profootballhof.com/heroes-of-the-game/hall-of-famers-by-draft-year/#1950s.
11. Pro Football Reference, http://www.pro-football-reference.com/teams/clt/1958_roster.htm.
12. *Ibid.*
13. "Life *Before* Indianapolis: A History of the Baltimore Colts," http://bonesaw.tripod.com/Baltimore.htm, accessed December 26, 2016.
14. *Ibid.*
15. "Colts Vindicate Weeb Ewbank."
16. Matt Schudel, "Buzz Nutter; Colts Center Was in 'Greatest Game Ever,'" *Washington Post*, April 18, 2008, http://www.washingtonpost.com/wp-dyn/content/article/2008/04/17/AR2008041704037.html.
17. *Ibid.*
18. *Ibid.*
19. Klingaman.
20. *Ibid.*
21. *Ibid.*
22. "Milt Davis, a Cornerback on 2 Title-Winning Teams, Dies at 79," *New York Times*, last modified October 1, 2008, http://www.nytimes.com/2008/10/02/sports/football/02davis.html.
23. *Ibid.*
24. *Ibid.*
25. Keith Yowell, "1953: Browns and Colts Conclude 15-Player Trade," Today in Pro Football History, March 26, 2012, https://fs64sports.blogspot.com/2012/03/1953-browns-and-colts-conclude-15.html.
26. http://www.profootballhof.com/news/the-nfl-s-largest-trade/.
27. Yowell, "1953," Today in Pro Football History.
28. http://www.profootballhof.com/news/the-nfl-s-largest-trade/.
29. Pro Sports Transactions, http://www.prosportstransactions.com/, accessed December 1, 2016.
30. *Ibid.*
31. *Ibid.*

The 1958 Draft

Bert Gambini

Head coach Weeb Ewbank had a lot on his mind. His Baltimore Colts were atop the National Football League's Western Conference heading into the tenth week of the 1957 season, trying to win a fourth consecutive game for the first time in franchise history. But the Colts were ailing. Both of their offensive guards, Art Spinney and Alex Sandusky, had leg injuries, and the player behind them on the depth chart, Ken Jackson, was already filling in at offensive tackle for starter George Preas, who was out with a partially torn ligament in his left knee. Ewbank was also watching Jim Mutscheller whose ankle injury clouded the offensive end's playing status.

It was Saturday, November 30, and Ewbank was fully absorbed in preparations for the next day's game against the Los Angeles Rams. A win was imperative if the Colts were to maintain their one-game lead over the San Francisco 49ers and Detroit Lions. That priority and the team's mounting injuries kept his attention from a list compiled by Keith Molesworth, the Colt's vice president and director of player personnel.

Molesworth served as the Colt's head coach when the city of Baltimore rejoined the NFL in 1953. Ewbank took over the following year as Molesworth assumed a role primarily concerned with leading the team's developing scouting effort and identifying their draft prospects. Often referred to as the Colt's talent director, Molesworth had devoted much of the past week trying to discuss the list with the coach. Ewbank, meantime, was focused on his game plan. The world around him, even the peripheral football world unrelated to the Rams, could wait.

But time was running out.

The annual players' draft was only two days away, scheduled to begin in Philadelphia at the Warwick Hotel less than 24 hours after the Rams' game in Baltimore. The list Ewbank had been ignoring had the names of 50 college players Molesworth felt would be a good fit for Baltimore. The Colts' drive toward the playoffs was Ewbank's immediate concern. The two-hour drive to Philadelphia was less appealing, but the coach knew he had to appraise the assembled talent to some degree before Monday.

Ewbank had a cursory knowledge of the class of '58, but nothing comprehensive.

He wanted a big defensive tackle, primarily because of uncertainty about how much longer 32-year-old Art Donovan would continue to play. Kentucky's Lou Michaels was the coach's personal favorite. He also liked tackles Charlie Krueger of Texas A & M and Pittsburgh's Jim McCusker along with Auburn end Red Phillips.[1] Aside from those three players, Ewbank had identified only areas of need, like defensive back, offensive guard, and a big halfback, in addition to tackle. Molesworth was the one responsible for crafting the specifics, and he finally had his chance to present that work to the coach.

Taking the papers in hand, Ewbank moved unenthusiastically through all of the names.

"The pickings are thin," Ewbank would later tell the *Baltimore Sun*.[2]

The assessment wasn't critical of Molesworth's efforts, but rather a measure of reality.

"I'm afraid there are only 12 outstanding college players available," said Ewbank. "We'll get one of them, but that's all."[3]

Yet the Colts may have gotten more than Ewbank expected, including first-round pick Lenny Lyles, a halfback from Louisville; Mississippi's Ray Brown, an all-around back, in round five; and Johnny Sample, a seventh-round defensive back from Maryland State (now the University of Maryland Eastern Shore), "one of the brightest pro prospects to come out of Maryland in years," wrote the *Baltimore Sun*.[4]

By the time Baltimore made its first-round pick, the 11th overall, the Rams had already tabbed Michaels with the fourth selection (via quarterback Rudy Bukich's trade to the Washington Redskins before the start of the season) and Phillips with their own pick, the fifth overall.[5] Krueger went to the 49ers with the ninth pick. McCusker was still available, but the Colts passed on him in favor of Lyles, who Ewbank and Molesworth felt was the best player available when Baltimore made its first-round pick.[6]

"We just couldn't let [Lyles] get out of our hands," said Ewbank. "He is a good receiver and could be used as a two-way back and end combination."[7]

His college head coach Frank Camp identified him as a pro prospect of equal potential to Camp's former quarterback at Louisville, John Unitas.[8] "There is no doubt in my mind that [Lyles] will be a great pro player," said Camp. "He has speed, size, change of pace, excellent balance, is a good pass receiver and most of all, he has guts."

With Lenny Moore in 1956, Jim Parker in 1957 and now Lyles in 1958, the Colts for the third consecutive year drafted an African American with their first selection.

The NFL was still not a fully integrated league in the late 1950s, but Lyles said years later that the succession of draft choices was an indication of change in the face of the era's persistent civil rights abuses.[9]

All told, NFL teams selected 28 African Americans in 1958, a number that had climbed slowly since 1949 when the Chicago Bears made George Taliaferro the first African American drafted by an NFL team.[10] The New York Giants, Philadelphia Eagles, 49ers and Rams each selected five black players in 1958. The Chicago Cardinals, Pittsburgh Steelers, and Washington Redskins—the only team in the league at that time yet to racially integrate—didn't draft any African American players that year.[11]

Lyles spent the 1958 season in Baltimore, mostly as a kick returner. He was waived before the start of the 1959 season and picked up by the 49ers. Lyles played two years in San Francisco only to return to the Colts in 1961 as a defensive back, a position he held for nine years in Baltimore until retiring after the 1969 season. His ten years with the team made him the longest tenured Colts from the '58 draft.

After Lyles, the team's 30 other draft picks accounted for only 12 years of experience with the Colts. Their second-round pick, Colorado's Bob Stransky, a single wing tailback; third-round pick West Virginia's Joe Nicely, an offensive guard; and fourth-round pick, Penn State end Les Walters, never made the team. All three were cut during Baltimore's 1958 training camp. Stransky and Nicely had brief careers in Canada while Walters played eight games for the Redskins in 1958.

Brown was one of the best backs in years to still be available late in the draft.[12] A quarterback in college, he became a defensive back and punter in Baltimore and was the only draftee to immediately enter the Colts' starting lineup in 1958, but a knee injury ended his career after three seasons.

Sample became a capable member of Baltimore's secondary as a backup in 1958 and 1959, before replacing Brown in the starting lineup in 1960. At the start of the 1961 season, the Colts traded Sample to the Steelers. He also played for the Redskins before later helping to defeat the Colts as a member of the New York Jets in Super Bowl III.

The draft class had plenty of other talent, but most of the blue chip players landed outside of Baltimore.

The Green Bay Packers drafted linebacker Dan Currie from Michigan State in the first round and Idaho offensive guard Jerry Kramer in the fourth, plus future Hall of Fame members Jim Taylor, LSU fullback, in the second round and Illinois linebacker Ray Nitschke, who the Packers took with their second third-round pick—compliments of a trade with the New York Giants—right after the Colts selected Nicely.

The Cleveland Browns also found a future Hall of Fame inductee in the seventh round when they picked Illinois halfback Bobby Mitchell with the 84th overall pick. Linebackers Chuck Howley, the Bears' number one selection who played most of his career with the Dallas Cowboys, and Wayne Walker, a 15-year Lions veteran, were also part of the class of '58.

From the start, Ewbank felt Baltimore's position in the draft was troublesome. With the same record as the Giants, the teams alternated the tenth and 11th picks in each round after a coin toss gave the earlier pick in round one to the Giants. Ewbank's fear, which materialized on draft day, was that his favorites would most likely be gone by the time Baltimore made its first selection.

Regardless of that forecast, all the variables facing the Colts and the other 11 teams would be in place only during the first four rounds because of a draft structure peculiar to the period.

For four years from 1956 through 1959, the NFL conducted a two-day player draft with a preliminary session held while the regular season was still in progress. A concluding session followed weeks later after that year's championship game. For the 1958 draft, the league held rounds one through four on December 2, 1957, and rounds five through 30 on January 28, 1958, also at the Warwick in Philadelphia.

Commissioner Bert Bell instituted the two-day draft in an effort to thwart Canadian teams from signing the most promising college players before the NFL's teams could even secure negotiating rights.

Canada's Western Interprovincial Football Union and its counterpart in the east, the Interprovincial Rugby Football Union had begun successfully luring players away from the U.S. in the early 1950s. By 1957, there was a belief the Canadian threat had largely dissipated.[13] Nevertheless, since the Canadians played their championship in November, they could easily start negotiating with college players before that NFL wrapped up its season at the end of December.

But the NFL's forced head start was problematic.

Awkwardly splitting the draft into two pieces meant conducting a preliminary session at a point in the regular season when teams were often fighting for titles.[14] Coaches had to balance their mental energies between the potential future represented by the draft with the critical present of trying to reach the postseason. That's why Ewbank couldn't immediately tear himself away from that week's game plan to review a list of prospects.

Ewbank was well aware that scouting had measurable value. As an assistant under Cleveland Brown head coach Paul Brown, a pioneer of football scouting, he learned first-hand how early identification of talent could help build a team. But scouting was still a developing practice for most of the NFL in the late 1950s. Beside the Browns, some teams, like the Rams, were early adopters. Los Angeles dedicated as much as $60,000 annually to its scouting budget by 1958.[15] But those two teams were the exceptions. The Colts had just begun to invest in their program. In fact, the 1957 season was the first that team owner Carroll Rosenbloom hired scouts and paid their travel expenses.[16]

For most teams, the draft was a matter of name recognition from press clippings or a player's performance in a college bowl game, the latter option not open to teams in 1958 since the first draft day preceded intercollegiate postseason play. Scouting was mostly a word-of-mouth enterprise, and the voices of authority were college coaches and sports writers.

A good deal of decision making actually took place on the spot in the Warwick. And 1958 was an apparently exhausting challenge for teams who consumed more time scrutinizing picks than in previous years. Traditionally four draft rounds took three hours to complete. More than five bloated hours were needed to make 49 selections for the preliminary 1958 session.[17]

"We hardly know a thing about the boys we're forced to pick prematurely," an unnamed coach told the *Washington Post*. "All we have to go on is the word of someone else."[18]

So limiting was the process that it wasn't unusual for coaches to skip the first draft session entirely. New York Giants head coach Jim Lee Howell, for example, didn't attend the 1958 draft's early session. Co-owners Wellington and Jack Mara represented the Giants on the first of the year's two draft days.[19]

Holding draft sessions both before and after the postseason also meant two different selection orders. The standings after ten weeks of play determined the order of the preliminary draft while the league's final standings dictated the order of day two.

The 1957 NFL champion Detroit Lions were 6–4 following Week 10. The Colts and Giants were 7–3. The Browns had the league's best record at 8–1–1. As champion, the Lions selected last in each round in January 1958, but in December 1957, they picked ahead of the Colts, Giants and Browns.

"The business of having two drafts," noted the *Washington Post*'s prize-winning columnist Jack Walsh, "is a lot nonsense."[20]

The league dismissed whatever foolishness the press perceived in the draft's structure, but it couldn't ignore a congressional subcommittee's probing interest in the draft's bonus selection.

Since 1947, an out-of-the-hat draw determined which team would have the first overall pick in the draft. Each year's winning team became ineligible for future selections until all 12 teams had won the draw. The Packers' Curly Lambeau originated the bonus pick during the battle years with the rival All-America Football Conference to ensure every NFL team would have a chance at making the first overall selection regardless of its previous season's record.

The subcommittee, led by Rep. Emanuel Celler (R–NY), took no issue with the overall draft, with its order determined by a team's performance, but the bonus pick smacked of a sweepstakes and lawmakers asked if the NFL might be conducting what amounted to an illegal lottery. Bell considered restructuring the bonus pick but owners could not agree on an alternative. Since all 12 teams had made a bonus selection, the owners dispensed with retooling and voted instead at their league meeting in January 1958 to eliminate the pick from the draft.

For the 1958 draft, the last year of the bonus selection, the Chicago Cardinals had the pick by virtue of being the only team in the league yet to win the drawing. They selected Rice quarterback King Hill to open the preliminary draft on December 2.

In announcing the bonus selection, Cardinals head coach Ray Richards praised Hill's ball handling, running, punting, placekicking, and defensive skills. Richards even commented on Hill's ability as a basketball player and a golfer, but he said nothing about his passing.

When pressed, Richards called Hill a "capable passer."

"They didn't throw much at Rice this year, but when Hill did pass he was effective," said Richards."[21]

However puzzling Richards' dismissive comments about a quarterback's passing ability might sound to modern ears, the coach's remarks were not so unusual in the late 1950s given a fundamental incongruity between college football and its professional counterpart.

If teams had Bell to thank for rushing the draft to keep prospects on the U.S. side of the border those same teams were however on their own when it came to deciding which side of the ball their draft choices would play professionally.

The 60-minute men were nearly extinct by 1958 as the NFL evolved into a two-platoon game. But college teams between 1953 and 1963 operated with a limited substitution rule that required everyone to play on both sides of the ball.[22] That meant some of the best offensive players in the draft also happened to be some of the best defensive players, according to the *Baltimore Sun*.[23]

For the Colts, all four of their preliminary selections were unsure on draft day about the positions they'd be playing professionally.

Lyles, a star runner in college, found his home on defense. Stransky, a 1,000-yard rusher his senior year, said he preferred playing offense, but felt his best chance of making the team was on defense. Nicely (offensive guard and linebacker) said it didn't make any difference to him if he played offense or defense.

"I like football from any position," he said.

Walters (offensive end and defensive back) was a good receiver but saw himself as a defensive back in the pros.[24]

Ray Brown's case was a bit different. With John Unitas, the league's Most Valuable Player in 1957, established as the Colts' starting quarterback and George Shaw, the team's bonus pick in 1955, behind Unitas, Baltimore told Brown from the start that he would be developed as a defensive back and possibly a third quarterback.[25]

Brown was the first player taken on the draft's second day thanks to a trade and a coin toss. He was number one on Molesworth's list for day two and was also highly sought by the Packers.

As was the case after ten weeks of play, the Colts and Giants ended the 1957 season with identical records. Since their position in the final standings relative to the other teams had changed from Week Ten, the two teams now alternated the eighth and ninth picks in each round. The Giants won the toss to pick before the Colts in round five, but the flip didn't have an impact in that round since New York already had Baltimore's selection.

The Colts, meantime, had the Cardinals pick in round five through a 1957 trade that sent Baltimore tackle Tom Finnin to Chicago. The Packers, tied with the Cardinals for the worst record of 1957, alternated picks one and two in each round after a coin toss gave the first pick in the fifth round to the Cardinals, which Baltimore used on Brown.

Ewbank entered the draft's second day with a better outlook than the previous

December. Trade possibilities fueled some of that optimism, and though the Colts didn't make any draft-day deals, Ewbank felt ready to explore the Colts' draft options.[26]

"For this draft we are better equipped. We have been studying motion pictures of many prospects since the season ended," said Ewbank. "In our first draft session in December we had to go pretty much on hearsay and opinion. This time we have a line on the talent."[27]

Since the Colts' 1957 season ended on December 15, as did the Giants' season for that matter, their draft preparations could proceed without distractions. With so much work to do, perhaps it was easy to overlook an Associated Press story from December 21, 1957, that ran in the *New York Times* and other papers across the country about both the Detroit Lions and San Francisco 49ers being unhappy with the NFL's "sudden death" rule should their Western Conference playoff game the next day be tied at the end of regulation play.[28]

Ewbank was likely watching game film, not reading the papers. He knew his conclusions about players were based on a few frames, and that the draft was still, in his words, "a calculated guess." But he considered any footage to be "an invaluable aid,"[29] especially with so few name players available.[30]

The *Washington Post*'s Jack Walsh said teams hoped only to be surprised by an underrated player coming through for them.[31] And the Colts had a slim history of that happening. They had previously picked end Raymond Berry in the 20th round in 1954. Guard Alex Sandusky came out of the 16th round that same year. Safety Andy Nelson was taken in the 11th round of the 1957 draft.

The team, however, wasn't as fortunate in 1958's draft.

Seventeen of the 27 Baltimore selections on the second day were future picks. This category of draft picks included players with remaining eligibility whose class had graduated, as well as those from service academies who had to complete their military commitment before playing professionally. Teams that made future picks retained negotiating rights until the players were ready to turn pro.[32]

If future picks were an even bigger gamble in a draft era already characterized by uncertainty, perhaps no Colts selection was more curious than Virginia tackle John Diehl, a pick obtained from the Steelers, who had never played a college football game when the Colts selected him in the seventh round.

He tried, but was ineligible as a freshman; flunked out of school as a sophomore; was injured the next year; and dropped out a year after that.

Diehl returned to Virginia and saw some playing time in 1958, his final year of eligibility, but went to work for a trucking company in Charlottesville, Virginia, rather than trying out for the Colts in 1959. Diehl's employer wanted him close to headquarters, and he obliged for four years after getting out of school. But football stayed on his mind and eventually, partly through the encouragement of his friends, Diehl decided to give pro football a shot.

"There are several reasons why I'm making a belated bid," he told the *Baltimore Sun* in 1961. "First, I was approached by another club, but if I was to play, I wanted to play for the team that was nice enough to draft me."[33]

Diehl, in turn, was nice enough to give the Colts four years of dedicated service from 1961 to 1964 and was the Colts only future pick of 1958 to play a significant role in the team's future.

1958 Colts NFL Draft Choices

RND	OVL	NAME	POS	COLLEGE
1	11	Lenny Lyles	B	Louisville
2	24	Bob Stransky	B	Colorado
3	35	Joe Nicely	G	West Virginia
4	48	Les Walters	E	Penn State
5	50	Ray Brown*	B	Mississippi
6	69	Bob Taylor	E	Vanderbilt
7a	79	Johnny Sample**	B	Maryland State
7b	82	John Diehl	T	Virginia
8	93	Floyd Peters	G	San Francisco St.
9	106	Hal Bullard	B	Lenoir-Rhyne
10	117	Ray Schamber	E	South Dakota
11	130	Bobby Jordan	B	VMI
12	141	Tom Addison	G	South Carolina
13	154	Jerry Richardson	E	Wofford
14	165	Ken Hall	B	Texas A & M
15	178	Les Carney	B	Ohio
16	189	Archie Matsos	G	Michigan St.
17	202	Jim Reese	B	Minnesota
18	213	Dave Lloyd	C	Georgia
19	226	John Murnen	G	Bowling Green
20	237	Tom Forrestal	QB	Navy
21	250	Jim Faulk	B	TCU
22	261	Bob McKee	E	Monmouth
23	274	Phil Parslow	B	UCLA
24	285	Bobby Sandlin	B	Tennessee
25	298	Jim Rountree	B	Florida
26	309	Bob Grimes	T	Central Michigan
27	322	George Dintiman	B	Lock Haven
28	333	Jim Murphy	T	East Tennessee St.
29	346	Doug Padgett	E	Duke
30	356	Gary Lund	G	Utah St.

from Chicago Cardinals for Tom Finnin

**from Pittsburgh Steelers for Dick Young*

Notes

1. "Colts Ready for Draft," *Baltimore Sun*, December 2, 1957.
2. *Ibid.*
3. *Ibid.*
4. "Sketches of the New Colts," *Baltimore Sun*, December 3, 1957.
5. Draft data from pro-football-reference.com.
6. "Colts Draft Lyles, Then Add Stransky, Nicely, Walters," *Baltimore Sun*, December 3, 1957.
7. *Ibid.*
8. "Sketches of the New Colts."
9. Dan Manoyan, *Alan Ameche: The Story of "The Horse"* (Madison, WI: Terrace Books, 2012), 220.
10. Selected in round 13 by the Bears, Taliaferro opted to play the 1949 season for the Los Angeles Dons of the AAFC. He moved to the NFL the following season with the New York Yanks (1950–51) and played for the Dallas Texans (1952), Baltimore Colts (1953–54) and Philadelphia Eagles (1955).
11. "NFL Teams Draft 28 Tan Players," *Baltimore Afro-American*, February 8, 1958.
12. "Colts Select Quarterback Ray Brown in Grid Draft," *Baltimore Sun*, January 29, 1958.
13. "Pro Football Looks Foolish with Two Drafts," *Washington Post*, January 26, 1958.
14. Although the NFL abandoned the two-day structure after 1959, the issue of drafting during

the regular season would persist and magnify in the early 1960s after the arrival of the American Football League (AFL).

15. "Pro Football Look Foolish with Two Drafts."

16. Mark Bowden, *The Best Game Ever* (New York: Atlantic Monthly Press, 2008), 69.

17. "Colts Draft Lyles."

18. "Pro Football Looks Foolish with Two Drafts."

19. *Ibid.*

20. *Ibid.*

21. "Cards Decided on Hill Morning of NFL Draft," *The Christian Science Monitor*, December 13, 1957.

22. Gerald Holland, "The Man Who Changed Football," *Sports Illustrated*, February 3, 1964.

23. "Colts Ready for Draft."

24. "Sketches of the New Colts."

25. "Brown Faces Defense Job," *Baltimore Sun*, January 31, 1958.

26. "Colts Eyeing Trade Talks," *Baltimore Sun*, January 27, 1958.

27. *Ibid.*

28. "Sudden-Death Rule in Football Irks Coaches of Lions and 49ers," *New York Times*, December 21, 1957.

29. *Ibid.*

30. *Ibid.*

31. *Ibid.*

32. Bob Carroll, Michael Gershman, David Neff, and John Thorn, eds., *Total Football II* (New York: HarperCollins, 1999), 1443.

33. "The Morning After," *Baltimore Sun*, July 20, 1961.

PART 2

The 1958 Season

1958 Training Camp and Preseason

Mark L. Ford

Training camp in the NFL is a daily process of putting a large group of players through difficult workouts, six days a week. Like all coaches, Coach Ewbank gradually had to whittle his training camp number (he had 60 players expected to show up) down to the NFL roster limit (35 men in 1958). Here is that day-to-day process, starting with Thursday, July 24, 1958, when the first rookies were scheduled to report to the campus of Western Maryland College in the town of Westminster....

July 24 (Thursday): The Baltimore Colts had signed 29 rookies, in addition to the 35 veterans from 1957. Twenty-five of them were required to check in by 6 o'clock that evening.[1] The other four (Lenny Lyles, Joe Nicely, Ray Brown and Johnny Sample) were excused because they were training for the Chicago College All-Star Game. Two of the 25 didn't show up that day. Jim Lehman (of St. John's College of Minnesota), had undergone two surgeries for a hernia, and was in no shape for a workout, while Mike Friedberg (from Millersville Teachers College) had opted for being a teacher and high school football coach in New Jersey.[2]

July 25 (Friday): Day one of camp was an academic workout, with Weeb Ewbank as the lecturer. The rookies took notes and were given materials to study after class, on which they would be tested later on. One player complained to a reporter, "This is more book work and writing than I did in college! I got cramps in my fingers."[3] One of the rookies, Harlan Geach (a tackle from the College of Idaho) had had the misfortune of arriving at Westminster with an injured back and didn't pass the physical. The Colts' 25th-round draft pick of 1957, Geach became the first man waived, and was sent home on the first full day of camp.[4]

July 26 (Saturday): Thirty-two of the 35 veterans arrived on Saturday, July 26, with training to begin on Monday with the first drills. Six of the vets hadn't come to terms on their new contracts, though Raymond Berry would sign the next week, followed by Ken Jackson, L. G. Dupre and Art Spinney.

July 28 (Monday): Coach Ewbank was optimistic, and told reporters (perhaps not for the first time), "For the first time, we are going to have difficulty in paring the squad down to the 35-man playing limit."[5]

July 30 (Wednesday): Jim Faulk (a back from Texas Christian) hadn't done well in the workouts, and became the next man to be released by Ewbank. Most of the others, however, would stay long enough to play in uniform at the August 11 Blue-White Game.[6]

August 1 (Friday): After doing their workouts the day before in 94-degree weather, the Colts' players "received their baptism of rain and mud" during their 90-minute morning workout in a downpour, in what *Sun* reporter Cameron C. Snyder would call "a pneumonia-testing practice."[7]

August 2 (Saturday): The first week ended with a game-like scrimmage at 2:30, played in front of a crowd of 2,500. Scrimmages are governed by whatever rules the coaching staff wants, and the lone game official was fine with allowing "fifth down"—and even "sixth"—if the offense couldn't gain ten yards in the usual four. The vets from 1957 were the stars that day; Alan Ameche crashed over from the one foot line, and quarterback Cotton Davidson ran 60 yards for a score when he was trapped while trying to pass. For the defense, Jack Patera picked off a George Shaw pass and ran it back 30 yards for the score. "It's nothing, gang," he told onlookers, "just my first touchdown of the season."[8] The same day, the Colts signed a new rookie, Ken Hall, who had quit Texas A & M early to play Canadian ball for the Edmonton Eskimos, then found that he couldn't get along with the Eskimo coach.

August 11 (Monday): The rookies in camp got their first (and for many, their only) chance of wearing a full Colts uniform and playing in front of a large crowd at Memorial Stadium. The occasion was the annual Blue-White Game, an intrasquad contest played for charity (for 1958, the Boys Club of Baltimore). "The situation is made for some rookie, who has failed to impress," wrote Cameron Snyder, "to emerge as star of the intra-squad game. Ewbank will trim his squad after hostilities tonight and the big hits will come from the rookie contingent. An outstanding performance can postpone a ticket to football oblivion indefinitely."[9]

The selection of teams was a foreshadowing of how Ewbank sized up the 54 players after two weeks. The White squad had the first-string offense and the second-string defense, and by the same token, the Blue squad was composed of the first-string defense and second-string offense. Kicker Steve Myhra handled the field goals and extra points for both sides, and a few other players were switched to the opposite squad late in the game. The event attracted its largest crowd up to that time, standing room only with 48,309 fans turning out to watch.[10] Rookie Ray Schamber would joke later, "I never saw so many people. This is more people than we have in the entire state of South Dakota."[11]

As for the game itself, Lenny Moore scored for the Blues with a 95-yard kickoff return, aided by Glenn Dillon's block of the White team's Jesse Thomas. Steve Myhra kicked the point after for the Blues and, later in the first quarter, connected on a 27-yard field goal attempt for the Whites.

Ray Krouse attempted a field goal for the Blues in the second quarter, which was blocked by Jack Patera. In the third, the Blues drove to the ½-yard line, but the Blues' Hal Bullard fumbled the ball away. Howard Cissell returned a punt 41 yards to start the Blues' next drive, and Unitas guided the Blue team all the way down to the ½-yard line again, but Art DeCarlo knocked down a pass attempt to Raymond Berry on fourth down. Down 7–3 in the fourth quarter, the Whites attempted a 30-yard field goal, which Myhra missed. Then, with 3:19 left, the Whites scored the winning touchdown on a George Shaw pass to Jack Call. Myhra made the point after, having scored four *points* for the Whites, and one for the Blues.

August 13 (Wednesday): Only two players were waived after the Blue-White game. Defensive End James Barton (of Marshall), and guard Floyd Peters (an eighth-round pick from UCSF who would develop into a Pro Bowl defensive tackle for the Eagles in the

1960s) were sent home. As for the other newcomers, Ewbank said, "I'm going to give the rookies a thorough test in our Hershey game with the Philadelphia Eagles."[12]

August 16 (Saturday): The game with the Eagles was the opener of the Colts' six-game preseason, fully half as long as the 12-game regular season. Players received $50 for a game.[13] Most of those summer tune-ups were played in non-league cities, with the clubs getting paid an appearance fee and expenses when they took their show on the road. The Colts' summer barnstorming tour began with a trip to Hershey, Pennsylvania, a midway point for the two teams, 90 miles north of Baltimore, and 95 miles west of Philadelphia, before a crowd of 16,894.

The Eagles had a new head coach, Buck Shaw, and a new quarterback acquired from the Rams, future Hall of Famer Norm Van Brocklin. Since early preseason games are for testing the abilities of rookies and second-string players, George Shaw started at quarterback instead of Unitas, and Shaw passed to L. G. Dupre for the first score, with Myhra converting to put Baltimore up, 7–0. Van Brocklin appeared for the first time in an Eagle uniform, but on his first play, the Dutchman threw an interception that the Colts' Don Shinnick ran back to the 24. On the next play, the Colts had first and goal on the three yard line. Tom Brookshier picked off Shaw's pass in the end zone and ran it back 100 yards for an apparent touchdown. Unfortunately for the Eagles, they had had 12 men on the field.[14] Moving half the distance, the Colts scored from one and a half yards out on Billy Pricer's run, and went up 14–0 after less than five minutes. Toward the end of that first quarter, second-round draft pick Bob Stransky of Colorado was called for pass interference. The Eagles got possession on the Colts' nine yard line. Less than a minute into the second quarter, Van Brocklin passed to Tommy McDonald for the touchdown, and Bobby Walston kicked the point after to make the score 14–7.

On their next possession, the Colts made no gain, and Ewbank sent in one of his rookies, Bob McKee, a 22nd-round choice from Monmouth College. McKee booted the ball to the Eagles' 17, and McDonald ran it the other 83 yards for a touchdown. Stransky redeemed himself by blocking Walston's point attempt, and the score was 14–13. Later in the second quarter, the Colts scored on an option play. Moore took a handoff and, given the choice of running or passing, opted for the latter, tossing to rookie Les Walters of Penn State for the Colts' third touchdown. Tempers flared in the August heat, and Colts veteran Doug Eggers was tossed out of the game for throwing a punch at Chuck Bednarik, who happened to be laying on the ground at the time. As the half ended, the Colts were up, 21–13.

Soon into the second half, the Colts' Art Donovan and the Eagles' Ken Huxhold were sent to the locker room after getting into their own fistfight. Walston closed the gap to 21–16 with a 43-yard field goal. Unitas entered the game at this point, but the drive fizzled. Ewbank picked another rookie to attempt a punt, 11th-round pick Bobby Jordan of VMI, who pinned the Eagles on the four. After going back to the two, Van Brocklin guided a 98-yard Eagle drive that ended on a touchdown pass to Walston, who also kicked the point after to give the Eagles their first lead, 23–21. As the quarter drew to a close, Unitas passed to rookie Glen Dillon of Pitt for a first down on the 24. Two plays later, Unitas passed to Moore to retake the lead, 28–23. Near game's end, Van Brocklin engineered another long drive that finished with a touchdown pass to Bob Gunderman, whose NFL career would consist of a single game in 1957. The Eagles were ahead again, 30–28. Late in the game, Myhra was sent in for a 51-yard field goal that fell far short of the goalposts, and the Colts lost.[15] After the loss, Ewbank told reporters, "Disappointed? Not me.

We found out what we wanted to know. We knew we could lose the game if we played our rookies exclusively. We didn't want to lose it, that's for sure, but if you don't play the newcomers, how can you uncover a Milt Davis or an Andy Nelson?"[16] Disappointment would come soon enough.

August 18 (Monday): Lyles, Nicely, Brown and Sample had reported to the Colts over the weekend after the College All-Star Game (which the college kids had won, 35–19, over the defending NFL champion Detroit Lions), but Ewbank waived quarterback Cotton Davidson (who promptly found a job up north with the Calgary Stampeders), and dropped his sixth-round draft pick, end Bob Taylor of Vanderbilt, who had missed a lot of practice with a back ailment.[17] The next day, tenth-round selection Ray Schamber of South Dakota was sent home after he had reinjured his leg, and veteran halfback Henry Moore was cut as well, after Billy Pricer's superior rushing against the Eagles.[18]

August 20 (Wednesday): The Colts finished their twice-a-day practices, and had light drills. Despite the heat, Ray Berry was in full uniform for the workout, commenting, "I like to practice the way I have to play." Berry made a "once in a million" pass reception, leaping high and hauling in a long pass with one hand. "Why did I have to waste that catch in practice?" he lamented. "I should have saved it for the opening game."[19]

For their next preseason meeting, 47 of the Colts flew the next day to Austin, Texas, to face the Chicago Cardinals. It was a five-hour commercial flight, arriving later than planned because the extra weight of the players supposedly slowed the plane down.[20]

August 23 (Saturday): About 14,000 fans came to watch the Chicago Cardinals "host" the Colts in Texas. Although the Colts had replaced the NFL's Dallas Texans after the 1952 season, the Cardinals had drawn a good crowd in Austin the summer before, and were scheduled to be there again in 1959. In the first quarter, both teams had to punt on their opening drives. When the Cardinals kicked the ball away on fourth down and 34, Lenny Moore fielded the ball and, with a key block by Carl Taseff, ran it back 66 yards for the first touchdown. The Colts went up, 7–0. After another exchange of punts, Cardinals quarterback Lamar McHan drove the team 59 yards in six plays and scored on a pass to Jimmy Sears. Tying the game at 7–7 was a kick by Bert Rechichar, who had played the previous five seasons for Baltimore until he was traded to the Cardinals during the offseason. Only 15 seconds later, the Cardinals scored again. Rookie Howard Cissell of Arkansas State fielded the kickoff for the Colts, and got to the 26 yard line before fumbling the ball, which the Cards' Jim Matheny ran back for a touchdown. Rechichar converted again, and the Chicago Cardinals were ahead, 14–7 as the first quarter ended.

A pass from Unitas to the Colts' 14th-round pick, Ken Hall of Texas A & M, gave the team a first down inside the ten, and within one yard of goal on fourth down, Unitas went for a touchdown. The pitch to Pricer failed and the Cardinals took over on downs. Baltimore had another chance when they made a fair catch on the Cardinals' 45. George Shaw passed to the Colts' first-round pick, Lenny Lyles, who ran 47 yards (behind a block by Sherman Plunkett) for the touchdown. Myhra's kick tied the game again, 14–14. In the final minute of the half, Shaw took to the air again and drove the team all the way to the one yard line where Steve Myhra kicked an eight-yard field goal to give the Colts a 17–14 lead at halftime.[21]

After the second half kickoff, the Cardinals drove 62 yards in two plays, ending with Lamar McHan's TD pass to Gern Nagler. Once again, Rechichar converted against his former team, and the men from South Chicago were up, 21–17. The Colts fumbled the ball away after three plays, but Leo Sanford, recently acquired from the Cardinals, got the ball back after his old teammate Ollie Matson lost the ball on the Colts' 42. Shaw went for it on fourth down twice in the drive, once on a fourth and nine play that got to the two-yard line, and again on fourth and goal to Berry. The Colts regained the lead, 24–21. On the Colts' next possession, Shaw drove the team to the two-yard line again, but was replaced by Unitas on fourth down. Johnny U's pass was batted down by Night Train Lane in the end zone. In the fourth quarter, the Colts had the ball back, and Unitas drove them to the two-yard line again on one pass and by running the ball himself three times, ending with a one-yard carry. The Colts widened their lead, 31–21. The Cardinals closed the gap again, 31–28, on a run by rookie passer M.C. Reynolds and Bobby Joe Conrad's conversion Unitas drove within 12 yards of another touchdown by the two-minute warning, but on fourth and six, Coach Ewbank sent Myhra in for a 19-yard field goal that the Cardinals' Jim Taylor blocked. With time running out, Reynolds threw long passes and got the Cards to the 22-yard line with five seconds left on the clock, close enough for Conrad to make the kick to tie the game, 31–31.[22]

August 26 (Tuesday): "We found out about a few more players," Coach Ewbank said after returning from Austin, "though we're through experimenting." Ninth-round draft choice Hal Bullard, a halfback from Lenoir-Rhyne (who had lost a fumble in the Blue-White Game), was the first cut after the return from Austin. The same day, Ewbank found a punter in 28-year-old Dick Horn, who was attending medical school at Stanford and who had stayed in shape over the years by playing rugby.[23] The next day, guard and 12th-round pick Tom Addison from South Carolina left to return to graduate school at his alma mater, and Howard Cissell (who had lost the ball while returning the kickoff days earlier) was sent home.[24] Thursday, Bob McKee of Monmouth College, who had been tested as a punter, was let go now that Horn had been acquired, bringing the roster down to 47 in time for the home game against Washington.[25]

August 29 (Friday): "We're not much better than the Colts," Washington owner George Preston Marshall would say after the game. "The Colts simply played bad football."[26] The home game didn't attract many fans from either city, filling less than half the seats (18,131 out of 48,000). The low attendance was blamed on the Labor Day weekend. Folks who paid to see the game probably wished they had stayed home.

The first quarter wasn't spectacular; the Colts made only three first downs, the Redskins just one, and the closest either team came to scoring was Myhra's 32-yard field goal try, which was blocked by rookie Frank Kuchta. Six minutes into the second period, however, things went awry. *Baltimore Sun* reporter Cameron C. Snyder would write the next day, "the supposedly strong Colt defensive line apparently showed the Redskins its press clippings, but, unfortunately, the Capital crew was too busy running over, through and around the Colts to read them."[27]

Eddie LeBaron drove the Skins 59 yards in ten plays, ending with Sid Watson running in from the one, and Sam Baker converting for a 7–0 Washington lead. Three plays later, Alan Ameche fumbled a handoff from Unitas, and the Redskins' Chet Ostrowski recovered on the Baltimore 37. LeBaron drove the Redskins down to the 14 and found Watson wide open in the end zone for a 14–0 lead. On the Colts' next play, Unitas tried to pass as he was being tackled, and Washington's Chuck Drazenovich ran the interception back for a third touchdown to go up 21–0. Besides the three conversions, Baker made a 17-yard field goal right before halftime. In less than nine minutes, the Skins had scored 24 points.[28]

We don't know what Ewbank said about the 24–0 deficit at halftime, but he substituted Shaw for Unitas. Shaw drove the Colts 80 yards in seven plays, concluding with Moore's 33-yard run through several tacklers for the touchdown. Myhra converted and closed the gap to 24–7. Milt Davis recovered a fumble late in the quarter, and as the drive continued into the fourth period, the Colts reached the three-yard line. On fourth and one, Alan Ameche's run was stopped and the Redskins took over. Even after the Redskins fumbled deep in their own territory, the Colts' possession was short-lived as Shaw threw an interception. Washington's Torgy Torgeson picked off Shaw's pass, and lateraled to Dick Lynch, who got to the Baltimore 39. Baker kicked a 17-yard field goal for the last score and a 27–7 Redskins victory. Adding insult to injury, Washington's coach Joe Kuharich told Ewbank, "Thanks, Weeb, your mistakes gave us the game."[29]

September 1 (Monday): "Colts to Get Bawling Out" was the headline of the Monday morning *Baltimore Sun*, with Ewbank announcing that he would be cleaning house, recounting Saturday's blunders, and promising that "further incidents of missed assignments and shoddy play like that revealed in the Redskin game will result in stiff fines."[30] With 47 players, Ewbank was required by the league to pare his roster to 43 by Tuesday. He started by waiving three defenders, including the team's second-round draft choice, Bob Stransky of Colorado. Stransky had been used as a defensive back despite having been college football's second leading rusher in 1957.[31] The next day, he gave the axe to two rookies, safety Joe Cannavino of Ohio State, and receiver Glen Dillon of Pitt, followed by three-year veteran safety Jesse Thomas.[32]

September 3 (Wednesday): Another veteran defender from 1957, defensive end Luke Owens, was dismissed on Wednesday, and the Colts made a trade to get back another defender from 1957, Bert Rechichar, from the Chicago Cardinals. Rechichar, described as "the victim of monetary circumstances" because he was "one of the highest paid defensive backs in the NFL," had been dealt away by the Colts during the spring for "an undisclosed draft choice."[33]

September 6 (Saturday): Buffalo was still a couple of years away from getting its AFL franchise, but in 1958, it hosted two preseason games, and even one of the Chicago Cardinals' regular season home games. While 14,000 fans bought tickets, only 8,661 of them went through the turnstiles after heavy rains were forecast. In the pouring rain, the Colts remained winless for their fourth consecutive week, this time losing to the Steelers. Unitas started at quarterback, while Pittsburgh was led by a future Baltimore Colts passer, Earl Morrall. Bert Rechichar was back on the Colts' roster, two weeks after he had been playing against his old teammates, and kicked off. The Steelers' opening drive ended with a punt by a future Buffalo Bills star (and a far future U.S. congressman), Jack Kemp. Baltimore didn't reach the end zone, but was able to get a 21-yard field goal from Myhra, and a 3–0 lead. In the second quarter, Pittsburgh intercepted a Unitas pass at its own 38, and Morrall drove the team 62 yards, finishing with a 31-yard pass to Ray Mathews in the end zone. Andy Nelson broke through the line, however, and blocked Tom Miner's conversion attempt, limiting the Steelers to a 6–3 lead. On their next possession, the Colts were halted at their 40, and Ewbank decided to give Bobby Jordan one more try as a punter. The ball went only 22 yards. With only 0:25 left in the half, Morrall completed a 48-yard pass attempt to one of the Steelers' practice squad players, Leon Jamison. With Miner's point after, Pittsburgh took a 13–3 lead into the locker room.

By the second half, the drizzle that started the game had turned into a downpour. A series of rushes by Lenny Moore got the Colts from their 33-yard line to the Steelers' 23-yard line. From there, Unitas passed to Berry, Myhra kicked, and the Colts closed the gap to 13–10. That would prove to be the end of the scoring. The field and the football were both slippery, and receivers couldn't hang on to the ball. Early in the fourth quarter, Myhra's 38-yard field goal try was wide right. Turnovers thwarted several chances for a Colts victory. The 13–10 loss gave the winless Colts a 0–3–1 record in the preseason, the worst of the NFL's 12 teams.[34]

To make matters worse, four of the Colts' players had to be treated for chemical burns after the game because the yardage lines were marked with calcium oxide, better known as "quicklime." Mixed with the rain, the chemical reaction can generate a temperature of 300 degrees. "I have never heard of anything so stupid as using unslaked lime for the yardage lines," said Colts trainer Ed Block. "Don Joyce received second degree burns, while Gino Marchetti, Don Shinnick and Raymond Berry were burned to a lesser degree. Suppose some of that lime got in the players' eyes? It would have blinded them."[35]

September 9 (Tuesday): Ewbank released only one player in the wake of the game at Buffalo, third-round draft choice Joe Nicely, who had been one of four Colts draftees who had been picked for the College All-Star Game. The time spent training with the college stars had caused him to miss the first three weeks at Westminster. Out of the first ten draft picks for 1958, Ewbank had only four left on his 41-man squad.[36] Sunday's exhibition would be at Memorial Stadium against the New York Giants, but by the end of the day, less than 3,000 tickets had been bought. *Sun* sportswriter Jesse A. Linthicum commented, "These tickets are priced at $4 each, a sum scarcely in keeping with the brand of football the Colts have been playing."[37]

September 10 (Wednesday): Classes had started up again at Western Maryland College, so the team practiced at Kirk Field, Baltimore's common ground for school sports, and concluded that even if it was adequate for high school players, it was "too dangerous for the Colts" because "the turf was rocky and baked almost to the thickness of brick." Thursday's workouts were relocated to another city property, Herring Run Park, which had its own problems including "the disadvantage of being unable to restrain spectators from wandering all over the practice area."[38]

September 14 (Sunday): Baltimore fans showed their disapproval of their .000 team by staying away from Memorial Stadium. The stands were more than three-fourths empty for the contest between the two clubs that would meet three months later for the NFL championship. In mid–September, however, the Colts and Giants were the worst in preseason play. The future NFL champs were 0–3–1, and their fated title game opponents were 1–3–0 after four exhibitions. "Maybe the Baltimore Colts are playing possum in their exhibition schedule," an Associated Press story noted, "but they aren't making the experts look good who picked them as a championship contender in the National Football League this year."[39] The NBC television network, however, had contracted in advance to broadcast both scheduled Colts vs. Giants exhibitions, so the 1 p.m. game was seen nationally (except for Baltimore, where it was blacked out). TV couldn't be blamed for the low turnout, nor could the weather, which was "sunny and pleasant" that afternoon. The paid attendance was only 11,111.

It was too bad, because the starting lineup for the Colts was identical to the one that would play in the December 28 game, and the Giants' lineup was almost the same as well. Earlier in the week, Ewbank announced that experimenting was over and that he would use his regulars for the rest of the preseason; Giants coach Jim Lee Howell pledged to do the same.[40] After the Colts' defense forced the Giants to punt, Baltimore's men showed what they could do. In seven plays, marked by Moore's running and Unitas' passing, the team drove from their 32 to the two-yard line, with Unitas finding Berry in the end zone and Myhra converting for the 7–0 lead. The Giants went one better, as Don Heinrich guided his team 87 yards in just seven plays, including a 51-yard pass to Alex Webster, and finishing with a nine-yard toss to Kyle Rote. Pat Summerall converted to tie the game 7–7.

In the second quarter, Cart Taseff picked off a Heinrich pass on the Colts' 37. On first down, Lenny Moore ran the other 63 yards behind the blocking of Jim Parker, and the Colts were up again, 14–7. Once again, the Giants responded in kind, this time with Charlie Conerly at the helm. After a 39-yard pass play from Conerly to Kyle Rote reached the 13-yard line, Conerly found Ken MacAfee alone in the end zone, and the game was tied at halftime, 14–14.

There was no scoring in the third quarter. At the end of the quarter, a Giants goal line stand netted them the ball at their own six-inch line. Having 11 men either partly or entirely in their own end zone, the Giants punted on first down. Carl Taseff fielded the punt on the 49 and ran it back to the 23. The Colts were at the 17 as the fourth quarter began. On the next play, they reached the four, and L. G. Dupre went over from there. The Colts were ahead once more, 21–14. After the Giants took the kickoff, Conerly drove them into Colts territory. Ray Brown picked off a pass on the 34, then ran 66 yards "behind a wall of blockers" for the Colts' fourth touchdown. Steve Myhra's extra point attempt was blocked, so the Colts' lead was 27–14. On their next possession, Conerly drove the Giants from their 38 and ended with a seven-yard pass to Kyle Rote. Summerall's kick was good, and the Giants were down by just six points, 27–21.

In the final minutes, the Giants made their way to the Colts' 47 and a first down. Conerly heaved a 40-yard pass and Frank Gifford came down with it at the seven-yard line—but not before he had shoved Andy Nelson out of the way. The offensive pass interference penalty moved the Giants a long way back; instead of being seven yards from a touchdown, they were now 62 yards away. After being slapped with another 15-yard penalty, the Giants repeated the down at second and 39, and fumbled the ball; they recovered it on their 14-yard line. Time ran out with the Giants running a play facing a third and 49 situation, and—not for the last time that year—the Baltimore Colts defeated the New York Giants by six points. Final score in the Colts' first win of the preseason, Baltimore 27, New York 21.[41]

September 16 (Tuesday): The league required all teams to be down to 38 players by day's end, so Ewbank had to send away three men. Only one was a rookie, Bobby Jordan from VMI who hadn't panned out as a punter. Ken Jackson was a six-year NFL veteran who had been a lineman with the Colts since their arrival in Baltimore in 1953, and one of the last remaining members of the Dallas Texans. Jack Patera had been on the Colts for three seasons as a middle linebacker, and Ewbank admitted that, "He's still a good middle guard … but we can't keep them all."[42] Patera would be picked up by the Cards two days later, and would later become better known as the Seattle Seahawks' first head coach. In another comment that day, Ewbank offered a bit of unassailable wisdom about the preseason closer with the Giants. "The only way we're going to lose this Sunday," he observed, "is for them to beat us."[43]

September 21 (Sunday): The final tune-up game for both the Colts and the Giants took place, not in Baltimore nor New York, but at the Kentucky State Fairgrounds in Louisville, Kentucky. This was the third consecutive preseason for a Colts game in the Derby City, with University of Louisville alumnus Johnny Unitas being the guest of honor.

This time around, the exhibition was even more appealing because it featured former another U of L star, the Colts' number one draft choice Lenny Lyles, whom Ewbank started at left halfback in place of L. G. Dupre. With the exception of Lyles, the starting lineups for both teams were the same as they would be in the NFL championship three months later.

The Kiwanis Club benefit organizers had hoped for at least 20,000 people; a local reporter optimistically noted before the game that "with the N.F.L. considering two additional franchises, a capacity turnout could enrichen Louisville chances."[44] Instead, a rain forecast kept away a lot of folks (and the pipe dream of a Louisville NFL team), and the turnout was 14,108.[45] Lyles took the opening kickoff, and on the first play, he was the recipient of what would have been a "sure touchdown pass" from Johnny Unitas, but the ball dropped off of his fingertips.[46] It took another drive for Unitas to guide the team to a score, starting from the 20 and ending with a 19-yard pass to Raymond Berry in the end zone. With Myhra's kick, the Colts took a 7–0 lead. As the first quarter drew to an end, the Colts were on the Giants' 15 and in a position to score again. Two plays into the second period, Unitas found Berry again on an 11-yard play, and the lead expanded to 14–0. On the first play after the Giants took the kickoff, Alex Webster fumbled and Big Daddy Lipscomb recovered on the Giants' 22. Lyles carried the ball on three of the next four plays, including a four-yard run around right end to score, and the Colts were now ahead 21–0.

After halting two Colts drives, the Giants got on the board with a 38-yard pass play from Charlie Conerly to Bob Schnelker, and the point after by Pat Summerall, to narrow the gap to 21–7. Moments later, the Colts were ahead by three touchdowns again, thanks to Lenny Moore's 91-yard kickoff return. At halftime, Baltimore was ahead, 28–7. After stymying the Giants' opening drive in the third quarter, the Colts were halted on the Giants' 16 and opted for a Myhra field goal on fourth and four, with Ray Brown as the holder; or so it seemed. Brown took the snap, then stood up and passed to Gino Marchetti for the Colts' fifth touchdown. Brown graciously allowed Myhra to make the next kick for the point after and a 35–7 lead.

In seven plays, Conerly drove the Giants 80 yards, finishing with a 12-yard pass to Schnelker, to be down once more by only three touchdowns and a 35–14 score.[47] Don Heinrich took over for Conerly, but the Colts' Dick Szymanski picked off Heinrich's third down pass and ran it back 26 yards to up the score to 42–14. A Frank Gifford touchdown pass to Kyle Rote concluded the scoring, 42–21.

With 38 players on the squad at game's end, and the league mandate to be down to 35 by 2 p.m. Tuesday, Ewbank waived veteran linebacker Doug Eggers[48] and the team's fourth-round draft pick, rookie end Les Walters of Penn State, then placed rookie halfback Ken Hall (the 14th rounder from Texas A & M) on injured reserve.[49] After their rough start, the Colts had finished the preseason with a two-game winning streak and a 2–3–1 record. Their regular season opener would be at home on September 28 against Detroit and, as with all NFL teams, they would start that Sunday at 0–0–0.

NOTES

1. "Colts Open Camp Today," *Baltimore Sun*, July 24, 1958.
2. "Twenty-One Rookies Reach Colt Training Camp," *Baltimore Sun*, July 25, 1958.
3. "Colt Rookies Indoctrinated with Ewbank's Book Work," *Baltimore Sun*, July 26, 1958.
4. "Vets Arrive at Colt Camp," *Baltimore Sun*, July 27, 1958.
5. "Colts Begin First Drills," *Baltimore Sun*, July 29, 1958.

6. "Colts Drop Rookie Faulk," *Baltimore Sun*, August 1, 1958.

7. "Colts Sign 2 Holdouts," *Baltimore Sun*, August 2, 1958.

8. "Ameche and Davidson Score as Colts Engage in First Scrimmage," *Baltimore Sun*, August 3, 1958.

9. "Colt Whites Face Blues at Stadium," *Baltimore Sun*, August 11, 1958.

10. "48,309 Watch as Whites Nip Blues in Colt Game, 10–7," *Baltimore Sun*, August 12, 1958.

11. "Rookies Impress Coach," *Frederick* (MD) *News*, August 13, 1958.

12. "Peters and Barton Go in First Colt Squad Cut," *Baltimore Sun*, August 14, 1958.

13. "17,000 to See Colts Tonight," *Baltimore Sun*, August 16, 1958.

14. Herb Good, "Eagles Edge Colts, 30–28, as Van Passes for 3 TDs," *Philadelphia Inquirer*, August 17, 1958.

15. "Eagles Beat Colts on Van Brocklin's Passing, 30–28," *Baltimore Sun*, August 17, 1958.

16. "Pricer, Shaw and Plunkett Praised by Coach Ewbank," *Baltimore Sun*, August 18, 1958.

17. "Colts Drop End Taylor; Squad at 52," *Baltimore Sun*, August 19, 1958.

18. "Colts Give Krouse Shot at End," *Baltimore Sun*, August 20, 1958.

19. "Injuries Help Colt Plan to Play Rookies," *Baltimore Sun*, August 21, 1958.

20. "Colts Fly for Texas Grid Game," *Baltimore Sun*, August 22, 1958.

21. "Chicago Cards Tie Colts, 31 to 31, in Last Minute," *Baltimore Sun*, August 24, 1958.

22. "Cardinals Tie Colts, 31–31, on Field Goal," *Chicago Tribune*, August 24, 1958.

23. "3 Colts Okayed to Play Friday," *Baltimore Sun*, August 27, 1958.

24. "Colts Push Defense in Heavy Drill," *Baltimore Sun*, August 28, 1958.

25. "Colts Seek First '58 Win Tonight Against Redskins," *Baltimore Sun*, August 29, 1958.

26. "Colts Look Sad in 27–7 Loss t o Redskins," AP report in *Hagerstown* (MD) *Daily Mail*, August 30, 1958.

27. Cameron C. Snyder, "Redskins Whip Colts in Stadium Exhibition, 27–7," *Baltimore Sun*, August 29, 1958.

28. "Fans Shake Heads in Disbelief as Visitors Roll Up 24 Points in Second Period," *Baltimore Sun*, August 29, 1958.

29. "'Ashamed, Not Discouraged,' Says Ewbank of Colt Loss to 'Skins," *Baltimore Sun*, August 31, 1958.

30. "Colts to Get Bawling Out," *Baltimore Sun*, September 1, 1958.

31. "Colts Place Stransky, No. 2 Pick, On Waivers," *Baltimore Sun*, September 2, 1958.

32. "Thomas Cut; Colts Down to 43 Limit," *Baltimore Sun*, September 3, 1958.

33. "Drill Taken by Rechichar," *Baltimore Sun*, September 4, 1958.

34. "Steelers Down Colts in Buffalo Exhibition, 13–10," *Baltimore Sun*, September 7, 1958.

35. "Colts' Horn Seeks School Leave," *Baltimore Sun*, September 9, 1958.

36. "Nicely, No. 3 Draft Choice, Cut by Colts; Squad at 42," *Baltimore Sun*, September 10, 1958.

37. Jesse A. Linthicum, "Sunlight on Sports," *Baltimore Sun*, September 10, 1958.

38. "Colts Move to Herring Run, Find Practice Fields Inadequate," *Baltimore Sun*, September 11, 1958.

39. "Colts Baffling Fans, Experts," AP report in *San Mateo* (CA) *Times*, September 8, 1958.

40. "Colts, Giants Plan to Start and Keep Regulars in Play," *Baltimore Sun*, September 13, 1958.

41. "Colts Win First Exhibition, Beating Giants, 27–21," *Baltimore Sun*, September 15, 1958.

42. "Patera Cut by Colts; Two More Go Today," *Baltimore Sun*, September 16, 1958.

43. "Colts Battle 'Jinx' Sunday," *Baltimore Sun*, September 17, 1958.

44. "20,000 Expected for Colts-Giants Today," *Louisville Courier Journal*, September 21, 1958.

45. "U.L.'s Unitas, Lyles Star as Colts Triumph 42–21 Over Sluggish Giants," *Louisville Courier Journal*, September 22, 1958.

46. Cameron C. Snyder, "Colts Trample Giants, 42–21, In Final Exhibition," *Baltimore Sun*, September 22, 1958.

47. *Ibid.*

48. "Doug Eggers on Waivers," *Baltimore Sun*, September 23, 1958.

49. "Colts Still Look for Aid," *Baltimore Sun*, September 24, 1958.

1958 Regular Season
Game Summaries

RICH SHMELTER, RUPERT PATRICK
AND SIMON HERRERA

September 28, 1958—Game 1: Detroit Lions vs. Baltimore Colts

Memorial Stadium

	Baltimore	Detroit
First downs	26	12
Yards rushing	166	73
Yards passing	250	163
Total yards (Net)	416	182
Passes	23–43	12–30
Intercepted by	3	1
Punts (Average)	6–30	6–48
Fumbles lost	0	1
Yards penalized	4–50	4–50

Detroit	0	9	6	0	15
Baltimore	7	7	0	14	28

Baltimore—Moore, 8 run (Myhra kick)
Detroit—Field Goal, Martin 31
Detroit—Cassady, 11 pass from Layne (Kick failed)
Baltimore—Berry, 26 pass from Unitas (Myhra kick)
Detroit—Cassady, 30 pass from Rote (Conversion failed)
Baltimore—Berry, 14 pass from Unitas (Myhra kick)
Baltimore—Dupre, 13 run (Myhra kick)
A—48,377

Rushing
(Attempts, Yards)
Baltimore—Ameche, 12–64; Dupre, 14–51; Moore, 7–36; Unitas, 3–15
Detroit—Rote, 5–27; Johnson, 6–20; Cassady, 1–12; Gedman, 6–10; Layne, 2–4; Webb, 4–0

Passing
(Attempts, Completions, Interceptions, Yards)
Baltimore—Unitas, 43–23–0–250–0
Detroit—Layne, 17–7–1–103; Rote, 13–5–2–60

Receiving
(Receptions, Yards)
Baltimore—Berry, 10–149; Moore, 6–59; Ameche, 4–2; Mutscheller, 2–41; Dupre, 1–(-1)
Detroit—Cassady, 4–65; Middleton, 3–42; Webb, 2–29; Johnson, 2–16; Doran, 1–11

The 1958 season opener against the defending NFL champion Detroit Lions no doubt had been circled on the calendars of Baltimore's players and fans since the schedule was released. Since entering the National Football League fold in 1953, the Colts' chances of being the alpha dog at the end of the season was never greater. Over their first five seasons, the Colts' fan base was one of the most passionate in all of professional sports despite the team's difficulties on the field. During the 1957 season, the Colts secured their first winning record. They were in the hunt for a Western Conference title, and ended one game shy of a trip to the NFL championship game with a 7–5 record.

With a solid team on both sides of the ball, it appeared that a run at the league's ultimate prize was within reach, and it all began against the Lions with a crowd of 48,377 in attendance at Memorial Stadium.

Carl Taseff set the Colts up for their first offensive series by returning a Yale Lary punt 49 yards before being stopped on the Detroit 42. Eight plays later the Colts hit pay dirt. On the seventh play of the drive from the Detroit 18, Johnny Unitas ran for ten yards and a first down at the eight. On the next play, Lenny Moore broke free of two tacklers en route to falling into the end zone. Moore finished the day with 36 yards on the ground in seven carries, but proved his worth as a multi-threat by catching six passes for an additional 59 yards. During the game, Moore also suffered a displaced fracture of the nose. Steve Myhra's conversion kick gave Baltimore a 7–0 lead at the end of the first quarter.

At the start of the second quarter, Yale Lary punted for Detroit, and the ball rolled out of bounds on the Baltimore 12. Dick Horn returned possession back over to the Lions on fourth down by punting from his own nine. Unfortunately, Horn's kick was not very good. The ball only traveled 20 yards to give Detroit exceptional field position. The Baltimore defense was a tough unit, and lived up to that reputation by forcing a three and out. Jim Martin was able to salvage the golden opportunity by connecting on a 31-yard field goal to cut Baltimore's deficit to 7–3.

The next time Horn punted, the ball once again traveled a short distance, on this occasion, a paltry nine yards, giving Detroit another excellent starting point on the Baltimore 37. Bobby Layne completed a pair of passes to advance the Lions to the Colts' 11. Layne then rolled out and threw in the direction of Howard "Hopalong" Cassady, who lived up to his Heisman Trophy days at Ohio State by making a headlong diving catch in the end zone to record an 11-yard touchdown reception. Layne's conversion attempt sailed wide, but the Lions claimed their first lead of the game at 9–7. Coming into the game Layne had successfully hit on 58 straight conversions.

Later in the second quarter, Baltimore went on a nine-play, 80-yard drive that allowed Unitas and company to regain the lead before heading into the locker room at the end of the first half. On a key play, Unitas completed a pass to Raymond Berry to the Detroit 26. From there, Unitas unleashed another pass toward Berry. After catching the ball, Berry twisted free of three would-be tacklers, and crossed the goal line. Myhra added the conversion kick to give the Colts a 14–9 lead at halftime.

The Lions wasted little time taking the lead back. With just four minutes and five seconds expired in the third quarter, Cassady capped a five-play, 59-yard drive with another touchdown reception. After catching a screen pass from Tobin Rote, Cassady ran behind great blocking for 30 yards all the way to the end zone. Another Detroit conversion attempt failed. The snap from center sailed over holder Rote's head and the kick was never tried. The Lions were now clinging to a slim 15–14 lead.

The Colts took the ensuing kickoff and got to the Detroit 19, but Myhra's field goal attempt from 26 yards out got caught up in the wind and sailed wide of the uprights. Later in the quarter, the Colts got a huge break when it appeared the Lions were heading for a sure touchdown. While passing out of his own end zone, Unitas was intercepted by Bob Long, who raced to the Baltimore ten before fumbling. Defensive tackle Alex Karras recovered for the Lions on the eight. Once again, the Baltimore defense forced a three and out. It looked like Martin would save the drive with an easy chip shot field goal from the 15 yard line, but the kick was wide.

The Colts received a big break, and made the most of it in the fourth quarter. On the first play from the Baltimore 20, Detroit's John Henry Johnson had an argument with a Colts linebacker, and hit him, causing penalty flags to fly. Aided by the penalty, the balanced Baltimore attack drove deep into Detroit territory. The Unitas-to-Berry combination struck again, this time from 14 yards out, and with Myhra's conversion kick, the Colts were up, 21–15. For the day, Berry caught ten passes for 149 yards, which was better than half of the Colts' aerial attack.

It looked like the Colts were going to go up by eight points after they recorded an apparent safety following a Tobin Rote fumble. Instead, a referee ruled that the Colts kicked the ball out of the end zone, which made it an automatic touchback for Detroit on the 20. The Baltimore defense held firm and the Lions' offense walked off the field with no additional points and had to punt.

Taseff returned the punt to the Detroit 44, but the Colts failed to advance, and on fourth down, Bert Rechichar attempted a whopping 53-yard field goal that rolled to the Detroit one where Big Daddy Lipscomb fell on it for Baltimore. The Colts quickly got the ball back when Andy Nelson intercepted a Rote pass at midfield and returned it to the Detroit 24. A clipping penalty moved Baltimore back to their own 45. A reception by Berry coupled with runs by Alan Ameche got the ball to the Detroit 12. After a beautiful fake from Unitas to Ameche, the ball was placed in the hands of L.G. Dupre. Dupre swept around the right end, and after receiving a key block from guard Alex Sandusky, he sprinted for a touchdown that sealed the victory. Myhra's conversion made it 28–15, which was how the game went into the record books. In the closing seconds, Milt Davis intercepted a Rote pass, but it was disallowed due to the Colts being offside. Davis enjoyed intercepting Rote so much that on the last play of the game, he did it again, and this time it counted. Davis picked the ball off on the Baltimore 25 and took it all the way to the Detroit 33.

The Baltimore defense allowed the defending NFL champions just 182 yards of total offense, while Unitas and the Baltimore offense rang up 416 yards. The Baltimore defensive line and linebackers tormented the Lions all afternoon. Linebackers Bill Pellington, Don Shinnick and Leo Sanford all caused fumbles, Eugene "Big Daddy" Lipscomb plunged his massive frame at anything wearing Detroit colors, and his fellow trench warriors, Gino Marchetti, Don Joyce, Ordell Braase and Art Donovan, applied constant pressure on pass rushes and stopped all running plays up the middle. They beat down both Layne and Rote, allowing only 12 completions in 30 pass attempts, and recorded three interceptions.

Coach Ewbank felt it was a true team victory, and singled out the defense for its tremendous work. This was the third straight win for Baltimore in a home opener, and the third time in 13 meetings with Detroit that they came away winners. All three of Baltimore's wins over Detroit came at Memorial Stadium.

Joining the Colts in victorious locker rooms across the league were the New York Giants, Washington Redskins, and Cleveland Browns in the East, and the San Francisco 49ers, and Chicago Bears in the West.

October 4, 1958—Game 2: Chicago Bears vs. Baltimore Colts

Memorial Stadium

	Baltimore	Chicago
First downs	17	20
Yards rushing	147	140
Yards passing	198	218
Total yards (Net)	325	316
Passes	10–23	16–35
Intercepted by	5	1
Punts (Average)	7–28	3–35
Fumbles lost	1	1
Yards penalized	6–68	5–64

Chicago	3	7	21	7	38
Baltimore	27	7	7	10	51

Baltimore—Moore, 28 run (Myhra kick)
Baltimore—Berry, 12 pass from Unitas (Myhra kick)
Baltimore—Moore, 9 run (Kick failed)
Chicago—Field Goal, Blanda 40
Baltimore—Moore, 77 pass from Unitas (Myhra kick)
Chicago—McColl, 11 pass from Brown (Blanda Kick)
Baltimore—Lyles, 103 kickoff return (Myhra kick)
Chicago—Morris, 5 run (Blanda kick)
Chicago—Brown, 1 run (Blanda kick)
Baltimore—Mutscheller, 2 pass from Unitas (Myhra kick)
Chicago—Galimore, 99 kickoff return (Blanda kick)
Baltimore—Moore, 33 pass from Unitas (Myhra kick)
Baltimore—Field Goal, Myhra 28
Chicago—McColl, 20 pass from Bratkowski (Blanda kick)
A—52,622

Rushing
(Attempts, Yards)
Baltimore—Moore, 10–71; Ameche, 8–35; Dupre, 10–30; Unitas, 4–11; Shaw, 1–1; Call, 5–(-1)
Chicago—Galimore, 11–96; Casares, 9–17; Brown, 4–16; Morris, 5–6; Caroline, 2–5

Passing
(Attempts, Completions, Interceptions, Yards)
Baltimore—Unitas, 23–10–1–198
Chicago—Brown, 27–12–5–166; Bratkowski, 7–4–0–52; Casares, 1–0–0–0

Receiving
(Receptions, Yards)
Baltimore—Berry, 4–63; Moore, 3–118; Mutscheller, 2–8; Ameche, 1–9
Chicago—Casares, 5–40; Jewett, 4–63; McColl, 4–62; Morris, 3–53

The celebration over defeating Detroit was short-lived for the Colts. Coach Ewbank made sure of it. The Chicago Bears were ready to invade Memorial Stadium and were definitely not taken lightly by the Baltimore head coach. Ewbank barked out to his team to forget about their win in the season opener during a tough practice in a short workweek leading up to a rare Saturday game. Ewbank wanted total focus on the task facing his team, not on past conquests. There would be plenty of time to relish all the victories after the goal of reigning supreme over the entire league was complete.[1]

Baltimore assistant coach Bob Shaw could not hold back his praise for the 1958 edition of the Chicago Bears under legendary head coach George "Papa Bear" Halas. Shaw felt Halas' team was the best he had ever seen, as they were solid on all three units. Fierce lineman Doug Atkins and linebacker Bill George were the leaders on defense. At 6'8", 260 pounds, Atkins was an unbridled, one-man wrecking machine that dominated opposing ball carriers. George was credited with being the game's first middle linebacker, and was once dubbed by a writer for *Sports Illustrated* as "the meanest Bear ever."[2] Both Atkins and George were considered two of the greatest to ever play their positions, and reside forever in the Professional Football Hall of Fame. The offense had a top-notch backfield duo in Willie "the Wisp" Galimore and the punishing Rick Casares.

The Bears came into Baltimore after disposing of the Green Bay Packers, 34–20, in the season opener. Galimore was the star by rushing for two touchdowns and catching three passes for 88 yards and another six-pointer.

The clash with the Bears would test Baltimore's mettle. Anticipation for this early season "clash of the titans" in the Western Conference ran so great that 46,745 tickets were sold in advance, the most in the Colts' history up to that time.

Opening the game with a 27-point first quarter barrage, the Colts gave their fans reason to believe that 1958 would finally be their year.

Baltimore's assault on the scoreboard began after they were awarded 34 yards on the first play of the game compliments of a pass interference call on Chicago's Erich Barnes against Lenny Moore. The infraction gave Baltimore the ball on the Chicago 40, and three plays later, Moore swept around the left side, outran defenders, and crossed the goal line standing up to complete a 28-yard scoring jaunt. Myhra's conversion gave the Colts a 7–0 lead with only 1:32 expired off the clock.

If that tally was not quick enough, the Colts gave their fans an immediate encore. Four plays after Moore's long trek to pay dirt, Baltimore was back on the attack. The Colts sent a fierce pass rush toward quarterback Ed Brown. Seeing the likes of Gino Marchetti, Art Donovan and Gene "Big Daddy" Lipscomb barreling in on him, Brown's survival instinct kicked in, and he unloaded a pass that had three options. A reception or incompletion were what the Bears could have hoped for, but the third option occurred instead, as linebacker Bill Pellington intercepted the ball on the Baltimore 45 and returned it to the Chicago 33.

The Colts moved to the eight due to a solid ground attack. The drive was capped when Johnny Unitas rolled out to his left and connected with his favorite target, Raymond Berry, who caught the ball on the goal line. Berry then jerked his body into the end zone for Baltimore's second touchdown. Myhra's conversion made it a 14–0 game with only 6:01 ticked off the clock in the opening quarter.

One play after the kickoff following Berry's touchdown, the Colts' offense once again had possession. Pellington made his second interception of the game, setting Unitas and company up with incredible field position, by returning the theft from the Chicago 35 down to the 15-yard line. Alan Ameche ran to the nine, and then Moore stamped his second ticket to the end zone by running it in from there. Myhra's extra point attempt was blocked, but the Colts led by a 20–0 margin with 7:11 still left in the first quarter.

In the season opener, the Colts' punting was atrocious, and it carried over into this game. A poor punt by Dick Horn coupled with a 15-yard penalty gave Chicago a scoring opportunity late in the first quarter at the Baltimore 36. Chicago's offense sputtered and they had to settle for a 40-yard field goal from George Blanda that made the score 20–3.

The Colts quickly got those three points back plus four more on their next offensive play. Unitas connected on a pass to Moore at the Baltimore 35-yard line. The fleet-footed Moore first faked out a defender on the sideline, and then outran Chuck Howley for a touchdown that covered 77 yards. Myhra's conversion made the score 27–3 at the end of the first quarter. That pass to Moore was only the third thrown by Unitas in the first quarter, and two of them went for touchdowns. Despite the lopsided score, the initial 15 minutes of this game produced incredibly hard hits that were so loud the reporters up in the press box were able to hear them.

Early in the second quarter, Blanda missed on a 47-yard field goal attempt, but the Bears quickly regained possession after Baltimore failed to move the chains. Horn's punting was still haunting the Colts. A weak 29-yard punt gave Chicago good field position at their own 43. On four plays, and with the assistance of a 15-yard penalty against the Colts, the Bears scored their first touchdown. Bill McColl capped the drive by making a great catch in the end zone of an 11-yard pass from Brown, and with Blanda's conversion, the Baltimore lead was cut to 27–10.

Lenny Lyles instantly got those seven points back when he returned the ensuing kickoff 103 yards for a touchdown. He received the ball three yards deep in the end zone, and after finding a clearing up the middle, Lyles outran the entire Chicago special team unit. Lyles' fantastic exploit was just three yards shy of the NFL record set by Green Bay's Albert Carmichael in 1956. Myhra's extra point kick was good, and the Colts were up by a 34–10 count. The rest of the first half was a struggle played out mostly at midfield, with the Colts incorporating a three-man defensive front designed to shut down Chicago's passing game.

Fifty members of the Dick Szymanski Fan Club of Toledo, Ohio, were the main focus during a halftime ceremony as they presented Colts owner Carroll Rosenbloom with a gold deputy sheriff's badge and a key to the city.

Following the halftime activities, the Bears returned to the field with a fighting spirit, and two quick touchdowns renewed their hope of a comeback. After receiving the second half kickoff the Bears drove 80 yards for a touchdown. Runs by Galimore and Casares, and a reception by Bob Jewett, moved the ball to the Baltimore five before Johnny Morris scored from there. Blanda added the conversion that cut the Chicago deficit to 34–17. Chicago went 72 yards for another touchdown on their next offensive series. Key plays included a 20-yard run by Galimore and a pickup of 24 yards on a pass from Brown to McColl that put the Bears on the Baltimore four. Two runs by Casares moved the ball to the one, and from there, Brown scored on a quarterback sneak. Blanda's extra point kick made the score 34–24.

Late in the third quarter, Unitas connected with Berry for a gain of 28 yards, but the drive ended on the Chicago 29 when a pass attempt popped out of Berry's hands and into those of linebacker Bill George. Baltimore flexed its defensive muscle and forced the Bears to punt. Baltimore couldn't sustain a drive and punted back to Chicago. The Colts finally received a break when Ray Brown intercepted an Ed Brown pass on the Chicago 45 and returned it to the ten-yard line. The Colts moved to the two, and from there, Unitas threw his third touchdown toss of the day, this time to Jim Mutscheller. Myhra added the extra point, and the Colts were again ahead by 17 with the score now at 41–24.

That breathing room was suffocated on the ensuing kickoff when Galimore turned on the jets and blazed his way across the field for a 99-yard kickoff return for Chicago's third six-pointer of the quarter. Blanda's conversion quickly brought the Bears back to within ten points at 41–31 going into the fourth quarter.

The Colts came back with ten points in the fourth quarter to secure a 51–31 lead as the game was winding down. Moore scored his fourth touchdown of the game early in the quarter on a 33-yard scoring strike from Unitas, and Myhra followed with his sixth conversion kick of the game. With that touchdown, Moore set an individual single game team scoring record. That scoring toss also gave Unitas four on the day. Another Ray Brown interception led to a 28-yard field goal by Myhra. The Bears then closed out the scoring when McColl hauled in a 20-yard pass from Zeke Bratkowski and Blanda's conversion made the final score in this wild shootout 51–38.

The combined 89 points were nine shy of the all-time NFL record set in 1948 when the defending league champion Chicago Cardinals beat the New York Giants 63–35.

After two weeks of NFL action, the Colts and the Browns led their respective conferences as the only undefeated teams in the league.

October 12, 1958—Game 3: Green Bay Packers vs. Baltimore Colts

Milwaukee County Stadium

	Baltimore	Green Bay
First downs	19	21
Yards rushing	152	61
Yards passing	243	320
Total yards (Net)	382	360
Passes	17–36	26–47
Intercepted by	4	1
Punts (Average)	7–27	6–45
Fumbles lost	1	0
Yards penalized	7–61	6–43

Baltimore	0	7	7	10	24
Green Bay	14	3	0	0	17

Green Bay—McIlhenny, 55 pass from Starr (Hornung kick)
Green Bay—Starr, 1 run (Hornung kick)
Green Bay—Field Goal, Hornung 19
Baltimore—Unitas, 1 run (Myhra kick)
Baltimore—Mutscheller, 54 pass from Unitas (Myhra kick)
Baltimore—Field Goal, Myhra 14
Baltimore—Nelson, 52 interception return (Myhra kick)
A—24,553

Rushing
(Attempts, Yards)
Baltimore—Dupre, 10–84; Unitas, 5–27; Moore, 6–21; Ameche, 6–20
Green Bay—Ferguson, 9–35; McIlhenny, 11–16; Shanley, 2–6; Hornung, 3–3; Starr, 1–1

Passing
(Attempts, Completions, Interceptions, Yards)
Baltimore—Unitas, 35–16–1–238; Shaw, 1–1–0–5
Green Bay—Starr, 46–26–4–320; Ferguson, 1–0–0–0

Receiving
(Receptions, Yards)
Baltimore—Moore, 6–108; Berry, 5–54; Mutscheller, 3–68;
Dupre, 1–8; Pricer, 1–5; Ameche, 1–0
   Green Bay—Howton, 7–92; McIlhenny, 5–90; Ferguson,
5–41; Meilinger, 4–50; McGee, 2–27; Knafelc, 1–9; Hornung,
1–6; Shanley, 1–5

Within a year, the Green Bay Packers would be on the verge of gaining everlasting fame as the "Sixties Team of Decade" under head coach Vince Lombardi. However, before Lombardi was able to transform Green Bay into "Titletown USA" the Packers found themselves on a disastrous path. The once proud franchise's last winning season was in 1947, with the exception of two years that saw them finish at .500. The team went through six head coaching changes, and was headed for their worst finish in the history of the organization at 1–10–1. Ray "Scooter" McLean was the head coach in 1958, and was very popular with the players and fans. Unfortunately, being too well liked caused a lack of discipline, which in turn created a major problem on the field and eventually in the standings.[3]

The Packers came into this meeting with the Colts posting a 0–1–1 record and with injuries to key personnel. Quarterbacks Bart Starr and Babe Parilli were hurting with a bad ankle (Starr) and ribs (Parilli). Veteran linebacker Bill Forester suffered a twisted ankle and that left the linebacker corps very young and inexperienced. However, despite the downward spiral the Packers were not to be taken lightly, and Baltimore head coach Weeb Ewbank wanted his team up and ready. The Colts seemed to play better at home, and even though they were seven-point favorites, they also played better when coming in as the underdogs.[4]

Despite Ewbank stressing to his players to be focused mentally and physically, the Colts came out flat in the first quarter. Baltimore's woes began when they failed to score a touchdown on their opening offensive series for the first time in 1958. Lenny Moore fumbled on the Green Bay 23 after picking up 43 yards on a pass from Unitas. The loose ball was recovered by defensive back Billy Kinard. The Colts' defense held and forced a punt on fourth down. Unitas had trouble connecting with his receivers on Baltimore's next series, and the Colts punted the ball back to the Packers. It was then time for Green Bay to seize an opportunity to light up the scoreboard. On second down, Starr, whose ankle was healthy enough for him to take the field, threw a pass from the Green Bay 45 down to the Baltimore 40. Defensive back Andy Nelson got a hand on the ball, but he never gained control, and it fell into the hands of halfback Don McIlhenny. McIlhenny wasted little time taking advantage of his good fortune, rambling the rest of the way for a 55-yard touchdown reception and the game's initial points. Paul Hornung added the conversion, and Green Bay held a surprising 7–0 lead with 8:57 remaining in the opening stanza.

The Packers enjoyed seeing what an opposing end zone looked like so much that they journeyed back there seven and a half minutes later. After taking the ensuing kickoff trailing by seven points, the Colts gained a huge chunk of real estate on a 39-yard run by L.G. Dupre that took the offense from their own 30 to the Green Bay 31 before rookie linebacker Ray Nitschke tackled Dupre. Despite the huge gain, the potent Baltimore offense continued to struggle. On fourth down, the Colts' brain trust decided to get creative by faking a field goal attempt, but the trickery failed just shy of the first down marker. Green Bay took over possession on their own 26-yard line, and ten plays later, were in the end zone. With Starr passing and Howie Ferguson plowing up the middle of the Baltimore defense, the ball rested on the one-yard line. It was from there that Starr called his own number and successfully plunged over the goal line on a quarterback sneak. Hornung added the extra point, and the Packers were up, 14–0, and looking like world-beaters with 1:31 left in the quarter.

The Packers began another serious drive in the closing seconds of the first quarter, and carried it over into the second. From the Green Bay 13, the Packers got deep into Baltimore territory in 15 plays before stalling. Hornung salvaged the drive with a 19-yard field goal that gave Green Bay what looked like an insurmountable 17–0 lead, plus headline-making material for the morning papers, after 6:27 expired in the second quarter.

Baltimore was reeling and still unable to move the ball through the air. Another punting situation arose, but the Packers quickly failed to expand their dominance. Andy Nelson made sure of that when he returned possession back over to the Colts on the magic of an unorthodox interception. Starr threw a low pass that careened off the foot of Billy Howton and shot up into the awaiting, but surely surprised, hands of Nelson at the Green Bay 46. Unitas now decided to attack the Packers on the ground, and the tactic paid off, as the Colts pounded out yardage all the way to the Green Bay 11. Dupre then capped the drive with a touchdown run, but Baltimore was called for holding, and the touchdown was nullified, thus thwarting Baltimore's first solid scoring opportunity. The penalty moved the Colts back to the 22-yard line, but a pair of runs got the lost yardage back plus an extra one for good measure. With the ball now at the ten, the Colts managed to pick up the needed yardage and get a fresh set of downs on the one-yard line thanks to a Unitas-to-Moore pass. Unitas then scored on a quarterback sneak that finally put the Colts on the scoreboard. Steve Myhra converted the extra point, and the Green Bay lead was cut to 17–7 with 2:07 left in the first half.

The Colts felt a swing of momentum, and looked to capitalize with another drive before halftime. Nitschke ended those hopes by intercepting Unitas on the Green Bay 23, and after 30 minutes of action, the Packers went to their locker room with their ten points lead intact.

The Colts scored the only points of the third quarter. The golden arm of Johnny Unitas awoke long enough to connect with Jim Mutscheller for a touchdown. From his own 46 yard line, Unitas focused in on Mutscheller slicing his way through a pair of defenders at the Green Bay 48. With Unitas' pass safely tucked in his grasp, Mutscheller plowed his way downfield until All-Pro defensive back Bobby Dillon's diving tackle brought him down. The tackle occurred with Mutscheller falling into the end zone for six points on a play that covered 54 yards. Myhra's conversion cut the deficit to three points at 17–14 with eight minutes ticked off in the third quarter.

The Packers tried to shake off the effects of the touchdown by rallying with a drive that got them to the Baltimore 19 as the third quarter expired. The drive came to an end when the Baltimore defense stopped the Packers inches shy of a first down on fourth down at the Colts' 11-yard line.

The Baltimore offense reverted back to ineptitude, as it failed to mount a serious threat yet again. It was up to the defense to come through. Linebacker Don Shinnick intercepted a pass midway through the fourth quarter on the Baltimore 46 and returned the ball to the Green Bay 38. Unitas looked to his legs to provide the offense with a spark, and his lower limbs carried the quarterback for big gains that got the Colts to the Green Bay five. Unitas was then dropped for a loss of five yards, and after another failed pass attempt, Unitas took off running again, but he fumbled on the eight, and Nitschke recovered for the Packers. However, a quick whistle by referee Robert Austin blew the play dead prior to the turnover, which allowed Unitas and company to still own possession thanks to a very lucky break. Facing a fourth down situation, coach Ewbank wisely decided to go for the tie with 4:11 remaining, and Myhra made it happen with a 14-yard field goal that knotted the game at 17.

The Packers had come too far to settle for a tie. They continued to play aggressively. On the fourth play of their next drive, Starr threw toward midfield, but safety Andy Nelson intercepted the ball on the Baltimore 48 and ran it back all the way for what proved to be the winning points. Myhra followed up Nelson's 52-yard interception return with the conversion that gave Baltimore a 24–17 lead.

Trailing for the first time all afternoon, the Packers were desperate. They got to the Baltimore 39 with 39 seconds remaining, but Shinnick killed any hopes of a comeback with his second interception of the day, and the Colts got out of Milwaukee still undefeated after a very close call.

Unitas had an off day, as he could only muster 16 completions out of 35 attempts. Despite an interception that provided the winning points (Nelson), and one that clinched victory (Shinnick), Starr, successfully pierced the Baltimore secondary with roll out passes that accounted for 320 yards. On the other side of the defensive spectrum, Baltimore's tremendous collection of trench warriors allowed a mere 61 yards on the ground. Even though the Baltimore defensive line turned in a dominant showing, tackle Art Donovan claimed that the Packers inflicted the hardest hits up to this stage of the season.

The Bears and Rams stayed a game behind the undefeated Colts in the Western Conference, as they both improved to 2–1 on the season.

The Cleveland Browns remained the leaders of the Eastern Conference after a 35–28 win over the Chicago Cardinals kept them undefeated and a game ahead of the Giants who improved to 2–1 with a 21–14 victory over the Redskins.[5]

October 19, 1958—Game 4: Detroit Lions vs. Baltimore Colts

Briggs Stadium

	Baltimore	Detroit
First downs	25	14
Yards rushing	316	79
Yards passing	221	148
Total yards (Net)	535	220
Passes	11–18	9–25
Intercepted by	1	0
Punts (Average)	3–37	7–45
Fumbles lost	2	2
Yards penalized	5–45	3–51

Baltimore	6	7	7	20	40
Detroit	0	7	0	7	14

Baltimore—Ameche, 1 run (Kick failed)
Baltimore—Ameche, 1 run (Myhra kick)
Detroit—Doran, 19 pass from Morrall (Martin kick)
Baltimore—Dupre, 3 run (Myhra kick)
Detroit—Lary, 71 punt return (Martin kick)
Baltimore—Moore, 11 run (Kick failed)
Baltimore—Mutscheller, 37 pass from Unitas (Myhra kick)
Baltimore—Lyles, 27 run (Myhra kick)
A—55,190

Rushing
(Attempts, Yards)
Baltimore—Moore, 12–136; Ameche, 19–76; Dupre, 11–39; Unitas, 5–36; Lyles, 1–27; Call, 1–2
Detroit—Rote, 3–21; Cassady, 8–16; Gedman, 8–15; Morrall, 2–14; Lewis, 2–13

Passing
(Attempts, Completions, Interceptions, Yards)
Baltimore—Unitas, 17–11–0–221; Brown, 1–0–0–0
Detroit—Rote, 17–7–0–107; Morrall, 8–2–1–41

Receiving
(Receptions, Yards)
Baltimore—Mutscheller, 5–99; Berry, 4–95; Moore, 1–15; Dupre, 1–12
Detroit—Middleton, 5–85; Doran, 3–56; Cassady, 1–7

The alluring mistress known as "Lady Luck" has long been a part of sports regardless of the level of competition. Many athletes have even claimed that they would rather be lucky than good. In the history of sports, how many times has a bounce of the ball turned out to be a key factor in victory? Therefore, even though professional athletes have reached the pinnacle of their chosen sport, superstitions still come into play on a huge scale.

The 1958 Baltimore Colts were no exception. Coach Ewbank had the same suit on in each of Baltimore's three victories, and refused to change it until the Colts lost a game. The team's general manager Don Kellett believed if he saw a truck carrying empty beer kegs that it was a sign of certain victory. Big Daddy Lipscomb had his hand bandages cut off late in games when the Colts were ahead, feeling that meant the team would not need him anymore in that game. Gino Marchetti always made sure never to place any article of clothing on backwards when suiting up for a game, and Marchetti's fellow defensive end, Ordell Braase, had to put his equipment on from the left, such a left sock and then the same side cleat before turning his attention to the right foot.[6]

The Colts had ample reasons to believe in superstitions going into their Week Four game in Detroit. Things had not gone well for anyone donning the blue and white of the Colts in the Motor City. The Lions had never lost to Baltimore in Detroit. The year before, the Colts held a 27–3 third quarter lead, only to see the Lions roar back with 28 points to win, 31–28.

The Colts were a totally different team coming into Detroit's Briggs Stadium than at any other time in their existence. They were a perfect 3–0, and confidence was growing with the passing of each weekend. On the other side of the field, the defending NFL champion Lions were at 0–2–1 and hoping to continue their dominance over the Colts at home and gain their first win. However a constant factor from Detroit's previous success over the Colts was now missing from the equation. The Lions had traded quarterback Bobby Layne, a proven winner, to the Pittsburgh Steelers on October 6.

With 55,190 in attendance at Briggs Stadium, the Colts moved into field goal range during their opening offensive series, but Steve Myhra missed on a 37-yard attempt that fell short of the goal posts and rolled out of bounds on the Detroit eight. Pinned down deep in their own territory, the Lions were unable move the ball and were forced to punt. Yale Lary's punt traveled to the Detroit 44, where Lenny Moore signaled for a fair catch.

Looking to establish a foothold on the scoreboard, the Colts drove downfield in seven plays for the game's first score. The key play in the drive was a 31-yard run by Moore. Unitas only threw one pass during the drive, a seven-yarder to Berry that put the Colts on the Detroit four. Unitas then turned things over to his hammering running back Alan Ameche. The former Heisman Trophy winner from Wisconsin plowed into the defense twice, the second time coming from the one-foot line for the touchdown. Myhra's conversion attempt sailed wide, but the Colts had a 6–0 lead with 9:21 expired in the first quarter. Later in the opening stanza, Baltimore looked to expand on their lead with a long field goal attempt from 45 yards out, but Bert Rechichar's kick dropped to the ground shy of the goal line.

The Colts began the second quarter by stopping the Lion offense once again. Baltimore then mounted another scoring drive that covered 80 yards of Briggs Stadium real estate in 12 plays with Unitas using a balanced attack that confused the Detroit defense. From the 17, Unitas again turned the heavy work over to Ameche, and "the Horse" again came through. Ameche got the ball three straight times, bullying his way to pay dirt on the final carry from one yard out. This time Myhra found the mark to give Baltimore a 13–0 lead with 6:11 left in the first half.

Things were looking good for Baltimore up to this point, but then the "jinx" tried to suffocate them on two occasions prior to halftime. The first mishap occurred when Yale Lary stripped the ball from Moore's grasp after "Lighting Lenny" tore off a gain of 16 yards. With the help of three penalties on the Colts, the Lions were able to get close enough for a Jim Martin field goal attempt from 45 yards out, but the kick failed to reach its mark. With 24 seconds left in the first half, the Colts had possession hoping to run out the clock. However, Moore fumbled and linebacker Bob Long pounced on the loose ball at the Baltimore 19. With time ticking away, Earl Morrall dropped back to pass, and avoiding a heavy pass rush, he threw to Jim Doran in the end zone for a 19-yard touchdown strike. Martin added the conversion, and the Lions cut the deficit to 13–7 as the first half came to a climax.

Baltimore received the kickoff to start the second half, and proceeded to drive 80 yards on seven plays. Dupre and Moore exhibited their running skills by quickly eating up yardage that got the Colts to the Detroit 16. Dupre carried for 14 yards on the Colts' first running play of the drive, and then Moore exploded for a gain of 50. Baltimore advanced to the five-yard line before needing a quarterback sneak by Unitas on fourth down to pick up a new set of downs at the four. The drive began with Dupre, and he proceeded to end it with a touchdown run from three yards out. Myhra's conversion split the uprights to give the Colts a 20–7 advantage with only 3:44 ticked off the clock in the third quarter.

Detroit twice threatened to score, but to no avail. The first occasion saw the Lions' drive from their own 26 to the front door of the Baltimore end zone at the one. Howard "Hopalong" Cassady then fumbled a golden opportunity away and Carl Taseff recovered for the Colts. Cassady's troubles continued. Another great scoring opportunity was stymied when Cassady fumbled again on the Baltimore four. Those costly turnovers appeared to deflate the Lions' spirit, but future Hall of Famer Yale Lary, a veteran of three NFL championships in Detroit during the 1950s, gave his teammates a jolt by returning a Ray Brown punt 71 yards for a touchdown in the fourth quarter. Jim Martin's extra point kick was good, and the Lions once again closed to within six points at 20–14.

In the past, the Colts had a reputation of folding under pressure, and memories of the Lions' huge rally a year before, were beginning to rise to the forefront. However, this was a different year, and instead of crumbling, the Colts rose up and got angry to the tune of 20 fourth quarter points that put the game away.

After taking the ensuing kickoff on their own 27, the Colts were in the end zone within four plays. The big play of the drive came when Unitas connected with Berry for a gain of 55 yards that placed the ball of the Detroit 11. Lenny Moore then took it across the goal line from there. Myhra's conversion attempt was no good, but the Colts still held a 26–14 lead.

Rookie safety Ray Brown returned possession back over to Unitas compliments of an interception that gave the Colts the ball on the Detroit 47. Ameche carried twice advancing the ball ten yards to the Detroit 37. From there, Unitas connected with Mutscheller for the touchdown. Myhra connected on this extra point attempt to give Baltimore a convincing 33–14 lead.

The Colts weren't done. On the final play of the game, Lenny Lyles tore through the Detroit defense for a 27-yard touchdown run. Myhra added his fourth conversion kick of the game, and the Colts ended their losing streak in Detroit with a decisive 40–14 victory. Defensive tackle Art Donovan was the last remaining member from the original Baltimore Colts team, and was present for all the losses in Detroit. To honor Donovan's long service to the team, the game ball was given to him by his teammates on the day they finally broke their losing streak in the Motor City.

Elsewhere in the National Football League, the defending Eastern Conference champion Cleveland Browns stayed even with the Colts as the only other undefeated team thanks to a 27–10 win over the Pittsburgh Steelers. The victory put the Browns up by two games in the East over the 2–2 Giants, Redskins, and Cardinals. In the Western Conference, the Chicago Bears stayed one game behind the 4–0 Colts in the standings at 3–1 with a 31–10 win over Los Angeles.[7]

October 26, 1958—Game 5: Washington Redskins vs. Baltimore Colts

Memorial Stadium

	Washington	Baltimore
First downs	11	21
Yards rushing	167	186
Yards passing	46	204
Total yards (Net)	183	390
Passes	4–16	12–20
Intercepted by	1	2

	Washington	*Baltimore*
Punts (Average)	6–47	5–31.5
Fumbles lost	1	1
Yards penalized	3–28	3–30

Washington	7	0	3	0	10
Baltimore	7	14	14	0	35

Washington—Zagers, 4 run (Baker kick)
Baltimore—Moore, 12 run (Myhra kick)
Baltimore—Berry, 17 pass from Unitas (Myhra kick)
Baltimore—Ameche, 4 run (Myhra kick)
Washington—Field Goal, Baker 31
Baltimore—Lyles, 101 kickoff return (Myhra kick)
Baltimore—Berry, 48 pass from Unitas (Myhra kick)
A—54,403

Rushing
(Attempts, Yards)
Washington—Olszewski 14–46; Zagers 11–60; Watson 5–27; Podoley 4–22; Sutton 3–16; Guglielmi 1–(-4)
Baltimore—Ameche 13–66; Dupre 10–46; Moore 7–60; Call 5–19; Lyles 4–(-10); Pricer 1–3; Unitas 1–2

Passing
(Attempts, Completions, Interceptions, Yards)
Washington—LeBaron 9–3–1–49; Guglielmi 4–1–0–(-3); Bukich 3–0–1–0
Baltimore—Unitas 15–8–0–183; Shaw 5–4–1–21

Receiving
(Receptions, Yards)
Washington—Zagers 1–19; Sutton 1–17; Walton 1–13; Olszewski 1–(-3)
Baltimore—Berry 4–92; Moore 2–62; Lyles 2–16; Call 2–11; Ameche 1–18; Rechichar 1–5

The 2–2 Redskins rolled into Baltimore for their annual meeting with the undefeated Colts. Washington was led by Eddie LeBaron, the shortest QB in pro football history at 5–7 and he was also leading the league in passing going into this game.[8] The Colts were tabbed as a favorite[9] by seven and a half points to run their record to 5–0.

Baltimore won the coin toss and started from their 23 after Sam Baker's kickoff, but failed to get a first down and Dick Horn's punt left the Redskins at their 25-yard line.

Two plays later, Sid Watson swept right and found 24 yards worth of daylight before Ray Brown caught him at the Baltimore 47. Jim Podoley got loose up the middle for nine more, followed by runs from Johnny Olszewski and Podoley that put the Redskins in the red zone. Facing a third and six from the 13, LeBaron stuck to his ground game, handing off to Bert Zagers, who carried to the four. On first and goal, Zagers swept left, diving in for the score. Baker's PAT gave the Burgundy and Gold a 7–0 lead midway through the first period.

Starting from their 25 following the kickoff, Number 19 went deep on third and seven for the Colts. Lenny Moore hauled in the bomb on the right sideline for 41 yards to the Washington 31 yard line. Runs by Moore and Ameche left the Colts a yard short of the first down marker, and then, Dupre took a draw up the middle for ten yards to the 12 yard line. From there, Unitas faked and then handed off to Moore, who swept left, with a block by Art Spinney clearing the path to the end zone. Myhra tacked on the extra point, and the score was tied at 7–7 with 3:35 left in the first frame.

After the Redskins' scoring drive, Colts middle linebacker Don Shinnick realized he was out of position on the initial drive which allowed Washington's runners to exploit the middle. When he got into the correct position on the next series, it shut down the middle to the Redskins for the rest of the game.[10] On the next Washington drive, three runs by the Redskins (including a running play on third and 12)[11] netted a negative two yards, but Baker got off a 54-yard punt that set the Colts back to their 28-yard line.

On the final play of the first period, Moore got loose on an end around for 15 yards to put the Colts into Washington territory. Runs by Moore and Ameche, along with a slant pass to Berry, put the ball at the 20-yard line. On a third and seven at the 17, Unitas put it up for Berry, who had two steps on Dick Lynch in the left corner of the end zone. The extra point made it 14–7 Baltimore with four minutes elapsed in the second period. The touchdown pass increased Unitas' streak to 20 consecutive games with a score through the air.

LeBaron finally dropped back to throw a pass on second down in the next drive but was smeared (which was the term used before Deacon Jones renamed it "sack" in the 1960s) by Gino Marchetti. An open Ed Sutton pulled in a LeBaron pass, good for 17 yards and a first down at the Washington 34. The drive stalled, and Carl Taseff returned the boot to the Colts' 38-yard line.

Moore took a pitch around the left side for 13 yards to cross midfield, but a Baltimore penalty negated a nice catch by Moore that would have put the Colts in field goal range. The pass on third and long was a little too high for even the lanky Berry to pull in, and the Redskins took over at their 28 after a short punt from Horn.

Two runs set up a third and four, and LeBaron dropped back to pass but Marchetti (who had a nine-inch height advantage on LeBaron) swatted the pass down. The ensuing punt was fair caught at the Baltimore 22 with about three minutes to play in the half.

Following a short run by Ameche, Unitas found Berry alone in the left flat for 17 yards to the Colts' 43. Moore took a screen and burst though the right side for 21 more yards before going out of bounds, sidestepping three diving tacklers along the way. Two plays later, Ameche, took a screen through a gap in the left side for 18 yards. Unitas handed off to Ameche on first down, who burst through the middle for 13 more yards to the Washington eight-yard line. Dupre went through the right side of the line for four more, and a final gallop from the Horse gave Baltimore a 21–7 lead with 1:17 left before halftime.

The Redskins ran out the remaining time in the half, knowing they would get the ball back to start the third period. Starting the second half at the Washington 35, LeBaron hit Zagers over the middle for 20 yards and combined with a roughing the passer penalty on the play, Washington had a first down at the Baltimore 23.[12] A pass to Zager in the middle on third and ten went off his hands, which led to a Baker field goal from 31 yards out to make it a 21–10 game.

Any thoughts of Washington getting back into the game were effectively dashed on the following kickoff when Lenny Lyles took the kick a yard deep in the end zone, waited for his blockers to form in front of him,[13] and broke right at the 20-yard line and ran untouched coast-to-coast. The extra point gave the Colts a 28–10 lead with 11:50 to play in the third quarter.

After an exchange of punts, Washington started from the Baltimore 45. On third down, LeBaron's pass that was intended for Watson was short and picked off by Ray Brown at the Colts' 23, with Brown returning it seven yards.

A left slant pass to Berry and a plunge by Ameche were enough for a first down, and then, Moore took a draw toward the right sideline, good for ten more yards to the Washington 48. On the next play, Unitas faked a pitch, then threw a quick left slant pass to Berry at the 40-yard line. Lynch almost got a hand on him when he was hauling in the ball, but Berry soon had a stride on the entire defense and outran them to the end zone for the score. Myhra tacked on the extra point to make it 35–10 with 5:05 to play in the third stanza.

Rudy Bukich came in at quarterback for Washington, but it only took Ordell Braase three plays to smear him for a big loss. Baltimore got the ball back and started moving the ball again before Jack Call fumbled, with Chuck Drazenovich smothering the loose ball at midfield for Washington. An interception by Leo Sanford on third down ended Bukich's day, with the Colts taking over at their 48-yard line.

There was no scoring in the fourth quarter. Ralph Guglielmi came in at quarterback for Washington, while George Shaw replaced Unitas for Baltimore, and Shaw was driving for another score but had a pass intercepted by Dick James. The final verdict was a 35–10 Baltimore triumph.

One casualty of the Colts' victory was punter Dick Horn, who was waived after the game and never played professional football again.

The Colts improved to 5–0 to maintain a one-game lead over the 4–1 Bears in the West. Cleveland also stayed undefeated in the East, with the Giants two games back at 3–2.

November 2, 1958—Game 6: Green Bay Packers vs. Baltimore Colts

Memorial Stadium

	Green Bay	Baltimore
First downs	8	30
Yards rushing	95	220
Yards passing	69	170
Total yards (Net)	142	390
Passes	5–26	15–29
Intercepted by	1	5
Punts (Average)	2–40	5–45
Fumbles lost	0	1
Yards penalized	8–57	5–45

Green Bay	0	0	0	0	0
Baltimore	7	21	14	14	56

Baltimore—Moore, 2 pass from Unitas (Myhra kick)
Baltimore—Ameche, 7 run (Myhra kick)
Baltimore- Ameche, 5 pass from Unitas (Myhra kick)
Baltimore—Lyles, 4 pass from Shaw (Myhra kick)
Baltimore—Mutscheller, 17 pass from Shaw (Myhra kick)
Baltimore—Shaw, 1 run (Myhra kick)
Baltimore—Pricer, 1 run (Myhra kick)
Baltimore—Rechichar, 6 pass from Shaw (Myhra kick)
A—51,333

Rushing
(Attempts, Yards)
Green Bay—Starr 2–32; Francis 3–21, McIlhenny 8–14; Ferguson 5–12; Carmichael 1–7; Taylor 3–7; Parilli 1–3; Shanley 1–(-1)
Baltimore—Call 10–73; Ameche 12–49; Dupre 6–34; Lyles 13–34; Unitas 2–17; Pricer 5–12; Shaw 1–1

Passing
(Attempts, Completions, Interceptions, Yards)
Green Bay—Starr 14–3–2–58; Parilli 11–1–3 6; Francis 1–1–0–5
Baltimore—Shaw 13–10–1–71; Unitas 16–5–0–99

Receiving
(Receptions, Yards)
Green Bay—McGee 3–58; Howton 1–6; McIlhenny1–5
Baltimore—Lyles 3–8; Moore 2–65; Berry 2–25; Rechichar 2–18; Ameche 2–16; Pricer 2–9; Mutscheller 1–17; Call 1–12

Ray McLean's Packers came into cold, rainy Baltimore in Week 6 for their second meeting with the Colts. Green Bay was 1–3–1, with Starr and Babe Parilli sharing the quarterbacking duties, and were fresh off a 38–35 victory over the Eagles the previous week and were optimistic about pulling an upset.

Green Bay missed a chance at a big gainer on the third play from scrimmage when Parilli's pass for Al Carmichael at the Packers' 40 went off Carmichael's hands. Carmichael had 20 yards of clear space ahead of him but the Packers instead had to settle for a punt.[14]

An interception by Bill Pellington on the next Green Bay drive led to a 42-yard field goal try by Steve Myhra that was wide left.[15] On the next Packer drive, Carl Taseff picked off Parilli at the Green Bay 34 and returned it to the 18. It took Unitas four plays to work the ball to the two-yard line.[16] From there, he flipped a shovel pass to Lenny Moore, who got in around the left side for the score. The 7–0 score held up through the first quarter.

After a fumble by Alan Ameche was recovered by Tom Bettis at the Green Bay 48, an unsuccessful series gave the Packers six yards,[17] which was just enough to put the ball in range for a field goal try by Hornung from midfield to start the second period. The three-point attempt was short and Taseff returned it to the Colts' 17 yard line.[18] Baltimore began a drive, taking eight plays to move 83 yards. Moore was again key on this drive as he and Unitas hooked up on a 15-yard pass that Moore turned into a 63-yard gain to put the ball at the seven-yard line. From there, Ameche ran off left tackle and into the end zone to make it 14–0 with three and a half minutes elapsed. The Colts had to go the rest of the way without L.G. Dupre, who dislocated a shoulder on the drive, but as it turned out, they didn't need him.

Andy Nelson picked off a Parilli pass at the Baltimore 40 and returned it to the Green Bay 25. Passes to Jack Call and Ameche would put the ball at the five-yard line where Unitas would connect with Ameche in the left side of the end zone for another score.

With Starr at the helm instead of Parilli, Green Bay finally started moving the ball, but lost it on downs at the Baltimore 25, and the Colts started moving again. With two minutes to play before halftime, Unitas was kneed by the Packers' John Symank during a QB draw and injured his ribs. George Shaw came in with the Colts at the Green Bay six-yard line and three plays later, tossed a short touchdown pass to Lenny Lyles to make it 28–0 at the half.

The deluge continued (which was literal, as the rain began to pour the entire second half)[19] when Carl Taseff returned the second half kickoff 50 yards and Baltimore drove 53 yards in four plays. Shaw connected with Jim Mutscheller from 17 yards out for the touchdown with less than two minutes elapsed in the third stanza.[20]

A later Packer drive resulted in another interception, this time by a diving Don Shinnick, who swiped a pass from Starr at the Green Bay 31 and returned it four yards. This time it took eight plays to get the ball into the end zone, with Shaw scoring on a keeper, and Baltimore led 42–0 after three periods.

A serious Packer drive was snuffed out when Nelson intercepted a Starr pass at the Baltimore two-yard line and returned it 69 yards.[21] The Colts started moving again, aided by two interference calls against the Packers. The drive ended with Pricer crossing the goal line on a one-yard plunge.[22]

With the score 49–0, Coach Ewbank began resting his starters in the fourth quarter, but the Packers still could not stop them. Call broke off a 35-yard run to the Green Bay 28, and Shaw hit Bert Rechichar with a six-yard pass for the final touchdown of the day.

Carmichael returned the Myhra kickoff 62 yards up the left sideline to the Baltimore 34, which set up the Packers last chance to avoid a shutout. Rookie Joe Francis came in at quarterback, and stuck to his running game, scrambling three times for 21 yards. Francis scrambled to the three-yard line, and on the last play of the game, Jim Taylor got the call, but was stopped at the Baltimore one-foot line.

The 56–0 massacre was the Colts first shutout in the six seasons the franchise had been in Baltimore and remains the most prolific victory in Colts history and the largest defeat the Packers have ever suffered. The most telling statistic of the game is that the Colts caught as many Green Bay passes (five) as the Packers receivers did.[23]

After the game, the Colts got additional bad news. Unitas had three broken ribs and was suffering from pneumothorax, which meant there was air in the chest cavity due to the rib injury, He could miss the next three or four games.[24]

It was also announced after the game that Dupre's shoulder separation would keep him out of the lineup for one to two weeks.[25]

Now 6–0, the Colts extended their lead in the West to two games over the 4–2 Bears who lost to the Rams. In the Eastern Conference, the Browns suffered their first loss of the season to the now 4–2 Giants to fall to 5–1. The Giants' victory allowed them to pull within a game of the Browns.

November 9, 1958—Game 7: Baltimore Colts vs. New York Giants

Yankee Stadium

	Baltimore	New York
First downs	19	18
Yards rushing	146	167
Yards passing	238	188
Total yards (Net)	384	341
Passes	12–30	13–20
Intercepted by	1	1

	Baltimore	*New York*
Punts (Average)	2–37	4–43
Fumbles lost	0	1
Yards penalized	2–10	5–35

Baltimore	7	7	0	7	21
New York	7	0	14	3	24

New York—Webster, 5 run (Summerall kick)
Baltimore—Moore, 36 pass from Shaw (Myhra kick)
Baltimore—Berry, 23 pass from Shaw (Myhra kick)
New York—Rote, 25 pass from Conerly (Summerall kick)
New York—Gifford, 13 run (Summerall kick)
Baltimore—Moore, 4 pass from Shaw (Myhra kick)
New York—Field Goal, Summerall 28
A—71,164

Rushing
(Attempts, Yards)
Baltimore—Ameche 18–87; Call 7–29; Moore 6–27; Shaw 1–3
New York—King 14–42; Webster 11–47; Gifford 7–38; Triplett 5–20; Chandler 1–15; Conerly 1–5

Passing
(Attempts, Completions, Interceptions, Yards)
Baltimore—Shaw 29–11–1–239; Brown 1–1–0–(-1)
New York—Conerly 18–12–1–125; Gifford 2–1–0–63

Receiving
(Receptions, Yards)
Baltimore—Moore 6–181; Berry 4–49; Mutscheller 1–9; Pellington 1–(-1)
New York—Gifford 5–48; Webster 3–23; Schnelker 2–66; Rote 2–39; King 1–12

An estimated 10,000 Colts fans[26] made the 200-mile trek from Baltimore to the Big Apple to see their undefeated Colts take on the 4–2 New York Football Giants. Jim Lee Howell's Giants had upset the Browns in Cleveland 21–17 the previous week and were seeking their second NFL title in three seasons. Led by stars such as Charlie Conerly, Frank Gifford, Alex Webster and Sam Huff, the Giants were clearly going to be the Colts' toughest opponent on their 1958 schedule. George Shaw would again get the start at quarterback for the Colts as Unitas was nursing a severe rib injury. Even without Number 19 behind center, the Colts came into the game as a three-point favorite.

With what was at the time the largest crowd ever to attend a pro football game in New York,[27] the Giants took the opening kickoff. On the first play from scrimmage, Conerly lateraled to Gifford, who rolled right on an option play and tossed a bomb to Bob Schnelker (who had just gotten past Andy Nelson) at the Baltimore 45. Schnelker was finally brought down by Milt Davis at the Baltimore 13 for a gain of 63 yards.[28] Gifford took a pitch to the left for five yards before going out of bounds, and the Giants faced a fourth and two from the five-yard line. Webster took a handoff through left tackle and in for the score. The extra point from Pat Summerall put the Giants ahead 7–0 three minutes into the contest.[29]

The Colts came roaring back, starting at their 28 and moving the ball well; however, the Giants' defense bent but did not break. A 16-play drive, which included a first and goal at the two-yard line, went for naught as the Giants took over on downs on their one-foot line following an epic goal line stand.

New York opted to punt on first down and Don Chandler's boot left the Colts at the Giants' 45. Following a draw by Alan Ameche that moved the ball to the 34, Shaw dropped back and put it up for Lenny Moore on the right corner of the goal line. Moore had to outleap Lindon Crow (who fortunately slipped at the last possible minute) for the ball and stepped into the end zone. Following the extra point by Steve Myhra, the game was tied at 7–7 with 32 ticks left in the first period.

In the second frame, the Colts got close enough to set up a field goal try, but it was a fake and Ray Brown threw to Bill Pellington. However, the pass came up short of the first down marker.[30]

On a fourth and one at the New York 28, Don Chandler decided to roll the dice and go with the fake punt, running with it. The ploy worked, and he picked up 15 yards and a first down. Conerly threw to Gifford over the middle, and when he was tied up, Gifford made the mistake of trying to lateral the ball to Webster, but the ball got loose, and Pellington fell on the ball for Baltimore. After four runs (which included a 15-yard draw by Ameche) moved the ball to the New York 23, Shaw connected with an open Raymond Berry in the left side of the end zone.[31] Baltimore opened up a 14–7 lead.

With time running out in the half, Nelson picked off a Conerly pass. At the midway point, Baltimore led by seven.

The second half kickoff went to Baltimore, who was unable to do anything, and punted to the Giants. Starting from their 42, it took nine plays for New York to put the ball in the end zone. The key play in the drive was when Conerly in the process of being smeared flipped the ball to Phil King at the last moment, with King turning a huge loss into a 12-yard gain and a first down. Two plays later, from the Baltimore 25, Conerly threw for Kyle Rote, who pulled the slip on Davis, (his cover), and made a diving catch in the back left corner of the end zone for the score. The score was tied at 14–14.

After another drive by Baltimore went nowhere, they punted to the Giants, who again began at their 42-yard line. This time it took New York 11 plays[32] to reach pay dirt, with Gifford skirting around the right side for the final 13 yards. Summerall's extra point gave the Giants a 21–14 lead.

Starting from the Baltimore 28, Shaw got the Colts offense in motion once again as the third quarter was winding down. After moving the ball to the 43, Shaw faked and aired it out for Moore on the right sideline, with Lenny pulling it in at the New York 20 yard line and making it to the six where he was stopped. After a short run by Moore, Shaw faked again, throwing to Moore in the right side of the end zone. Moore made a bobbling catch but held on, and the conversion by Myhra knotted the game at 21 two minutes into the final quarter.

After New York failed to get anything going, they punted to Baltimore, and Shaw hooked up with Moore for 33 yards to the New York 25. From there, Shaw threw for Lyles in the end zone, but the pass went off his hands. Shaw's next pass was his only mistake in the game, as his pass was intercepted by Huff at the Baltimore 15-yard line and returned to the 23.

Conerly had the clock on his side, and took his time, handing off to Webster for eight yards and then, throwing to Webster for 13 more. A pass to Gifford was good for 12 yards, and a scramble put the Giants at the Baltimore 28. The Colts stopped them on the next series, and on fourth and three at the 21, Summerall came in to kick. The

28-yard field goal split the goalposts, and gave the Giants a 24–21 lead with only 2:40 to play.

With the game on the line, Shaw began his final drive, hooking up with Moore on a 37-yard pass which put the Colts at the Giants' 38, but his luck started to run out. Incompletions on first and second downs was followed by a pass to Lenny Lyles in the end zone that went off his hands, which brought up a fourth and ten.[33] Opting not to try a 45-yard field goal, Shaw went for broke, and his last ditch effort was broken up.[34] The whistle blew, and the Colts suffered their first defeat of the 1958 season as they came up on the short end of a 24–21 decision to the Giants.

After the game, Coach Ewbank gave the Giants praise, but ultimately laid the loss at the feet of his boys, "We lost to good ball club, and it was a game that could have gone either way. We have nobody to blame but ourselves."[35]

The Colts loss tightened the Western Conference race, as the Bears defeated the Packers to pull within a game of Baltimore and set up a showdown in Week Eight. The frontrunners in East (New York and Cleveland) were now tied with identical 5–2 record as the Browns lost for second week in a row (this time to the Lions).

November 16, 1958—Game 8: Baltimore Colts vs. Chicago Bears

Wrigley Field

	Baltimore	Chicago
First downs	14	8
Yards rushing	159	107
Yards passing	131	72
Total yards (Net)	285	161
Passes	10–23	8–26
Intercepted by	3	1
Punts (Average)	9–45	8–46
Fumbles lost	1	2
Yards penalized	8–75	6–72

Baltimore	0	14	0	3	17
Chicago	0	0	0	0	0

Baltimore—Berry, 7 pass from Shaw (Myhra kick)
Baltimore—Ameche, 4 run (Myhra kick)
Baltimore—Field Goal, Myhra 12
A—48,664

Rushing
(Attempts, Yards)
Baltimore—Ameche 26–142; Moore 7–19; Call 7–6; Pricer 1–3; Shaw 1–(-11)
Chicago—Galimore 10–22; Douglas 5–31; Casares 5–10; Morris 4–5; Caroline 3–11; Brown 1–28

Passing
(Attempts, Completions, Interceptions, Yards)
Baltimore—Shaw 23–10–1–131
Chicago—Bratkowski 12–3–1–44; Ed Brown 9–3–2–9; Blanda 5–2–0–19

Receiving
(Receptions, Yards)
Baltimore—Moore 4–39; Mutscheller 3–54; Berry 3–38
Chicago—Hill 3–41; Casares 3–7; McColl 1–15; Morris 1–9

The Colts blew into the Windy City in Week 8, with the Bears needing a victory to give them a share of first place alongside Baltimore in the West. The largest home crowd of the season showed up to see the hometown Bears take on the Colts.

With Unitas still nursing rib injuries, George Shaw got his second consecutive start behind center. Unitas was suited up and could have played in an emergency, as he was wearing a wire apparatus that resembled a bird cage, and this early prototype of the flak jacket would have protected his ribs.[36] L.G. Dupre would miss another start as he was still suffering from a shoulder separation. Shaw and Alan Ameche would have to pick up the slack.

In the first quarter the Bears got as close as the Baltimore 17, where the drive stalled. George Blanda attempted a 29-yard field goal that failed. Another Chicago drive led to an Ed Brown punt that rolled dead at the Baltimore three-yard line. The Colts were unable to move the ball and punted.

After another punt pinned Baltimore at their seven-yard line, Ameche took a handoff and got loose for 22 yards on the final play of the first period. The Colts continued their drive from there, taking nine more plays to move the remaining 71 yards. The drive included Shaw connecting on six straight passes, starting with a pass to Raymond Barry for 12 yards, and then he connected with Jim Mutscheller for 25 yards to the Bears' 45 yard line. Despite tight coverage from Charlie Sumner, Berry hauled in a pass that was good for 22 yards. After moving the ball to the ten-yard line, a short toss to Moore was followed by a pass to a diving Berry in the end zone for the game's first score,[37] as four minutes were gone in the second period.

Later in the second quarter, Carl Taseff returned a Brown punt 15 yards to the Baltimore 40-yard line. Shaw connected with Moore in the right flat on a pass that was good for 23 yards. After a short run by Ameche, Shaw went deep for Moore on a post pattern, but Erich Barnes picked off the bomb at the Chicago four and returned it 37 yards. But wait, there was a flag on the play. Chicago was called for interference, giving the Colts a first down at the Bears' four-yard line. Ameche went off left tackle and into the end zone for the score. Myhra tacked on the PAT to make it 14–0 at the half.

Chicago began the second half with tremendous field position when Willie Galimore received the kickoff at the two-yard line and broke off a 65-yard return before Art DeCarlo took him down at the Baltimore 33-yard line. A sweep to the right by Johnny Morris was read by the Colts' defense, costing the Bears ten yards, but rookie Merrill Douglas came through, taking a draw 18 yards through the middle. Two plays later, Douglas took a handoff to the 16 where the ball came loose and Ray Brown recovered for Baltimore.

After a change of possessions, Ed Brown got off another excellent punt, pinning the Colts at their two-yard line. The Colts started to move again, but Shaw was intercepted at the 32 by Barnes. Here, the Colts defense clamped down, only allowing the Bears one yard on three offensive plays, and forcing a punt.

Late in the third quarter, the Bears started moving again. On the initial play of the fourth quarter, Chicago faced a fourth down at the Baltimore 27. Zeke Bratkowski dropped back to pass to Galimore in the end zone. The Colts had Galimore double-covered, and the pass didn't have a chance. The play was doubly damaging to the Bears as end Harlon Hill suffered a ruptured tendon during the play and would be lost for the remainder of the season.[38]

Down by two TDs in the fourth frame, Bratkowski was going to the air on virtually every play. At this point, Baltimore's stellar pass defense (their 35 interceptions during the season led the league in 1958) started forcing interceptions. Carl Taseff picked off a deflected pass at the Chicago 40 but the Colts were unable to take advantage of the turnover.

On the next possession, Ed Brown was in at quarterback, and Andy Nelson swiped a pass that led to an unsuccessful 32-yard field goal attempt by Myhra.[39] On the next play, Ray Brown got his paws on another Ed Brown pass and returned it 30 yards to the Chicago ten-yard line. The Bears' defense kept Baltimore out of the end zone and Myhra got another shot at a three-pointer, this time from 12 yards away. The kick was good, and Baltimore had a 17–0 lead with five minutes to play.

There was no further scoring, and the shutout was Chicago's first in 149 games since they were blanked by the Giants in 1946.[40] The game ball went to Ameche,[41] who rushed 26 times for 142 yards and a score.

Coach Ewbank said after the game, "We stopped a great Bear team…. Today our deep secondary was 100 percent better than a year ago."[42]

The Colts did suffer a loss during the game when Dick Szymanski was placed on injured reserve and would miss the remainder of the 1958 season after tearing knee ligaments during the game.[43]

The Colts' victory allowed them to extend their lead over the Bears and Rams (who were now also 5–3) to two games in the West. In the East, the Browns defeated the Redskins to improve to 6–2, and regain a one-game lead over the Giants who were upset by the Steelers.

November 23, 1958—Game 9: Baltimore Colts vs. Los Angeles Rams

Memorial Stadium

	Los Angeles	Baltimore
First Downs	19	19
Yard Rushing	75	151
Yards Passing	358	239
Total yards (Net)	419	369
Passes	25–45	14–20
Intercepted by	4	0
Punts (Average)	2–41	7–37
Fumbles Lost	5	0
Yards penalized	5–30	6–59

Los Angeles	0	0	7	0	7
Baltimore	7	6	0	21	34

Baltimore—Moore, 58 pass from Unitas (Myhra kick)
Baltimore—Moore, 8 run (Kick blocked)
Los Angeles—Wilson, 4 run (Cothren kick)
Baltimore—Mutscheller, 12 pass from Unitas (Myhra kick)
Baltimore—Unitas, 1 run (Myhra kick)
Baltimore—Dupre, 6 run (Myhra kick)
A—57,557

Rushing
(Attempts, Yards)
Baltimore—Ameche 15–68; Dupre 8–36; Call 2–26; Moore 6–22; Pricer 2–6; Unitas 4–3; Lyles 3–(-10)
Los Angeles—Marconi 4–22; Wilson 4–20; Arnett 8–15; Wade 1–11; Ryan 1–7

Passing
(Attempts, Completions, Interceptions, Yards)
Baltimore—Unitas 18–12–0–218; Shaw 2–2–0–21
Los Angeles—Wade 41–23–2–356; Ryan 3–1–1–2; Wilson 1–0–1–0

Receiving
(Receptions, Yards)
Baltimore—Moore 6–157; Berry 3–37; Mutscheller 2–17; Rechichar 1–11; DeCarlo 1–10; Dupre 1–7
Los Angeles—Shofner 8–110; Lundy 6–103; Arnett 4–75; Wilson 2–32; Phillips 2–23; Marconi 2–13; Clarke 1–2

Week 9 for the Colts pitted them against their conference rival the Los Angeles Rams. The Colts stood atop the Western Conference at 7–1 while the Rams were just two games behind. The *Baltimore Sun* reported that the game was the biggest of the season for the Colts. The fans appeared to agree. On the Thursday night prior to the game a sellout was announced, the first in Colts history.[44]

That Sunday 57,557 packed into the sold-out Memorial Stadium. Neither the crowd nor the Rams were entirely sure who would be starting for the Colts at quarterback. Johnny Unitas, who was nursing his injured ribs, shared snaps all week with George Shaw at practice. Coach Ewbank refused to name a starter during the week, not because he wasn't sure if Unitas could go but because he wanted to keep the Rams guessing.[45]

Despite the uncertainty surrounding the Colts' quarterback situation the Colts were favored by six points. Rams coach Sid Gillman didn't seem to care who was starting for the Colts, stating, "it makes no difference, both worry me."[46]

Kickoff was set for 2:05 local time. Prior to the game Unitas warmed up in the sun-filled stadium with an aluminum brace protecting his ribs.[47] On their first possession the Rams were forced to punt. Carl Taseff returned the punt 16 yards out to the Colts' 42. Unitas lined up under center for his first play back after the injury. Perhaps trying to get in an early hit on Unitas, the Rams brought pressure up the middle. Frank Fuller bull-rushed over center and then in one motion knocked left halfback L.G. Dupre (returning from his shoulder injury) backwards and almost into the backpedaling quarterback. Unitas gave a quick pump fake and with linebacker Dick Daugherty barreling down on him he sidestepped and moved up in the pocket. He spotted his receiver downfield and lunged forward as he released the ball. Lenny Moore had broken free along the right sideline. The pass to Moore hit him in stride at the 22-yard line and he was able to easily jog into the end zone.[48] Steve Myhra kicked the extra point and the Colts led 7–0.

On the next drive the Rams drove into Colts territory. Quarterback Bill Wade hit left end Lamar Lundy for a gain but as he was tackled the ball came out. Milt Davis scooped up the ball and advanced it six yards before being brought to the ground. The Colts began their second drive from their own 36-yard line. During the drive the Rams again pressured Unitas. On a play near midfield Fuller zeroed in on the quarterback and it looked like the big tackle was going to bring him down. Unitas stood tall and was able to get a pass off to Moore all while in Fuller's grasp. The Colts' drive stalled out in Rams territory and Myhra attempted a 39-yard field goal. The kick missed wide and short.[49] On the Rams' final drive of the first quarter Wade threw a pass that was intercepted by Taseff. The quarter ended with the Colts holding a 7–0 lead.

To start the second quarter the Colts took over at the Rams' 18-yard line. Two plays later Moore took the handoff from Unitas and ran in for an 8-yard touchdown. The extra point try by Myhra was blocked. The Colts now led 13–0.

Following the kickoff, the Rams drove into Colts territory. The drive came to a halt and the Rams lined up for a 44-yard field goal attempt. On the play 6'6" Gene "Big Daddy" Lipscomb[50] broke through and blocked Paige Cothren's kick.

With time running out in the half the Rams made one more push into Colts territory. The ball rested on the Colts' 21-yard line to start the final play of the drive. Wade took the snap and dropped back to pass. He hit Del Shofner on a pass who took it towards the goal line. At the three-yard line the ball came out and safety Ray Brown fell on the ball to preserve the first half shutout. The Colts held the ball until the whistle blew ending the half.

The two teams battled back and forth in the third quarter with the Rams being the only team to put together a drive. Wade and the Rams began the drive on their own 17-yard line. Wade completed pass after pass as they marched down the field.[51] From the 34-yard line Wade dropped back to pass and pump faked to the back in the right flat. He then fired a strike over the middle to Lundy for a 25-yard gain to the Colts' nine. Left halfback Jon Arnett took the ball down to the four. On the next play Tom Wilson followed great blocking from pulling guard Duane Putnam and fullback Joe Marconi. A hole opened up on the right side of the line and Wilson lowered his head and burrowed into the end zone. Cothren kicked the extra point and the Rams were within six.[52]

The fourth quarter began with the Colts clinging to a six point lead. The Rams held the Colts and they were forced to punt. Arnett was back to receive the punt. The ball slipped through his hands and the Colts came up with the recovery at the Rams' 19-yard line.

The Rams put pressure on Unitas but he was able to get off a pass while in the grasp of end Glenn Holtzman. The ball was lofted with touch over the goal line and into the arms of Jim Mutscheller for a touchdown. After a successful kick by Myhra the lead was back to 13 at 20–7.[53]

On the ensuing drive with time running out the Rams went for it on fourth down. The pass was batted down and the Colts took over on their 32-yard line. On the second play of the drive Unitas dropped back, looked off the safety deep over the middle and fired a bullet deep down the sideline to an open Lenny Moore. Moore had a step on safety Don Burroughs whose diving attempt caught just enough of Moore's foot to trip him up and bring him to the ground.[54] The play resulted in a 50-yard gain for the Colts. Alan Ameche carried the ball to the Rams' four and then to the one. On the next play Unitas ducked behind Buzz Nutter and snuck into the end zone. The extra point was good and the Colts led 27–7.[55]

Tom Wilson of the Rams fumbled the ensuing kickoff and two plays later Dupre carried the ball in from six yards out. Myhra's extra point was good and the Colts led 34–7. The Rams suffered their ninth turnover of the game just a few minutes later. Deep in Colts territory, Wilson fumbled the ball and the Colts recovered it on their two-yard line. The final gun sounded and the Colts secured their eighth win of the season.[56]

With three games remaining the Rams were essentially out of the running for the Western Conference. The Chicago Bears beat the Lions to move to 6–3 and stand as the only real threat to the Colts. In the Eastern Conference, the 7–2 Cleveland Browns, the 6–3 New York Giants and the 5–4 Pittsburgh Steelers all still had a realistic shot at the title.

November 30, 1958—Game 10: Baltimore Colts vs. San Francisco 49ers

Memorial Stadium

	San Francisco	Baltimore
First Downs	22	24
Yard Rushing	155	219
Yards Passing	168	229
Total yards (Net)	313	415
Passes	15–29	17–33
Intercepted by	5	1
Punts (Average)	3–40	3–28
Fumbles Lost	0	1
Yards penalized	4–50	5–46

San Francisco	7	20	0	0	27
Baltimore	7	0	7	21	35

San Francisco—Tittle, 1 run (Soltau kick)
Baltimore—Unitas, 4 run (Myhra kick)
San Francisco—Tittle, 3 run (Kick blocked)
San Francisco—McElhenny, 1 run (Soltau kick)
San Francisco—Hazeltine, 13 interception return (Soltau kick)
Baltimore—Ameche, 1 run (Myhra kick)
Baltimore—Ameche, 1 run (Myhra kick)
Baltimore—Moore, 73 run (Myhra kick)
Baltimore—Berry, 7 pass from Unitas (Myhra kick)
A–57,557

Rushing
(Attempts, Yards)
Baltimore—Moore 8–114; Ameche 17–78; Dupre 9–15; Unitas 5–12
San Francisco—Perry 14–113; McElhenny 11–36; Tittle 5–6

Passing
(Attempts, Completions, Interceptions, Yards)
Baltimore—Unitas 33–17–1–229
San Francisco—Tittle 29–15–5–168

Receiving
(Receptions, Yards)
Baltimore—Berry 9–114; Mutscheller 3–77; Moore 5–38
San Francisco—Wilson 4–48; Perry 4–41; Conner 3–37; Owens 2–29; McElhenny 2–13

In Week 10, the Colts faced the San Francisco 49ers. With a record of 8–1 the Colts held a two-game lead in the Western Conference while the 49ers were out of the running with a record of 4–5. With a Colts win and a Chicago Bear loss the Colts would win the

Conference. Excitement was building around the team and for a second week in a row the game was a sellout.[57]

A couple of days prior to the game Week Ewbank and scout Ed Shaw told the *Baltimore Sun* that the 49ers were "a much better club than their record indicates."[58] The statements were based on the fact that the 49ers had the same core of players from just a year earlier. In 1957 the team tied the Detroit Lions with eight wins to force a playoff game for the Western Conference.[59] The difference between the Colts and Niners was bad luck and injuries.[60] Despite everything pointing to a good matchup the Colts were favored by 13. That didn't faze the strong-armed and former Colts quarterback Y.A. Tittle. "I don't want to sound overconfident but we are going to beat the Colts Sunday," he stated in an interview with the *Baltimore Sun*.[61]

Kickoff was at 2:05 local time. The temperature hovered around 24 degrees and a ten-mile per hour breeze blew out of the west. Under blue skies[62] the captains met for the coin flip and the 49ers elected to receive the ball.[63] The Colts' kick was downed in the end zone and the 49ers started their first drive at the 20-yard line. On the first play Tittle handed the ball to fullback Joe Perry who ran around the left end and into the clear for a 23-yard gain. Tittle's first pass attempt was incomplete but after that he hit five of his next six to drive his team down to the Colts' one-yard line. After an offside penalty Tittle called his own number and snuck the ball in from the half-yard line. Soltau kicked the extra point and the 49ers led 7–0.[64]

The Colts' first drive started at their 22-yard line. A roughness penalty on defensive end Bob Toneff kept the drive alive and the Colts were able to get the ball out near midfield before punting.[65]

The 49ers took over at their 18-yard line and appeared to be on their way to scoring another touchdown. From the Colts' 47 Tittle threw the ball to left end Clyde Conner but the pass was intercepted by Milt Davis who ran it back to the Colts' 35-yard line.[66]

With some momentum after the turnover the Colts started a drive. Lenny Moore took the handoff and ran around the left end for a 22-yard gain. Raymond Berry made a leaping catch for a 20-yard gain bringing the Colts to the 49ers' 22-yard line.[67] Once the Colts were inside the 20 Unitas took over with his legs. He pump faked a pass and then tucked the ball and ran for nine. On the next play he ran for three more. After giving Dupre a carry Unitas ran for three more off right tackle and then around the left end for a four-yard touchdown. Myhra put the kick through and the game was tied at 7–7.[68]

The 49ers opened the second quarter with the ball and were forced to punt. The Colts drove into field goal range and missed a 38-yard field goal. Here the 49ers began another march down the field. Perry again broke free for a 20-yard run. Tittle hit right end Billy Wilson for 16 yards and then halfback R.C. Owens took a screen pass for 22 more. Linebacker Don Shinnick made matters worse on the play to Owens by hitting him late and getting called for a roughness penalty. Not wanting to be outdone by Unitas, Tittle completed two more passes to get the 49ers to the Colts' three-yard line. On the next play Tittle bootlegged and ran the ball around the right end and in for a three-yard touchdown. The extra point attempt was blocked and the San Francisco lead was 13–7.[69]

The Colts started their next drive from their 20-yard line. On third down Unitas dropped back to pass. Toneff broke through the line and knocked the ball free. After a mad chase for the loose ball the Colts recovered the fumble at their own one-yard line. A bad punt was fair caught at the Colts' 27-yard line.[70]

On the first play Tittle hit Conner for a 20-yard gain and then Perry carried the ball for six more to the one-yard line. The Colts failed to capitalize on two mistakes by the 49ers. Tittle fumbled the ball but Perry recovered it for a three-yard loss. On the next play halfback Hugh McElhenny fumbled the ball; again the 49ers recovered. Perhaps not wanting to risk another blocked kick, 49ers coach Frankie Albert decided to go for it from the half-yard line. This time McElhenny held the ball tightly and broke through right tackle and into the end zone for a touchdown. Soltau made the kick and suddenly it was 20–7 49ers.[71]

The Colts' misfortunes continued. The kickoff by Soltau was caught in the end zone by Colts returner Lenny Lyles. Instead of downing the kick he brought the ball out trying for a big return. Lyles was immediately hit which caused him to fumble. Luckily the Colts were able to recover the ball at their five-yard line. Two plays later on third down Unitas was throwing from his own end zone. The pass was tipped and sent high into the air by lineman Leo Nomellini. Matt Hazeltine snagged the ball at the Colts' 13 and charged through several Colts defenders including Alan Ameche. Nobody could bring him down and he took the ball into the end zone.[72] Soltau added the extra point and after a couple of more minutes the half ended with the 49ers leading 27–7.

Needing a score to get back in the game the Colts opened the second half with a steady drive down the field. Soon the ball rested on the 49ers' three-yard line. Unitas handed to Dupre who gained one yard up the middle. Then it was Ameche up the middle for one more. On third down Ameche ran behind left guard for another yard and into the end zone. Myhra added the extra point and the Colts trailed 27–14.[73]

By this time it had been announced that the Pittsburgh Steelers had defeated the Chicago Bears. The crowd and the Colts realized that a comeback win over the 49ers was now also worth a Western Conference championship. The Colts' defense stiffened and forced the 49ers to punt on their next possession. Two plays later Bill Herchman broke through the line and hit Unitas so hard he fumbled the ball. Jerry Tubbs of the 49ers fell on the ball at the Colts' 23-yard line.[74]

With the game well into the third quarter and the 49ers just 23 yards from making it a three-score game it appeared the Colts might have to wait another week for a chance to clinch the title. Tittle threw two incomplete passes. On third down Tittle lofted one of his famed alley-oop passes into the back of the end zone. Colts defender Ray Brown who had position on the high ball to Owens intercepted the pass.[75]

Unitas took advantage of the turnover and hit end Jim Mutscheller for a 50-yard gain over the middle. The third quarter ended with the Colts on the 49ers' three-yard line. On the third consecutive carry by Ameche he broke over right guard and in for a score. Myhra kicked the extra point and the Colts were within six as they trailed by a score of 27–21.[76]

Nothing was going right for the 49ers; they even fumbled the ensuing kickoff but were able to recover it in their own end zone for a touchback.[77] After a brief drive and one first down the 49ers punted the ball. The punt was downed at the Colts' 33-yard line. On the first play from scrimmage Moore took the ball and cut to his left. Behind great blocking by Art Spinney and Berry he navigated his way through the broken field for a 73-yard touchdown run. After a critical kick by Myhra the Colts were in the lead 28–27.[78]

The 49ers had no answer and Tittle threw his fourth interception. The Colts scored on a seven-yard pass from Unitas to Berry with three minutes to go to officially seal the victory.[79] Tittle threw his fifth interception and the Colts ran out the clock.[80] The final score stood at 35–27 in favor of the Western Conference champion Baltimore Colts.

Thousands of fans rushed the field to celebrate. Several players were carried off of the field by the mob.[81] The players continued the conference winning celebration in their locker room. The general feelings of the players were happiness and disbelief. A great feeling of accomplishment was felt as is evident by Art Spinney's comments: "This is the greatest day of my life. We worked long and hard for this and now we are reaping the rewards."[82]

Mayor D'Alesandro sent a telegram to Colts owner Carroll Rosenbloom: "Congratulations to the entire team on the greatest and most thrilling victory in Baltimore's football history. The whole city is proud of your unbeatable spirit and unbreakable will to win. I am confident that after this great comeback, the Colts will go on to win the world's professional football championship."[83]

December 6, 1958—Game 11: Baltimore Colts vs. Los Angeles Rams

Memorial Coliseum

	Los Angeles	Baltimore
First Downs	12	26
Yard Rushing	44	156
Yards Passing	257	214
Total yards (Net)	279	359
Passes	11–26	23–41
Intercepted by	2	3
Punts (Average)	7–46	5–40
Fumbles Lost	1	2
Yards penalized	5–35	1–5

Baltimore	14	0	7	7	28
Los Angeles	3	13	7	7	30

Baltimore—Berry, 3 pass from Unitas (Myhra kick)
Los Angeles—Field Goal, Cothren 43
Baltimore—Moore 5, pass from Unitas (Myhra kick)
Los Angeles—Wilson, 2 run (Cothren kick)
Los Angeles—Daugherty, 12 interception return (Kick failed)
Los Angeles—Morris, 44 interception return (Cothren kick)
Baltimore—Ameche, 2 run (Myhra kick)
Los Angeles—Shofner, 69 pass from Wade (Cothren kick)
Baltimore—Mutscheller, 22 pass from Unitas (Myhra kick)
A–100,202

Rushing
(Attempts, Yards)
Baltimore—Ameche 16–92; Dupre 12–32; Moore 6–19; Unitas 3–11; Pricer 1–2
Los Angeles—Arnett 9–30; Marconi 4–10; Wade 4–2; Wilson 2–2

Passing
(Attempts, Completions, Interceptions, Yards)
Baltimore—Unitas 38–22–3–214; Shaw 3–0–0–0
Los Angeles—Wade 26–11–2–257

Receiving
(Receptions, Yards)
Baltimore—Berry 8–78; Moore 6–52; Dupre 5–29;
Mutscheller 3–47; Ameche 1–8
Los Angeles—Shofner 5–175; Lundy 2–34; Arnett 2–13;
Phillips 1–24; Wilson 1–11

After a couple days of celebrating and practice the Colts headed out West for two games. First the Colts would face the Rams in Los Angeles and then they would travel on to San Francisco to play the 49ers.

The team had several obstacles facing them as they prepared for the final two games. Coach Ewbank addressed his concerns with the media and the team. With the Western Conference title secured he warned the team against a letdown. "In this league you can't play half-hearted football and escape with no scars. We either hit them as hard as they hit us or we are going to get hurt."[84] Some of the other obstacles his team faced were a short week, (the game in Los Angeles was on Saturday) a three-hour time change, temperatures in the 80s and the travel itself.[85] When asked about his plans for the players, Ewbank told the *Baltimore Sun* that George Shaw was scheduled to substitute at quarterback for Unitas and to avoid injuries he planned on playing the reserves as much as possible.[86]

Despite all of the obstacles and the fact that the Colts essentially had nothing to play for, it was announced that they were favored by two points. Kickoff was scheduled for 1:30 local time. A crowd of over 75,000 was expected but when the final count was tallied 100,202 filled the Coliseum making it the third largest crowd to see an NFL game at the time.[87]

The Rams received the kickoff and on the second play from scrimmage quarterback Billy Wade dropped the snap and Baltimore defensive end Jim Mutscheller raced around from end and fell on the loose ball. The Colts took over at the Rams' 29-yard line. Unitas took the first snap and threw a flare to Lenny Moore in the flat for a 17-yard gain. After runs by Alan Ameche and L.G. Dupre, Unitas found Raymond Berry in the end zone for a three-yard touchdown. The touchdown pass marked the 24th straight game in which Unitas had thrown a touchdown pass. This gave Unitas the record for consecutive games with a touchdown pass surpassing Cecil Isbell of the Green Bay Packers, a record which had stood since 1942. Steve Myhra hit the extra point and the Colts led 7–0.[88]

Later in the quarter the Rams took possession at their 30-yard line. Wade completed several passes driving the home team down to the visitor's 35-yard line. The Colts' defense stiffened and Paige Cothren booted a 43-yard field goal bringing the Rams within four. The score stood at 7–3 in favor of the Colts.[89]

Billy Pricer fielded the kickoff and weaved his way out to the Colts' 38-yard line. Unitas drove the Colts down the field with a mix of runs and passes to the flats. Eleven plays later the Colts had the ball on the Ram five-yard line. Unitas took the snap and looked over the middle. Moore raced out of the backfield and put a move on defensive halfback Jimmy Harris.[90] Unitas floated a perfect pass leading Moore just past Harris for the touchdown. Myhra converted the extra point and the Colts' lead was 14–3.[91]

Early in the second quarter the Rams had the ball at their own 35-yard line. Wade dropped back to pass and found his end Del Shofner. The big end reeled in the pass and broke tackle after tackle as he raced down the field. After a 62-yard gain he was finally wrestled to the ground at the Colts' three-yard line. Two plays later back Tommy Wilson carried the ball in from two yards out. Cothren added the extra point and the Colts' lead was back to just four.[92]

Ewbank had subbed in some of his second string running backs at the start of the quarter. He also wanted to get a look at Jackie Simpson, a 1957 draft pick from Florida that had just completed his military obligations. Following the score Simpson was back to receive the kick. Simpson took the ball and headed up field. As he crossed his own 20-yard line he was hit and the ball came loose, Ram defender John Houser fell on the ball and the Rams took possession in scoring position.[93]

The Colts' defense got Simpson off the hook when Carl Taseff intercepted a Wade pass at the nine-yard line. The Colts again marched down the field but the drive ended on a Dupre fumble. The Rams moved the ball out near midfield before being forced to punt. The punt pinned the Colts deep in their own territory. With just a little under four minutes remaining in the half the Colts came out throwing the ball. Unitas dropped back and tried to hit an open receiver. The ball was blocked at the line by Glenn Holtzman. The ball deflected into the air and linebacker Dick Daugherty caught it and ran it 12 yards into the end zone. The extra point try failed and the Rams took the lead into the half, 16–14.[94]

The Colts took the ball to start the third quarter. After exchanging punts the Colts started a drive at their 29-yard line. A few plays later they were across the 40-yard line for a first down. On the next play Unitas dropped back to pass and was tackled for a seven-yard loss. On second and long Unitas again dropped back to pass. He got the throw off but it hit Ram defensive back Jim Morris in the hands. Morris already with momentum broke free and raced 44 yards for the touchdown. Cothren added the extra point and the Rams now led 23–14.[95]

The Colts responded with an 18-play drive. Lenny Lyles took the kickoff in his end zone and brought the ball out to the 18 yard line. Ameche smashed his way through the defense for a 20-yard gain. Dupre took the ball on a handoff and cut back for a gain of six. Unitas flipped a short pass to Dupre on the following play for a gain of 19 yards. From the Rams' 37-yard line Ameche ran around end for another gain of nine. Unitas gained another first down with a sneak of his own. Once the Colts got inside the Ram ten-yard line Ameche took a draw up the middle for six and then a play later he lowered his head and rammed over the goal line for a touchdown. Myhra converted the extra point try and the Ram lead was just 23–21.[96]

Late in the third quarter the Rams faced fourth down and inches from their own 30-yard line. Instead of punting coach Sid Gillman left his offense on the field. On the critical play the Rams ran the ball and got just enough for the first down. The referees waived off the play and signaled that time had expired prior to them getting the play off. The two teams took a break and then switched sides. Again Gillman sent his offense back onto the field. The Rams ran the ball again for a short gain. After a measurement the referees signaled first down Rams, by an inch.[97]

The series of plays appeared to rattle the Colts' defense. On the next play Wade hit Shofner for a short pass. Shofner broke free from rookie defender Johnny Sample and was off to the races for a 69-yard touchdown. Cothren's kick was good and the Ram lead was back to nine as the score stood at 30–21 with 14 minutes remaining in the game.[98]

The Colts stuck with most of the starters again but they failed to cross midfield. The two teams exchanged punts and for the Colts precious time ran off the clock. The next Colts drive started at their 14-yard line. Unitas was tackled back at his eight-yard line and then floated a ball to defender Les Richter who dropped the ball in what would have been a game ending interception. On third down Unitas hit Berry on a long gain and after a penalty they were at midfield. A few plays later from the 22-yard line Unitas took three shots at the end zone. On the third attempt he hit Mutscheller on a perfect pass for a touchdown. Myhra hit the kick to make it 30–28 Rams.[99]

The Colts kicked off and the Rams held the ball for a couple of minutes before punting. With just a few seconds to go Unitas hit Berry for five and on the next play the final gun sounded as another pass fell incomplete.[100]

Ewbank was pleased with the performance and felt good about things going forward. The Colts escaped with only one injury during the game. Since the game was played on Saturday they now enjoyed an extra day off and only had to travel a short distance up to San Francisco for their final regular season game.

In the Eastern Conference both the Browns and Giants won so it meant that the Browns held a one-game lead on the Giants heading into the final week. Unfortunately for the Browns they had to travel to New York to face the Giants that week. The Giants would need to win to force a playoff game.

December 14, 1958—Game 12: Baltimore Colts vs. San Francisco 49ers

Kezar Stadium

	San Francisco	Baltimore
First Downs	23	12
Yard Rushing	128	109
Yards Passing	241	200
Total yards (Net)	368	289
Passes	24–38	14–38
Intercepted by	0	0
Punts (Average)	5–37	6–44
Fumbles Lost	3	1
Yards penalized	6–40	3–24

San Francisco	0	7	7	7	21
Baltimore	3	3	0	6	12

Baltimore—Field Goal, Rechichar 48
San Francisco—Conner, 8 pass from Tittle (Soltau kick)
Baltimore—Field Goal, Myhra 12
San Francisco—Smith, 1 run (Soltau kick)
San Francisco—Smith, 3 run (Soltau kick)
Baltimore—Mutscheller, 38 pass from Unitas (Kick failed)
A—53,334

Rushing
(Attempts, Yards)
Baltimore—Moore 7–73; Dupre 5–23; Ameche 9–14; Unitas 1–5; Shaw 1–3; Brown 1–(-9)
San Francisco—Perry 7–50; Smith 6–49; McElhenny 11–17; Pace 2–9; Atkins 1–5; Babb 1–2; Tittle 3–(-4)

Passing
(Attempts, Completions, Interceptions, Yards)
Baltimore—Unitas 25–11–0–157; Shaw 13–3–0–43
San Francisco—Tittle 36–24–0–241

Receiving
(Receptions, Yards)
Baltimore—Dupre 4–56; Mutscheller 3–67; Moore 3–44; Ameche 3–28; Call 1–5
San Francisco—Conner 8–86; Wilson 5–56; Owens 4–55; McElhenny 4–27; Perry 2–16; Pace 1–1

Weeb Ewbank gave the Colts players Sunday and Monday off and then Tuesday the team flew to San Francisco.[101] During the week when asked which team the Colts would rather play in the championship, Ewbank refused to give an answer. "I don't want to give them any psychological weapons. If I did, both Jim Howell of the Giants and Paul Brown of the Browns would use it to arouse their players." Not only would Ewbank not answer the question, he asked his players to refrain from making any selection.[102]

Going into the game the Colts were just two-point favorites.[103] This was partially due to the fact that Ewbank wanted to play his starters to keep them sharp but he also admitted that he wanted to rest them up and keep them fresh for the title game.[104]

The kickoff was set for 1:35 local time. A crowd of 53,334 fans packed into Kezar Stadium to see the game.[105] 49ers coach Frankie Albert had announced that this would be his last game coaching the team so the feeling of the players and around the stadium was, let's win the last one for Frankie.[106]

The Colts won the coin toss and elected to receive.[107] George Shaw opened the game for the Colts at quarterback as expected. The Colts failed to gain a first down and punted. The 49ers first possession started on their 43-yard line. On the second play Jim Mutscheller hit Hugh McElhenny hard causing a fumble. Colts linebacker Don Shinnick fell on the ball on the Colts' 47-yard line.

Shaw and the offense marched down the field and into scoring position. From the three-yard line Shaw floated a pass over Lenny Moore's head. After the play Unitas ran onto the field to take over at quarterback. On third down Unitas threw to Raymond Berry in the left flat, but the pass fell incomplete. Unitas and the offense stayed on the field for fourth down. A pass to Mutscheller in the end zone was broken up and the 49ers came away with a moral victory.[108]

The 49ers failed to take advantage of the early momentum. They were forced to punt from deep in their own territory. Billy Atkins hit a good punt and after a 20-yard return the Colts started their next drive at the 49ers' 44-yard line. The 49ers' defense held again. Bert Rechichar came onto the field to attempt a 48-yard field goal. The snap to Ray Brown was good and Rechichar sent the ball through the uprights to give the Colts a 3–0 lead.[109]

On the next 49ers possession Y.A. Tittle came out firing. He hit left end Clyde Conner for 15 and then Joe Perry carried the ball for 19. The drive stalled and on fourth down the 49ers lined up to punt from near midfield. Atkins took the snap and ran forward on a fake which failed.[110]

The Colts took over and three plays later the quarter came to a close. On the first play after the break the Colts lined up for a 49-yard field goal. This time Brown could not handle the snap and he was tackled for a nine-yard loss.[111]

The 49ers capitalized on the Colts mistake. Perry took a handoff and ran straight up the middle and into the open. It appeared he was going to take the ball the distance but he was held up and tripped over his own man after a 19-yard gain.[112] The mishap didn't slow down Tittle. He hit Billy Wilson on consecutive plays for 14 and then six yards. From the eight-yard line Tittle faked a handoff right and then kept the ball on a bootleg left. As soon as the Colts defenders committed to him he flipped a short pass over their heads to Conner who was standing all alone in the end zone. Gordie Soltau converted the extra point and the 49ers led 7–3.[113]

Baltimore sent Shaw out at quarterback but the Colts were forced to punt. Tittle and the 49ers drove deep into Baltimore territory. On first down from the 21-yard line Tittle pitched the ball out wide to Perry. The lateral pass hit the ground with the Colts recovering.[114] On the first play of the ensuing drive Shaw handed to Moore who broke through a hole at left tackle and ran 57 yards before being pushed out of bounds by Jimmy Ridlon at the 49ers' 22-yard line. The 49ers' defense held and the Colts kicked a field goal bringing the score to 7–6 in favor of the 49ers.[115]

The 49ers tried to answer the score by putting together a drive that featured the arm of Tittle. He completed four passes as they marched into field goal range. On fourth down Soltau came on for a 30-yard attempt; the kick sailed wide left.[116]

With just a few minutes remaining in the half Unitas was sent out at quarterback. He remained ineffective and the Colts punted the ball. The 49ers held the ball until the whistle blew signaling the end of the half.[117]

Both teams opened the half with drives that ended in punts. On the 49ers second possession they took over at their own 18-yard line. Tittle opened with a pass to Wilson for 16 and then to McElhenny in the left flat for nine more. McElhenny then carried for seven more up the middle. Tittle hit R.C. Owens for nine over the middle and then back to the left flat to Conner for 12 more. After a couple of short runs the 49ers faced fourth down and two from the Colts' 21-yard line.[118] The crowd roared and started yelling, "No, no, no" as the field goal unit started onto the field. Hearing the uproar and probably figuring he had nothing to lose, Albert waved his offense back to the field. McElhenny took a pitch and ran wide around left end for an 11-yard gain and a first down.[119] Two plays later, on third down, Tittle hit Perry on a swing pass and Perry fought his way down to the one-foot line. On fourth down there was no question that Albert was going to go for it. He sent in J.D. Smith for Perry. Smith took the handoff and smashed into the end zone. Soltau added the extra point and the 49ers led 14–6.[120]

The Colts started their second drive of the half again with Unitas. The drive fizzled out and they could not convert on a fourth down near midfield. To start the fourth quarter the 49ers held the ball on their 39-yard line but two plays later they were forced to punt. Unitas and the Colts moved the ball to midfield and then they punted the ball out of the 49ers' end zone. San Francisco took over on the 20-yard line after the touchback and started another march down the field. Smith stayed in the game and ran the ball five times on the drive for 48 yards. On the final play of the drive Smith carried the ball three yards over the middle and into the end zone. Soltau's kick was good and the 49ers were up 21–6.[121]

Down by three scores the game was essentially over. Ewbank decided to leave Unitas in the game and again the Colts punted. After a 49ers three and out Unitas was back on the field. The drive started on the Colts' 31-yard line. Unitas took to the air and hit Jack Call for five yards. Three plays later Unitas hit Moore for a 21-yard gain. On the next play Unitas dropped back and threw a deep pass over the middle. Mutscheller made a juggling catch at the eight and carried the ball over the goal line for a touchdown. Brown again fumbled the snap and the extra point attempt failed.[122]

Final score, Niners 21–12.

Fortunately for Ewbank leaving Unitas in the game paid off. Unitas wasn't injured and he was able to extend his consecutive touchdown passes in a game streak to 25. The other positive for the entire Colts team was that it reminded the players how potent their offense could be, something they may have needed after a long day and as they turned their attention to the championship game.

In New York, the Giants had rallied from a 10–3 deficit in the fourth quarter to beat the Browns 13–10 and force a playoff game for the title. The following week the Giants beat the Browns by a score of 10–0 to win the Eastern Conference and the right to play the Colts for the NFL championship.[123]

NOTES

1. Sports Section, *Baltimore Sun*, September 29, 1958.
2. https://en.wikipedia.org/wiki/Bill_George_(linebacker).
3. https://en.wikipedia.org/wiki/List_of_Green_Bay_Packers_seasons.
4. Sports Section, *Baltimore Sun*, October 10, 1958.
5. Sports Section, *Baltimore Sun*, October 13, 1958.
6. Sports Section, *Baltimore Sun*, October 15, 1958.
7. Sports Section, *Baltimore Sun*, October 20, 1958.
8. *Washington Post*, October 27, 1958.
9. *Ibid.*
10. *Ibid.*
11. *Ibid.*
12. *Baltimore Sun*, October 27, 1958.
13. *Washington Post*, October 27, 1958.
14. *Green Bay Press Gazette*, November 3, 1958.
15. *Chicago Tribune*, November 3, 1958.
16. *Baltimore Sun*, November 3, 1958.
17. *Green Bay Press Gazette*, November 3, 1958.
18. *Chicago Tribune*, November 3, 1958.
19. *Green Bay Press Gazette*, November 3, 1958.
20. *Baltimore Sun*, November 3, 1958.
21. *Chicago Tribune*, November 3, 1958.
22. *Baltimore Sun*, November 3, 1958.
23. *Ibid.*
24. Cameron Snyder, "Unitas Due to Miss 3 or 4 Games," *Baltimore Sun*, November 5, 1959.
25. *Annapolis Evening Capital*, November 4, 1958.
26. *Baltimore Sun*, November 10, 1958.
27. *Los Angeles Times*, November 10, 1958.
28. *New York Times*, November 10, 1958.
29. *Ibid.*
30. *Baltimore Sun*, November 10, 1958.
31. *Ibid.*
32. *Ibid.*
33. *Washington Post*, November 10, 1958.
34. *Baltimore Sun*, November 10, 1958.
35. *Ibid.*
36. *Baltimore Sun*, November 17, 1958.
37. *Washington Post*, November 17, 1958.
38. *Chicago Tribune*, November 17, 1958.
39. *Washington Post*, November 17, 1958.
40. *Hartford Courant*, November 17, 1958.
41. *Baltimore Sun*, November 17, 1958.
42. *Chicago Tribune*, November 17, 1958.

43. *Baltimore Sun*, November 18, 1958.

44. Cameron C. Snyder, *Baltimore Sun*, November 23, 1958.

45. Cameron C. Snyder, *Baltimore Sun*, November 20, 1958.

46. Cameron C. Snyder, *Baltimore Sun*, November 23, 1958.

47. Cameron C. Snyder, *Baltimore Sun*, November 24, 1958.

48. "Baltimore Colts and Los Angeles Rams Play a Game of Football at Baltimore Memorial Stadium in Baltimore, Maryland," http://www.criticalpast.com/video/65675022488_Baltimore-Colts-and-Los-Angeles-Rams_Baltimore-Memorial-Stadium_football.

49. Cameron C. Snyder, *Baltimore Sun*, November 24, 1958.

50. http://www.kencrippen.com/Scouting-Reports/Lipscomb_Big_Daddy.pdf.

51. Cameron C. Snyder, *Baltimore Sun*, November 24, 1958.

52. "Baltimore Colts and Los Angeles Rams Play a Game of Football at Baltimore Memorial Stadium in Baltimore, Maryland," http://www.criticalpast.com/video/65675022488_Baltimore-Colts-and-Los-Angeles-Rams_Baltimore-Memorial-Stadium_football.

53. Cameron C. Snyder, *Baltimore Sun*, November 24, 1958.

54. "Baltimore Colts and Los Angeles Rams Play a Game of Football at Baltimore Memorial Stadium in Baltimore, Maryland," http://www.criticalpast.com/video/65675022488_Baltimore-Colts-and-Los-Angeles-Rams_Baltimore-Memorial-Stadium_football.

55. *Ibid.*

56. Cameron C. Snyder, *Baltimore Sun*, November 24, 1958.

57. Cameron C. Snyder, *Baltimore Sun*, November 30, 1958.

58. Cameron C. Snyder, *Baltimore Sun*, November 25, 1958.

59. *Ibid.*

60. *Ibid.*

61. Cameron C. Snyder, *Baltimore Sun*, November 30, 1958.

62. Ernest B. Furgurson, *Baltimore Sun*, December 1, 1958.

63. November 30, 1958, Colts–49ers Gamebook.

64. *Ibid.*

65. Darrell Wilson, *San Francisco Chronicle Sporting Green*, December 1, 1958.

66. *Ibid.*

67. *Ibid.*

68. November 30, 1958, Colts–49ers Gamebook.

69. *Ibid.*

70. *Ibid.*

71. *Ibid.*

72. Wilson.

73. November 30, 1958, Colts–49ers 1958 Gamebook.

74. Wilson.

75. *Ibid.*

76. November 30, 1958 Colts-49ers Gamebook.

77. *Ibid.*

78. Wilson.

79. November 30, 1958, Colts–49ers Gamebook.

80. *Ibid.*

81. Wilson.

82. Cameron C. Snyder, *Baltimore Sun*, December 1, 1958.

83. *Ibid.*

84. Cameron C. Snyder, *Baltimore Sun*, December 4, 1958.

85. *Ibid.*

86. *Ibid.*

87. Cameron C. Snyder, *Baltimore Sun*, December 7, 1958

88. *Ibid.*

89. *Ibid.*

90. *Ibid.*

91. http://losangeles.cbslocal.com/photo-galleries/2016/09/12/la-rams-through-the-years/.

92. Cameron C. Snyder, *Baltimore Sun*, December 7, 1958.

93. *Ibid.*

94. *Ibid.*
95. *Ibid.*
96. *Ibid.*
97. *Ibid.*
98. *Ibid.*
99. *Ibid.*
100. *Ibid.*
101. Cameron C. Snyder, *Baltimore Sun*, December 8, 1958.
102. Cameron C. Snyder, *Baltimore Sun*, December 9, 1958.
103. Cameron C. Snyder, *Baltimore Sun*, December 12, 1958.
104. Cameron C. Snyder, *Baltimore Sun*, December 14, 1958.
105. Cameron C. Snyder, *Baltimore Sun*, December 15, 1958.
106. Cameron C. Snyder, *Baltimore Sun*, December 14, 1958.
107. December 14, 1958 Colts- 49ers Gamebook.
108. *Ibid.*
109. *Ibid.*
110. *Ibid.*
111. *Ibid.*
112. Art Rosenbaum, *San Francisco Chronicle Sporting Green*, December 15, 1958.
113. *Ibid.*
114. December 14, 1958, Colts–49ers Gamebook.
115. *Ibid.*
116. *Ibid.*
117. *Ibid.*
118. *Ibid.*
119. Rosenbaum.
120. *Ibid.*
121. December 14, 1958, Colts–49ers Gamebook.
122. *Ibid.*
123. http://www.pro-football-reference.com/teams/nyg/1958.htm.

1958 NFL Championship Game

Rupert Patrick

December 28, 1958—NFL Championship: Baltimore Colts vs. New York Giants

Yankee Stadium

	Baltimore	New York
First downs	27	10
Yards rushing	138	88
Yards passing	349	200
Total yards (Net)	452	266
Passes	26–40	12–18
Intercepted by	0	1
Punts (Average)	4–50.8	6–45.7
Fumbles lost	2	4
Yards penalized	3–15	2–22

| Baltimore | 0 | 14 | 0 | 36 | 23 |
| New York | 3 | 0 | 7 | 70 | 17 |

New York—Field Goal, Summerall 36
Baltimore—Ameche, 2 run (Myhra kick)
Baltimore—Berry, 23 pass from Unitas (Myhra kick)
New York—Triplett, 1 run (Summerall kick)
New York—Gifford, 15 pass from Conerly (Summerall kick)
Baltimore—Field Goal, Myhra 20
Baltimore—Ameche, 1 run
A—64,185

Rushing
(Attempts, Yards)
Baltimore—Ameche 14–65; Dupre 11–30; Moore 8–23; Unitas 6–20
New York—Gifford 12–60; Webster 9–24; Triplett 5–12; Conerly 2–5; King 3–(-13)

Passing
(Attempts, Completions, Interceptions, Yards)
Baltimore—Unitas 40–26–1–349
New York—Conerly 14–10–0–187; Heinrich 4–2–0–13

Receiving
(Receptions, Yards)
Baltimore—Berry 12–178; Moore 6–101; Mutscheller 3–46; Ameche 3–17; Dupre 2–7
New York—Rote 2–76; Schnelker 2–63; Webster 2–17; Triplett 2–15; MacAfee 1–15; Gifford 3–14

The 1958 NFL championship is the most written about and talked about game in pro football history, with only Super Bowl III and the Ice Bowl game coming close, and 60 years after the fact is still one of the most famous pro football games ever played. Many fans consider it *the* greatest game ever played.

At the time this game was played, baseball and college football were more popular than pro football, and this game was definitely a turning point in the sport, and showed that the NFL was a game that was designed for television. It could also be argued that the national interest in pro football that was generated in the wake of this game led to the creation of the AFL in 1960, which brought pro football to a number of cities and regions of the country that were not covered by the NFL. A number of men who were involved in this game—Gifford, Unitas, Huff, Lombardi, Landry, Summerall to name a few—would become household names. From a historical standpoint, this was the most important game in pro football history.

New York was two years removed from winning the NFL championship, with their main offensive weapon, one Frank Gifford, who led the team in rushing yards and receptions. Sam Huff was the heart and soul of the Giants' defense that gave up the fewest points in the NFL. The head coach of the Giants was Jim Lee Howell, and his offensive coordinator was a fellow named Vince Lombardi. The Giants' defensive coordinator was a former Giants defensive back by the name of Tom Landry. The Colts led the league in offense, and were second in the league in defense behind New York. Those who set the odds had the Colts favored to beat the Giants by three and a half points.[1]

At the House That Ruth Built, Bert Rechichar kicked off for Baltimore, with the ball being downed for a touchback. On the first play from scrimmage, Don Heinrich's pass was batted down by a leaping Gino Marchetti. Heinrich flipped a pass to Alex Webster, good for seven yards, and on third and three, the pass to Kyle Rote was high and went off his hands. Don Chandler punted to Carl Taseff, who made a fair catch at the Baltimore 30.

On first down, Moore took a handoff and swept to the left, but the Giants were all over him and he was taken down for a loss. Horse Ameche went through the line for seven yards, setting up a third and six. Unitas went for the quarterback draw, but he took several hits and the ball popped loose, with Jim Patton falling on it for New York at the Baltimore 37. A handoff to Webster lost a yard, but on second down there was a bad snap from center, and Marchetti recovered for Baltimore at the Colts' 45.

Unitas dumped it off to L.G. Dupre in the left flat for four yards, and then, Dupre took a handoff a yard to the midfield stripe. Number 19 went to the air on third and five, but his pass to Raymond Berry was a little short and Linden Crow intercepted, returning the pick a couple yards to the Giants' 46. Runs by Gifford and Mel Triplett were unsuccessful and on third and 11, Heinrich's pass to Triplett came up short of the first down marker. Chandler's punt was returned to the Baltimore 15 by Taseff with about eight minutes to play in the first period.

Unitas rolled the dice and went deep on first down, with Moore hauling it in (despite tight coverage from Crow) along the right sideline at midfield and taking it to the New York 25 before Patton took him down after a gain of 60 yards. Ameche ran it up the gut to the 19, and Dupre lost a yard on second down. A delay penalty cost the Colts five yards, and a screen to Moore gained nothing. On fourth down, Baltimore set up for a field goal attempt but an offside flag against the Colts moved the ball to the 19. Still four yards short of a first down, Steve Myhra attempted a 27-yard three-pointer but Huff blocked the kick, and New York took over at their 22.

Charlie Conerly went in behind center for the Gothams, and on second down, he connected with Triplett for nine yards. Facing a third and one, Gifford took a pitch and got loose down the left side for 38 yards before Bill Pellington tackled him at the Baltimore 31. Triplett ran for two yards on first down, but incompletions on second and third downs were followed by a 36-yard field goal by Pat Summerall to put the Giants ahead by 3–0 with two minutes to play in the first quarter.

Lenny Lyles took the kickoff at the goal line and returned it to the 20, and a pass to Moore on the right sideline gained six yards. Dupre ran to the 28, and on third and two, Unitas put it up for Moore on the right flat at the 40 but Crow very nearly intercepted the pass. On the final play of the first period, Ray Brown's punt went to Crow at the Giants' 28 and Crow tried to return it but he wound up being pushed back to his 18 where he was tackled. With one period played, the Giants led 3–0.

On the first play of the second period, Gifford fumbled a pass from Conerly and Ray Krouse pounced on the loose ball at the Colts' 20. Moore took a handoff to the 15 before Huff manhandled him to the ground, and Ameche rolled through the middle for four yards. Unitas handed to Ameche on third and one, barely making the first down to set up a first and goal at the ten. Moore swept left on first down, going to the one before Patton knocked him out of bounds. From there, Ameche went off tackle and into the end zone. With two and a half minutes played in the second frame, Baltimore had a 7–3 lead.

The kickoff from Rechichar went to Triplett, who returned it 23 yards to the New York 38. Two plays later, a pass to Rote was good for 14 yards to the Giants' 48. On the next play, Conerly dropped back to pass but Pellington got to him and applied the smear at the Colts' 39. Webster took a reverse left for four yards, and on third and 15, Conerly threw to Gifford but the pass bounced off his chest and fell to the ground. Chandler's punt went to Jackie Simpson at the 19, but the ball came loose after a jarring hit from Billy Lott, with Buzz Guy recovering for New York at the Baltimore ten-yard line. Turnovers often seem to happen in pairs, and on the next play, Gifford took a pitch and started right but Milt Davis slammed into him and knocked the ball loose, with Don Joyce recovering for the Horseshoes at their 14-yard line.

Unitas tried a bomb similar to the one to Moore in the first period, but was unsuccessful. Berry hauled in a five-yard pass before Unitas converted the first down with a pass to Ameche for ten yards to the 29. Lenny cut through the middle for ten yards and another first down. Runs by Ameche and Moore left the Colts just short of a first down, and just short of midfield. Handing off to Ameche on third and one was like money in the bank, and Unitas did just so, with the Horse picking up two yards to the New York 49. After an incompletion to Berry on first down, Dupre ran for three yards. On third and seven, Unitas dropped back and could not find an open receiver, and ran for it, breaking left for 16 yards to the Giants' 30. An illegal motion penalty against Baltimore set up a second and 13 from the 34, and Berry pulled in a pass on the left sideline for 13 yards as two minutes remained in the half. Needing one yard on third down, you know who would get the call, and Ameche took a handoff left for six yards to the 15-yard line. On first down, Unitas dropped back and fired to Berry in the end zone. Berry had found a gap in the coverage between Patton and Emlen Tunnell, and pulled in the pass. The score came with 80 seconds left in the half, and gave Baltimore a 14–3 lead.

After the kickoff went for a touchback, a handoff lost a yard. On second down, Conerly dropped back and slipped and went down at the ten-yard line, with Art Donovan falling on top to register an easy smear. Conerly handed off to Webster for nine yards on the final play of the first half, with the Giants trailing by 14 to 3.

Lyles caught the second half kickoff underneath the goalposts and returned it to the 19 where he went out on the right sideline. A five-yard run by Moore and an eight-yard toss to Jim Mutscheller were enough for a first down at the 32. Moore took a reverse and tried to sweep left but future Rams and Chargers head coach Harland Svare took him down for a seven-yard deficit. A pass to Berry on the left sideline was good for 15 yards, but left the Colts two yards short of the marker. Huff applied what some might consider a late hit on Berry, which compelled Weeb Ewbank to take a swing at Huff, and Huff swung back before the two were separated, although no punches actually landed. (Ewbank said after the game, "Huff should have been kicked out of the game.")[2] An offside penalty against Baltimore made it a third and seven, and a screen to Dupre in the left flat only gained three yards. Brown got off a 53-yard punt to rookie Don Maynard at the New York 12, and it was returned to the 21.

Gifford took a handoff into the line on first down but Donovan stuffed him for no gain. A screen to Gifford in the left flat was read by Myhra, who took down Gifford for a three-yard loss. Conerly dropped back to pass on third and long, but the Colts blitzed and Donovan recorded his second smear of the game at the New York 18. Chandler's punt went to Moore, who opted for a fair catch at the Baltimore 41 with about five minutes gone in the third quarter.

Johnny U aired it out to an airborne Mutscheller for 32 yards over the middle, putting the Colts at the Giants' 27. A short run by Dupre and an incompletion on second down was followed by a pass to Berry on the left side for 11 yards and a first down inside the red zone. One play later, a right slant pass to Moore was good for 12 yards, giving Baltimore a first and goal at the three. On first down, Ameche swept left, and was forced down at the one. Unitas tried to sneak it in, but was unsuccessful, and Ameche was stopped short on third down. On fourth and goal, with the game on the line (a Colts TD here would have made the score 21–3 and likely put the game out of reach), the pitch went to Ameche, who went right in a pass option, but Cliff Livingston got through and took him down at the five. After one of the great goal line stands in the history of pro football, the Giants were still in the game with about six minutes to play in the third.

Gifford and Webster ran the ball for five and three yards, respectively, and on third down, Conerly dropped back to pass. At this point, the most bizarre play of the game occurred, as Conerly went deep to Rote at the New York 33, who was charging downfield. Nelson caught Rote at the 35 and took him down, but the ball came loose and continued rolling toward the Colts end zone. Webster, who was running behind Rote, picked up the ball at the 22 and continued down the right side until Taseff pushed Webster out of bounds at the Baltimore one-yard line after a gain of 85 yards. After Webster failed to put the ball across on first down, Triplett hit the line and broke the plane for the score. With less than four minutes to play in the third, the Giants were suddenly back in the game, trailing 14 to 10.

Simpson returned the ensuing kickoff to the Colts' 25, and a short run by Dupre was followed by a smear courtesy of Dick Modzelewski. On third down, Unitas dropped back but ran for it, picking up nine yards to the 29, four yards short of a first down. Brown booted a 56-yard punt to Maynard at the New York 15, with Maynard returning it four yards.

After a short run by Webster, Conerly connected with a leaping Bob Schnelker for 17 yards over the middle to the New York 39 on the final play of the third period. On the next play, Conerly went deep on a post pattern to Schnelker at the Baltimore 27, with Schnelker making it to the 15 where Nelson stopped him after a 46-yard gain. With the hot hand, Conerly went airborne again, this time on a right sideline route to Gifford at the seven and Gifford got past Davis for the score. With 14 minutes to play in regulation, the Giants stormed back to take a 17–14 lead.

The kickoff went for a touchback, and Unitas hit on passes to Moore for 11 yards and Berry for 13 to the Baltimore 44. After overthrowing Dupre on the left sideline on first down, Unitas scrambled for a yard to put Baltimore in a third and nine. Unitas threw to Mutscheller at the New York 38 but Crow was all over him, and the referee ruled interference, giving Baltimore a first down. Incompletions on second (a bomb to Dupre at the five that went off his fingertips) and third downs were followed by a 46-yard field goal attempt by Rechichar that hit the grass at the goal line.

Following a four-yard run by Phil King, Conerly connected with Ken McAfee for 15 yards to the New York 39. Gifford took a handoff on first down but Donovan caught him in the backfield for a two-yard loss, and a sweep left by Triplett picked up seven yards. On third and five, Gifford swept right but changed direction and cut through the line for ten yards, putting the Giants into Colts territory with a fresh set of downs. Conerly went to Gifford again on first down, and the run right was good for four yards. On second down, a handoff to King went disastrously bad when Big Daddy Lipscomb got through the line and separated King from the ball. Ray Krouse fell on the loose ball at the New York 42 midway thru the fourth quarter.

Unitas went for broke on first down (he did like to throw deep on first down to keep the defense honest) as he aired it out to Moore on the right sideline, but Lenny caught the ball while his foot was on the sideline. The pass on second down was batted down by Carl Karilivacz, but Unitas came through on a pass to Berry for 11 yards to the Giants' 31. Dupre ran for a couple yards on first down, but sacks on second and third down by Andy Robustelli and Modzelewski pushed them out of FG range and brought on the punting team.

The punt was returned to the New York 19 by Patton, and Webster ran for five yards on first down, but Gifford was stopped at the line by Marchetti and Donovan. On third and five, Conerly hit Webster on the right sideline for ten yards to the 34, moving the chains. Nursing a lead with less than four minutes to go in regulation, Conerly chose to burn up the clock by keeping the ball on the ground; handing off to Webster for a yard and Gifford for five yards. The next play was the most controversial play of the game, a third down and four. Gifford ran right and he may have gotten the four yards, but Marchetti broke his right ankle[3] on the play. In the chaos as teammates and coaches and trainers ran on the field to tend to Marchetti, the refs may not have properly spotted the ball. After getting Marchetti off the field and bringing out the chain gang, the Giants were a little short, although Gifford swore he had the first down. "I made that first down but the officials ruled it otherwise so what can you do,"[4] said Gifford after the game. New York decided to play it safe and punted to Baltimore.

The Colts had 2:20 left on the clock and were 86 yards from the end zone and down by three. After barely overthrowing Mutscheller on a bomb on first down, Unitas threw to Dupre, Dupre trapped the catch on the ground and it was ruled incomplete. A pass to Moore near the right sideline gained 11 yards to keep the drive alive, but Moore did not get out of bounds. After an incompletion on first down, Berry took a pass 25 yards up the middle to midfield with 1:04 remaining. Unitas hooked up with Berry on the next play, this time for 15 yards to the New York 35 as 40 seconds remained. Berry hauled in another pass and took it to the 13. With seven ticks left, Steve Myhra booted a 20-yard FG to tie the game at 17 apiece. There was just enough time for a kickoff and Conerly taking a knee to end regulation. For the first time, the NFL championship was going to sudden death.

New York won the toss, and Rechichar's kickoff went to Maynard, who returned the ball to the Giants' 20. Gifford swept left on first down, picking up four yards, and Conerly was unable to connect on a pass to Schnelker at the 45 yard line. Conerly took the snap on third down and bootlegged right, gaining five yards but coming up short of the first down. Chandler got off a 52-yard punt to the 19, which was returned a yard by Taseff.

On first down, Unitas handed off to Dupre, who swept right but cut inside and picked up 11 yards. Johnny U went deep on first down, but his pass intended for Moore was broken up by Crow at the New York 20.[5] A run by Dupre and a screen to Ameche for eight yards in the left flat were just enough for a first down at the Baltimore 41. After another run by Dupre, this time for four yards, a smear by Modzelewski set up third and 14. Unitas and Berry collaborated on a pass on the left sideline for 21 yards to the Giants 42, with Berry getting free when Karilivacz fell down.[6]

Ameche took a trap draw through the middle and galloped through the line for 22 yards to the 20 yard line. This was the play that pretty much put the Colts in scoring position and sealed the game. Unitas said after the game, "When we noticed that Huff was laying back just a bit for pass protection, we figured that Modzelewski would come flying through there. He did and everything worked out as it was supposed to. Ameche went clean up the middle."[7] Ewbank also agreed the play call from Unitas was brilliant, and said, "That was the big play in the drive. It helped our pass protection on the next few plays too."[8]

It was at this point when television audiences across the country were treated to two and a half minutes of dead air when somebody on the sidelines apparently knocked a TV power cable loose. NBC (who was broadcasting the game) suddenly found themselves in the position of possibly not being able to show the winning score live.[9] As the story goes, in order to hold up the game momentarily, an NBC employee on the sidelines was ordered to run onto the field and cause a commotion, and the delay while he was chased down and hauled off the field gave the technicians sufficient time to fix the problem and get the network feed reestablished. Only two plays were missed by TV audiences.

Dupre tried to run right but was stopped at the line, and on second down, Unitas threw to Berry on a slant pattern to the eight, setting up a first and championship. (The NBC technical problems were resolved at this point in the game.) Ameche went through the line for a yard on first down, and Unitas threw to Mutscheller in the right flat, with Mutscheller going out of bounds at the one yard line. Ameche took the handoff and rolled through a hole on the right side of the line, and into the end zone. Many of the 15,000 Colts fans who attended the game charged the field immediately and tore down the goal posts.[10] After 8:15 of sudden death, the Colts were NFL champions with a 23–17 victory.

Johnny Unitas was voted the MVP of the game (26–40–349–1–1), although an argument probably could have been made for Raymond Berry, who caught 12 passes for 178 yards and a touchdown. Unitas became the proud owner of a new sports car that was awarded by *Sport Magazine*.[11]

NFL Commissioner Bert Bell (who died less than a year later) said after the game, "I never thought I would live to see sudden death"[12] and also it was the "greatest game he had ever seen."[13]

Coach Howell gave the Colts their due: "We were only a few feet and seconds away from taking it all but they are great and we have nothing to be ashamed of."[14]

NOTES

1. *Baltimore Sun*, December 28, 1958.
2. *Baltimore Sun*, December 29, 1958.
3. *Ibid.*
4. *Hartford Courant*, December 29, 1958.
5. *Chicago Tribune*, December 29, 1958.
6. *Ibid.*
7. *Ibid.*
8. *Chicago Defender*, December 29, 1958.
9. *Washington Post*, December 29, 1958.
10. *New York Times*, December 29, 1958.
11. *Baltimore Sun*, December 29, 1958.
12. *Baltimore Sun*, December 26, 1999.
13. *New York Times*, December 29, 1958.
14. *Hartford Courant*, December 29, 1958.

Final 1958 NFL Standings

Eastern Conference

Team	W	L	T	PCT	PF	PA
New York Giants	9	3	0	.750	246	183
Cleveland Browns	9	3	0	.750	302	217
Pittsburgh Steelers	7	4	1	.636	261	230
Washington Redskins	4	7	1	.364	214	268
Chicago Cardinals	2	9	1	.182	261	356
Philadelphia Eagles	2	9	1	.182	235	306

Western Conference

Team	W	L	T	PCT	PF	PA
Baltimore Colts	9	3	0	.750	381	203
Chicago Bears	8	4	0	.667	298	230
Los Angeles Rams	8	4	0	.667	344	278
San Francisco 49ers	6	6	0	.500	257	324
Detroit Lions	4	7	1	.364	261	276
Green Bay Packers	1	10	1	.091	193	382

Courtesy Wikipedia.

1958 Colts Statistics

RUPERT PATRICK

Team Statistics

Category	Offense	Defense
First Downs	253	188
Rushing–Passing–Penalty	117–120–16	70–106–12
Rushes–Yards–Yards per Rush	456–2127–4.7	331–1291–3.9
Pass Attempts–Completions	354–178	363–168
Completion %	50.3	46.3
Yards Passing	2537	2248
Yards Lost Passing	125	255
Net Yards Passing	2412	1993
Net Yards per Att–Net Yards per Comp	6.81–13.55	5.49–11.86
Total Yards Gained	4539	3284
% Yds Rushing–% Yds Passing	46.86–53.14	39.30–60.70
Offensive Plays–Yds per Play	810–5.6	694–4.7
Had Intercepted–Yards–TDs	11–169–3	35–514–1
Punts–Yards–Average per Punt	62–2276–36.7	62–2736–44.1
Punt Returns—Yards–Average–TDs	39–237–6.1–0	40–176–4.4–1
Kickoff Returns–Yds–Ave–TDs	34–864–25.4–2	43–1241–28.9–1
Penalties–Yards Penalized	55–518	60–555
Fumbles	26	31
Own Recovered–TDs by Own Rec	15–0	14–0
Opp Recovered–TDs by Opp Rec	17–0	11–0
Points Scored	381	203

Category	Offense	Defense
Touchdowns (Total)	53	27
TD's Rushing–Passing–Ret & Rec	24–26–3	13–9–5
Extra Points	48	23
Safeties	0	0
Field Goals Made–Attempted	5–14	6–17
FG % Successful	35.7	35.3

Individual Statistics

Rushing	No.	Yards	Ave	Long	TDs
Alan Ameche	171	791	4.6	28	8
Lenny Moore	82	598	7.3	73	7
L.G. Dupre	95	390	4.1	39	3
Jack Call	37	154	4.2	35	0
John Unitas	33	139	4.2	28	3
Lenny Lyles	22	41	1.9	27	0
Billy Pricer	10	26	2.6	4	1
George Shaw	5	-3	-0.6	3	1
Ray Brown	1	-9	-9.0	-9	0

Passing	Att	Cmp	% Cmp	Yds gained	TDs	Long	Int	% Int	Yds/Gain
John Unitas	263	136	51.7	2007	19	77	7	2.7	7.63
George Shaw	89	41	46.1	531	7	57	4	4.5	5.97
Ray Brown	2	1	50.0	-1	0	0	0	0.0	0.00

Receiving	No.	Yards	Ave	Long	TDs
Raymond Berry	56	794	14.2	54	9
Lenny Moore	50	938	18.5	77	7
Jim Mutscheller	28	504	18.5	54	7
L.G. Dupre	13	111	8.5	22	0
Alan Ameche	13	81	6.2	18	1
Lenny Lyles	5	24	4.8	11	1
Bert Rechichar	4	34	8.5	12	1
Jack Call	4	28	7.0	12	0
Billy Pricer	3	14	4.7	6	0
Art DeCarlo	1	10	10.0	10	0
Bill Pellington	1	-1	-1.0	-1	0

Interceptions	No.	Yards	Ave	Long	TDs
Andy Nelson	8	199	24.9	69	1
Ray Brown	8	149	18.7	30	0
Carl Taseff	7	52	7.4	17	0
Bill Pellington	4	44	11.0	21	0
Milt Davis	4	40	10.0	28	0
Don Shinnick	3	23	7.7	16	0
Leo Sanford	1	7	7.0	7	0

Punting	No.	Yards	Ave	Long	Block
Ray Brown	41	1635	39.9	60	0
Dick Horn	19	617	32.5	48	0
Avatus Stone	1	28	28.0	28	0
L.G. Dupre	1	-4	-4.0	-4	0

Punt Returns	No.	Yards	Ave	Long	TDs
Carl Taseff	29	196	6.8	33	0
Bert Rechichar	7	29	4.1	11	0
Lenny Moore	2	11	5.5	11	0
Jackie Simpson	1	1	1.0	1	0

Kickoff Returns	No.	Yards	Ave	Long	TDs
Lenny Lyles	11	398	36.2	103	2
Billy Pricer	9	168	18.7	28	0
Lenny Moore	4	91	22.8	25	0
Bert Rechichar	3	50	16.7	22	0
Jackie Simpson	3	59	19.7	24	0
Jack Call	2	48	24.0	26	0
Carl Taseff	1	50	50.0	50	0
A DeCarlo	1	0	0.0	0	0

Scoring	TDs All–Rush–Rec–Ret	XPA–XPM	FGA–FGM	Saf	Points
Lenny Moore	14–7–7–0	0–0	0–0	0	84
Steve Myhra	0–0–0–0	51–48	10–4	0	60
Alan Ameche	9–8–1–0	0–0	0–0	0	54
Raymond Berry	9–0–9–0	0–0	0–0	0	54
Jim Mutscheller	7–0–7–0	0–0	0–0	0	42
Lenny Lyles	4–1–1–2	0–0	0–0	0	24
L.G. Dupre	3–3–0–0	0–0	0–0	0	18
John Unitas	3–3–0–0	0–0	0–0	0	18
Bert Rechichar	1–0–1–0	0–0	4–1	0	9
Andy Nelson	1–0–0–1	0–0	0–0	0	6
Billy Pricer	1–1–0–0	0–0	0–0	0	6
George Shaw	1–1–0–0	0–0	0–0	0	6

Field Goals	1–19 Yds	20–29	30–39	40–49	Over 50	Total	Ave Att	Ave Make	Ave Miss	Long
Steve Myhra	2–2	2–3	0–3	0–2	0–0	4–10	30.2	20.5	39.3	28
Bert Rechichar	0–0	0–0	0–1	1–2	0–1	1–4	46.0	48.0	45.3	48

Statistics courtesy 1959 NFL Record and Rules Manual and pro-football-reference.com.

1958 Colts Superlatives

RUPERT PATRICK

Despite missing two full games and half of a third game, Johnny Unitas still managed to be the consensus All-Pro QB. Johnny U was elected First Team All-Pro by the Associated Press (AP), United Press International (UPI), *The Sporting News* (SN), *The New York Daily News* (NYDN) and Newspaper Enterprise Association or NEA.

In 1958, passers were rated strictly on average yards per pass attempt, and Unitas finished fifth in the NFL with a value of 7.63 yards per pass. His 19 TD passes led the league, and he had the lowest interception percentage of 2.7 percent. When the modern passer rating formula (which was first adopted by the NFL in 1973) is retroactively applied to 1958 statistics, Unitas led the NFL in passer rating in 1958 with a rating of 90.0. Unitas was fourth in passing attempts (263), completions (136) and yards (2007).

Alan Ameche finished third in the loop in rushing attempts with 171 and his 791 rushing yards was barely half of Jim Brown's league leading total of 1527 yards. Ameche's eight rushing TDs tied for third in the league. He was voted Second Team All-Pro by the AP, UPI, NEA and NYDN.

Raymond Berry's 56 receptions tied with Philadelphia's Pete Retzlaff for best in the NFL, and Berry's nine TD catches tied the Eagles Tommy McDonald for the league lead. Berry's catches went for 794 yards, good for fourth in the NFL. Berry was a consensus First Team All-Pro for 1958.

Lenny Moore was an explosive combination of runner and receiver, whose 598 rushing yards were eighth in the NFL in 1958 and was fourth in the league with 50 receptions. He finished tied for sixth in rushing TDs with seven, and was tied for fifth in pass reception TDs with seven. Moore's total of 14 trips to the end zone was second in the league, and his 84 points scored tied with Rams kicker Paige Cothren for second-best in the NFL. Moore was voted a consensus First Team All-Pro.

Colts end Jim Mutscheller was also tied with Moore at fifth in the league with seven TD receptions.

Future Hall of Famer Jim Parker was a First Team All-Pro at tackle as named by the AP, UPI, NYDN and NEA. Guard Art Spinney was voted a First Team All-Pro by the SN and Second Team All-Pro by the AP, UPI and NEA.

On the defensive side, tackle Big Daddy Lipscomb was a consensus First Team All Pro, as was end Gino Marchetti. Tackle Art Donovan (who would join Marchetti in Canton) was voted First Team All-Pro by the NYDN and Second Team All-Pro by the AP, NEA and UPI.

Linebacker Bill Pellington was voted a First Team All-Pro by SN and Second Team All-Pro by the NEA.

Safety Andy Nelson intercepted eight passes, tied for third in the league. Nelson's 199 yards in interception return yards led the league. For his efforts, Nelson was voted First Team All-Pro by the NYDN and SN and Second Team by the NEA, UPI and AP.

Ray Brown also picked off eight passes, tying Nelson for third-most in the NFL. His 149 interception return yards ranked fifth in the league.

Carl Taseff was tied for fifth in the circuit with seven interceptions. Taseff's 29 punt returns led the league, and was tied for second in punt return yards with 196. He was voted a Second Team All-Pro by the AP and UPI, and 1958 was the only year he was named to an All-Pro team.

Steve Myhra's 48 extra points led the NFL.

Statistics, category ranking and All-Pro information courtesy of Pro-Football-Reference.com

PART 3

The Team

Alan Ameche

Rick Schabowski

When Lino Dante "Alan" Ameche carried the football, Baltimore Colts fans felt their hearts beat as fast as the horses' gallops at the Preakness. Well, pretty close.

Ameche's accomplishments on the gridiron boosted an icon status for the Wisconsin native, who won the Heisman Trophy at the University of Wisconsin in 1954; played in four NFL Pro Bowls; and scored the winning touchdown—in overtime—in the 1958 NFL championship against the New York Giants.

Born on June 1, 1933, in an upstairs apartment in Kenosha, Ameche weighed more than 11 pounds; when he was two, he wore clothes made for four-year-olds. Parents Augusto and Benedetta were immigrants—they Americanized their names to August and Betty. Augusto came to the United States in 1914 and became a citizen in 1921. Six years later he returned to Italy and married Benedetta on June 29, 1927. The newlyweds moved back to Kenosha later that year. Their first child was born in 1928—Lyndo.

Betty missed Italy and went there with her two sons in early 1937. With Mussolini coming to power, turmoil escalated. Four-year-old Lino had to wear the Fascist Youth uniform prescribed by Mussolini. "I don't remember much about it, thank God,"[1] said Ameche.

They returned to Kenosha in late 1937; changes abounded: the family's last name "Amici" became "Ameche," Lyndo became Lynn, and the Ameche matriarch became a U.S. citizen.

The family adjusted well to being back in the United States, and young Lino took a liking to sports and weight lifting. Lynn helped make a set of weights using a broom stick and attaching coffee cans filled with cement.

Cupid's arrow struck the younger Ameche in high school—he fell in love at first sight with Yvonne Molinaro, his future wife. Ameche changed his first name to "Alan" during his time at Kenosha Bradford High School, which he started attending at age 16. Yvonne said the reason for selecting "Alan" was because Ameche liked actor Alan Ladd.

Ameche won the Wisconsin state championship in the shot put during his junior year, with a toss of 50 feet, nine inches. He was also a terrific sprinter, posting a time of 10.2 seconds in the 100-yard dash. Football was where he really excelled, though.

In Ameche's senior year, 1950, Kenosha Bradford had one of the greatest teams in Wisconsin high school football history, scoring more touchdowns than their opponents scored points—Ameche was responsible for 108 points. There was only one close game, an 18–13 win against perennial power Madison East. Kenosha Bradford trailed 13–0 at halftime, but rebounded on Ameche's three touchdowns in the second half.

For the season, Ameche and his teammates had a 342–48 point differential against their opponents. Their coach, Chuck Jaskwich, kept his starters out for about half of every game, except the one against Madison East. Ameche was named to the Wisconsin All-State football team at fullback. A number of his teammates received scholarships.

One of Ameche's closest high school friends, Bobby Hinds, recalled the future Colts star's ability: "He was not a stylish runner, he just bullied ahead. He was super strong. He wasn't a ballet dancer; he went right through you."[2]

Tom Braatz, who later served as executive vice president of the Green Bay Packers, was also a teammate and a close friend. He and Ameche often double dated with their girlfriends, stayed close for several years, and became godparents for each other's children. "Starting in high school, he was very blessed with talent," remembered Braatz. He got the nickname 'Horse' from the players because he was kind of built like a racehorse, very strong physically but with very skinny, long legs."[3]

Ameche attracted interest from several colleges, but he narrowed it to three—Wisconsin, Notre Dame, and USC. His second cousin, Don Ameche, also born in Kenosha, made his name as a Hollywood movie star and became a huge fan of USC football. Don's advocacy for USC included mentioning the gorgeous female actresses in Los Angeles, but it was to no avail—Ameche already had Yvonne, the love of his life.

Notre Dame made a strong sales pitch with a personal connection—Ameche's high school coach, Chuck Jaskwich played quarterback and basketball at Notre Dame, graduating in 1932.

Fred Miller, the president of the Miller Brewing Company, was a Notre Dame alumnus.

Alan Ameche.

Miller played for Knute Rockne, earning All-America honors at offensive tackle. He sparked controversy with his vigorous recruiting efforts on behalf of the Irish—it got so heated that some Wisconsin beer drinkers threatened a boycott of Miller Beer if Ameche went to Notre Dame.

In the end, Wisconsin won the battle. Badgers assistant and later head coach Milt Bruhn reflected on the decision. "I think Al came to Wisconsin because Ivan [head coach Ivy Williamson] took about five of his high school buddies. If it hadn't been for that, he probably would have gone to Notre Dame." Wisconsin did sign Bradford stars Mario Bonfiglio, Ameche's good friend and high school quarterback, tackles Ed Ronzia and Dick Nicolazzi, end Frank Aiello, linebacker/center Ruel McMullen, and fullback Bobby Hinds. Wisconsin also offered a scholarship to Tom Braatz, who opted to attend Marquette.[4]

Williamson promoted Ameche to the varsity for his freshman season in 1951 after an impressive pre-season practice. It did not appear likely, though, that Ameche would get much playing time—Badgers captain Jim Hammond performed with aplomb at fullback. NCAA rules at the time allowed freshmen, with no restrictions, to play in JV games and varsity games. Ameche did not start the first JV game against Iowa on September 28, but he scored two touchdowns, and suited up for the varsity game the next day against Marquette, gaining one yard on one carry.

On October 6, in a game against Illinois, Ameche got another varsity opportunity when he spelled Hammond. He gained 40 yards on ten carries in the 14–10 loss, but impressed Illinois coach Ray Elliot, who said, "I like that kid Ameche. Did you see him hit our line? He's the finest freshman back I've seen. He's a great prospect."[5]

The Badgers finished the season at 7–1–1 with one of the best defenses in the country, but the loss to Illinois cost them the Big Ten title. Ameche had a great season, leading the conference with 774 yards on 147 attempts, both Big Ten records. It was the first time a freshman led the Big Ten in rushing. Overall he finished with 824 yards on 157 carries, both Wisconsin school records.

Burt Hable, who later became a successful coach at Madison West High School, was a junior during Ameche's freshman year. "From the beginning, I could see he was a nice guy. He looked to older players for direction and advice and he wasn't a showoff or anything. We all recognized his talent, but he was just himself."[6]

Yvonne visited Madison late in Ameche's freshman season. During the short time she spent there, the telephone rang 11 times, indicating Ameche's gloried status among the UW women. This ended on Thanksgiving Day, November 27, 1952, when the couple married at the Holy Rosary Church in Madison.

Nineteen fifty-two was also a great season for Wisconsin football. The Badgers upset number two- ranked Illinois on October 4, 20–6, a game in which Ameche gained 116 yards on 32 carries against a defense designed to stop him with an eight-man line. The Badgers tied Purdue for the Big Ten title with a 4–1–1 conference record and finished with a 6–3–1 overall mark. Ameche led the Big Ten in rushing with 721 yards and was named first team All-Big Ten. Overall, prior to the Rose Bowl, he finished with 946 yards on 205 carries, breaking his own school records in both categories.

A 7–3 vote by the Big Ten athletic commissioners sent 11th ranked Wisconsin to the 1953 Rose Bowl, where they would play fifth-ranked USC. The Badgers lost a hard-fought defensive game, 7–0, with Ameche rushing for 133 yards on 28 carries.

The NCAA implemented a big rule change for the 1953 season—elimination of two-platoon football. Under the new paradigm, only one player could be substituted between plays. When a player left the game for a substitute in the first half, he could not return until the second half. When a player left the game in the second half, he could not play in the remainder of the game.

To circumvent the rule, offensive players had to find a position to play on defense, and vice versa. Though Ameche had some experience playing defensive back in high school; he played linebacker for Wisconsin.

"You bet it hurt [Ameche] playing both ways," said teammate Dick Nicolazzi. "It was a stupid rule. I guess the idea was to cut down on the number of scholarships they were giving out, but it took a hell of a toll on a running back to play linebacker too."[7]

Wisconsin had another solid season in 1953, finishing 4–1–1 in Big Ten play and 6–2–1 overall, ranked 15th in the final polls. Ameche finished the season with 801 yards on 165 carries. The *Milwaukee Sentinel*'s Frank Graham reflected on Ameche's 1953 season: "Ameche is the kind of kid for whom football was invented. He enjoys hitting and being hit, and it required the abolition of the two-platoon system to bring out the best there was in him. He's a nice kid, gentle and considerate of his classmates and all others on campus when he's off duty, but once he puts on that football suit he is sparked by a lust for violence and a ball carrier who falls into his hands is marked for destruction."

Ameche was named to seven All-America teams.[8]

In 1954, Ameche's senior year, Wisconsin finished 7–2, ranking #9 in the polls at the end of the season with road losses to Ohio State (31–14) and Iowa (13–7). Ameche finished with 641 yards in 146 carries, and was a consensus first team All-American. In addition, Ameche was named the Big Ten MVP by the *Chicago Tribune*, UPI's Back of the Year, and Senior Bowl MVP. For his career, he scored 25 touchdowns and rushed for 3,212 yards on 673 carries, both NCAA records (his 1953 Rose Bowl statistics are not included in the final totals).

On December 9, 1954, Ameche received college football's biggest award—the Heisman Trophy. At the Downtown Athletic Club in New York, Ameche said that he was "proud and humble"[9] because "I know many other deserving players could have received this honor."[10] He credited everyone who had helped him, especially his coaches. Yvonne received the spotlight, too, when Ameche said, "I want to thank the most understanding and helpful one of all, my wife."[11] Coach Williamson praised, "You can be a great football player, you can be a great guy, but you have to prove it to yourself. He has proved it."[12]

Ameche's manner, performance, and personality led to respect among his Badger teammates. "As a person, he was fun loving and went out of his way to help everybody," said Jim Haluska, the quarterback for the 1952 Big Ten title team that played in the 1953 Rose Bowl. "He had his buddies on the team and off the team, and he was as friendly as he could be with all of them. He went out of his way to take care of them."[13] Don Voss, an All-American defensive end on the 1952 team, noted, "Al had a great sense of humor. As much as he was the star, he was never big-headed. He was down to earth and as friendly to the sixth stringer as he was to the first stringer."[14]

At the Eagles Club in Kenosha, a banquet honoring Ameche sold out all 1,000 tickets in two days. Generosity swarmed him at the event held on January 12, 1955—gifts included a 1,500-pound horse, a watch, toys for his kids, a brand new Hudson automobile, and 3,212 one-dollar bills representing the number of yards he gained at Wisconsin.

Des Moines promoter Pinkie George offered Ameche $100,000 to become a professional wrestler, exclaiming, "I don't have fundamental objections if Ameche also wants to play pro football. But in that event, I could offer him only $50,000 for about six months of wrestling a year."[15] Though it was a tempting offer, Ameche veered toward the NFL.

The 1955 NFL draft took place at the Warwick Hotel in New York on January 27–28. With the bonus pick the Baltimore Colts selected Oregon's George Shaw, an All-American quarterback. The Chicago Cardinals selected Max Boydston, an Oklahoma end, with the second pick. Ameche's waiting game ended when the Colts used the third pick to select the Wisconsin star, who learned of his destiny through a telephone call to his Madison home.

The Colts offered a one-year deal, but Ameche wanted to lock in three years. They compromised with a two-year deal with a salary of $15,000 for Ameche's rookie season.

At that time, Ameche's salary was the highest ever offered a rookie. In turn, it created friction among the Colts. Teammate and future Hall of Fame defensive end Gino Marchetti recalls the first time that he met Ameche:

> It was really strange. I remember it was before camp opened, and I was walking with Weeb Ewbank. We were coming from a meeting and heading to chow, and Alan was walking ahead of us. I remember it because Weeb made a really strange comment that stuck with me over the years. He sees Alan in front of us and he says, "There is our big draft choice. He was babied in college. He was spoiled at Wisconsin." It was so strange because here Weeb hadn't even had a chance to know the guy and he'd already made up his mind about him. The really strange thing is that Weeb never changed his mind about Alan. He never liked Alan for some reason, and I could never figure it out. Alan worked hard, he played hard, he was a good blocker. He did everything that was asked of him, but Weeb wouldn't give the guy a break.[16]

Indeed, Ewbank and Ameche feuded throughout the latter's tenure in Baltimore.

During training camp, Ameche started at fullback; he stayed there for the entire pre-season.

Hall of Fame broadcaster Ernie Harwell worked in Baltimore during Ameche's emergence in the NFL; his biggest sports thrill of 1955 happened in Ameche's first game against the Chicago Bears, on September 25. "It was the opening game of the year. A big crowd was still moving into Baltimore [Memorial] Stadium when Ameche took the ball on the first Colt play from scrimmage and galloped 79 yards for a touchdown, sparking the Colts to a 23–17 upset over the Chicago Bears."[17]

When Gino Marchetti congratulated Ameche on his first-ever NFL carry, a touchdown, Ameche replied, "You know, Gino, I didn't think it was going to be this easy. I never ran 79 yards in my life."[18]

The rookie finished the day with 194 yards on 21 carries.

Carrying the pigskin 213 times in his first season, Ameche led the NFL with 961 yards and caught 27 passes for 141 yards. His was named first team All-Pro and 1955 NFL Rookie of the Year; the feat of being both the Heisman Trophy winner and Rookie of the Year would not happen again until Tony Dorsett's rookie season in 1976.

Four games into the 1956 season, the Colts offense changed its complexion. George Shaw injured his knee in a game against the Bears and, as a result, Johnny Unitas became the starting quarterback. The excellence of Unitas was immediately apparent. Unitas had a 55.6 percent completion mark for the season, a record at the time for a first-year quarterback. With Unitas at the helm, and the improved performance of Raymond Berry at end, the Colts now had an enhanced two-dimensional offense. Ameche gained 858 yards on 178 carries and scored eight touchdowns. Again, Ameche had a place on the All-Pro team.

Unitas lead the Colts to a 7–5 record in 1957, the first winning record in franchise history. Ameche gained 493 yards on 144 carries with five touchdowns and caught 15 passes for two touchdowns. For the third straight year, he earned a spot in the Pro Bowl.

The change in offense definitely affected Ameche's role with the Colts. Gino Marchetti noted, "When Unitas got here, they had such confidence in his passing that it got so Alan would get the ball on third and one, third and two. They were the only times he'd even touch the ball. Sometimes he'd carry the ball six times a game, and before Unitas he carried the ball twenty-five, thirty times a game." He elaborated further, "It was the way Weeb designed the offense. To be honest, Alan was lost out there. Weeb just put him aside. I'm sure he figured as long as John can do it, let him do it. I'm not saying Weeb should have taken the ball out of Johnny's hands, though. He was a great quarterback.

But as time went by, there were games when Alan would get like six carries in a game. A running back can't get a rhythm like that. Sometimes it takes 15 or 18 carries for a running back to get warmed up."[19]

For Ameche, negative feelings stirred. "I was bitter as hell when it happened, but you can't argue with the success we had," admitted the Colts' star. "I can't argue with what they did. I got to be a better blocker, and after all, how many times do you get a Unitas?"[20]

The Colts' newest icon spoke highly of Ameche. "Back in the years when we were winning everything in sight, we had one of the best fullbacks the National Football League has ever seen—Alan Ameche. The Horse could bull his way through anything, and he was a wicked blocker, too. He could get the job done."[21]

The 1958 Colts galloped out of the gate, winning six straight to start the season. They beat the defending NFL champion Detroit Lions twice, one of the wins a 40–14 rout at Briggs Stadium on October 19. Ameche scored two touchdowns, gaining 76 yards on 19 carries.

The Chicago Bears were the closest team in the Western Conference standings to the Colts, and they had a key game in Chicago on November 16. For the first time since 1946, the Bears were shut out, losing to the Colts, 17–0. Ameche was more of a bull than a horse, gaining 142 yards on 26 carries, and scoring a touchdown. He was awarded the game ball for his performance. On November 30, a loss by the Bears and a 35–27 Colts victory over the 49ers clinched the Western Conference title for the Colts. The Colts finished the season with a 9–3 record. Ameche gained 791 yards on 171 carries with eight touchdowns, and he caught 13 passes for 81 yards and a touchdown.

The Eastern Conference champion was decided by a playoff game between the New York Giants and the Cleveland Browns, who both finished the regular season with 9–3 records. The Giants won the game, 10–0, at Yankee Stadium on December 21 for the right to play the Colts.

In what many football fans call "The Greatest Game Ever Played," the Colts beat the Giants 23–17 for the NFL title in the league's first overtime championship game. Before the contest, Ameche stated, "The Giants are more versatile. They do a lot of different things well, and the New York defense forced Cleveland to do something it didn't want to do and that was pass. We're the same type of team as the Giants, and I've never felt so confident in my life as I do right now that we can beat them. This is the biggest game of our life."[22]

It was a battle that teetered back and forth like a seesaw. The Colts jumped to a 14–3 lead. In the third quarter, on third down from the Giants' one-yard line, Ameche got stopped. Ewbank decided to go for it on fourth down. Unitas called play "428," a pitchout to Ameche, who would then throw a pass to Jim Mutscheller. Ameche did not hear the "4" and thought the play was "28," which required the fullback to run through the "8" hole. Again, the Giants stopped Ameche. Mutscheller, meanwhile, was open in the end zone.

The Giants clawed back, taking a 17–14 lead. Colts' kicker Steve Myhra tied the game with a 20-yard field goal as seven seconds remained on the clock to send the game into overtime.

With the Giants winning the coin toss to start the overtime period, the Colts' defense rose to the occasion and held them. After the Giants punted, the Colts drove down the field 80 yards in 13 plays and scored the winning touchdown. Ameche made several critical plays on the drive—catching an eight-yard pass on third and eight from the Colts' 33-yard line and later rushing 22 yards to the Giants' 20-yard line. He scored on third and goal from the Giants' one-yard line to win the game.

Johnny Unitas, who called the game-winning play, told the Associated Press, "A lot of people remember him [Ameche] from that particular run, but he was instrumental in keeping that game alive with his pass catching and running ability. We knew he wouldn't fumble."[23] Ameche commented, "We were on the right hash mark and everybody thought we'd run off tackle to the left. That way if we didn't make it, we're lined up on the goalpost for the field goal. Instead, John [Unitas] called off tackle right. The Giants were looking left, just like everybody else. The hole was so big, I waltzed right in."[24]

When asked if this was the greatest thrill in his career, Ameche answered, "You know, I can't think of a better one. But I can say, too, that when those fans mobbed me in the end zone and took the ball away, I was hit harder than any time in football."[25] Colts center Buzz Nutter retrieved the football and headed with Ameche to the locker room.

In his book *Johnny U*, Tom Callahan wrote, "Immediately after the game, a representative from *The Ed Sullivan Show* offered Unitas $500 to appear on that evening's telecast. John declined, saying he wanted to fly home with the team. When the offer was sweetened to $700, Unitas responded, 'Give it to Ameche.'" Callahan continued, "Trading in his uniform for a suit and tie (and for the original $500), Ameche stood in the wings as Sullivan introduced him and recapped the game: 'This is Alan Ameche of the Baltimore Colts, who today, in the first sudden death playoff in professional football, went across the goal line with the winning touchdown. So, let's have a tremendous hand for Alan Ameche.'"[26]

Sam Huff compared the running backs the Giants played against in the playoffs. "Jim Brown is faster, but Ameche hits quicker into the line. Both are tough boys, particularly Ameche."[27]

In 1959, the Colts went 9–3 to win the Western Conference, giving them an opportunity to play against the Giants for the NFL title. They won, 31–16. Ameche had a good season, gaining 679 yards on 178 carries.

In 1960, Ameche gained 263 yards on 80 carries, playing in ten games. In a game against the Detroit Lions on December 4, 1960, he tore his Achilles tendon. Ameche recalled, "We were playing Detroit and I was pass protecting against Alex Karras. Just as I lunged toward him to take his charge, the tendon in my right leg gave way. It snapped, severed completely. That was it. I never played again. The leg still bothers me occasionally."[28]

Ameche ran the idea of retiring past coach Ewbank, and Ewbank didn't object saying he thought that it might be a good idea; feeling unwanted and very hurt, Ameche retired on June 21, 1961. He ended his career with 4,045 rushing yards, 101 receptions for 733 yards, and 44 touchdowns.

In 1957, Ameche received an invitation to invest in a fast food business with teammate Joe Campanella and former Ohio State player Lou Fischer. A carry out business named Ameche's Drive-in began, with its signature item named the "Powerhouse," a hamburger similar to the Big Mac at McDonald's. It had a special sauce called "35" (Ameche's number) and a popular slogan—"Meetcha at Ameche's." Later, Ameche had a radio show called *Ameche's Powerhouse Sports News and Views*.

In 1958, Ameche joined with Gino Marchetti in another fast food establishment—Gino's. Ameche's Wisconsin teammate Jim Haluska commented, "I remember when he went into business, he said he was going to open a little hamburger stand. It became the McDonald's of the East." There were more than 300 locations. After the Marriott Corporation bought the chain in 1980, Ameche was a multi-millionaire.[29]

The Wisconsin fans voted Ameche to the Wisconsin All-Time team in 1969 and the College Football Hall of Fame inducted him in 1975. In 1984, Ameche donated his Heisman Trophy to his alma mater. "It was the appreciation and the love I have for the school, and I guess that's gotten stronger, too, as the years have worn on."[30]

On August 8, 1988, Ameche died of a heart attack at Methodist Memorial Hospital in Houston, two days after a bypass and valve surgery. He had a history of heart problems; a bypass operation took place ten years earlier.

Alan Ameche was a generous, thoughtful man loved by his teammates, family and friends. Son Alan, Jr., recalled, "He felt a tremendous responsibility to help people less fortunate than himself. My father's greatest gift was that he had an incredible ability to understand what it must be like to be in someone else's shoes less fortunate than himself. And I think it was because of his upbringing…. He felt a tremendous obligation to share his good fortune. I never loved anyone more in life than my father."[31]

NOTES

1. "Alan Visited Italy as a Child, but He's Eager to Forget It," *The Sporting News,* October 27, 1954.

2. Gary D'Amato, "Kenosha Bradford Proud to Claim Two of the Best Backs in State History," *Milwaukee Journal Sentinel*, December 12, 2014.

3. Vic Watia, "Alan Ameche Mourned by Football Friends," UPI Archives, August 13, 1988.

4. Bob Wolf, "Ameche Valued Friends, Not Glory," *Milwaukee Journal*, August 11, 1988.

5. Bob Russell, "Another Ameche Taking Bows for Hit Play," *The Sporting News.* November 7, 1951.

6. Wolf.

7. Dan Manoyan, *Alan Ameche: The Story of "The Horse"* (Madison, WI: Terrace Books, 2012), 143.

8. *Ibid.*, 153.

9. *Ibid.,*170.

10. *Ibid.*

11. "Ameche, 'Proud and Humble' as He Accepts Heisman Football Trophy," *Milwaukee Journal,* December 10, 1954.

12. *Ibid.*

13. Bob Berghaus, "Ameche Recalled as a Great Player and Person," *Milwaukee Journal*, August 9, 1988.

14. *Ibid.*

15. Manoyan, 181.

16. *Ibid.*, 195–196.

17. "Ameche's TD Gallop in Pro Bowl Highlight for Harwell," *The Sporting News*, January 4, 1956.

18. Manoyan, 201.

19. *Ibid.*, 207

20. Dave Klein, *The Game of Their Lives* (New York: Random House, 1976), 58.

21. Johnny Unitas and Ed Fitzgerald, *Pro Quarterback: My Own Story* (New York: Simon & Schuster, 1965), 84.

22. Cameron J. Snyder, "Best Effort of Year Needed to Win Title in Opinion of Coach," *Baltimore Sun*, December 22, 1958.

23. Manoyan, 6.

24. "UW Heisman Winner Ameche Dies," *Milwaukee Sentinel*, August 9, 1988.

25. John Steadman, "Ameche, Long Shot in '54, Champion Charger in '58," *The Sporting News,* January 14, 1959.

26. Tom Callahan, *Johnny U: The Life and Times of John Unitas* (New York: Crown, 2006), 172.

27. Cameron Snyder, "Giants Coach Praises Colts' Play In Winning NFL Championship," *Baltimore Sun,* December 29, 1958.

28. Milton Richman, "Alan Ameche Atypical of Former Players," *Reading Eagle*, November 29, 1982.

29. Berghaus.

30. "Obituaries," *The Sporting News*, August 22, 1988.

31. Manoyan, 10–12.

Raymond Berry

John Vorperian

Teammates Lenny Lyles and Gino Marchetti called him a "genius" and the greatest receiver of all time, and legendary *Los Angeles Times* columnist Jim Murray colorfully stated that he "saw more film than Darryl Zanuck" and "could run a pattern through a crowded subway rush hour and shake loose."[1] Wide receiver Raymond Berry terrorized Colts opponents from 1955 to 1967 with his analytically precise pass patterns, earning Pro Bowl honors six times (1958–61; 1963–64). The 6'2," 187-pound Texan led the NFL in receptions for three consecutive seasons, 1958, 1959, and 1960, helping the Colts win back-to-back NFL championships in 1958 and 1959.

Raymond Berry.

Raymond Emmett Berry was born on February 27, 1933, in Corpus Christi, Texas, to Mark Raymond and Bess (née Hudgins) Berry. He was the couple's second child. They also had a daughter, Peggy, three year older than him. His father went, not by the given first name of Mark but rather as Raymond Berry. The senior Berry was a high school teacher and football coach. Bess tended the household.

Berry's birthplace Corpus Christi translates from the Spanish as "the body of Christ." The family lived there until Raymond was about five years old. They then moved to Paris, Texas. His father became head football coach for the Paris High School Wildcats. Football reigned so supreme within this East Texas community that in addition to his high school teaching and football coaching duties, Raymond's father founded what could be termed as the Paris elementary school football conference. He proposed and the education district approved and fully funded football to be played by all six Paris elementary schools.

Raymond's earliest experience of playing organized football was in the fifth grade. His first official coach was his dad. As a high school junior, Raymond weighed 135 pounds so although he was on the varsity football team his playing time was quite limited. During his senior year Raymond experienced a physical growth spurt now standing 5'10½" and weighing 150 pounds. He was an extremely good defensive player. On offense he was positioned at left end and although he was not the quarterback he called the plays. The Paris passing game was non-existent. They ran the single wing and all Berry ever did was block. Berry estimates during his entire high school football career he probably caught about 28 passes.

As a senior he was chosen a consensus All-District player and made second team All-State. Berry cited an interscholastic match as a key memorable game. In the final regular season fixture of his senior year, the Paris Wildcats journeyed 100 miles from home. A 13–7 triumph over Gainesville High School resulted in the first District title in Paris High School history.

"Believe it or not, I rank the thrill of winning that game as highly as winning my first championship in the NFL in 1958."[2] Asked about that grading, Berry said, "I'd say that for a sixteen-year-old it really was in the same category as being twenty-five years old and winning my first world championship in New York … you'd have to be from Texas to understand it."[3]

Upon graduation Berry enrolled in Schreiner Institute (now known as Schreiner University) a junior college located in Kerrville, Texas. He made that decision because it was the only school to offer him a scholarship. Here he experienced football for the first-time primarily as a wide receiver. He had never been with an offense that shun the run and simply threw the ball. During the 1950 season, Berry led the junior college Pioneer Conference in pass receiving with 67 receptions as the Mountaineers finished 7–3, their best record in ten years.

After one year, Raymond left Schreiner to play for Rusty Russell, head coach at Southern Methodist University. Russell's offensive designs featured the passing game. He liked to throw the ball with spread formations. Berry said of Russell's Mustangs, "double wings triple wings motion-he had everything. I think he was throwing 75 percent of the time and that played to my strengths."[4]

Under Texas rules a junior college transfer who had played only one year was ineligible for varsity play because they were required to "lay out" a year. Over Russell's career he coached various players who made it to the NFL such as Doak Walker, Kyle Rote, Bobby Layne and Forrest Gregg. Meeting with Berry, Russell gave him an honest assessment, "I don't know if you're going to be big enough to play in the Southwest Conference or not … but … you'll play on our redshirt team working against our varsity.… I'll watch you … and if I think you can play in this conference, I'll give you a full scholarship at that point."[5]

In practice, with Berry at end, the redshirt offense played against the varsity defense running the schemes of the upcoming week's opponent. Additionally, three times a week in half hour sessions, Berry handled passes from SMU's legendary throwing specialist-tailback Fred Benners. Drafted in 1951 by the New York Giants, Benners played a single season in 1952, and then left the NFL to pursue a legal career.

A team meeting called by Coach Russell at mid-season placed Berry front and center before the squad. The offensive guru said, "If you varsity receivers went after that ball like this little broomstick receiver, we wouldn't have any problems out there on Saturday afternoons."[6]

Berry earned his full scholarship, but after Berry's sophomore year, head coach Russell was fired. His replacement Chalmer "Woody" Woodard favored the straight T formation in which the Mustangs ran the ball and threw sparingly. As a result, Berry's key role offensively was to block. He primarily opposed the defensive end or picked up an oncoming linebacker. He credited this extensive blocking experience at SMU in aiding him later on in the pros. Berry snagged 11 passes for 144 yards and one touchdown in his junior term. Berry also played defense lining up either at linebacker or end, and actually felt that defense was the strongest part of his game.

Most pro scouts assessed Berry as too slow and too small to play in the NFL. He also used eye glasses. In the era's conventional thinking those birddogs thought his vision would be too poor to catch pro passes.

On January 28, 1954, the National Football League held its draft at the Bellevue-Stratford Hotel in Philadelphia. The Colts selected Berry as a "future draft pick" in the 20th round (232nd overall). This designation meant the Colts would have to wait a year for the prospect to report to their training camp.

Berry entered his senior year voted by the team as Co-captain. In 1954 SMU went 6–3–1 with road wins over #4 ranked Arkansas and #15 ranked Rice, and Raymond totaled 16 receptions for 217 yards. He was named All-Southwest Conference, and also earned credit as an Academic All-American.

On New Year's Day 1955, Raymond was in San Francisco for the East-West Shrine Game. Although the East prevailed 13–12, defensively Berry had a good game for the West. Earlier in December 1954 SMU faced Notre Dame. Fighting Irish All-American Ralph Guglielmi was quarterbacking the East squad. At the game's outset Berry immediately recognized that Guglielmi was calling out plays with Notre Dame's signal system. All day Berry knew well in advance whether to stay with his man or move and cover another opponent.

The Colts' 1955 training camp was held at Western Maryland College (now McDaniel College) in Westminster, Maryland. The 22-year-old was determined to make not just the team but the NFL. Baltimore had no veteran receivers. Berry felt that was the reason the Colts had taken a chance on him and he wanted to prove them right.

Head coach Weeb Ewbank employed a pro-set offense with his Colts. Berry had to learn the split-receiver position and master running pass routes against man-to-man coverage. Berry was up for the challenge. He had a strong work ethic, paid keen attention to details and strove for perfection in his pass-catching skills.

Before Raymond signed his initial contract he contacted other pro receivers and probed about their salaries. Armed with that information Berry asked for $10,000. Colts general manager Don Kellett offered $8,500 with a $1,500 bonus. A deal was met.

Assistant coach Charley Winner and some Colts veterans noticed that Berry was very different from other novice pros. He didn't spend his paychecks on cars, booze or women. Instead, Raymond bought a 16-millimeter projector. After each day's practice, while his teammates were out on the town, Berry would be in his room studying game films, in particular, watching how other receivers ran their routes and how defensive backs covered those pass catchers.

During a time when they were considered a novelty Raymond purchased contact lens. He obtained a custom fitted tooth guard to protect himself from concussions. Noticing the team issued canvas-like sweatpants became too heavy once they were damp; Berry contacted a clothes manufacturer and acquired a special light weight set. In order that those specific pants were not lost among the team's mass of soiled uniforms Raymond did his own laundry daily.

Berry also enlisted the help of another 22-year-old in honing his football skills. Leroy Vaughn, a native Baltimorean and free agent star quarterback out of Virginia Union, was one of four black players trying to make the Colts. Vaughn didn't make the official 1955 roster but was placed onto the club's taxi squad. He left the pros after that season, and went onto a successful career as a high school principal and football coach. His son Maurice "Mo" Vaughn became a major league baseball player and in 1995 was named the American League's MVP.

Texas may have been part of the Confederacy but Raymond Berry was no subscriber to Jim Crow. The shackles of legal segregation and social codes of overt racism were present in U.S. Society but as Berry put it, "I wasn't raised to think that way."[7] As for their friendship, Vaughn said "We hit if off real good. Who would have thought, back then, that the best friend of a guy from Texas would be a black quarterback?"[8] They would eat together in the camp cafeteria and away from campus catch a movie or shoot pool.

But more importantly, on days off the two would, with Berry driving his vehicle, go to a public park and exercise. As Vaughn recalled, "He'd pick me up in that beat-up old car … and we'd go to Druid Hill or Clifton Park to practice his pass patterns."[9] "When we got there, he would park, then open the hood and tape his key to the carburetor, so no one would steal the car. Then we'd go to work. He had me throw balls high and low, at his feet, to make him dive left and right. If he had dropped a pass on Sunday, we ran that play again and again until he figured out why. He left nothing to bear."[10]

Baltimore completed the 1955 campaign 5–6–1 for fourth place in the NFL Western Conference. Berry had just 13 receptions. Out of the 12 franchises the Colts finished tenth in passing yardage. However, a new signal caller would radically alter that statistic the next season and well into the future.

John Unitas, a semi-pro ballplayer, came to Baltimore in April of 1956 for a tryout. Unitas had been a quarterback at Louisville. In 1955, he was drafted by the Pittsburgh Steelers in the ninth round but cut before that season's start. Unitas felt Pittsburgh never gave him a fair shake. He was determined the Colts staff get a good look at his talents. Two individuals in the Baltimore organization clearly bolstered Unitas' fortune in making the roster, Ewbank and Berry.

Ewbank utilized the Cleveland grading system (developed by Paul Brown) which ignored pedigree and judged players strictly by performance. Players were assessed on a scale from zero to five. A missed assignment tabbed a zero whereas a remarkable play registered a four. Fives were rarely recorded. Ewbank, along with his coaches, saw Unitas' arm strength and throwing abilities and came to believe Pittsburgh had made a significant mistake.

The Colts had several receiver prospects in camp. Berry felt his 1955 statistics were inadequate. If he was going to remain a Colts receiver Berry needed and desired more pass-catching training. In Unitas, Raymond found a new quarterback friend who was more than willing to remain after official practice and do just that.

The pair had Ewbank's blessing. Berry recalled many times when he and John were out on the field he could see Coach Ewbank observing the duo.

After-hours practice was simply unheard of in this time period. When Baltimore veterans, many who were hard drinkers and chain-smokers learned what Berry was doing in addition to the two-a-days it added to the collective view that Raymond was a peculiar sort. Lineman Art Donovan, a notorious jokester, hefty imbiber and overeater chortled that punishment for the diet conscious, alcohol abstaining, non-smoker Berry must be not being allowed to practice. Gino Marchetti chimed, "Wouldn't it be awful if the whole team were Raymond Berrys? The only way to punish them would be to say, 'You have to stop practice and go to the movies tonight.'"[11]

Game Four of the 1956 season starting quarterback George Shaw was injured during a 58–27 debacle against the Chicago Bears. Coach Ewbank inserted Unitas. Johnny U became Ewbank's steady signal caller, and the Unitas-Berry tandem was born.

In the very next game, 40,086 Memorial Stadium faithful saw Berry snag three passes for 70 yards and a touchdown as the Colts downed the Green Bay Packers 28–21. All but five of Berry's 68 career receiving touchdowns came from the right arm of John Unitas, a record for one quarterback throwing to one receiver that stood until 1992 when the Miami Dolphin tandem of Dan Marino and Mark Clayton broke the mark.

Unitas recalled Raymond Berry's dedicated commitment to perfection. He "ran the 40 in about 4.9, 4.8 … had uncanny moves … and he worked on every one of these different moves."[12]

On Tuesday of game week, after studying film Sunday and Monday nights, Berry would report to practice with a list on a yellow pad and inform Unitas, "These are the things I can do against this guy we're playing this week. I've got an inside move, like an outside move."[13] After practice for nearly an hour they would run those specific pass plays.

Football lore claimed Berry had 88 different moves. Raymond explained, "I don't know the precise number…. I had variations…. I compare this to baseball Hall of Famer Juan Marichal … [he]had several pitches but … [threw] … from a variety of angles … as if he had an endless supply."[14]

The 1956 Colts again finished fourth in the NFL Western Conference, but now Baltimore ranked fifth in passing touchdowns and sixth in passing yardage with Berry catching 37 balls for 601 yards and two touchdowns.

After three losing seasons Ewbank's Steeds had a turnaround in 1957 with a 7–5 mark for third place in the Western Conference. The club was now tops in the NFL in passing yardage and passing touchdowns. Raymond had 47 receptions with six touchdowns and a league leading 800 receiving yards.

The Colts opened the 1958 season with six consecutive wins. Local sportswriters inked columns about the city's latest craze "Coltsaphrenia." In Week Seven, the Colts traveled to New York. Berry nabbed a touchdown pass but Baltimore lost its first game 24–21 to the Giants.

That night Raymond appeared on the TV show *What's My Line*. A four-person panel had to guess the guest's occupation. With celebrity guests the panel normally would be blindfolded, but such was not the case with the Colts' number 82. Raymond came on as a regular guest. However, in the approaching weeks, Berry and his teammates would soon gain national notoriety.

The Colts finished atop the Western Conference with a 9–3 record. On December 28, 1958, Baltimore traveled to Yankee Stadium to face the New York Giants for the NFL title. In the second quarter, Unitas connected with Berry from 15 yards out to give the Colts a 14–3 lead. The Giants fought back and late in the fourth quarter they led the Colts 17–14.

With the championship on the line, Ewbank trusted his quarterback to make the right calls, and Johnny U trusted Raymond to tell him what routes they could employ. As Berry, remembered, "There was no time for huddles. We were trying to beat the clock. The plays were called from the scrimmage line and we stuck with the basic stuff. We merely reacted the way we've been trained to react all year. I recall that one of the big gainers developed from a slant that I ran inside a Giant linebacker who was playing on my nose. We'd practice it many times."[15]

Three consecutive passes to Berry totaling 62 yards placed the Colts 13 yards out where kicker Steve Myhra's 20-yard field goal knotted the score 17–17 at the end of regulation and sent the game into overtime.

Giants Hall of Famer Frank Gifford recalled the Colts' game tying drive: "At this point, I could just say, 'Unitas to Berry, for twenty-five yards, Unitas to Berry, for fifteen yards, Unitas to Berry, for twenty-two yards.' And that would pretty much cover it. I heard the words then, and I hear then now. That we had to hear them then, echoing from the Stadium speakers, spoken in our home announcer's dulcet tones, somehow made it even more painful."[16]

During the decisive overtime drive, Berry caught two more passes for 33 yards as the Colts came away with a dramatic 23–17 victory. For the game, Berry caught a record-setting 12 passes for 178 yards and a touchdown. Berry later stated, "It certainly was the best game that Unitas and I had together."[17]

Berry, along with his teammates, each got $4,718.77 as their winning share from the league. Baltimore owner Carroll Rosenbloom equaled that sum. Colts management had also created a Victory Fund. For every victory $10,000 went into the pot. $90,000 was evenly split among the players. Sponsor National Brewing Company also tossed $25,000 into that pot which was matched with another $25,000 by an anonymous donor (some accounts contend the donor may have been Owner Rosenbloom).

Raymond was named to his first Pro Bowl game in '58. He had led the NFL with 56 receptions and nine receiving touchdowns. However, upon contract renewal GM Kellett began negotiations not at $10,000, but at $8,500.

Heading into the 1959 NFL season, the country's sports media buzzed that the Unitas-Berry hook-up was the NFL's most powerful scoring combo. In 1959, Berry led the NFL with 66 receptions, 959 receiving yards and 14 receiving touchdowns (a then franchise record). He scored 84 points with only two men bettering him in that category: Green Bay's Paul Hornung scored 94 points to lead the league in scoring followed by New York's Pat Summerall with 90. However, those players were also kickers. Take away field goals and PATs and Summerall had zero points and Hornung's adjusted number tapped out at 42.

The Colts hosted the Giants in the December 27, 1959, NFL championship clash and bested New York 31–16 with Berry catching five passes for 68 yards.

In the spring of 1960, John Bridgers, Baylor University head coach and a former Colts assistant coach, asked Berry to mentor his Bear receivers during spring football. In April, on a blind date Raymond met a Baylor co-ed. After an August 20, 1960, pre-season away game against Dallas, Berry got married in Tyler, Texas. As of this writing, Raymond and his bride, Sally, have been together for 48 years.

Berry led the NFL in receptions (74) and receiving yards (1298) yards in 1960, scoring ten touchdowns and earning Pro Bowl honors. The 27-year-old had seven 100-yard games (then a club record and still fourth for the franchise).

In 1961, the Colts went 8–6 in the NFL's first 14-game regular season. Raymond made his fourth consecutive Pro Bowl with 75 receptions for 873 yards but no touchdowns.

The Colts were mired in mediocrity from 1960 to 1963. In '63 Ewbank was released. Thirty-three-year-old Don Shula took over the team.

From 1962 to 1966, Berry continued to excel for the Colts, with two final Pro Bowl berths in 1963 and 1964.

In 1967 the NFL expanded to 16 teams split into four divisions. The prior season Berry ranked in the NFL's top ten in receptions (56) and touchdown catches (7). But in '67 his body was breaking down. He played the first two games but was out for the next three contests. In Week Six against the Vikings a defender dislocated Berry's left shoulder. The gritty pass catcher returned to the Colts line-up for the last three games, but for the season he caught only 11 passes for 167 yards and one touchdown.

In March 1968 the 35-year-old announced his retirement. Berry finished his playing career with 631 receptions for 9,275 yards and 68 touchdowns. At the time he was the NFL career leader in receptions and receiving yards.

A day after Berry hung up his cleats, Cowboys head coach Tom Landry offered him an assistant coaching position. This began a long term coaching career for Berry. Raymond coached at both the professional and collegiate level, spending time with the Cowboys (1968–69), Arkansas Razorbacks (1970–72), Detroit Lions (1973–75, 1991), Cleveland Browns (1976–77), New England Patriots (1978–81 as an assistant and 1984–89 as head coach), and Denver Broncos (1992).

Berry was inducted into the Pro Football Hall of Fame in 1973. A first ballot enshrinee, his presenter was Weeb Ewbank, who said, "Raymond's pass patterns were so minutely perfected that he was almost unstoppable. I don't believe that he had in his career 13 dropped balls."[18]

On October 25, 1984, eight games into the NFL season, he took a phone call from Patriots owner Billy Sullivan. New England was 5–3 with eight games left. Pats general manager Pat Sullivan had fired coach Ron Meyer. Looking outside the organization for a replacement, Pat's father appealed to Berry to take the helm. Berry response was he wanted to talk with his wife and pray before answering Sullivan's inquiry, which he did.

Berry debuted as the Patriots head coach on October 28 defeating the New York Jets 30–20 in Foxboro. New England won four of their last eight games for a 9–7 record, second place in the AFC Eastern Division.

Berry believed talent wise the Patriots were a championship club. With Steve Grogan, Berry saw some quarterback and leadership traits that were similar to Unitas. Berry stressed communication, concentration and consistency. He also emphasized that everyone with the squad be treated with respect-even the ball boys. Running Back Tony Collins commented, "Raymond Berry earned more respect in one day than Ron Meyer earned in three years."[19]

Indeed, the next year New England improved further to 11–5 and made the playoffs as a wild card. The 1985 Patriots became the first team in NFL history to head into the Super Bowl by winning three road playoff games. Berry was named AFC Coach-of-the-Year by the AP.

The Pats magical ride ended as Mike Ditka and his Chicago Bears mauled New

England 46–10 in Super Bowl XX. Buddy Ryan's 46 defense reigned havoc on the Pats. Berry honestly stated, "We couldn't protect the quarterback, and that was my fault. I couldn't come up with a system to handle the Bears' pass rush."[20]

In 1986, the Pats finished on top of the AFC Eastern Division at 11–5, but lost to Denver in the divisional round 22–17 at Mile High Stadium. In the 1987 strike-shortened season, Berry's 8–7 Pats missed the playoffs, and again missed the playoffs in 1988 with a 9–7 record.

After suffering through a 5–11 record in 1989 season, new Patriots owner Victor Kiam dictated Berry give up control over personnel and change his staff; Raymond declined and was dismissed. Berry's final head coaching record stood at a respectable 48–39 (.552) and 3–2 (.600) in the postseason.

Presently, Raymond and his wife reside in Tennessee. They have three married children, Suzanne, Mark and Ashley. The Berrys also have nine grandchildren. Raymond has business activities in the financial services industry. Additionally he speaks before various organizations like the Salvation Army, Campus Crusade for Christ and the Fellowship of Christian Athletes.

How will he be remembered in the NFL annals?

Jim Murray wrote of Berry, "He didn't play a game of football, he engineered it. He checked the temperature, lighting, humidity, even the position of the sun in the sky. He studied the terrain as if he had to putt on it, not run on it…. He could catch in handcuffs…. He could hold onto a football in an avalanche."[21]

NOTES

1. Raymond Berry with Wayne Stewart, *All the Moves I Had: A Football Life* (Guilford, CT: Lyons Press, 2016), 194–195.
2. *Ibid.*,10.
3. *Ibid.*, 11.
4. *Ibid.*,14.
5. *Ibid.*, 15.
6. *Ibid.*, 16.
7. Mike Klingaman, "Ex-Colts Connecting Again," *Baltimore Sun*, October 8, 2008.
8. *Ibid.*
9. *Ibid.*
10. *Ibid.*
11. Berry, 196.
12. Lou Sahadi, *Johnny Unitas: America's Quarterback* (Chicago: Triumph Books, 2004), 273.
13. *Ibid.*
14. Berry, 43–44.
15. Sahadi, 61.
16. Frank Gifford with Peter Richmond, *The Glory Game* (New York: HarperCollins, 2008), 205.
17. Lou Sahadi, *One Sunday In December* (Guilford, CT: Lyons Press, 2008),178.
18. "Raymond Berry Enshrinement Speech," Pro Football Hall of Fame, July 23, 1973, www.profootballhof.com/players/raymond-berry/enshrinement.
19. http://en.wikipedia.org/wiki/Raymond_Berry.
20. *Ibid.*
21. Berry, 195.

REFERENCES

Bowden, Mark. *The Best Game Ever*. New York: Atlantic Monthly Press, 2008.
Kelley, Craig. "Catching Up with: Raymond Berry." www.colts.com, posted September 24, 2013.

The NFL Century: The Complete Story of the National Football League 1920–2000. New York: Smith-mark & NFL, 1999.

Smith, Ron. *Pro Football's Heroes of the Hall*. St. Louis: Sporting News Books, 2001.

Summerall, Pat. *Summerall On and Off the Air*. Nashville: Nelson Books, 2006.

Sykes, Bill, ed. *Sports Illustrated Football's Greatest*. New York: Time Home Entertainment, 2012.

Unitas, John, with Harold Rosenthal. *Playing Pro Football to Win*. Garden City, NY: Doubleday, 1968.

"Where Are They Now: Raymond Berry." BaltimoreRavens.com, posted November 30, 2009.

Whittingham, Richard. *For the Glory of the Game*. Chicago: Triumph Books, 2005.

http://en.wikipedia.org/wiki/Raymond_Berry.

www.profootballhof.com/raymond-berry/biography.

www.profootballreference.com.

Ordell Braase

JAY ZAHN

The crack of the pads echoed around Memorial Stadium. Two rookies were going at it, so intensely that coach Weeb Ewbank had to ask the battlers to tone it down after first encouraging the combat. It's a sight common during training camp days, but far less frequent during the season. Yet it was a daily occurrence for these two. One, a tackle from Ohio State, was Jim Parker; All-American and bound for the Hall of Fame. The other, a defensive end from South Dakota, was Ordell Braase; a late-round draftee from three years ago, delayed by an Army stint. The desire and work ethic demonstrated on that day in 1957 were everyday life for Ordell Braase, on and off the gridiron.

Ordell Wayne Braase was born March 13, 1932, in Mitchell, South Dakota. Mitchell is a town of about 15,000, best known as the home of the Corn Palace. The Corn Palace also hosts the basketball games of the local high school team, the Mitchell Kernels. It was as a Kernel hoopster that Ordell first achieved a measure of fame and greatness. Braase transformed himself from an awkward junior reserve to an all-state center, helping lead the Kernels to a state basketball championship.

Ordell's efforts led to a basket-

Ordell Braase.

ball scholarship offer from the University of South Dakota. The Vermillion campus is about 100 miles southeast of Mitchell. Ordell continued to play basketball as well as football there, making the all-league team as a senior in 1953, as well as honorable mention Little All American.

While at USD, Braase also made a good impression on one Janice Rademacher, from Garretson. "He was an all-around athlete and taller than anyone else on the campus. I could wear high heel shoes and still look up to him,"[1] said the 5–8 Janice. Ordell and Janice would marry in June 1954.

By that time, Ordell had already signed a football contract with the Baltimore Colts. The Colts had drafted Ordell in the 14th round of the 1954 college draft. He was the first Coyote player ever drafted. Of his selection, Ordell would later say, "I still run into people who ask, 'How in the world could they ever have drafted someone from South Dakota back then?' I can't answer that."[2] In fact, the Colts had acted upon the recommendation of Doug Eggers, a recently signed free agent who'd played against Ordell at rival South Dakota State.

Ordell would sign a contract with the Colts in March of 1954, after his senior basketball season had ended. New Colts coach Weeb Ewbank said at the time, "He is a tall well boned boy and can get his weight up to 225 or so without losing any of his agility. We feel he has a fine chance to make the grade with the Colts as an offensive lineman."[3]

Braase wouldn't get much of a chance to make the grade in 1954, due to a pending armed services commitment. He did make a brief appearance at Colts camp between stints at Fort's Lewis and Benning, but military life would keep Ordell occupied for the next three years. The military obligation was nothing unusual to young men in the early to mid–1950s; in Ordell's case, it turned out to be a blessing in disguise.

Ordell attended paratroop school while still at Fort Benning. Since he was married, he was allowed to live off base. Ordell and wife Jan graciously hosted dinners for his squad mates. Later Ordell was transferred to Japan, then Korea. Ordell kept his football skills up, playing in the Rice Bowl (a service all-star game) in Tokyo in 1955.

Braase was discharged in 1957 and prepared to resume his career. The time away had helped his prospects. When he'd left the Colts in 1954, he weighed 215 pounds, 15 to 25 pounds lighter than his peer linemen. The Army had given him a chance to bulk up. Teammate Art Donovan took notice, saying, "[Braase was a] little guy. Then he went into the Army for two years, and when he came back I couldn't believe it was the same guy. He had arms on him then like a side of beef."[4]

Ordell would need the added bulk to make a Colts team that was improving itself. Slotted at defensive end, he didn't have immediate hope of starting with perennial All-Pro Gino Marchetti and long term starter Don Joyce in place. Instead, he'd have to compete for a backup spot with Bill Danenhauer, a taxi squadder from the 1956 team. Ordell won the battle when Danenhauer was released in mid–September. Ordell would get a little help from fellow rookie Luke Owens, but he would be the main defensive line reserve for his rookie season.

As Ordell watched and learned, he put in extra time to improve his skills. Another rookie on the 1957 Colts was a coach, Johnny Bridgers. Bridgers had been hired to coach the defensive line after a few years coaching at nearby Johns Hopkins. "I became his pet project," Ordell said of Bridgers. "John stuck with me, kept me focused, and encouraged me to stay after practice and continue working after Weeb blew the whistle. He taught me the principles of balance and how to rush the passer and get rid of those blockers fast. John was a really smart guy."[5]

For the 1958 season the Colts beefed up their defensive line by adding Ray Krouse as a backup tackle. The Colts took advantage of their improved depth by inserting Braase and Krouse frequently as relief; they played nearly as much as the starting line. Eventually the entire group would earn the collective nickname "Six Tons of Fun."

Ordell also made his mark on the special teams in 1958. In a November game against the Rams, in the fourth quarter he recovered a Jon Arnett fumbled punt on the Rams 19. Leading 13–7 at the time, the Colts scored two plays later and wound up winning 34–7. The next week, Ordell blocked a key extra point in the Colts' 35–27 win over the 49ers. "I went through a gap inside their tackle. I think it was No. 75 [John Gonzaga] and he just blocked a piece of me as I went by him,"[6] he said. That game would clinch the Western Conference title for the Colts. Ordell quipped after the game, "All I want to know is do I get a hat from Weeb? You know he gives a hat away if you block a kick."[7]

Braase continued his special teams and reserve role into the NFL championship game at Yankee Stadium. When Gino Marchetti broke his leg late in the game, Ordell replaced him. In overtime, Ordell had a tackle of Frank Gifford to help with the one final stop the Colts' defense needed before their winning touchdown drive.

Still pushing to improve himself, Ordell worked during the off season in a special training program. Under the direction of trainer Ed Block and Bill Neill, physical therapy director at Kernan Hospital, Ordell used workouts on a progressive resistance exercise table to increase his weight and improve his other measurements as well. "Take a look at him," said Neill. "He has increased his chest girth by more than an inch and his upper arm by at least half an inch…. Ordell is building up muscles in the right spots. He will be much stronger and more agile this season."[8]

Ordell continued to press Don Joyce in particular for playing time in 1959. He even started four mid-season games when Joyce was hampered by a sprained ankle. When Ray Krouse was lost to the Dallas Cowboys in the 1960 expansion draft, Joyce moved to a backup utility role and Ordell took over as starting right end. Braase made a good first impression, as he was named second team All-NFL in 1960 by the *New York Daily News.*

The Colts faded from title contention in the early 1960s, but Ordell continued to gain experience as a starter. He generally played a clean football game reliant on quickness. But in 1961, the Rams' Roy Hord broke Ordell's jaw with a forearm shot, causing him to miss the final game of the season. Ordell considered retaliating the following year but took the high road and forgave the incident after talking it over with his wife, Jan.

In 1964 the Colts took a big step forward both offensively and defensively under coach Don Shula. A 12–2 record was enough to win the Western Conference title again. The championship game against Cleveland ended in a disappointing 27–0 loss, but Braase still had his moments, collaborating on a sack with Gino Marchetti and tackling Jim Brown for a four yard loss. Dick Schafrath, the Browns tackle who faced Braase that day, recalled preparing for Ordell. "The man was tough and he was quick," Schafrath said. "I was stronger, so I didn't worry too much about him on running plays. I knew that I could take him, one-on-one. But passing plays, where I had to back up—especially at [Cleveland] Stadium in December, where I knew the turf would be wet and I could slip—that worried me. I was fast, but Braase was just as quick."[9]

Marchetti retired before the 1965 season, making Ordell the senior member of the Colts' defensive line. Though slowed by a groin pull, Ordell had another fine year, again earning second team All-Pro honors. He repeated those honors in 1966, adding his first Pro Bowl selection. Ironically, though a Pro Bowl rookie, at 34 he was the oldest player in the game.

Ordell repeated both second team All-Pro and Pro Bowl honors in 1967. Known as the "other end" when he played opposite the legendary Marchetti, he was one of the leaders of a "no-name" defense that gave up less than 200 points for the first time in Colts history. Braase would comment on the team's change in defensive approach over the years. "[In 1967] we were No. 2 in giving up the least amount of points," he said. "We missed out by two to the Rams. That's one of the things we're shooting for. Back in the old days we'd start off in a 4–3 defense and stay there 90 percent of the time. We had the all-pros then—Donovan, Marchetti, Lipscomb. Now we make up for it with slants and overshifts."[10]

Now into his 11th season as a pro, the veteran Braase wasn't above the occasional on-field mischief. In a 1967 game against the Falcons, the canny Braase managed to loosen Falcon quarterback Randy Johnson's shoe while Atlanta was mounting a last-ditch comeback. Ordell threw the shoe away, then made a half-hearted effort to retrieve it, causing the Falcons to waste valuable seconds of their comeback bid. The Colts held on for a 38–31 victory.

After several years of near misses, the 1968 Colts roared back into the playoffs with a 13–1 record. In the NFL championship game, Braase again matched up against the Browns' Dick Schafrath. Ordell and the Colts had the better of it this time; the Colts won 34–0, and Ordell recorded three sacks. Ordell was modest over his achievement. "Sometimes, you get too much credit," he said of his play that day. "For some reason, the way Cleveland's defense [sic] was set up, I had little opposition. I had a clear shot at their quarterback [Bill Nelsen] on almost every play. As the game went on, I thought, 'Hey, this is all right. I wish I could do this every Sunday.'"[11]

Ordell would see a reversal of that fortune in his next and last pro football game, Super Bowl III. Ordell was not only matched up against former coach, Weeb Ewbank, but a former pupil, Jets tackle Winston Hill. Hill had gone to camp with the Colts in 1963 but had struggled so badly against Braase in practice that he had been cut from the team. Five years later, Hill had the upper hand, as the Jets ran against the Colts' right side and Braase regularly and with success. Ordell needed relief from rookie Roy Hilton in the second half as the Colts lost in a big upset. Ordell retired shortly after the game.

During and after retirement from football, Ordell proved to be as hardworking and industrious off the field as on. Though he maintained connections to friends and family in South Dakota, the Braases made Baltimore their year-round home. After his career he owned the Flaming Pit restaurant, a popular hangout for Colts players. He was president of a transportation company and on the Maryland Track Commission. Ordell was also active in the Lutheran church as a social worker.

Ordell also got into the broadcasting game. He was a sideline reporter and color commentator for Colts radio broadcasts. Later he co-hosted the local TV show *Braase, Donovan, and Fans* with the dapper Braase acting as straight man to his rumpled former teammate. "Good gracious, you don't go head-to-head with Artie," Ordell said. "I'd throw him a line and let him run with it. We didn't need dialogue; Artie had his own."[12]

During his career, Ordell served a two-year term as president of the NFL Player's Association. At the time the union was in its infancy with few rights. "It was an interesting time. I'm not going to say we got a lot accomplished, but we got our foot in the door,"[13] he said. One important step was getting the union formally recognized. On the advice of a lawyer, Braase accomplished this by getting the owners to agree to a few negotiated points at a 1965 owners' meeting. Braase also campaigned for increased preseason pay, and continued lobbying for improved pensions for former players while Gene Upshaw was head of the NFLPA.

As his former teammates aged, Ordell continued to stay involved and in touch. Wife Jan Braase died of ALS (Lou Gehrig's disease) in 1997, and the next year Ordell organized a 40th anniversary reunion benefit of the 1958 Colts that raised $230,000 in her memory and to fight ALS.

Ordell currently resides at a Validus senior living community in Florida. Validus has contracted with the NFL to provide special treatment to former players with dementia. Ordell's work with the NFLPA and on behalf of alumni has fortunately paid off in better care and awareness of the health issues of pro football players.

NOTES

1. Cameron C. Snyder, "Mrs. Braase Saw World Watching Ordell Play Ball," *Baltimore Sun*, November 4, 1959.
2. Mike Klingaman, "Catching up with Former Baltimore Colts Defensive End Ordell Braase," *Baltimore Sun*, November 1, 2012.
3. Cameron C. Snyder "Ordell Braase, South Dakota Tackle, Signs Contract with Colts," *Baltimore Sun*, March 7, 1954.
4. Joe Snyder, "With Gino Retired, Braase Now Rates the Bouquets," *Hagerstown Morning Herald*, February 5, 1966.
5. Mike Klingaman, "Former Baylor Football Coach John Bridgers Passes Away," *Baltimore Sun*, November 27, 2006.
6. "Colt Flash Explains Run," Associated Press, December 1, 1958.
7. Cameron C. Snyder, "Lipscomb Says Victory Is 'My Happiest Day'; Spinney Echoes Mate," *Baltimore Sun*, December 1, 1958.
8. Cameron C. Snyder, "Colts Take Physical Therapy to Prevent Injuries in Fall," *Baltimore Sun*, June 21, 1959
9. Terry Pluto, *When All the World Was Browns Town: Cleveland's Browns and the Championship Season of '64* (New York: Simon & Schuster, 1997), 128.
10. Seymour S. Smith, "Top Defense Braase Goal," *Baltimore Sun*, November 24, 1968.
11. Klingaman.
12. *Ibid.*
13. Jon Morgan, *Glory for Sale* (Baltimore: Bancroft Press, 1997), 161–163.

Ray Brown

RICK GONSALVES

Ray Brown was born in Clarksdale, Mississippi, on September 7, 1936, but was raised in Greenville several miles away. At age seven, he suffered a hip injury while playing with a friend on a wagon that nearly ended any hopes of him ever playing football. From the injury, he developed osteomyelitis, an inflammation of a bone which was so serious, that doctors thought he may never walk again. Ray was then taken to the Campbell Clinic in Memphis, Tennessee, where doctors did treat him successfully.[1]

He went on to play football for Greenville High School as a quarterback, defensive back and punter and led the team to the Mississippi Big Eight championship in 1953. During his four-year high school career, he earned 11 letters in sports for football, baseball, basketball and track. Ray was voted team captain for the football team in 1953, the same year he was selected All-Big Eight MVP. Along with being a two-time All-State, All-American in football, he won First Team All-Southern honors in 1952 and 1953.[2]

Ole Miss was so impressed by Ray's athletic abilities that they recruited him in 1954. Because of NCAA rules, Ray, a freshman, could not play football for the varsity that year. Starting the following year, Ray played on both defense and offense for Ole Miss in addition to handling the punting under famed coach Johnny Vaught. With his passing and rushing, Ray helped lead the Rebels to the 1956 Cotton Bowl, beating TCU, 14 to 13 and to the 1958 Sugar Bowl defeating Texas 39 to 7.[3] Brown's play in the Sugar Bowl was simply outstanding. He opened the scoring with a one-yard touchdown run. As the game progressed, he completed a three-yard touchdown pass then set up another touchdown with an interception.

Late in the fourth quarter, Ray dropped back to punt from his own end zone. He took a high snap but before he could get the punt away, he saw a Texas lineman bearing down on him. To avoid getting the kick blocked for a score, Ray circled to his right and took off downfield to complete a 92-yard touchdown run. It not only set the record for the longest touchdown run from scrimmage in Sugar Bowl history but he also became the only player to be selected MVP by a unanimous vote from all 116 media voters.[4]

During his college career, Ray was the SEC passing champion in 1956, SEC total offensive leader in 1957, and All-SEC that same year.[5]

Ray, at 6'2", 192 pounds, was drafted by the Baltimore Colts in the fifth round (50th overall) in 1958. As a rookie, he picked off eight passes and was part of a defensive backfield that allowed only nine touchdowns. He also punted 41 times for a 39.9-yard average. Against the Chicago Bears on November 16, Brown had a fumble recovery and interception. He also punted the Colts out of trouble nine times for a 45-yard average as the Colts shut out the Bears, 17 to 0.[6] In the 1958 NFL championship game, Ray kept the Giants at bay with four punts for a 50.8 yard average. After this historic game was settled in overtime, Ray drove from New York City back to Baltimore with his family.

"What a fantastic time we had," said Brown. "On the way home, I remember stopping for

Ray Brown.

dinner at a Howard Johnson's and having the waitress say, 'Mr. Brown, your family's meal has been paid for by a Colts fan who had already left the restaurant.'"

"The guy hadn't even asked for an autograph. That's how grateful people were that we had won."[7]

Once Ray signed his contract prior to the 1958 season, he enrolled in law school at Ole Miss and completed a portion of his coursework at the University of Maryland Law School. "I would go to classes in the morning and practice with the team in the afternoons," Ray explained. "In the spring, I would go to Oxford and take courses at Ole Miss."[8]

In 1959, Ray did little punting. But playing defense, he made five interceptions. Once more, the Baltimore Colts met the New York Giants in the NFL championship game and beat them 31 to 16 for their second consecutive title.

During the 1959 exhibition season, coach Weeb Ewbank tried Ray out as a quarterback because the Colts had traded George Shaw, their backup, to the Giants. If John Unitas were to get injured, there was no one else with quarterbacking experience to fill in for him.

Playing the Philadelphia Eagles on September 15, during the preseason, Ray got his first start as a quarterback. He responded by completing 16 of 33 passes for 199 yards and one touchdown although the Colts lost the game 35 to 13.

"We lost a game but we found a quarterback," Ewbank said.[9]

Brown's play also drew praise from the Eagles crusty old quarterback, Norm Van Brocklin.

"I like him," he said. "He'll be a good quarterback. You don't need to worry about a number two man with him around."[10]

Ray, however, got only one chance to play quarterback that season going one for four on passes and then six for 13 in three appearances the following year.

He became the Colts' regular punter again in 1960, with 52 kicks good for a 38.5-yard average. In 1961, after his third year with the team, Brown decided to leave football and pursue a career in law.

"The Colts had slipped to fourth place that year and I injured my knee which required surgery to repair. I was also near to getting my law degree which would come in 1962."[11]

That year, Ray received his degree from the University of Mississippi School of Law, where he was associate editor of the *Mississippi Law Journal*. He then clerked for a year for U.S. Supreme Court justice Tom Clark before returning to Mississippi to practice law in Pascagoula.[12]

Brown was inducted into the M-Club Hall of Fame in 1988; Ole Miss Alumni Hall of Fame in 2000; and Mississippi Sports Hall of Fame in 2006.[13]

Ray continued to practice law until his death on December 25, 2017, proudly wearing his 1958 championship ring and, on occasion, the blue and white team jacket that the Colts gave him. In 2007, the *Wall Street Journal* selected an all-time law football team which included former president Gerald Ford, Supreme Court Justice Byron "Whizzer" White and Ray Brown.

"When I saw that article, I thought, 'My goodness,'" Brown said. "Then I framed it and hung it on the wall next to the photographs of the 1958–59 Colts' championship teams."[14]

NOTES

1. Annie Rhoades, "Alumni Profile: Raymond Brown," https://www.olemissalumni.com/alumni-profile-ray-brown.
2. "Raymond Lloyd Brown," http://msfame.com/hall-of-fame/inductees/raymond-lloyd-brown.
3. *2016 Ole Miss Media Football Guide.*
4. Rhoades.
5. "Ray Brown," *2016 Ole Miss Football Media Guide.*
6. "Ray Brown," *1959 Baltimore Colts Press Guide.*
7. Mike Klingaman, "Catching Up with Former Colt Ray Brown," *Baltimore Sun,* June 23, 2009.
8. Rhoades.
9. Mike Rathet, "Ray Brown 'Found' as Colt Quarterback," *Tuscaloosa News,* September 15, 1959.
10. *Ibid.*
11. Klingaman.
12. *Ibid.*
13. "Raymond Lloyd Brown," http://msfame.com/hall-of-fame/inductees/raymond-lloyd-brown.
14. Klingaman.

Jack Call

David Standish

Drafted by the Baltimore Colts in the 13th round of the 1957 NFL draft—arguably the best collection of talent in the history of the NFL—John Arthur "Jack" Call enjoyed a brief but stellar tenure in the environs of Chesapeake Bay. Playing halfback for the Colts in 1957 and 1958, Call had a record of excellence at Colgate University, where he played multiple sports and competed during the collegiate heydays of Paul Hornung and Jim Brown. A combination of speed and size—about 200 pounds—made Call a solid offensive threat.

Born on July 30, 1935, in Cortland, New York, a working class manufacturing town in the Empire State's Southern Tier region, near the Pennsylvania border, Call remembers his hometown as the type of town where many people worked in local industry.[1] Brockway Motor Company and Smith Corona called Cortland home.[2] His grandfather started a trucking business, his father was a truck driver, and his mother was a registered nurse at a hospital in Cortland County, later working as a visiting nurse.

Sports were much more simple and bare-bones when Call was a child. There was no little league football, and baseball for children was informal. Nevertheless, Call had athletics in his blood, as his father played both football and basketball for Cortland High School. A tackle on the football team, the elder Call was part of the first undefeated football team in the history of Cortland.[3]

Call showed natural promise as an athlete in his high school years at Cortland High. His speed was recognized early, as he ran track as a sprinter in the 100- and 220-yard events. He was also a running back on the football team. Though he would go on to renown as a football player in college, his high school sports experience focused on basketball due to his father's wishes. He was a center on the Cortland High basketball team despite standing only 6'1". He was first team All-Southern Tier Conference in his senior year and went on to attend Colgate University in Hamilton, New York, on a full basketball scholarship in 1953.

At Colgate, Call decided that basketball would not be in his future after his freshman year. Football and track became his focus, leading to a lauded college career in both sports. Because of his gridiron success, Colgate kept Call on a full scholarship, despite his initial commitment to play basketball.

Call lettered in football for three years, 1954–56, and has fond memories of playing for Colgate head coach Hal Lahar, a former offensive guard for the Chicago Bears (1941) and the Buffalo Bills (1946–48); Lahar mentored his players through the college experience ensuring success with academics, as well as athletics.[4]

Jack Call.

Call led the Colgate Red Raiders in rushing for the 1955 and 1956 seasons with 402 and 479 yards, respectively.[5] On October 15, 1955, Call recovered a fumbled snap and rushed for more than 50 yards to score a touchdown—it made the pages of *Ripley's Believe It or Not*. In 1956, Call averaged 5.8 yards per carry and scored 11 total touchdowns (nine rushing, two receiving), ranking ninth in rushing touchdowns and sixth in touchdowns from scrimmage in the NCAA.[6]

In track, Call lettered twice—in 1955 and 1956—and set Colgate records for the 100-yard sprint and 200-yard sprint. Further, he lettered in lacrosse as a center midfielder in 1957 without ever playing the sport before taking it up at the direction of Baltimore Colts head coach Weeb Ewbank upon being drafted in 1957. Ewbank believed that lacrosse could help Call sharpen the skills he would need on the football field, particularly because Colgate had one of the few competitive collegiate lacrosse teams in the region.[7] Call's speed allowed him to excel in the sport.

When the Colts drafted Call in 1957, he joined an amazing roster of prospects, including nine future Hall of Famers[8]; the 1964 draft surpassed it with 10.[9] Others selected in the first round included Jim Brown (sixth overall); Paul Hornung (first overall); Len Dawson (fifth overall); and Jim Parker (eighth overall). Later rounds saw drafts of Tommy McDonald (third round); Sonny Jurgensen (fourth round); Henry Jordan (fifth round); Gene Hickerson (seventh round); and Don Maynard (ninth round).[10]

Call's father telephoned him to relay the news about the Colts, a team that was unfamiliar to the Colgate star.[11] The salary was $6,000 per year[12]; in contrast, Call's wife worked as a teacher in Massapequa, New York—on Long Island—and made $4,200.[13] The most that Call ever made in one year as a professional football player was $9,000.

Call remembers the Colts of the late 1950s as a team of camaraderie despite, or perhaps because of, the tough atmosphere. He recalled that the size of the active roster and coaching staff was much more bare-bones than those we see today. Due to the smaller squads, players would play through injuries lest they be summarily dropped from the roster for a quick replacement.[14] Ewbank was a distant manager, unlike the involved mentor that Call had in Colgate's Lahar.[15]

Sharing time in the same backfield as Lenny Moore and Alan Ameche, Call described Moore as being able to "run as fast sideways as he could [forward]."[16] Between 1957 and 1958, Call rushed for 299 combined yards on 70 attempts (4.27 yards per carry).[17]

Call recalls the confusion surrounding the novelty of "sudden death" in the 1958 championship game between the Baltimore Colts and the New York Giants. Neither he nor many of his teammates knew how this overtime paradigm worked, so they huddled to hear referees discuss the rules.[18]

Call was released after the 1958 season and signed with the Pittsburgh Steelers after passing on the New York Giants. While the Giants still had a backfield that included Frank Gifford, the Steelers offered an immediate job and had a greater need for running backs. He played for the Pittsburgh Steelers for the 1959 season under head coach Buddy Parker a former NFL player with the Detroit Lions and Chicago Cardinals. As a coach, Parker led the Cardinals, Lions, and Steelers, guiding the Lions to two NFL championships in 1952 and 1953.[19]

Parker was a good coach and a good man, but a mercurial character.[20] He was simultaneously known as a tough and loyal coach, but also a manager who would terminate players with very little deliberation. Call played in Pittsburgh during 1959 until a leg muscle tear while returning a kick at Soldier Field in Chicago ended his career.[21]

After leaving football behind, Call returned to New York and pursued a teaching career. During spare time in his playing career, he had earned a master's degree in education, which prompted him to work in New York's Mohawk Valley before working at Harford Community College in Churchville, Maryland. There, Call helped launch a football program that he coached for eight years before becoming athletic director and associate professor of health. About six years after his retirement, Harford discontinued its football program because of costs.[22]

Call lives in Maryland with his wife Mary. They dated briefly in high school, then reunited during Call's time on the Colts. They have a son, a daughter, and three grandchildren. After operating a profitable antique business for almost 20 years, the Calls enjoy the freedom of retirement and travel to exotic locales, including Israel and Mexico.[23]

NOTES

1. Jack Call, interview with author, January 9, 2017.
2. https://en.wikipedia.org/wiki/Cortland,_New_York.
3. http://www.gocolgateraiders.com/hof.aspx?hof=76&path=&kiosk.
4. https://en.wikipedia.org/wiki/Hal_Lahar.
5. http://www.gocolgateraiders.com/hof.aspx?hof=76&path=&kiosk.
6. http://www.sports-reference.com/cfb/players/john-call-2.htm.
7. Interview.
8. http://www.pro-football-reference.com/years/1957/draft.htm.
9. "The Ten NFL Draft Years That Yielded the Most Hall of Famers," http://www.therichest.com/sports/football-sports/the-10-nfl-draft-years-that-yielded-the-most-hall-of-famers/.

10. http://www.pro-football-reference.com/years/1957/draft.htm.

11. Interview.

12. *Ibid.*

13. *Ibid.*

14. *Ibid.*

15. *Ibid.*

16. *Ibid.*

17. http://www.pro-football-reference.com/players/C/CallJa20.htm.

18. Interview.

19. https://en.wikipedia.org/wiki/Buddy_Parker.

20. Interview.

21. *Ibid.*

22. *Ibid.*

23. *Ibid.*

Milt Davis

Nick Ritzmann

Vice president and general manager of the Pittsburgh Steelers Kevin Colbert noted, "The first thing anybody would tell you is that he was a great man."[1] Milton Eugene Davis lived much of his life near Hollywood, California, which was appropriate, because his was a life movies are made about. Born on May 31, 1929, on the Fort Gibson Indian Reservation near Muskogee, Oklahoma, to Clifford Davis and Leola Haynes Davis, his family soon joined many others fleeing the Oklahoma Dust Bowl for the promise of a better life in California.

The family broke apart in California and when Milt graduated from Jefferson High School in Los Angeles in 1947, he was working and living at Vista Del Mar, a Jewish orphanage. He shoveled coal and spent part of a year loading and unloading sacks of walnuts on boxcars to earn money to attend college, initially at Los Angeles City College, a public school where he ran on the track team and was noticed by longtime UCLA track coach Ducky Drake, who offered him a partial scholarship.[2]

Davis ran track for the Bruins in the Spring of 1951, and came to the attention of their football coaches, particularly Tommy Prothro, who had come west from Vanderbilt University in 1949 with head coach Henry "Red" Sanders. The Bruin coaches had not recruited him out of high school, nor had any other colleges, because he did not play high school football. A story goes that when Red Sanders questioned the ability of the newcomer from the track team as they watched practice together, Davis said, "Tell me…. Who is it that I got to kill?. That stopped [Sanders] from talking."[3]

Davis made a strong initial impression, and after being quickly moved up from the junior varsity on September 12, he earned playing time for the Bruins in 1951, intercepting a pair of passes vs. Oregon on October 20. After running track for the Bruins in the Spring of 1952, he was a top contributor for the 1952 football team, intercepting six passes on a defense that allowed only 55 points all season, for a team that finished ranked sixth in the nation.

In 1953 UCLA's defense allowed only 76 points and 65 pass completions all season, and only five of those completions went for touchdowns, while 20 passes were intercepted by the Bruins. After playing the final game of his college career vs. Michigan State in the 1954 Rose Bowl, the two-time defending world champion Detroit Lions chose him with the last selection in the eighth round (97th pick) in the NFL draft and he agreed to contract terms with the Lions in March.

The United States Army also drafted Davis, and he spent the 1954 and 1955 seasons overseas and away from professional football. Davis rejoined the Lions in 1956 after his obligation was completed, but in October was placed on the "band" or "taxi" squad, meaning he was a player who practiced with the team and received a weekly wage but was not a member of the active roster.

As Davis was finishing up the 1956 season, the Lions' front office neglected to sign him to a contract, which opened the door for another team to extend an offer. Davis was told that the Lions didn't have a black teammate to go with him on road trips so he couldn't stay with the team.[4]

After the 1956 season Davis returned to Los Angeles and continued to live at the orphanage and work as a science tutor while attending graduate school at UCLA. He worked out at Denker Playground in Los Angeles with Baltimore Colts defensive end Eugene "Big Daddy" Lipscomb and (future Hall of Fame) Chicago Cardinals defensive back Dick "Night Train" Lane. Lipscomb recommended Davis to Colts general manager Don Kellett, while Lane taught him about playing cornerback in the National Football League.[5]

Milt Davis.

Kellett apparently saw enough in Davis to sign him away from Detroit. As one Baltimore writer noted, "he was the steal of the decade." Years later the Lions paid back the Colts by snatching a practice player off their bench, eventual Hall of Fame defensive back Dick LeBeau.[6]

When Milt Davis arrived in Maryland for the Colts' 1957 training camp he was 28 years old and also 15 pounds heavier than when he left Detroit.[7] He got off to an outstanding start in the Colts' first scrimmage by intercepting a pass, recovering a fumble, batting down another pass, and coming up to the line of scrimmage to make several sharp tackles.[8]

Nine days later during the Colts' annual scrimmage in Memorial Stadium it was noted that he "showed remarkable agility, batting down several passes and putting pressure on all receivers in his area."[9]

On August 24, 1957, the Colts played to a 24–24 tie in an exhibition game against the Chicago Bears in Cincinnati, Ohio. Davis was noted as a defensive standout "who looked like he owned the great Chicago end Harlon Hill."[10] In August 1957, Hill had been in the National Football League for three seasons, and had been voted All-Pro in each of them.[11]

Davis started the season opener at right halfback against his former team, and began with a bang, picking off Lions quarterback Bobby Layne. During the twelve-game regular season Davis intercepted ten passes, which he returned for 219 yards and a pair of touchdowns as the Colts finished 7–5. The ten interceptions tied Davis with future Hall of Fame members Jack Butler and Jack Christiansen for the league lead, and a poll of Maryland press and radio representatives awarded him the Sports Boosters Trophy as the Colts' "rookie of the year" for 1957.[12] As the calendar turned to 1958, he was one of three Colts defenders (the others being Art Donovan and Gino Marchetti) voted first-team on the Associated Press All-Pro team.

Davis suffered a hip injury during a training camp scrimmage on August 5, 1958.[13] On August 11 he received his trophy for being the top Colts rookie before a record sellout crowd of 48,309 fans for the team's annual intra-squad benefit game. Davis commented that "all of us are lifetime rookies, because no two minutes of life are alike, and no two football plays are alike."[14]

Davis returned to play during the Colts' exhibition games, and intercepted a pass on the final play of the team's opening day win in Baltimore over the Detroit Lions. After the Colts' win over the Bears in the second game of the season, star Bear end Harlon Hill "complained to Owner-Coach George Halas that Davis stuck so close to him that he didn't have a chance to get open."[15]

In the Colts' October 19 game at Detroit, Davis deflected a pass to teammate Ray Brown for an interception, then recovered a pair of fumbles in a home victory over the Los Angeles Rams on November 23. He had a pair of interceptions as the Colts defeated the visiting 49ers 35–27 on November 30 to clinch the Western Conference title, but the following week he broke the metatarsal bone in his right foot when he and teammate Steve Myhra bumped into each other during a loss to the Rams in the L.A. Coliseum.[16]

After sitting out the final game of the regular season in San Francisco, he played in the championship game in Yankee Stadium on December 28 wearing low-cut sneakers because they better accommodated the swelling and helped disguise his injury, then took a shot of Novocaine to ease the pain, but "the fallout was painful when it wore off in the 4th period" and the coaching staff decided to remove him from the game.[17] "I didn't ask to be taken out of the game. They took me out. When you're hurt, you do the best you can."[18] Before leaving he forced a fumble by the Giants' Frank Gifford.

The 1959 season began for Davis and the Colts on a hot summer night in Chicago in the College All-Star Game, where he intercepted a pass and ran in back for a touchdown just before halftime. The Colts again opened their season by hosting the Lions, and again they won, this time by a score of 21 to 9. Davis suffered a fractured thumb, but started the next game as the host Colts lost to the Chicago Bears 26–21. The interceptions kept coming. Despite missing the final game of the regular season with a leg injury, Davis tied teammate Don Shinnick and Pittsburgh's Dean Derby for the most interceptions in the league with seven, and played top defense on a team that repeated as NFL champions. The Colts managed to pick off 40 passes during 1959, leading the league for the second year in a row.

Davis' 1960 season also began with another victory in Chicago at the College All-

Star Game. He nabbed his first interception in the regular season's second game, one of seven interceptions by the host Colts in a 42–7 rout of the Chicago Bears. He intercepted another pass in a win against the expansion Dallas Cowboys on October 30, then intercepted two more passes a week later in a 38–24 home victory over the Green Bay Packers. In mid–November, he was one of four Colts nominated for the Pro Bowl. The Colts tailed off a bit in the second half of the year and finished with a 6–6 record, but Davis ended up with six interceptions.

Davis, nicknamed "Pops" by his Colts teammates, retired at age 31 on March 13, 1961, to complete his master's and doctoral degrees at U.C.L.A. He played in 45 games during his four seasons with the Colts, intercepting 27 passes and was a starting defensive back on two championship teams.

The leading physicist Joseph Kaplan, also a professor at UCLA, "once said Davis was the smartest athlete he had ever taught."[19] After returning to Los Angeles, he obtained his doctorate in education and taught and coached at John Marshall High School in Los Angeles until 1964. He then worked as a professor of zoology field ornithology and natural history at Los Angeles City College from 1964 to 1989 and spent more than 30 years as a scout for a series of NFL teams including the Colts, Dolphins, Browns, and Lions, for which he was elected to the Ourlad's Scouting Services Scout Hall of Fame.[20]

He retired to a 50-acre farm near Eugene, Oregon, in 1989 and raised animals, including sheep, cattle and llamas. He also liked to swap bird calls with former Steelers coach Chuck Noll when they met.[21] Milt Davis passed away on September 29, 2008, from cancer and is buried in Oregon.

NOTES

1. Ron Bellamy, "Cancer Takes Davis at 79," *The Register-Guard*, October 1, 2008.

2. Ron Bellamy, "Wings of Fire," *The Register-Guard,* February 5, 2006.

3. *Ibid.*

4. "Milt Davis, a Cornerback on 2 Title-Winning Teams, Dies at 79," *New York Times*, last modified October 1, 2008, http://www.nytimes.com/2008/10/02/sports/football/02davis.html.

5. Bellamy, "Wings of Fire."

6. Cameron C. Snyder, "Milt Davis Will Retire," *Baltimore Sun*, March 14, 1961; John F. Steadman, *From Colts to Ravens* (Centreville, MD: Tidewater, 1997), 130.

7. Cameron C. Snyder, "Milt Davis Is Rare Colt," *Baltimore Sun*, September 4, 1957.

8. Cameron C. Snyder, "Davidson Stars in Colts Drill," *Baltimore Sun,* August 4, 1957.

9. Cameron C. Snyder, "Blues Defeat Whites, 23 to 21, in Colt Squad Game," *Baltimore Sun*, August 13, 1957.

10. Cameron C. Snyder, "Graham Here to Aid Colt Passing," *Baltimore Sun*, August 26, 1957.

11. pro-football-reference.com.

12. *Baltimore Sun*, December 29, 1957.

13. Cameron C. Snyder, "Davis Hurts Hip in Colt Workout," *Baltimore Sun*, August 6, 1958.

14. Edward C. Burks, "48,309 Turn Out for Colt Night," *Baltimore Sun*, August 12, 1958.

15. Cameron C. Snyder, "Colt Sample Injures Hand," *Baltimore Sun*, October 9, 1958.

16. John Steadman, "Ex-Colt Milt Davis Blends Intellect, Humanism," *Baltimore Sun*, November 22, 1998.

17. *Ibid.*

18. Bellamy, "Wings of Fire."

19. Snyder, "Milt Davis Will Retire."

20. http://blogs.ourlads.com/2012/09/06/milt-davis-ourlads-nfl-scouts-hall-of-fame/.

21. Mike Klingaman, "Colts Grew with 'Pops' at Their Side," *Baltimore Sun*, October 2, 2008.

Art DeCarlo

Rick Schabowski

Arthur Anthony DeCarlo had a six-year career in the NFL, playing for the Pittsburgh Steelers, Washington Redskins and Baltimore Colts. His greatest achievement was being on the back-to-back Colts championship teams in 1958–59.

DeCarlo was born in Youngstown, Ohio, on March 23, 1931. His parents were Josephina and Antonio DeCarlo, who worked as a contractor. Both of his parents died when he was young, so he was raised by an older brother.

Youngstown was a hotbed for football. Frankie Sinkwich, the 1942 Heisman Trophy winner, attended Chaney High in Youngstown. DeCarlo played high school football at Youngstown East High School. Many star players from the Youngstown area attended the University of Georgia during the 1940s and 1950s including George Poschner, Al Bodine, and Anthony Joseph (Zippy) Morocco.

After high school graduation, DeCarlo had scholarship offers to play for some colleges in Ohio. He spent the summer working in a steel mill.

Bodine, who played as a running back at Georgia in 1947–48, recommended DeCarlo to Georgia coach Wally Butts. A friend of Bodine's gave DeCarlo a train ticket to Athens, Georgia, and DeCarlo made the trip. Art stood 6'3" and weighed 167 pounds at the time. Butts was skeptical.

DeCarlo's high school coach, Dick Barrett, contacted Butts. He told him, "Don't worry a minute about Art DeCarlo. His tremendous competitive spirit will more than make up for any weight shortage. He carries thirty pounds of character."[1] DeCarlo was really put through a tough test for the tryout. In one session, 15 running backs tried to go over him one at a time, DeCarlo stopped them all. He had earned the right to be a member of the Bulldogs.

DeCarlo wasn't expected to play until his junior season, but the first four games of his sophomore season changed things. Art recovered eight fumbles and was a four-time selection on the AP's SEC Team of the Week.

The Georgia coaches had high praise for DeCarlo. Backfield coach

Art DeCarlo.

Bill Hartman said, "In fifty years, I never saw a player with a better attitude than DeCarlo. Wherever we played him, he loved it. He had tremendous agility and quickness. Talk about versatility, he played everywhere. To my knowledge, he never criticized any player or any coach. He had tremendous team loyalty."[2] Coach Wally Butts called him "one of the finest competitors to play for the Red and Black."[3]

Indeed, DeCarlo did play many positions while at Georgia. He'd be at center one play, wide receiver on another, and linebacker or defensive back when the opposition had the ball. Although he gained weight and weighed 195 pounds his senior year, he still maintained his speed and quickness. His senior year he played linebacker and caught 18 passes for three touchdowns as an end. His honors included being named twice to the All-SEC Team and twice receiving honorable mention on the All-America team. He was also selected to play in the Senior Bowl, the Blue-Gray game, and the College All-Star Game. He graduated from Georgia with a bachelor of arts degree in business adminis-tration.

Reflecting on his years at Georgia, DeCarlo talked about their strenuous practices. "We were expected to beat down the guy in front of us, not outsmart him. The practices were brutal, much more so at Georgia than with the Colts or Steelers."[4]

The 1953 NFL draft was held on January 22, 1953, at the Bellevue-Stratford Hotel in Philadelphia. The Chicago Bears selected DeCarlo in the sixth round, the 65th overall pick. He was traded to the Pittsburgh Steelers, and he played in 12 games that season, intercepting five passes and recovering a fumble.

Another draft took place after the season. Uncle Sam drafted DeCarlo, and he missed the next two seasons while serving in the Army. During his service stint, DeCarlo met Mary Kerr on a blind date, and they got married three months later. While in the military, DeCarlo was traded to the Washington Redskins.

DeCarlo loved playing in the defensive backfield for the Redskins. "Playing the cor-ner is a lot of fun, although you have a lot of responsibilities. Sometimes they get you betwixt and between, when you don't know whether to move up to stop a run or play back for a pass."[5] He played 12 games in 1956, with one interception and two fumble recoveries. He was released by Washington after playing in two games in 1957.

In the fourth game of the 1957 season in a game against the Lions, John Henry John-son had a questionable hit on the Colts' Carl Taseff on an extra point attempt. Taseff's nose was broken, and he was sidelined for the remainder of the season. The Colts signed DeCarlo as a free agent to fill in. He played in six games and intercepted one pass. DeCarlo was very humbled to play for Baltimore, saying it gave him the opportunity to be on a team "with some of the greatest football players ever to play the game."[6]

One of the standout players during the Colts' 1958 preseason camp was DeCarlo. Cameron Snyder of the *Baltimore Sun* stated, "DeCarlo was a pleasant surprise as an offensive end but really reveled as a defensive halfback, making several good saves on passes and coming up with teeth-jarring tackles on runs."[7]

Ewbank used DeCarlo as a utility player during the 1958 season, and he played on all the special teams in the championship game victory over the Giants. DeCarlo's son James shared his father's memories of the game: "My father vividly recalled the pregame prayer and the photo of it published in *Sports Illustrated*. He contrasted that emotion with the arrival back in Baltimore where the team bus at the airport was mobbed by a frenzied 2,000 fans. But the game itself was not as special as the men who played around him. He told me they won that day because of their unity and the love they had for each other."[8]

DeCarlo played two more seasons for the Colts, 1959 and 1960. He missed the last four games of the 1959 season due to injury, and in 1960, he was also used as a receiver, filling in for injured Jim Mutscheller, catching eight passes for 116 yards.

Before the 1961 season, DeCarlo retired from football, and he received many compliments, one of which was from his coach, Weeb Ewbank. "If I had a son, I would want him to be like Art DeCarlo. If the Colts had 36 Art DeCarlo's, they would have no personnel problems, no egos to deflate or inflate for each game, no prima donnas with fiery tempers to soothe."[9] Teammate Jim Mutscheller added, "He was a pass receiver and a defensive back and played both positions well. He was a good friend of mine and Art Donovan too."[10]

After retirement, Art stayed busy. He coached a semi-pro football team, the Harrisburg Capitols, a member of the Atlantic Coast Football League, and in 1965, he was a football coach and mathematics teacher at Loyola Blakefield High in Towson, Maryland, a job he held for two years.

Using the education he received at Georgia, DeCarlo went into the construction business. He built homes and owned a number of miniature golf courses. He later converted one of the courses into a restaurant, DeCarlo's Beef and Beer. He became a national sales manager for Panasonic, a job he kept until the late 1980s. In 1966, he received the post graduate achievement award from the National Football Foundation College Hall of Fame's University of Georgia Chapter and was selected to Georgia's All-Time Football team in 1976. He wrote a novel, *Fumbled Kidnap*, which was released in 2002. He enjoyed spending time with his family and grandchildren and playing golf.

Members of his family were concerned about his increasing memory loss, and he was diagnosed with a form of injury-induced Alzheimer's disease. This affliction led to his death from complications of dementia on December 21, 2013, at the age of 82. He was survived by his wife, Mary Helen Kerr, sons, James, Arthur, and Thomas, two daughters, Linda and Donna, and 14 grandchildren.

After his death, DeCarlo's brain was sent to Boston University for testing. The results were positive for CTE (Chronic Traumatic Encephalopathy), an Alzheimer's-like disease caused by continual head injuries.

The DeCarlo family opted out of the NFL CTE Class Action lawsuit that was settled in 2015 and filed a wrongful death case against the NFL in New York. The lawsuit, which has been settled and sealed, claimed that DeCarlo's death was caused by CTE and that information concealed and/or withheld by the NFL contributed to his death.

NOTES

1. Gene Asher, "Meet Mr. Nice Guy," November 2, 2004, www.georgiatrend.com.
2. Gene Asher, *Legends: Georgians Who Lived Impossible Dreams* (Macon: Macon University Press, 2005), 70.
3. Asher, "Meet Mr. Nice Guy."
4. Asher, *Legends*, 70.
5. Mal Mallette, "Cornerman Needs 'Heart' for Grid—So Joe Got Job," *The Sporting News*, October 9, 1957.
6. *The Youngstown Vindicator Archives*, December 26, 2013.
7. Cameron C. Snyder, "Cotton Goes for 60 Yards," *Baltimore Sun*, August 3, 1958.
8. Jacques Kelly, "Art DeCarlo, Colts Defensive Back," *Baltimore Sun*, December 26, 2013.
9. *Ibid.*
10. *Ibid.*

Art Donovan

NEAL GOLDEN

Arthur "The Bulldog" Donovan, Jr., was one of two Pro Football Hall of Fame defensive linemen on the Baltimore Colts' 1958 and 1959 National Football League championship teams.

He weighed a whopping 17 pounds[1] when he was born on June 5, 1924, in a tough neighborhood in the Bronx, New York. His father, Arthur Donovan, Sr., was the most famous referee in all of boxing during the 1930s and 1940s.[2] His grandfather, "Professor" Mike Donovan, was the world middleweight boxing champion in the 1870s. Both Mike and Arthur Sr. are enshrined in the International Boxing Hall of Fame.[3]

Art played football at Mount Saint Michael Academy[4] in the Bronx despite suffering from osteomyelitis at a young age, a malady, he later admitted, he hid "from every coach and team doctor I've played for since."[5] Young Arthur received a football scholarship to Notre Dame, but freshmen were not eligible for varsity play. After one semester in South Bend, he joined the Marine Corps. It was April 1943. He served in the Pacific during World War II and participated in some of the fiercest battles in that theater, including the Battle of Iwo Jima and the Battle of Luzon. He earned the Asiatic-Pacific Campaign Medal and the Philippine Liberation Medal. Years later, he became the first pro football player inducted into the U.S. Marine Corps Sports Hall of Fame.[6]

After the war, Donovan tried to enter hometown Fordham University, his first college choice all along. When that didn't happen, he decided to continue his college football career at another Jesuit school, Boston College.[7] The arrival of the six-foot-tall, 250-pound "son of the famous fight referee of New York" for spring practice in 1946 was duly noted in the Boston press.[8] One of his teammates on the line was Ernie Stautner, who also be elected to the Pro Football Hall of Fame.[9] Another member of the well-stocked line was Art Spinney, a future Colts teammate of Donovan.[10] Since the NCAA had made freshmen eligible during the war, Art lettered four times at tackle or guard and helped the Eagles compile a 20–13–3 record.[11] Donovan's #70 jersey was retired by his alma mater.[12]

Art Donovan.

The New York Giants picked Donovan in the 22nd round of the 1947 NFL draft but, even though the Giants were his hometown team, he chose to stay in school.[13] After his senior year, Baltimore chose him with their extra pick in the third round (40th overall) of the 1950 NFL dispersal draft of All-America Football Conference (AAFC) Players.[14] The Colts were one of three AAFC teams that were absorbed by the NFL for the 1950 season.

The 26-year-old rookie played in all 12 games at right defensive tackle for the Colts, who emerged victorious just once and became the only NFL team to surrender more than 50 points in four games.[15] At the end of the year, the Colts' owner, Abraham Watner, in financial distress, sold the team to the league,[16] which folded the franchise and dumped all the players into the 1951 draft.

The Cleveland Browns drafted Donovan in the fourth round, but he started the pre-season camp on the injured list.[17] To get down to the roster limit for the regular season, the Browns sent Art and another player to the New York Yanks, who played their home games at Yankee Stadium, where Art Sr. had refereed many championship bouts.[18] The Browns got a 1952 draft choice in return. Art again played in all 12 games during the '51 season.[19] The Yanks did slightly better than the '50 Colts, winning one game but also tying two.

In a recurrence of what happened to Art's first NFL team, the Yanks' financially-strapped owner Ted Collins, who was also singer Kate Smith's manager, sold the team back to the league. The NFL decided to grant a franchise to a Dallas-based group and assigned the entire Yanks roster to the new team. So Donovan moved again.

It didn't seem possible that his third NFL season could end worse than either of the other two, but it did. The winless Texans didn't even make it to the end of the season before the owners, unable to make payroll, threw in the towel after seven games. For the remainder of the season, the NFL operated the team out of Hershey, Pennsylvania. The team played its final "home" game on Thanksgiving at the Rubber Bowl in Akron Ohio, where they upset the Chicago Bears 27–23 to make it three seasons in a row that Dono-van's club won but a single game.[20] Art suffered a cracked bone in his ankle and a damaged knee in the sixth game that ended his season.[21]

The next incarnation of Art's franchise would provide the stability he needed to fashion a Hall of Fame career. Wooed by NFL commissioner Bert Bell, Carroll Rosen-bloom agreed to head up a group of investors that purchased the Dallas franchise and moved it to Baltimore.[22]

The new Colts started 3–9 under coach Keith Molesworth—a poor record but for Donovan as many wins as he experienced in his first *three* NFL seasons combined. He started a streak of five straight seasons making the Pro Bowl.[23] The next year, Weeb Ewbank came from the Cleveland Browns to take over the club and started building the foundation for a championship team four years later. 1954 began another five-year streak for Donovan of making at least one first team All-Pro team each year.[24]

Finally able to sink some roots, Art married Dottie Schaech, a local Catholic girl, and spent the rest of his life in Baltimore. One of the most popular Colts, Art started a liquor store that he owned for 21 years.[25]

When the Colts advanced to the championship game in 1958, how fitting that it was played in Yankee Stadium in Donovan's old stomping grounds in the Bronx. He helped the Baltimore defense hold the Giants to only 88 yards rushing on 31 attempts, a paltry 2.8 yards per carry.

The following season, the Colts and Giants met again for the championship. Baltimore's 31–16 triumph was not nearly as exciting as the previous year's classic.

Art characterized the great defense of the championship years like this: "We were in the same formation, a four-three, ninety-nine percent of the time. We never blitzed. They figured we should put pressure on the passer without the blitz, and we didn't want to blitz because we figured we were all doin' our job."[26]

Donovan played through the 1961 season, missing only two games in his nine years with the Colts.[27] The franchise retired his number 70 in 1962. In 1968 he became the first member of the Baltimore Colts to be inducted into the Pro Football Hall of Fame.[28]

Hall of Fame center Jim Ringo of the Green Bay Packers said this about Donovan: "Some of the greatest football ever played by a defensive tackle was played by Art Donovan. He was one of the greatest people I played against all my life."[29]

After retiring from football, Art fashioned a career as a self-deprecating comic storyteller, football's version of baseball's Bob Uecker (except that Uecker was not a Hall of Fame player). Donovan's teammates already knew that side of him. Dick Szymanski said, "Wherever Artie goes, people always crowd around him, and he makes them laugh. Isn't that a gift?"[30] Art appeared on *The Tonight Show* with Johnny Carson and on *Late Night with David Letterman* on multiple occasions. Letterman issued this statement on the occasion of Art's death: "We always looked forward to Art coming on the show because he would not only tell a great story, he just made you happy he was there. He was always humble and self-effacing, a guy from a different era of professional football who could make anyone laugh. We will miss him."[31]

Perhaps Donovan's most famous line dealt with one of his main themes—his weight. "I was a light eater. When it got light, I started eating."[32] And another: "Some people call it junk food. I call it gourmet food."[33] On getting into shape: "The only weight I ever lifted weighed 24 ounces. It was a Schlitz. I always replaced my fluids."[34]

Donovan died of a respiratory ailment on August 4, 2013, at age 89, surrounded by his family.[35]

Notes

1. www.nytimes.com/2013/08/06/sports/football/art-donovan-a-behemoth-of-modesty-dies-at-89.html.

2. www.ibhof.com/pages/about/inductees/nonparticipant/donovanarthur.html.

3. www.ibhof.com/pages/about/inductees/pioneer/donovanmike.html.

4. en.wikipedia.org/wiki/Mount_Saint_Michael_Academy#Notable_alumni.

5. www.theguardian.com/sport/2013/aug/06/art-donovan-jr-baltimore-colts.

6. www.wwmcmillan.info/awards_MCSHOF.html.

7. www.theguardian.com/sport/2013/aug/06/art-donovan-jr-baltimore-colts.

8. *Boston Traveler*, April 13, 1946.

9. *Boston College 2016 Football Media Guide*.

10. *Boston Herald*, October 24, 1947.

11. www.bceagles.com/news/2013/8/6/Football_Great_Art_Donovan_Dies_at_89.aspx.

12. *Boston College 2016 Football Media Guide*.

13. http://www.pro-football-reference.com/years/1947/draft.htm.

14. www.prosportstransactions.com/football/DraftTrades/Years/1950AAFCDisp.htm.

15. en.wikipedia.org/wiki/1950_Baltimore_Colts_season.

16. R.D. Griffin, *To the NFL: You Sure Started Somethin': A Historical Guide to All 32 NFL Teams and the Cities They've Played In* (Pittsburgh: Dorrance, 2012), 26–27.

17. *Columbus Dispatch*, July 31, 1951.

18. *The Repository* (Canton, OH), August 31, 1951.

19. www.pro-football-reference.com/players/D/DonoAr00.htm.

20. en.wikipedia.org/wiki/Dallas_Texans_(NFL).

21. *Dallas Morning News*, November 6, 1952.

22. "What If Carroll Rosenbloom Had Kept the Colts?" www.stampedeblue.com, March 31, 2015.

23. www.pro-football-reference.com/players/D/DonoAr00.htm.

24. *Ibid.*

25. William Gildea, *When the Colts Belonged to Baltimore* (New York: Ticknor & Fields, 1994), 271.

26. *Ibid.*, 275.

27. www.pro-football-reference.com/players/D/DonoAr00.htm.

28. "Baltimore Colts Great Art Donovan Dies," ESPN.coM, August 5, 2013.

29. *Ibid.*

30. *Ibid.*

31. ftw.usatoday.com/2013/08/looking-back-at-art-donovans-best-late-night-appearances.

32. "Baltimore Colts Great Art Donovan Dies."

33. profootballtalk.nbcsports.com/2013/08/04/art-donovan-great-player-and-great-character-dies-at-88/.

34. *Ibid.*

35. en.wikipedia.org/wiki/Art_Donovan.

L.G. Dupre

GREG SELBER

Louis George Dupre always had the potential to go all the way, and advanced from Texas City High School to Baylor University and eventually to the NFL as a breakaway threat, picking up the nickname "Long Gone" in his college days from legendary Southwest Conference broadcaster Kern Tips.

He may not have lived up to his considerable potential on the highest level, but Dupre, a 5'11", 190-pounder with great speed and elusive running ability, did make his mark for the 1958 Baltimore Colts. Since arriving in the league back in 1955 as a third-round draft choice, Dupre had seen his carries reduced by a 1956 rookie, the eventual Hall of Famer Lenny Moore.

In the Greatest Game Ever Played, the former Baylor All-American gained 30 yards on 11 carries, caught 2 passes for 7 yards, and played a key role in the Colts 80-yard drive to victory in overtime, but Dupre narrowly missed catching a Johnny Unitas pass during the famous game tying final drive that covered 86 yards in the waning minutes, typifying the career trajectory of one of Texas' favorite gridiron sons: so close, not quite close enough.

Dupre was not a native Texan, having been born in New Orleans in 1932, but he got to the Lone Star State as soon as he could. As a high school football and basketball star at Texas City he was good enough to warrant a look from Baylor University coach George Sauer, Sr.

In a three-year Baylor career from 1952 through 1954, Dupre rushed for 1,423 yards with 19 touchdowns and also contributed 805 yards in returns. L.G. was part of the Fearsome Foursome backfield in 1953 which also featured Jerry Coody, Allen Jones, and Cotton Davidson.

Also on the squad during Dupre's Baylor career were Del Shofner, Jim Ray Smith, and Hank Gremminger, all future pros. And it was the first athlete who introduced a pattern of play that followed Dupre from here onward. After Dupre led the Bears in rushing in 1952 and 1953 he was supplanted as the number one option by Shofner, who became the leading ball carrier in 1954. Shofner would go on to catch 349 passes for 51 touchdowns in an 11-year career with the Rams and Giants, surpassing 1,000 yards in four separate campaigns. At every step, it seemed there would be someone taking playing time from the Texas City grad.

The Bears won seven games each in 1953 and 1954 with a Gator Bowl appearance in December 1954. In the Gator Bowl loss to Auburn, L.G. raced 38 yards for a score. Getting an invite for the Senior Bowl and the College All-Star Game after his senior season, Dupre ran for 74 yards in 12 carries and caught three passes for 49 yards in the latter affair versus the champion Cleveland Browns. He gained mention in *Sports Illustrated* for "disproving the old axiom that you can't run against the pros, by sifting through the defense all night, almost at will."[1]

L.G. Dupre.

During the 1953 season he had engaged in a battle with a pair of Rice backs, Dicky Moegle and Kosse Johnson, for the Southwest Conference scoring title, and despite sharing the load with Shofner and fullback Allen Jones the next season, was high on the draft boards for 1955. Years later, in 1981, he would be elected to the Baylor Athletics Hall of Fame.

Although he was a fast back who could catch the ball, Dupre was also a tough customer, and he came by this grit naturally. L.G. explained, "Back in Texas City, my daddy would take my brothers and me around from saloon to saloon, pair us off against each other in bare knuckle boxing matches, and pass the hat. Made a pretty good dollar, too. That's why, when the fights break out today I'm the only one in the league throwing jabs!"[2]

The Colts selected Dupre in the third round of the 1955 NFL draft with the 27th pick overall. As a rookie, he rushed for 338 yards, caught ten passes, and zoomed on a 60-yard run to show his talents. His big games came against the Packers (88 yards in a 14–10 win) and Giants (80 yards in a

17–7 loss). Fellow rookie Alan Ameche was the Colts' featured back, leading the league in rushing carries, yardage and touchdowns.

In 1956, Johnny Unitas and Lenny Moore became members of the Colts' roster. Dupre punted 25 times during his second season but got just 49 trips for 182 yards on the rush (two TDs), adding 16 catches for two scores. He did jet for 61 yards on just six attempts in a 28–21 victory over the Bears in Week One and notched 81 yards receiving in a 31–14 loss to the Lions in Week Two. He was also used as a kick returner in 1956 averaging 21.1 yards per return.

The next season, the Colts went 7–5 and almost made the playoffs for the first time in franchise history, losing their last two games to fall out. Dupre enjoyed one of his best seasons in the pros with 375 rushing yards and 32 receptions for 339 yards. His highlights were against Detroit (five catches for 70 yards and two touchdowns in a 34–14 Week One victory) and in late season, when he rushed for 178 yards in four games and added 14 catches.

By now an established veteran, Dupre was once again productive during the championship season of 1958, running for a career-best 390 yards and a 4.1 yards per carry average, also his best as a pro. He gained 51 yards with one score in the season opener- a 28–15 victory over Detroit. On October 12 he rambled for 84 yards on just ten carries against Green Bay in a 24–17 victory and scored rushing touchdowns in Week Four and Week Seven triumphs over the Lions and the Rams. Though the Colts lost the regular season finale to San Francisco, Dupre contributed four catches for 56 yards.

Late in his run with the Colts, Dupre had the honor of playing a touch football game with the fabled Kennedy family, along with Baltimore teammate Billy Pricer. Ted Kennedy arranged to bring the "ringers" in for the family's game before John Kennedy's inauguration.

Ted Kennedy hedged his bet before the match, telling Bobby Kennedy that the two big, strong studs were "a couple of guys who were working on the campaign" to elect brother Jack to the presidency.[3]

The 1958 season was the high water mark for L.G. in Baltimore. In 1959 he played in just four games due to a series of injuries suffered in an automobile accident, and though the Colts repeated as champs, Dupre was done. He ended up with the expansion Dallas Cowboys for 1960 and was to have some big moments for the new team.

Dupre scored three times in a late season 31–31 tie against the Giants en route to leading the Cowboys with 362 rushing yards. He added 21 catches for 216 yards, with five total touchdowns. Dallas went winless save for the tie with the Giants that season. Dupre's last bout of '60 saw him run for 83 yards on 15 carries with a touchdown in a 23–14 season ending loss to the Lions.

The next season was his last in the NFL, and the Baylor-ex finished with just 60 yards rushing on 16 trips and six receptions, failing to get into the end zone for the first time in seven seasons.

Later in life Dupre found himself staying in Dallas, where he lived for the next 40 years before his death in 2001. He had worked for General Electric and Bethlehem Steel during his NFL days.

Though he did not live up to the promise he had shown as an All-American at Baylor, he did earn a pair of championship rings with the Colts. Lifetime, he gained 1,761 yards rushing with a 3.7 yards per carry average and 11 touchdowns, adding 104 receptions for 1,131 yards for a 10.9 yards per catch average and seven scores.

Dupre once said that he had no regrets about the way his career shook out, speaking of his Colts days with satisfaction: "We had a great team, I tried my hardest. One out of 1,000 make a pro team and I was so happy to have made the ball club … my role on the Colts was as more of a supporting player…. I didn't make the big money but the friendships last forever."[4]

NOTES

1. Irwin L. Stein, "Events and Discoveries: Unsung Heroes," *Sports Illustrated*, August 22, 1955.
2. Tom Callahan, *Johnny U: The Life and Times of John Unitas* (New York: Crown, 2010), 64.
3. Robert H. Boyle, "The Pleasure of Dying on Sunday," *Sports Illustrated*, December 13, 1965.
4. Ted Patterson and Dean Smith, *Football in Baltimore: History and Memorabilia* (Baltimore: Johns Hopkins University Press, 2013), 149.

Dick Horn, Avatus Stone and Gary Kerkorian

MARK L. FORD

Even on a healthy NFL team, not everyone lasts the full season. Coaches are continually tinkering with the roster. The three players discussed here were all born within 16 months of one another, and each played a part in the Colts' 1958 championship run, just not a large one.

Dick Horn and Avatus Stone were both tried out as punters in 1958, as Weeb Ewbank attempted to shore up the weak link in the Colts' game, but neither of them lasted for long. Horn appeared in five NFL games, Stone in but one, and both were put on waivers. Backup quarterback Gary Kerkorian never even got on the field. Nevertheless, all three got a small chunk of the title game proceeds.

In 1957, Baltimore had the best passing in the league, and the second best offense and point differential. While they didn't have to punt very often, the Colts were 12th in a 12-team league when it came to punting, the only club to average less than 35 yards per attempt. So it was that, late in August, Ewbank decided to hire a specialist; and late in October, hired a different one. Both men had been outstanding punters in college, Horn at Stanford and Stone at Syracuse, but neither fared too well during their brief stay in the NFL. On the other hand, they both went on to do very well in life after football.

Dick Horn

For instance, consider Richard H. Horn, M.D., who was still in medical school when he got the call from Coach Ewbank. Born on March 18, 1930, in Santa Monica, California, Dick Horn was a star quarterback at Santa Monica High in L.A., but ended up at Stanford University as the backup for another future Colts player profiled here, Gary Kerkorian. Once Kerkorian proved a success, Stanford coach Chuck Taylor switched Horn to the defense.[1] Horn would recall later that when the coaches read off the assignments, "much to my chagrin, I was going to be a defensive back." But, he added, "it worked out great because at least I was starting."[2] He was a pretty good punter as well, averaging 40.1 yards per attempt in his senior season in 1951.[3]

Despite his talents as a defender and a punter, Horn didn't get picked until the 17th round of the 1952 draft[4] when he was selected by New York Yanks NFL team, which would soon become the Dallas Texans.[5] Before he could start his pro football career, though, he became a draft pick for a higher authority, the Selective Service System, and spent two years in the United States Air Force. Set to be discharged in the summer of '54, he signed a Colts contract with Weeb Ewbank as a defensive back and to be "available for emergencies for quarterback."[6] Horn stayed on the Colts' roster until six days before the season opener, and was waived (but not forgotten) by Ewbank on September 20.[7]

Dick Horn (courtesy Stanford University).

Though he had envisioned a coaching career at one time, Horn returned to Stanford in 1955, this time with their College of Medicine. He also stayed in shape while away from football, and kept his punting skills fine-tuned while playing rugby in California.[8] Before Horn was going to begin his fourth and final year of med school, he got a call from Coach Ewbank, who had been unable to find a decent punter during training camp.[9]

Colts vice president Don Kellett told a reporter, "We think we've got that solved this fall in a kid named Dick Horn…. All he can do is kick—but what a job he does at that."[10] A few days later, Horn was the lone "encouraging note" in an otherwise terrible Colts preseason drubbing by the Redskins, averaging almost 45 yards per punt on three attempts.[11] He comported himself well during the remaining exhibition games, and would make the 35-man roster, not as a quarterback, not as a defensive back, but "solely for punting, making him one of the most specialized of specialists" as one reporter described it.[12] Horn still needed a doctor's excuse of sort, in the form of permission from Stanford Medical School to take an academic leave. "I told Dick that the Colts didn't want to stand in his way of becoming a doctor," Kellett told the *Baltimore Sun*. "If he can't get permission to play for us, we don't want him to quit school."[13]

Stanford allowed him to transfer to Baltimore's Johns Hopkins University for the autumn semester, and he appeared in the Colts' last three preseason games. He was given jersey number 18, a digit below the #19 worn by Unitas. In practices, Hunt was making punts as long as 45 yards, and it looked like Ewbank had found the right man. His stellar ability, in the dress rehearsals of preseason, left him on opening day against Detroit on September 28. "I can't believe that Horn is a 2 o'clock kicker," Ewbank would say after the Colts' 28–15 win that day in trying to defend his new punter,[14] using an expression for someone who performs excellently until the game actually starts. "Dick Horn, a young back retained by the Colts for his punting ability, betrayed them with two weak kicks," the *Detroit Free Press* would comment the next day.[15] "Dick Horn, who was to put the foot back into Colt football, presented the Lions with nine points," the *Sun*'s Cameron C. Snyder would write.[16]

His punt from the Colts' nine-yard line traveled only 20 yards, leaving the Lions close enough to score a field goal. On the next Colts drive, Horn booted the ball and it traveled only nine yards, to the 37 yard line, and Detroit drove for a touchdown. It got worse. The day after the next game, against the Bears, the headline in another paper was "Colts Lead West Division Despite Poor Punt Showing." "The Colts still don't have a punter," the story continued. "Poor kicks set up most of the opposing scores."[17] The Colts kept winning, and were at 5–0–0 at October's end, but Horn had averaged only 32.5 yards on 19 punts and he was waived on October 29. "He got his last chance to prove his worth as a kicker in Sunday's game with the Redskins," read the obituary to Horn's NFL career. "He failed miserably, punting five times for a 31.5 yard average."[18]

The good news was that Horn no longer had to coordinate medical school and pro football, and, with his entire attention focused on his studies, Horn received his M.D. in the spring of 1959. After an internship at UCLA and a residency at Stanford University Hospital, Dr. Horn became a successful pediatrician in Palo Alto, California.[19] Horn's departure from the NFL led Ewbank to look for another punter, and he chose Avatus Stone, a former Canadian football standout.

Avatus Stone

Avatus Stone had one of the briefest NFL careers of all time, playing but a single down for the Colts. Signed on a Saturday, waived on Monday, he worked only three days for the Colts. But, like the man he replaced, he got more than $1,400 after Baltimore won the NFL championship game; and, like Dick Horn, he went on to great success after leaving football.

Born on April 21, 1931, in Washington, D.C., Avatus Harry Stone played quarterback at the all-black Armstrong High School from 1944 to 1946. A talented basketball player, he might have gone on to an NBA career. The legendary Red Auerbach, at the time the coach of the Washington Capitols, tried to persuade Stone to play at Columbia University.[20]

Stone, however, preferred the gridiron, and decided on Syracuse University, where he was on the roster as a halfback, a punter, and the third-string quarterback. In 1951, the Orangemen's Pat Stark broke his leg[21] and was replaced by Bruce Yancey; a month later, Yancey's leg was broken.[22] Stone suddenly found himself calling the plays. After a shaky first game, he threw three touchdowns in a 33–20 upset of Fordham.[23] The United Press described him the next day as a "quadruple threat,"[24] a designation higher than mere triple threats like Slingin' Sammy Baugh. He could pass, he could run, he could tackle, and he could punt. With an average of 40.2 yards per punt, he was the best in his conference[25] and 1952 looked to be even more promising.

Unfortunately, it was Stone's turn to get injured. In the intersquad game that closed spring training, he broke his left arm[26]; no sooner did he recover from that, he tore the ligaments of his left knee during punting practice, and was out for the season.[27]

Avatus Stone (right; courtesy Syracuse University).

Since he missed all of '52, Stone was still eligible for another season even after his class graduated, but he opted for a professional career. He went on to become a star, albeit north of the border. The Chicago Cardinals drafted him in the ninth round, and he signed a contract with them in July, getting a cash bonus of $200 and a $500 advance on his salary.[28] Then, while training camp was going on, Stone went to Canada and inked a deal with the Ottawa Rough Riders. Aware that he was still under contract in the States, a reporter noted, "There is no explanation as to how he comes to Ottawa, but he wasn't cut from the Cardinals."[29] For a while, Cards owner Walter Wolfner threatened a lawsuit for an injunction to stop Stone's Canadian career,[30] but that dispute was settled, and Avatus Stone became a star in the "Big Four," the Interprovincial Rugby Football Union— the Canadian Football League hadn't been formed yet—and was third in scoring in his rookie Canadian season. In 1955, he won the IRFU's Player of the Year Award, the Jeff Russell Memorial Trophy.[31] The black football star was extremely popular with his mostly white fans, and was featured in an ad for Ottawa's dairymen, which had a photo of "Stoney" and noted, "He says: 'Professional football takes all you've got. I drink milk because I know it gives that 'something extra' you need when the going's tough.'"[32] Then, in 1956, he re-injured his knee.[33] The following season, the Riders traded him to Montreal, where he played seven games for the Alouettes before hanging up his cleats at the end of 1957 and going back to the U.S.

Stone's name kept showing up in print, however, as the subject of brief filler items in the newspaper. If you followed newspapers in the days when they were still being composed on a linotype machine, or have seen almost any old paper from that era, you've seen fillers, usually a boring little factoid tossed in to fill an empty space on the page, like "Within the last 20 years, the United States has emerged as the largest producer of soybeans." So it was that, several years after his college days, there was a Twitter-sized filler that told readers, "Best punter of footballs in Syracuse University history was Avatus Stone. His 96 punts during the 1950–51 campaigns averaged 39.7 yards."[34] In 1958, that info (which also appeared in the Cumberland, Maryland, paper on March 5) may have been enough to fill in a vacant space on the Baltimore Colts. Whether someone on Coach Ewbank's staff happened to spot that or not, the Colts signed Stone on November 1, the day before the game against the visiting Packers.[35]

Unfortunately for Stone, November 2 was a rainy day and, playing against the worst team in the NFL, the Colts only had to punt twice on the way to a 56–0 win. Sent in on fourth down, Stone had the opportunity to demonstrate how far downfield he could punt the football; but the ball spun off the side of his foot, and traveled only 28 yards. Ewbank sent defensive back Ray Brown to handle the next punt, and found the man who would handle the duties for the rest of the season. On Monday, Stone was put on waivers.

When the new AFL was launched in 1960, Stone signed a contract with the New York Titans and reported for training camp in July. His coach was a more famous quarterback-punter-defender, Sammy Baugh. The former "quadruple threat" did not impress the legendary "triple threat," and Stone was one of 14 players to get the ax on July 24.[36]

His playing days over, Stone coached at Washington's Phelps High School football for a couple of years. In 1966, he became a recruiter for the Peace Corps, and was assigned to bring in volunteers at historically black colleges.[37] He later went into business as a consultant, became wealthy and influential,[38] and passed away on November 2, 2000, 42 years to the day after his lone game in NFL. Summing up Stone's day in in the rain, *Baltimore Sun* reporter Cameron C. Snyder would write, "one kick proved the beginning and end of Avatus Stone's short career with the Colts."[39] Even as he was sending Stone away, Coach Ewbank was contacting yet another replacement player, Gary Kerkorian.

Gary Kerkorian

"My biggest contribution to the game is quitting," Gary Kerkorian once said.[40] When the Colts opened camp in 1956, Kerkorian decided that he needed to finish law school rather than spend another year as backup quarterback, so he retired from the NFL on August 8 and announced he would be going to Georgetown University.[41] The Colts, suddenly forced by Kerkorian's inconvenient timing to find a new understudy for George Shaw, took a chance on a sandlot player named Johnny Unitas, and the rest is history.

Kerkorian was part of the 1958 championship team, albeit very briefly, and he never actually got into a game. For a guy who never played a single down for the '58 Colts, he made a lot of headlines on November 5 of that year. More than one newspaper implied that the retired Colts veteran was not only returning to professional football, but that he was actually going to take over as the Colts' starting quarterback. One paper's headline got it doubly wrong, proclaiming "Law Student Kerkorian to Replace Injured Unitas At

Quarterback Spot" and running an Associated Press story that began "Lawyer Gary Kerkorian of Inglewood, Calif., is trading his briefcase for a football to get the Baltimore Colts out of a hole."[42] Other papers lured readers in with the suggestion that Kerkorian would be taking the place of Johnny U in time for the crucial November 9 game in New York before revealing in the lead that his actual role was "as an understudy to George Shaw."[43]

Gary Ray Kerkorian goes down in history as an interesting footnote. Born in Los Angeles on January 14, 1930, he was a star passer for Stanford University in the early 1950s, but he was also a pretty decent placekicker, and was one of the few NFL players to have been a rugby player. Kerkorian started at quarterback for Stanford from 1949 to 1951, setting passing records for the school. As a senior

Gary Kerkorian.

in 1952, he drew some All-America notice while leading the 9–1 Stanford Indians to the Rose Bowl where they lost to Illinois 40–7. With fellow Armenian Harry Hugasian, a halfback, the duo was known as the "Shish Kebab Twins." Hugasian was also Kerkorian's teammate on the Colts for a couple of games in 1955.

Four years before their championship season, when the Colts weren't so good, Kerkorian had been their starting quarterback. In later years, he would be the backup for former Colts backups. Like Unitas, Kerkorian had been signed by the Pittsburgh Steelers when he first got out of college; Gary was a 19th-round draft pick in 1952. Unlike Unitas, Kerkorian got a chance to appear in a few Steelers games, mostly as a placekicker in 1952, but sometimes to toss a pass in place of starter Jim Finks.

After the '52 season ended, Kerkorian changed sports. In May of 1953, the United States fielded a national rugby team for the first time, and Kerkorian was one of the 22 selected for a tour of Australia and New Zealand.[44] The NFL backup became a rugby star for the "Los Angeles All-Stars" in their first game, a 52–25 loss before a crowd of 65,000 in Sydney; Kerkorian's field goal kicking skills came in handy as he made all eight of the Yanks' "tries," good for 16 points.[45] At the end of their 19-game tour, the Americans had just two wins for a 2–16–1 record Down Under.[46] Kerkorian had been traded by the Steelers to the Rams during the off-season,[47] but he started law school at Stanford University for the 1953–54 school year, and he got traded to Baltimore after the spring semester.[48]

Sent to the east coast, he arranged a transfer to Georgetown University and took off a semester to be the Colts' starter for 1954, missing two of their 12 games due to injury.

He led the Colts on their only winning streak in '54, with two consecutive wins in late November on the way to a 3–9–0 record, and a sixth place finish in the six-team Western Conference. Baltimore had the bonus pick in the 1955 draft and selected a new quarterback, George Shaw, and Kerkorian was a backup again. When 1956 arrived, Kerkorian didn't report to training camp and, on August 8, announced that he was quitting pro football to complete his legal education at Georgetown University[49] (leaving a vacancy filled by Johnny Unitas). Then, when George Shaw was injured on October 22, and Unitas moved to first string, the Colts asked Kerkorian to work out with the team, just in case Shaw didn't respond to treatment.[50] When Shaw was placed on the injured reserve list on the day before the Colts' game with Green Bay, Kerkorian signed a contract for 30 days, the amount of time that Shaw would be required to stay out of the game.[51] Unitas excelled, and there was little need for a backup's services, but on the last game during that 30-day contract, Kerkorian was called to the field late in the fourth quarter in a game at Los Angeles, when the Colts were enjoying a 49–21 lead. He completed both of his pass attempts, one of them to Billy Vessels for his last NFL touchdown.[52]

The following June, Kerkorian received his juris doctor degree from Georgetown and notified the Colts on July 1, 1957, that he definitely was retired from professional football, and with good reason—he was preparing to take the California state bar examination on September 9.[53] He passed the exam, became a member of the California bar, and was in practice in Inglewood in 1958, with no plans to don an NFL jersey again. Then came the Colts' November 2 game; Unitas suffered broken ribs, and George Shaw took over as starter. The Colts hired attorney Gary R. Kerkorian to appear on their behalf, although it would be more accurate to say that they had him "on retainer." As #18 on the roster, Kerkorian rode the bench during the Colts games against the Giants and the Bears while Shaw called the plays, and was there, just in case, when Unitas was back in action against the Rams and the 49ers. During the interlude, Coach Ewbank told reporters that "if something had happened to Shaw … I'd have used Gary Kerkorian, who is a good football player."[54] After the November 30 game, as the Colts were preparing to travel to Los Angeles to face the Rams at the Coliseum, Kerkorian went ahead of them and returned to his office in the L.A. suburbs, waived in order to make room for a new player, Jackie Simpson.[55]

Kerkorian spent the rest of his life in the practice of law, moving from L.A. to Fresno in 1971, and becoming the unofficial leader of the area's Armenian-American community. In 1989, he found himself on the bench again, this time as a Fresno County Superior Court judge. Despite a diagnosis of lung cancer near the end of his career, he didn't retire until his 70th birthday, then passed away four months later on May 22, 2000.[56] He was survived by his wife Joyce and their six children. Kerkorian is a member of the Stanford Hall of Fame.

Although Horn, Stone and Kerkorian were long gone from the Colts by the time the NFL championship took place, they were voted a share of the receipts by their teammates. Each of 41 players got $4,718 as their share of the winning team's money. In the week before the game,[57] the Colts voted to have "1 1/2 shares to be divided among five players who were with the club at various times during the season"[58]—Jackie Simpson and Fuzzy Thurston were the other two—so each man came away with $1,415.40. In Stone's case, pretty good pay for one down of football; in Kerkorian's, not bad for sitting on the bench.

Notes

1. "Taylor Named Coach of Year," *Oakland Tribune*, December 7, 1951.
2. Reggie Burton, "Horn's Dream Quickly Dashed at Stanford; Star Defensive Back Came in '48 as a QB," *San Jose Mercury News*, October 23, 1991.
3. "Rose Bowl Bound: Dick Horn, Defensive Back," *Oakland Tribune*, December 25, 1951.
4. "Vandy's Bill Wade Drafted by Los Angeles Rams," *Shreveport* (LA) *Times*, January 18, 1952.
5. "Texans' Roster Lists Vets, Top Rookies," *Odessa* (TX) *American*, March 19, 1952.
6. "Stanford's Dick Horn Signed by Baltimore," *Los Angeles Times*, June 20, 1954.
7. "Colt Eleven Drops Three—Courtre, Horn and Embree Placed on Waivers," *Baltimore Sun*, September 21, 1954.
8. "Colts Study Films with Eye on Cuts," *Baltimore Sun*, August 26, 1958.
9. "Horn Added to Roster," *Frederick* (MD) *News*, August 26, 1958.
10. "Colts Beaming Over Len Lyles," *Louisville Courier-Journal*, August 28, 1958.
11. "'Ashamed, Not Discouraged,' Says Ewbank of Colt Loss to 'Skins," *Baltimore Sun*, August 31, 1958.
12. Jack Russell, "Unitas' Passing Makes Baltimore a Dangerous Opponent," *San Mateo Times*, September 20, 1958.
13. "Colts' Horn Seeks School Leave," *Baltimore Sun*, September 9, 1958.
14. Jesse A. Linthicum, "Colts Click at Key Time," *Baltimore Sun*, September 9, 1958.
15. George Puscas, "Colts Spoil NFL Opener for Our Champion Lions," *Detroit Free Press*, September 29, 1958.
16. Cameron C. Snyder, "Colts Rally in Last Period to Beat Lions, 28 to 15," *Baltimore Sun*, September 9, 1958.
17. "Colts Lead West Division Despite Poor Punt Showing," *Salisbury* (MD) *Daily Times*, October 6, 1958.
18. "Colts Ask Waivers on Horn, Failure as Punt Specialist," *Baltimore Sun*, October 29, 1958.
19. Burton.
20. Hugh Fullerton, Jr., "The Sports Roundup," *The Daily Mail* (Hagerstown MD), March 12, 1949.
21. "Syracuse Loses Its Quarterback," *Pittsburgh Press*, September 23, 1951.
22. "Syracuse Loses Yancey," *Binghamton* (NY) *Press*, October 15, 1951.
23. "Avatus Stone Leads Syracuse to 33–20 Win Over Fordham," *Elmira* (NY) *Sunday-Telegram*.
24. "Fordham Upset by Syracuse, 33 to 20," *Brooklyn Daily Eagle*.
25. "Stone Top Punter in Eastern Group with 40.2 Average," *Norwich* (NY) *Sun*, November 29, 1951.
26. "Hill Intra-Squad Football Game Costly as Stone Breaks Arm," *Syracuse* (NY) *Post-Standard*, May 4, 1952.
27. "Syracuse Loses Stone for Season," *Rochester* (NY) *Democrat and Chronicle*, September 17, 1952.
28. "Cards Sign Back from Syracuse U.," *Chicago Daily Tribune*, July 8, 1953.
29. "Ex-Syracuse Negro Back Joins Ottawa," *Ottawa Journal*, August 17, 1953.
30. "Card Grids to Sue Ottawa Over 'Jumper,'" *Los Angeles Times*, August 21, 1953.
31. "Avatus Stone Captures Canadian Grid Trophy," *Baltimore Sun*.
32. Advertisement in *Ottawa Journal*, September 12, 1956.
33. "Tom Tracy to Play Against Argos, Avatus Stone to Rest Injured Knee," *Ottawa Journal*, September 21, 1956.
34. "Top Kicker," *Lansing* (MI) *State Journal*, March 23, 1956.
35. "56,000 Fans Expected to Watch Colts Play Packers Here Today—Stone to Try Punt Talents," *Baltimore Sun*, November 2, 1956.
36. "Baugh Trims Titan Roster to 50 Men," *Abilene* (TX) *Reporter-News*, July 25, 1960.
37. "Avatus Stone Was One of D.C.'s Best Athletes," *Washington Times*, November 20, 2000.
38. "Wilder's Inaugural Ball Brought in $1.5 Million," *Richmond Times-Dispatch*, November 29, 1990.
39. "Dupre Out of Game with Giants; Unitas Has Chance," *Baltimore Sun*, November 4, 1956.
40. "Kerkorian, Ex-Stanford QB, Dies of Lung Cancer at 70," *San Francisco Chronicle*, May 27, 2000.

41. "Kerkorian Quits Colts to Resume Law Studies," AP report in *The Evening Sun* (Hanover PA), August 10, 1956.

42. "Pro Club Gets Emergency Aid; Law Student Kerkorian to Replace Injured Unitas at Quarterback Spot," *Tallahassee* (FL) *Democrat*, November 5, 1958.

43. "Kerkorian Takes Unitas' Place," *Pittsburgh Press*, November 5, 1958.

44. "Sol Naumu on American Rugby Team," *Honolulu Advertiser*, May 18, 1953.

45. "Kerkorian Star but U.S. Bows," *Independent Press-Telegram* (Long Beach CA), May 31, 1953.

46. "Harold Han of U.S.C. Names U.C.L.A. for '54 Rose Bowl," *Honolulu Star-Bulletin*, July 30, 1953.

47. "Rams Acquire Gary Kerkorian from Steelers," *Los Angeles Times*, June 25, 1953.

48. "Gary Kerkorian Traded to Colts," *Los Angeles Times*, July 1, 1954.

49. "Kerkorian Quits Colts to Resume Law Studies," AP report in *The Evening Sun* (Hanover PA), August 10, 1956.

50. Cameron C. Snyder, "Colts to Use Kerkorian in Emergency," *Baltimore Sun*, October 24, 1956.

51. Cameron C. Snyder, "Packers Play Colts Today," *Baltimore Sun*, October 28, 1956.

52. Jack Geyer, "Colts Race to 56–21 Victory Over Rams," *Los Angeles Times*, November 26, 1956.

53. "Kerkorian Quits Gridiron for Law," AP report in *Kansas City Times*, July 2, 1957.

54. "Colt Coach Confident, Not Cocky," *Kansas City Times*, November 17, 1958.

55. "Colts to Play at Los Angeles Today Before 75,000; Club Adds Simpson in Last Deal; Kerkorian on Waivers; Champs Are Favored by Two Points," *Baltimore Sun*, December 6, 1958.

56. "Judge Kerkorian Dies in Fresno Home at 70," *Fresno Bee*, May 25, 2000.

57. "Colts Decide on Fund Split," *Baltimore Sun*, December 13, 1958.

58. "Giants and Colts Reveal Division of Playoff Cash," *Hartford Courant*, December 28, 1958.

Don Joyce

Neal Golden

Don Joyce played right defensive end opposite Gino Marchetti on one of the finest defensive lines in National Football League history, that of the 1958–59 world champion Baltimore Colts.

Joyce was born in Steubenville, Ohio, on October 8, 1929. Weighing 190 pounds going into his senior year, Don switched from end to quarterback for the Steubenville Wells Big Red the second half of the season and handled the punting chores.[1]

When Henry Frnka moved from Tulsa to Tulane of the Southeastern Conference as head coach in 1946, he threw out a recruiting net over a wide area that included the Midwest. One of the fish he caught was Don Joyce, who joined the Green Wave freshman class in 1947.[2] Listed at six feet tall and 190 pounds,[3] Don made the traveling squad,[4] but a leg injury knocked him out of action for a month.[5] He played right end on the "B" team and did some punting.[6]

Joyce moved to tackle for the 1948 season. "Don has gained some weight over the spring and summer and he is a rugged fellow, and I believe that he just fits in better as a tackle," explained Frnka.[7] Tulane enjoyed a 9–1 season but did not make a bowl game.

By his junior year, Joyce had bulked up to 230 pounds.[8] Moved back to end, he was singled out for praise after a rough and tumble game with Vanderbilt by the *Times-Picayune*. "Joyce, who made life miserable for [quarterback] Jamie Wade, took a beating

Don Joyce.

that two or three men shouldn't take."[9] The Green Wave were on their way to the undisputed SEC title and a Sugar Bowl bid until they were upset by LSU 21–0 in the annual finale finishing the season 7–2–1 and conference co-champs with the Tigers.

The highlight of Don's senior season came against Notre Dame at Tulane Stadium. "Tulane tackle Don Joyce, who … pestered the Irish all afternoon, dropped [quarterback Bob] Williams in the end zone for the two-pointer."[10] When you shine against Notre Dame, you receive national attention. Joyce made the United Press All-American watch list the week after the game[11] as well as the list of candidates for the Associated Press' All-Southern team[12] and All-SEC team.[13] He also received several nominations for national Lineman of the Week.[14]

Joyce was part of a senior class that helped Tulane compile one of the best three-year records in school history: 22–5–2. He was inducted into the Tulane Athletic Hall of Fame in 1979.[15]

The Chicago Cardinals chose Joyce in round two of the 1951 NFL draft (pick #18). Listed at 253 pounds,[16] Joyce played three full seasons with the Cards at right defensive tackle. Just before the start of the 1954 season, he was traded to the Baltimore Colts for guard Bill Lange and an undisclosed draft choice. He became the "other end" to Gino Marchetti with Art Donovan and Tom Finnin the tackles on Weeb Ewbank's first Baltimore eleven. The Colts improved from three wins his first year, to five the second and third seasons, then seven in 1957 when Gene Lipscomb replaced Finnan next to Joyce.

According to his son, Don Joyce, Jr., the most Don ever earned in pro football was $12,000 a year.[17] So in 1956, he began supplementing his income for his family of three children by wrestling in the off-season. He worked primarily in the Baltimore area for promoter Vince McMahon, Sr. Joyce's NFL contract would not allow him to work as a "heel" (bad guy), so he wrestled exclusively as a "face" (good guy), sometimes with "Big Daddy" Lipscomb.[18]

Wide receiver Raymond Berry spoke highly of Joyce. Berry stated,

> He was such a popular player, very well known. He was a big part of our defense. In our championship years, the offensive players were aware that there was so much talk about our offense, but we knew the defense was always going to get us the ball. If we didn't get any first downs or scores, we knew the defense would get the ball back to us. Our defense was the backbone of our team. That's what we all knew. Don was one of our toughest guys.... His size and strength was an unusual combination.... He had a reputation for being the type that you could not block him or move him, you had to maneuver around him. You were not going to be running over him.[19]

Berry remembered Joyce off the field as "more of an introvert. He was a team player. The guys on the team just loved Don Joyce. He was one of the most popular guys we had. He was the type of person teammates gravitated toward."[20]

Joyce used the head slap in his battles with opposing tackles. During a 1958 game, Don broke the cheekbone of Roosevelt Brown, sending the New York Giants' All-Pro tackle to the hospital.

Don Jr. once related an incident that illustrates his father's toughness: "In 1954, the Los Angeles Rams had a $100 bounty on my dad for anyone who could knock him out of the game. My dad warned the player, Les Richter, that he'd rip his head off. It happened again, and my dad ripped the guy's helmet off and beat him with it. A hundred dollars was a lot of money back in those days."[21]

Joyce earned a reputation as the biggest eater on the Colts—quite an accomplishment on an NFL team filled with giants like Marchetti, Lipscomb, and Donovan. Teammates also remembered Don's odd preparation for each Sunday's game: "He ingested uppers, pills he got from long-haul truckers, that he bragged enabled him to stay up all night drinking beer, and that turned him into a demon on the field. Joyce would stop eating and drinking completely every Wednesday night, and starve himself for the team's weekly weigh-in on Friday.... He would treat himself to a feast immediately afterward."[22]

Marchetti told a humorous story about Joyce's eating habits: "I asked my mother to send me some spaghetti sauce. She made homemade spaghetti sauce and spaghetti. Donovan was there and Joyce had just joined us.... So we sat there and we drank wine and ate the spaghetti. Joyce musta ate three pounds.... And then he reaches in, pulls out this little pill and puts it in his coffee. I said, 'What's that for?' He said, 'I gotta watch my weight.'"[23]

After the 1960 season, Baltimore made Joyce one of eight Colts who would be available for the expansion draft. He was the most prominent of the three teammates taken by the Minnesota Vikings. Don played in all 14 games for the Vikings during the 1961 season.[24]

Released by the Vikings, Joyce signed with the Denver Broncos of the American Football League and played in six games in 1962 before retiring. He returned to Minneapolis and coached football for five years at De La Salle High School.[25]

Joyce spent most of the rest of his life scouting for NFL teams. He began with the Vikings, then became a regional scout for BLESTO (Bears Lions Eagles Steelers Talent

Organization). Bill Tobin, who worked in the front office of several NFL teams, including the Indianapolis Colts,[26] praised Joyce's skill:

> He had a knack for scouting. He didn't overwhelm you with his opinion, but you sure knew where he stood. When I got to Indianapolis in 1994, he was with the Colts.... It was a big thrill to him that he played for the Colts, then was able to work with the Colts. It was comforting to have him in the draft room on draft day. He could identify players, and he was a great person.... You hear stories about him as a player, how determined and how vicious he was. As an individual off the field, he was very warm, very gracious, made great appearances on college campuses when he was scouting.[27]

Don Joyce died on February 26, 2012, at the age of 82. While he made just one Pro Bowl in his 12-year NFL career (in 1958), he was fondly remembered as a fierce competitor and respected teammate on the field and a gentle giant off it.

Notes

1. *The Repository* (Canton, OH), October 24, 1946, and June 18, 1947.
2. *Times-Picayune* (New Orleans, LA), September 5, 1947.
3. *Tulane vs. Alabama Souvenir Program*, September 27, 1947.
4. *Times-Picayune*, October 10 and November 20, 1947
5. *Times-Picayune*, September 26 and 30, 1947
6. *Times-Picayune*, October 9 and November 3 and 30, 1947.
7. *Times-Picayune*, August 31, 1948.
8. *Times-Picayune*, September 7, 1949.
9. *Times-Picayune*, November 14, 1949.
10. *Times-Picayune*, October 15, 1950.
11. *Times-Picayune*, October 17, 1950.
12. *Morning Advocate* (Baton Rouge, LA), October 17, 1950.
13. *Morning Advocate*, October 31, 1950.
14. *States Times Advocate* (Baton Rouge, LA), November 1, 1950.
15. "Tulane Athletics Hall of Fame," tulanegreenwave.com.
16. "1951 Chicago Cardinals Roster," www.justsportsstats.com.
17. Paul McEnroe, "Obituary: Ex–Viking Don Joyce Was Ferocious on Field, Kind Off It," *Minneapolis Star Tribune*, March 11, 2012.
18. Greg Oliver, "Don Joyce Was Famed Defensive End, Part-Time Qrestler," slam.canoe.com, 12/18/2012.
19. Craig Kelley, "Colts Remember: Don Joyce," www.colts.com, February 27, 2012.
20. *Ibid.*
21. McEnroe.
22. Mark Bowden, *The Best Game Ever* (New York: Atlantic Monthly Press, 2008), 38.
23. *Ibid.*, 226.
24. McEnroe.
25. *Ibid.*
26. "Bill Tobin (American football)," en.wikipedia.org, last modified December 15, 2016.
27. Kelley.

Ray Krouse

Bill Lambert

Raymond Francis Krouse was born in Washington, D.C., on March 21, 1927. This was during the Calvin Coolidge administration and right in the middle of prohibition.

It was the period affectionately known as the Roaring Twenties and still a few years before the Great Depression engulfed the country.

Ray attended high school at the old Western High School in D.C. Western was open from 1890 to 1977 (notable alumni include Gloria Steinem and David Scott, an astronaut that walked on the moon). It has since become the Duke Ellington School of the Arts (comedian Dave Chappelle is an alumnus).[1]

After high school, Ray served in World War II as part of the U.S. Navy. He then entered the University of Maryland and lettered all four years under coach Jim Tatum. Maryland had solid teams during Ray's tenure. They went 7–2–2 in 1947 and played in the Gator Bowl, tying Georgia 20–20. The 1948 season saw them go 6–4, then 9–1 in the 1949 season ending with a 20–7 Gator Bowl win over Missouri and 7–2–1 in 1950 (with a solid win over Michigan State). Tatum called Krouse "the best tackle ever coached or seen."[2]

Ray earned honorable mention Associated Press All-America in 1948 and second team Associated Press All-America honors as a tackle in 1949. He played with future Hall of Famer Stan Jones, and Dick Modzelewski, both of whom would follow Ray and become All-America tackles at Maryland (Ray would subsequently be traded for Modzelewski when they were in the NFL). Other All-America teammates of Ray included Bob Ward (G) and Jack Scarbath (QB). Ray worked on construction of the new stadium at Maryland during the summer of 1949 and even took time out to get married.[3]

Upon completion of his college career, Ray was drafted by the New York Giants in the second round with the 25th overall pick of the 1951 Draft. Looking back at the players selected in that draft, Ray compared quite favorably, particularly in games played in his career. Out of 361 players drafted only ten played more games in their careers than Ray's 118.[4]

The 1951 New York Giants were led by Hall of Fame coach Steve Owen and compiled a 9–2–1 record, second in the American Conference. Both losses came at the hands of the Cleveland Browns, eventual winners of the American Conference and losers to the Los Angeles Rams in the 1951 NFL championship game. Hall of Fame teammates included Tom Landry, Arnie Weinmeister, and Emlen Tunnell. Ray played in 12 games that year. The 1951 Giants defense allowed the fewest total yards and rushing yards in the NFL that season.[5]

Ray Krouse.

The New York Giants fell to 7–5 in 1952. A notable addition to that team was rookie running back and future Hall of Famer, Frank Gifford. Ray played in all 12 games and recovered two fumbles during the season. The team finished second once again in the American Conference.[6]

The 1953 season was Steve Owen's last as coach of the Giants. The team struggled to a 3–9 record and finished fifth in the NFL's Eastern Conference. Ray played in ten games that season. Future Hall of Famer Rosey Brown joined the team in 1953.[7]

Jim Lee Howell took over the Giants in 1954. The team bounced back a bit by finishing third in the NFL's Eastern Conference with a 7–5 record overall. Ray recovered one fumble in 1954 and made the Pro Bowl. He was also named second team All-NFL by the Associated Press and first team by the *New York Daily News*. He played in all 12 games during the season.[8]

The 1955 Giants took a slight step back to 6–5–1. Ray had another solid year earning second team All-NFL with both the *New York Daily News* and UPI. He also played in all 12 games again.[9]

The 1956 New York Giants won the NFL championship. Unfortunately for Ray, he was dealt to the Detroit Lions prior to the season for former college teammate, Dick Modzelewski. It had to be a tough pill for Ray to swallow but he left a team on the cusp of a championship to another one loaded with future Hall of Famers and stars. Detroit held Krouse in high regard. Lions GM Nick Kerbawy called Krouse, "one of the biggest and fastest tackles in pro football," further stating that they finally got the man they wanted.[10]

The Detroit Lions of 1956 were led by coach Buddy Parker and finished 9–3. Future Hall of Famers on their roster included Jack Christiansen, Lou Creekmur, Yale Lary, Bobby Layne and Joe Schmidt. Ray stepped into his new team and played in 12 games that year while recovering two fumbles. He was voted first team All-Conference by *The Sporting News*.[11]

The 1957 season started out slowly for the Detroit Lions. The sudden departure of coach Buddy Parker and subsequent replacement by George Wilson couldn't have helped. After six games they were 3–3. They won five of their last six regular season games to finish in a tie for the Western Conference lead with the 49ers. In a one game Western Conference playoff, the Lions defeated the Niners 31–27, and went on to destroy Cleveland in the championship game 59–14. Ray played in 12 games during the season and started both playoff games for the league champions.[12]

The high of winning a league championship had to be brought down quickly when Ray was once again traded in the off-season, this time to the Baltimore Colts for a third-round draft choice (eventually pick number 36 in 1959—future Major League Baseball umpire Ron Luciano).[13]

Once again though, Krouse was traded to a solid team building toward a championship. In 1958 Colts finished the season 9–3 and won the NFL Western Conference, and Ray played in all 12 games.[14]

In the 1958 NFL championship game against the Giants there were eight fumbles. Krouse led all players with two fumble recoveries. Ray's first recovery was a Frank Gifford fumble early in the second quarter. His second recovery came in the fourth quarter on a Phil King fumble. In the end, the Colts won in overtime 23–17 for Ray's second straight NFL championship.[15]

The Baltimore Colts repeated as NFL champions in 1959. Ray played in all 12 games again and the NFL championship game.[16]

At this point, Ray's run of championships took a bit of a downturn as he was selected by the Dallas Cowboys in the 1960 NFL expansion draft. He ended up not playing for the Cowboys as he was traded to the Washington Redskins on June 23 for center Frank Kuchta. Ironically, he appeared in the 1960 Topps' football card set as a member of the Dallas Cowboys.[17]

Ray played one season for the Washington Redskins. That season was a letdown after three straight NFL championships.

Washington Post reporter Dan Steinberg related fellow *Post* reporter Jack Walsh's account of Krouse's training camp experience with the Redskins in August 1960: "Rookies get a gentle hazing at dinner time when they're called on to stand, put their hand over their hearts and sing their school song. Clown Bob Toneff made this request the other day: 'Ray Krouse, the best rookie in the history of the National Football League, will you stand and sing your song?' Krouse, 10-year pro vet from Maryland, just went on eating, saying 'I not only forget the song, I forget where I went to school it's been so long ago.'"[18]

The 1960 Redskins finished 1–9–2 under second year coach Mike Nixon. Ray was the oldest player on the team as the roster was filled with youth and mostly non-distinguished players. He did recover his sixth career fumble during the season and once again saw action in all 12 games.[19]

Nineteen sixty turned out to be Ray's last season. He finished his NFL career with three championships, one Pro Bowl appearance (1954), and he was voted first or second team all NFL in 1954 and 1955.[20]

Ray Krouse passed away on April 9, 1966, at the age of 39 leaving behind his wife Marjorie and four daughters. The *Washington Post* on April 10 reported, "Raymond Francis Krouse, one of the finest athletes ever to come out of Washington, died yesterday at Georgetown University Hospital of a liver ailment."[21]

Ray was posthumously inducted into the University of Maryland Athletic Hall of Fame. He must have made quite an impression at Maryland, as the team awards the Ray Krouse award to its most valuable football player each season.[22]

Notes

1. "Duke Ellington School for the Arts," http://www.ellingtonschool.org/, accessed April 17, 2017.

2. https://en.wikipedia.org/wiki/Ray_Krouse, accessed April 11, 2017; https://en.wikipedia.org/wiki/Maryland_Terrapins_football_under_Jim_Tatum, accessed April 11, 2017; "Ray Krouse, Ex-Grid Star Dies at 39," *Schenectady Gazette*, April 11, 1966, 23.

3. "Maryland Football All-Americans," Umterps.com, accessed April 11, 2017; University of Maryland Men's Football Media Guides, https://www.lib.umd.edu/univarchives/football, accessed April 11, 2017.

4. "1951 NFL Draft Listing," Pro-Football-Reference.com, accessed April 11, 2017.

5. "1951 New York Giants Statistics & Players," Pro-Football-Reference.com, accessed April 11, 2017.

6. "1952 New York Giants Statistics & Players," Pro-Football-Reference.com, accessed April 11, 2017.

7. "1953 New York Giants Statistics & Players," Pro-Football-Reference.com, accessed April 11, 2017.

8. "1954 New York Giants Statistics & Players," Pro-Football-Reference.com, accessed April 11, 2017.

9. "1955 New York Giants Statistics & Players," Pro-Football-Reference.com, accessed April 11, 2017.

10. "1956 New York Giants Statistics & Players," Pro-Football-Reference.com, accessed April 11, 2017; "Lions Obtain Giant's Krouse," *Ludington Daily News*, April 27, 1956.

11. "1956 Detroit Lions Statistics & Players," Pro-Football-Reference.com, accessed April 11, 2017.

12. "1957 Detroit Lions Statistics & Players," Pro-Football-Reference.com, accessed April 11, 2017.

13. "1959 NFL Draft Pick Transactions," Pro-Football-Reference.com, accessed April 11, 2017.

14. "1958 Baltimore Colts Statistics & Players," Pro-Football-Reference.com, accessed April 11, 2017.

15. "Championship—Baltimore Colts at New York Giants—December 28th, 1958," Pro-Football-Reference.com, accessed April 11, 2017.

16. " 1959 Baltimore Colts Statistics & Players," Pro-Football-Reference.com, accessed April 11, 2017.

17. "1960 NFL Expansion Draft," www.profootballarchives.com, accessed April 11, 2017; Keith Yowell, "1960: Cowboys Obtain Eddie LeBaron from Redskins," *Today in Pro Football History*, accessed April 11, 2017.

18. Dan Steinberg, "Great Moments in Redskins Hazing," *Washington Post*, November 6, 2013.

19. "1960 Washington Redskins Statistics & Players," Pro-Football-Reference.com, accessed April 11, 2017.

20. "Ray Krouse," Pro-Football-Reference.com, accessed April 11, 2017.

21. Raymond Francis "Ray" Krouse (1927–1966), https://www.findagrave.com, accessed April 11, 2017.

22. https://en.wikipedia.org/wiki/Ray_Krouse, accessed April 11, 2017.

Gene Lipscomb

GEORGE BOZEKA

At 6'6" and nearly 300 pounds, "Big Daddy" Lipscomb was once characterized as the prototype for the modern NFL defensive lineman. A dominating combination of strength, size, agility, and speed at defensive tackle, Lipscomb was an effective defender against both the run and the pass. Paul Brown remembered, "We never ran at Big Daddy. Well, now and then we ran a sucker play to keep him at home. But that was all. What was the use of wasting a play." Hall of Fame linebacker Chuck Bednarik added that Lipscomb "had the best lateral movement of any big man I've ever seen. He put on a good pass rush, and when he hit a man head-on it made you shudder."[1] His career and life would come to a premature and self-destructive end.

Eugene Allen "Gene" Lipscomb was born during the height of the Great Depression on August 9, 1931, in Uniontown, Alabama. Agriculture was predominant in Alabama, and Gene's family was cotton pickers. Lipscomb had a tragic childhood. He never knew his father, who died in a Civilian Conservation Corps camp, one of the many New Deal work programs established by FDR. When he was three, Gene and his mother Carrie moved to the Black Bottom ghetto on Detroit's east side. When Gene was 11 years old his mother was violently murdered at a bus stop on Lafayette Street, stabbed 47 times by her boyfriend. Lipscomb carried photos of the horrific murder scene with him as an adult. Teammates like Ordell Braase of the Colts remembered Lipscomb being haunted by his childhood—unable to sleep and subject to mood swings. "He was a troubled guy. I remember waking up at four in the morning, and he'd be pacing those halls. I think the haunts of his childhood pursued him to the end of his life."[2]

After his mother's murder, Lipscomb lived with his paternal grandfather, Charles Hopkins. Hopkins was a harsh disciplinarian who charged Gene room and board. Gene worked odd jobs to pay his grandfather.[3]

In the sixth grade, Gene was an oversized 6'4," 220-pound man-child who felt like a freak. He was mercilessly bullied by classmates over his outgrown clothes, specially sized desk and academic shortcomings.[4]

Lipscomb was a star football player at Miller High School in Detroit, but he never attended college. Ineligible for his senior season because he had played semipro basketball and softball, Lipscomb joined the Marines at the suggestion of high school coach Will Robinson. He was later awarded a diploma at a special program in 1960 at the age of 28.[5]

Pete Rozelle, then a young public relations director with the Los Angeles Rams, discovered Lipscomb playing football for the Marines at Camp Pendleton in California where Gene served from 1949 to 1953. The Rams picked him up as an undrafted free agent in 1953 for the final two games of the season. Lipscomb had matured physically during his time with the Marines.[6]

Lipscomb's next two seasons with the Rams were chaotic both on and off the field. Lacking in the basic fundamentals that most players learn in college, Lipscomb was an easy target for opposing teams. Lou Creekmur, the Detroit Lions' Hall of Fame offensive lineman, recalled that Lipscomb "was as raw as liver with the Rams. In the service he could get away with standing up straight and muscling people around, but he couldn't do that in the pros. All you had to do was get under his arms and hands, and his body was so huge that once you got it moving in one direction, it was going over."[7]

Gene Lipscomb.

Off the field, Ram teammates recalled a conflicted man—a warm and gentle person with a terrible dark side characterized by associations with unsavory parasites, excessive drinking, indiscriminate womanizing, and violent outbursts. Deacon Dan Towler recalled, "He had this gentle spirit. He was a prince. He had no control over himself. He was a paradox. The way he acted in my house and out of my house, it was like Dr. Jekyll and Mr. Hyde. His animal nature often was unchecked."[8]

Lipscomb acquired his famous nickname while playing with the Rams. He started calling teammates "Little Daddy." Since some Ram linemen of that era weighed as little as 200 pounds, they in turn started calling him "Big Daddy."[9] He also became known derisively as "Fifteen Yard Daddy" because his undisciplined, roughhouse play resulted in so many penalties. Lipscomb recalled in 1960, "I just thought if I hurt an opponent enough to get him out of the game it would make my teammates like me. But it didn't help. They kept right on razzing me and laughing at me."[10]

In 1956, the Rams grew tired of his carousing and lack of improvement on the field.[11] He was available for a $100 fee. The 49ers had the first claim as a result of having the worst record from the previous season, with the Colts second in line. Both teams were interested, but the 49ers notified Commissioner Bert Bell's office by telegram, whereas the Colts made a telephone call. The delivery of the wire was delayed because of the Labor Day holiday weekend. Bell ruled in favor of the Colts because he received their phone notification first. The Niners complained, but soon dropped their claim.[12]

In Baltimore, over the next five seasons, Lipscomb totally assumed the larger than life persona of "Big Daddy." He drove around town in a gold Cadillac and wore fancy clothes,[13] and became a beloved folk hero in the community, finding beds for derelicts and giving poor ghetto children shoes and clothes.[14]

On the field, he flourished under the structured environment instituted by Weeb Ewbank. Fellow defensive linemen Gino Marchetti, Art Donovan, and Don Joyce were mentors for Lipscomb. According to Marchetti, "there was not much formal coaching on the line in those years, so the players would gather on the field and share their tricks and techniques. It was like an on-field seminar. What Big Daddy learned, he learned through watching us…. From sideline to sideline, I don't think anybody ever did a better job than Big Daddy did."[15]

In 1957, Big Daddy's on field play started to mature. Lipscomb later stated, "By the grades Weeb Ewbank gives us after running films of the games, I had a fine season in 1957. Nobody else made 135 tackles like I did…. I knew beyond a doubt that both Baltimore and Daddy were on the way."[16] During the Colts' championship seasons of 1958 and 1959 Lipscomb earned first team All-Pro honors and was named to the Pro Bowl. Ewbank gushed, "He just got better and better."[17]

Lipscomb had morphed into a ferocious yet disciplined lineman with a touch of kindness. He would crunch opponents into the ground, and then help them up, and pat them on the behinds as they headed back to their huddle. Lipscomb explained, "Nobody is going to say Big Daddy is a mean man."[18]

Big Daddy also became very popular with the writers, who loved his colorful quotations. On his practical, yet efficient style of line play, Lipscomb said, "If a player starts holding, I smack my hand flat against the earhole of his helmet. When he complains about dirty playing, I tell him to stop holding and I'll stop slapping. That's what I call working out a problem." On his unique tackling methods, Lipscomb said, "I just reach out and grab an armful of players from the other team and peel them off until I find the one with the ball. I keep him."[19]

Not everyone associated with the Colts was a fan of Lipscomb's. Art Donovan was not a fan of Lipscomb's play, calling him a marginal player at best[20]:

> To be frank, Big Daddy was pretty much of a bully as a football player. Baltimore brought him over from the Rams in 1956, and for all the legends that grew up around Big Daddy, he never really played for Los Angeles except special teams, when they would send him in to try to block a kick. He was six-seven, about 290 pounds, and I don't think he liked to be hit. At any rate, when Weeb brought him in here, Weeb got the public-relations machinery rolling to try to build Big Daddy into the second coming of Colossus. To an extent, it worked. But it didn't fool anyone who played with him.[21]

Donovan was in the minority regarding Big Daddy's skill set. Hall of Fame running back Jim Brown gave the following assessment of Lipscomb:

Daddy rose up in the middle of the enemy line like the Empire State Building with a mustache. He had the strength of an elephant and was so fast he frequently ran down backfield men from behind. He was the one player in the league who could practically control a play. What gave me pause was the known fact that Daddy could stop a ball carrier in his tracks with a giant bear-hug, then straighten him up like a board, then bend him every way imaginable. There was nothing illegal or dirty bout this sort of thing. But just thinking about it, you could feel your spine tingle. You knew it wouldn't take much to give Daddy an excuse for twisting you into a piece of abstract sculpture. For one thing, he was the supreme showman: His shirttail always hung loose so it could flap in the wind when he ran. Crowds tittered when Daddy considerately leaned over and helped us little 230-pounders to our feet after smashing us into the ground. But above all, Daddy had the sensitive soul of an artist.[22]

Assistant coach Charley Winner remembered Lipscomb's mischievous side. Lipscomb was in the midst of a prostate exam administered by a team doctor, when the doctor approached him with a rubber covering over his finger. Lipscomb queried the doctor about the rubber covering on his finger. It's "'a prophylactic,' said the doc. 'Take that thing off,' Big Daddy deadpanned. 'I'm a Catholic.'"[23]

In addition to his teammates, another person who mentored Lipscomb in Baltimore was former Colts running back Buddy Young. Young tried to teach him to take control of his chaotic life. Young's wife Geraldine remembered, "You should have seen this raw man when he came to Baltimore. He talked about how raggedy his shoes were when he went to school and how his pants were always too short. Deep down, he felt, There's more to life than what I've lived. He was scared, and he didn't know why. People talked to him as if he were a child. They all thought he was this big lummox who had no brains. He saw this, and there was this real hurt. Here he saw rewards for fulfilling a commitment and following orders."[24]

Lipscomb's fears were deep seated. His teammates remembered him crying himself to sleep, keeping a gun under his pillow, and his bed against the door so nobody could get into his room.[25] He was acutely sensitive about his lack of education.[26]

As a result Lipscomb was never able to completely escape his past or his insecurities, and he would continue the self-destructive carousing off the field.

In 1960, the Colts failed to repeat as champions, but Lipscomb had another stellar season, as he was again named first team All-Pro.

During the summer of 1961, Colts nation was shocked when Big Daddy was traded to Pittsburgh. Winner explained that the trade was made because of Lipscomb's off field issues. "It was always something. Money problems. Legal and personal problems."[27] Good friend and teammate Lenny Moore elaborated, "I think it was because the management was afraid they couldn't control Big Daddy anymore, who wouldn't tolerate any more mistreatment of blacks on the team. Also, many coaches thought that big Daddy's drinking had caught up with him and that he'd lost a step. Either way, I was devastated to see my best friend leave the team."[28]

In the off season Lipscomb wrestled to make some extra money and stay in shape. He teamed with fellow pro football players Leo Nomellini and Verne Gagne.[29] He also toyed with idea of joining NASA: "I'm not kidding. I want to be an astronaut. And I sure would like to be the first guy to land on the moon. Why, I'd look around. Wave the American flag, declare the territory for America and pick up a little glory for Big Daddy, too." "I wonder if those cats up there on the moon have a football team. If they do, Big Daddy would have himself a ball. And when those scientists look at the planet at night and see somebody making tackles all over the surface they'll be able to say, 'There's the man in the moon and it's Big Daddy.'"[30]

Lipscomb played for the Steelers for two seasons, earning first team All-Pro from the NEA in 1961, and Pro Bowl honors in 1962. He was at the top of his game in 1962 being chosen Steeler of the Year and lineman of the game in the Pro Bowl with a dominating performance that included 11 tackles, a blocked punt, one forced fumble, and one recovered fumble. Coach Buddy Parker claimed that Big Daddy was "the best man I ever saw at knocking people down."[31]

Off the field, Lipscomb's life was an unbridled Roman bacchanalia. Hard-living quarterback Bobby Layne and other Steelers teammates were bad influences. Big Daddy would drink whiskey by the bottle and satisfy his huge libido indiscriminately. Defensive back Brady Keys recalled picking up Lipscomb in the morning with orgies in progress. "There would be three or four women, and they would be half naked. Big Daddy had enough energy for them all. He was always drunk. And he always had cash lying all over the place. Big Daddy did three things: He drank, he screwed, and he dominated football games."[32]

During the off season, Lipscomb still lived in Baltimore. On May 9, 1963, he played in a softball doubleheader. As was his habit, Lipscomb then proceeded to party into the early morning hours of May 10 with an acquaintance named Timmy Black. According to Black, the carousal included the purchase and use of heroin. Lipscomb shot up first, and overdosed. Black claimed that he and a third man tried to revive Lipscomb with ice and a shot of saline solution. They failed. An ambulance was called and Lipscomb was dead on arrival at Lutheran Hospital. He was 31. The autopsy showed an alcoholic content of .09 and five times the amount of heroin that would be considered a safe dosage in his system.[33] Black was later arrested but ultimately acquitted on a charge of possessing narcotic equipment.

Many friends of Lipscomb were skeptical of Black's story believing instead that Black was an unsavory character who shot Lipscomb up to steal money. Black alleged that Lipscomb was a regular heroin user. Friends claimed that Lipscomb had a mortal fear of needles.[34]

According to the Pittsburgh team physician, Dr. Raymond Sweeney, "Big Daddy was no addict. I was too close to him over the last two years. I could have recognized it easily."[35] Sweeney stated, "We wanted to shoot him with Novocaine [at halftime after an injury], but he said he never had a needle in him in his life and would rather play hurt."[36]

In 2006, the Professional Football Researchers Association named Lipscomb to its Hall of Very Good, honoring players not in the Pro Football Hall of Fame. Gino Marchetti believes that Lipscomb deserves to be inducted into the Hall, but that the manner in which Lipscomb died has kept him out. "I doubt he ever will be," Marchetti says. "What they said about him with drugs may be held against him."[37]

Thousands attended Big Daddy's visiting hours. The *Hanover Evening Star* reported that "at one point the line at the Baltimore funeral establishment was four abreast and more than a block long as people filed by the casket."[38]

William Nack described the scene in *Sports Illustrated*:

> One thousand people were at Lipscomb's funeral in Detroit, and symbols of the life he had led surrounded the gravesite in Lincoln Memorial Cemetery. There were those eight football greats—Erich Barnes, John Henry Johnson, Dick (Night Train) Lane, Lenny Moore, Luke

Owens, Jim Parker, Sherman Plunkett and Johnny Sample—carrying the coffin draped in the U.S. flag, a reminder of Lipscomb's service in the Marine Corps. There were his friends from Black Bottom. And there were all those honeys, at least one fiancée wearing a ring and two others claiming they were engaged to Big Daddy. They were around there screaming and hollering, "What are we gonna do without him." The preacher said, "He did some good, he did some wrong..." A spring wind rustled in the trees, whispering, Amen to that.[39]

Big Daddy Lipscomb died as he had lived—on the edge. A talented football player and, deep down, a good man whose abilities and innate kindness were sadly consumed by his uncontrollable demons.

NOTES

1. "Big Daddy," *NFL GameDay Program Colts at Steelers*, August 28, 1992, 33.
2. William Nack, "The Ballad of Big Daddy Lipscomb," *Sports Illustrated*, January 11, 1999, 74.
3. Lew Freedman, *Clouds Over the Goalpost: Gambling, Assassination, and the NFL in 1963* (New York: Sports Publishing, 2013), 35.
4. Nack, 76.
5. Nack, 76; Eugene (Big Daddy) Lipscomb as told to Robert G. Deindorfer, "I'm Still Scared," *The Saturday Evening Post*, November 12, 1960, 92.
6. Nack, 76; Greg Oliver, "The Brief Career of Big Daddy," *Slam Sports*, http://slam.canoe.com/Slam/Wrestling/2005/09/01/1197832.html, accessed August 8, 2017.
7. Nack, 76.
8. *Ibid.*, 76–80.
9. "Big Daddy," 36.
10. Lipscomb, 92.
11. "Melvin Durslag, Big Daddy Changed Pro Game," *Los Angeles Herald Examiner*, May 12, 1963, CC.
12. John Steadman, *From Colts to Ravens* (Centreville, MD: Tidewater, 1997), 133.
13. "Big Daddy," 36.
14. Nack, 73.
15. *Ibid.*, 80.
16. Lipscomb, 94.
17. Nack, 80.
18. "Big Daddy," 36.
19. Nack, 82.
20. Arthur J. Donovan, Jr., with Bob Drury, *Fatso: Football When Men Were Really Men* (New York: Avon Books, 1987), 204.
21. *Ibid.*, 186.
22. Jim Brown with Myron Cope, "Off My Chest," in *The NFL Literary Companion: A Game of Passion*, John Wiebusch and Brian Silverman, ed. (Atlanta: Turner Publishing, Inc., 1994), 197.
23. Tom Callahan, *Johnny U: The Life and Times of John Unitas* (New York: Crown, 2006), 92.
24. Nack, 80.
25. Michael Olesker, *The Colts in Baltimore* (Baltimore: Johns Hopkins University Press, 2008), 136.
26. Freedman, 36.
27. Nack, 82.
28. Lenny Moore with Jeffrey Jay Ellish, *All Things Being Equal* (Champaign, IL: Sports Publishing, 2005), 101–102.
29. Oliver.
30. "'Big Daddy' Asks Flight to Moon to Wave the Flag," *Charlotte Daily News*, August 8, 1962, 14.
31. "Big Daddy," 33.
32. Nack, 84.
33. Edward Linn, "The Sad End of Big Daddy Lipscomb," *The Saturday Evening Post*, July 27, 1963, 76.
34. Nack, 86.

35. "Big Daddy," 36.

36. Cameron Snyder, "Lipscomb's Death Shocks Colts," *Baltimore Sun*, May 11, 1963, 17.

37. Nack, 86.

38. "Fans Pay Respect to Gene Lipscomb," *Hanover* (PA) *Evening Star*, May 13, 1963, 8.

39. Nack, 86.

Lenny Lyles

Ed Gruver

Only a handful of people participated in the two most important and iconic games in pro football history.

Lenny Lyles is among the select few.

A native of Nashville, Tennessee, Lyles was a rookie return specialist for the Baltimore Colts in the 1958 NFL championship game, an overtime classic in which the Colts rallied in dramatic fashion to defeat the New York Giants 23–17 in Yankee Stadium. The game is widely recognized as the starting point for pro football replacing major league baseball as the American pastime.

Ten years later, Lyles started at right cornerback for the Colts, who endured a humiliating 16–7 upset loss to another New York team, the upstart Jets of the rebellious American Football League, in Super Bowl III. The stunning victory by a Jets team that was an 18-point underdog is seen as the game that legitimized the Super Bowl as America's single most important sporting event every year.

Born January 26, 1936, Leonard Everett Lyles helped pave a path for African American athletes at the University of Louisville. Lyle was three years old when his parents moved the family from Tennessee to Louisville. A star athlete at Louisville's Central High School, Lyles was recruited by Louisville and in 1954 broke the school's color barrier for scholarship athletes.[1] Later in life Lyles blazed another path when he became the first African American admitted to Rover Road Country Club.[2]

The speedy Lyles starred for the Cardinals in football and track. As a freshman, he joined senior

Lenny Lyles.

quarterback John Unitas in the Louisville backfield in 1954. A running back, he was known as the "Fastest Man in Football" and was timed at 9.4 seconds in the 100-yard dash. Lyles was a four-year starter for the Cardinals rushing for 2786 yards for his career. During his senior season in 1957 he ran for 1,207 yards, the most in college football, as he became the first Cardinal to rush for more than 1,000 yards in a season.[3]

For his senior efforts, Lyles was named to the Little All-America team after helping the Cardinals go 9–1 and record a victory in their first bowl appearance, a 34–20 decision over Drake in the 1958 Sun Bowl. Lyles was injured in the first quarter and fellow running back Ken Porco earned Most Valuable Player honors after rushing for 119 yards and one touchdown on 20 carries.

Lyles left Louisville having scored 49 total touchdowns, 42 rushing touchdowns and averaging 7.0 yards per carry during his college career, all school records. His 300 points scored is also a school record for non-kickers.

Selected in the first round of the 1958 NFL draft, Lyles was converted to cornerback by the Colts, Baltimore being well-stocked in the backfield with speedy right halfback/flanker Lenny Moore, shifty left halfback L.G. Dupre and bruising fullback Alan "The Horse" Ameche. Lyles did see time on offense his first two years in the NFL, totaling 126 yards rushing and receiving and scoring three touchdowns.

In joining the Colts Lyles joined ex–Cardinal teammate Johnny Unitas. Wearing No. 26 in his first season in Baltimore, Lyles returned 11 kickoffs for 398 yards and led the league with two returns for touchdowns and a long of 103 yards in a 51–38 victory over visiting Western Conference rival Chicago on October 4. Three weeks later on October 26 Lyles returned a kick 101 yards for a score in a 35–10 win over Washington.

By season's end Lyles averaged 36.2 yards per return. On defense, he was credited with three fumble recoveries. Lyles also saw action on offense, starting in Week Four against Detroit in Briggs Stadium on October 19. Lyles capped the Colts' scoring in a 40–14 romp when he raced 27 yards to the end zone on his lone carry of the game. The following week he had four carries for minus-10 yards in a 25-point win over Washington but still contributed two catches for 16 yards. In Week Six Lyles gouged Green Bay for 34 yards on 13 carries and added eight yards and a touchdown on three catches during a 56–0 Colts romp.

Lyles didn't get another carry until Week Nine and while he was limited to minus-10 yards on three carries the Colts still routed the Rams 34–7. In Los Angeles for the penultimate game of the regular season Lyles carried one time for no gain in a 30–28 loss.

Lyles' play-making abilities helped Baltimore finish with a 9–3 record and win its first Western Conference title. On December 28 the Colts faced the Eastern champion Giants in the NFL title game at Yankee Stadium.

The Giants had rallied to edge the Colts 24–21 on a Pat Summerall field goal in New York in Week Seven of the regular season on November 9.[4] Amid unseasonably warm conditions for Christmas week in New York, the rematch was also tight. Writing a script as dramatic as any penned by Madison Avenue ad men, the underdog Giants held a 17–14 fourth quarter lead until Steve Myhra's 20-yard field goal tied the game at 17 in the closing seconds and forced pro football's first sudden death championship game.[5]

With a national television audience gripped by the drama unfolding in sport's greatest cathedral, Unitas and the great Giants defense matched up one final time in overtime. As darkness settled on Yankee Stadium, Unitas handed off to Ameche and the Horse galloped in from a yard out to give Baltimore a 23–17 win. It's been called the "Greatest Game Ever Played" and while that may be debatable the game's historical significance is unassailable.

"Of all the games, the 1958 sudden-death against the New York Giants was something I'll never forget," Lyles told John Steadman of the *Baltimore Sun* in 1994. "Look at my championship ring. Being a rookie in a title game was a nervous experience. I was praying I wouldn't fumble one of those kicks. I didn't want to make a mistake to take us out of the game."[6]

Lyles, who returned two kicks for 39 yards with a long of 20 in the title game, was a champion in his first season in pro football. As a number one pick Lyles had a lot to live up to in Baltimore—Moore and future Hall of Fame offensive tackle/guard Jim Parker were the team's two previous top selections. Due to his difficulty relaxing during his rookie season Lyles was placed on waivers and selected by San Francisco. Lyles told Steadman the move surprised him since the Colts chose to keep injured Harold Lewis, whose hand was in a cast. "That was a low day for me. I had my bag packed and went out the door."[7]

In San Francisco Lyles led the NFL in 1959 in kick returns (25) and return yardage (565). He had a long return of 46 yards and averaged 22.6 yards per return. Lyles stayed with the 49ers through 1960 and led the NFL in return average (30.9) that season, including a 97-yarder for a touchdown against his former team, the Colts, on December 18 in San Francisco's Kezar Stadium. Lyles' score stood as the league's longest return in 1960 and helped spark a 34–10 win, ending Baltimore's two-year reign as Western Conference kings and ushering in Vince Lombardi's decade of dominance in Green Bay.[8]

By 1961 Lyles was back in Baltimore after being reclaimed on waivers by the Colts and was bearing the more familiar uniform number of 43. Lyles told Steadman the turning point for him came upon his return to Baltimore when star defensive end Gino Marchetti told him the Colts had made a mistake letting him go.

"I'm glad you're back," Marchetti told Lyles.

"That gave me a feeling I never had before," Lyles told Steadman. "The Colts wanted me."[9]

The NFL expanded from a 12-game schedule to 14 games in 1961 and the 6'2," 202-pound 25-year-old played in every game, resuming his duties as return specialist and averaging 24.0 yards on 28 returns. Lyles was limited to six games in 1962. The Colts went 7–7, and their fourth-place finish led to head coach Weeb Ewbank's firing by principal owner Carroll Rosenbloom and the hiring of former Baltimore defensive back Don Shula.

The architect of the great Detroit Lions defensive units of the early 1960s, Shula gave Lyles his first full-time starting position in pro football, installing him at right cornerback for the 1963 season. Lyles recorded two interceptions and Baltimore returned to its winning ways, finishing 8–6.

The 1964 regular season was the greatest in team history to that point. The Colts cruised to the conference crown with a 12–2 record that was the NFL's best and ranked number one in the league in both offense and defense. Lyles had two interceptions and a fumble recovery and played a pivotal role in Baltimore surrendering just 225 points.[10]

The Colts were seven-point favorites in the NFL championship game in Cleveland's muddy Municipal Stadium on December 27. But Browns quarterback Frank Ryan filled the steel-gray skies with footballs and found wide receiver Gary Collins for three touchdowns. Lou Groza kicked two field goals and Cleveland's unheralded defense forced four turnovers in a stunning 27–0 win.

The 1965 season saw the Colts challenge for another conference title. Despite losing Unitas, the reigning NFL MVP, and his backup Gary Cuozzo to injuries, the Colts turned the QB duties over to versatile halfback Tom Matte. Lyles contributed an interception and two fumble recoveries to a defense that wasn't as dominant as the season before but still ranked among the league's best in fewest points allowed.

The Colts clinched a first-place tie in the West with Green Bay on the final day of the regular season to force the NFL's first one-game playoff since the Browns-Giants Eastern showdown in 1958. Baltimore had dropped its two previous decisions to the Packers in 1965 but it was the Colts who struck first in the playoff game on the day after Christmas in frozen Lambeau Field.

Lyles provided an immediate impact. On the game's first play from scrimmage Green Bay quarterback Bart Starr passed to tight end Bill Anderson in the left flat. Lyles drove his helmet and shoulders into Anderson's midsection, forcing a fumble that was scooped up by Don Shinnick. The Colts' right linebacker returned the loose ball 25 yards down the sideline for a 7–0 lead. Left-footed Lou Michaels made it 10–0 in the second quarter with a 15-yard field goal. Playing without the injured Starr—Green Bay's field general having suffered bruised ribs in attempting to tackle Shinnick on the fumble recovery—the Packers rallied behind backup Zeke Bratkowski. Halfback Paul Hornung plowed to pay dirt from a yard out in the third quarter and Don Chandler's disputed 22-yard field goal in the fourth tied the game at 10-all and forced the NFL's first overtime postseason game since the 1958 Colts-Giants classic.

The Packers prevailed in overtime when Chandler's second field goal cleared the cross bar from 25 yards out. The loss left Lyles and the Colts out of the championship game and prevented Baltimore from a championship rematch with Cleveland. Lyles and Co. would have to wait three years to get another postseason shot at the Browns.

The 1966 season resulted in Lyles' lone Pro Bowl appearance. He registered an interception and three fumble recoveries for a Colts squad that went 9–5 and dropped two decisions to the Packers—24–3 in the season opener on a Saturday night in Green Bay and 14–10 in mud-caked Memorial Stadium in Baltimore in another Saturday night game, this on December 10. Unitas' turnover late in the second game has been referred to as the "Million Dollar Fumble" for it clinched another conference championship for Green Bay and put the Packers on the path to the historic first Super Bowl meeting with the champion of the American Football League, the Kansas City Chiefs.

The 1967 season saw the start of a new era in the NFL as the league switched from two conferences to four divisions and expanded the playoffs from two teams to four. For Lyles and the Colts, 1967 was another hard-luck story. Dueling throughout the season with the Los Angeles Rams in the newly-formed Coastal Division, the Colts took an NFL-best 11–0–2 record into the Los Angeles Coliseum in the season finale. Lyles and the defense, coached by future legends Bill Arnsparger and Chuck Noll, had allowed just 164 points through their first 13 games. Lyles produced five interceptions and a fumble recovery and Baltimore ranked with the Rams' renowned "Fearsome Foursome," Dallas' "Doomsday" and Green Bay's defense as one of the top units in the NFL. For the fourth straight season the Colts failed to win the big game that really mattered and yielded a season-high 34 points in a lopsided loss to Los Angeles.

In 1968, a year which saw Cliff Nobles' instrumental "The Horse" peak on the pop charts, the Colts romped through the league and produced a 13–1 record that matched the 1962 Packers as the best in modern NFL history to that point. Lyles pirated five passes and teamed with fellow veteran cornerback Bobby Boyd and safeties Rick Volk and Jerry Logan in a smothering secondary. The Baltimore defense led the league with just 144 points allowed, produced three shutouts and held ten of 14 opponents to ten points or less.[11]

Journeyman Earl Morrall earned NFL MVP honors after replacing an injured Unitas and the Colts captured the Coastal crown and then mauled Joe Kapp and the Minnesota Vikings 24–14 in a muddy Western Conference championship game in icy Memorial Stadium.

In the NFL championship game against a Browns squad that supplied the lone blemish on Baltimore's regular-season record, a 30–20 upset of the Colts in Memorial Stadium on October 20, the Colts buried Cleveland 34–0 in cold, cloud-shrouded Municipal Stadium. Baltimore's shutout was its fourth of the season and sent the NFL champions into Super Bowl III as heavy favorites to defeat a Jets squad coached by former Baltimore boss Ewbank.

The game featured key figures from the 1958 NFL overtime classic played a decade earlier—Lyles, Shinnick, Unitas and Ordell Braase; former Colts Ewbank and cornerback Johnny Sample; and ex–New York Giant Don Maynard. Considered by many the greatest team in NFL history after having won a then league-record 15 games, the Colts were expected to exceed the dominance displayed by Green Bay over AFL champions Kansas City and Oakland in Super Bowls I and II.

What wasn't known outside the Colts locker room at the time was that the right side of the Baltimore defense was suffering physically. Lyles was battling a flu that weakened him significantly and Braase, Baltimore's right defensive end, had a bad back. Since the strength of the Jets' ground game lay in a left side that listed all-stars in ex–Colts' training camp attendee Winston Hill at tackle and former Oilers' great Bob Talamini at guard, Ewbank had planned to attack the right side of Baltimore's defense. Also, with Maynard limping, Jets quarterback Joe Namath, who brashly "guaranteed" a Jet victory the Thursday prior to Super Sunday, was planning on using split end George Sauer as his primary target.

The Colts' injuries and the Jets' planning produced a perfect storm that led to New York's shocking 16–7 upset. A weakened Lyles struggled to stop Sauer, who hauled in eight catches for 133 yards, and Lyles and Braase could not close down a left-handed running attack that saw fullback Matt Snell batter his way to 121 yards and New York's lone touchdown. Snell's second-quarter score marked the first time the AFL led the NFL in the Super Bowl and he became the first 100-yard rusher in Super Bowl history.[12]

Lyles returned for the 1969 season but lost his starting job to rookie Tommy Maxwell. Baltimore never recovered from its stunning defeat in Super Bowl III and finished 8–5–1 and a distant second to the Rams in the Coastal standings. Lyles finished his career with 16 interceptions, two of which were returned for touchdowns, 201 interception return yards and 13 fumble recoveries. As a kick return specialist he produced 2,161 return yards and averaged 26.7 yards per return.

The final season of Lyles' 12-year pro career was also the final year the NFL and AFL would operate as separate leagues. The warring leagues merged for the 1970 season and Baltimore joined Cleveland and Pittsburgh in the newly formed American Football Conference. Had Lyles stayed with the Colts for one more season he would have gained another NFL championship and an elusive Super Bowl victory, Baltimore beating Dallas 16–13 in Super Bowl V.

Lyles returned to Louisville and was a successful businessman, developer, and entrepreneur.[13] He helped revitalize the Smoketown area where he had grown up and served as a role model and mentor for minority youths.[14] Lyles contributed generously to several area charities, particularly those that were minority-based. In 1994, he returned to Baltimore to help support the Baltimore Ravens' Ed Block Courage Award and its cause of aiding abused children.[15] He was recognized by the National Junior Chamber of Congress as one of the country's top ten young business executives, an honor rarely bestowed upon former athletes.[16]

Lyles died at age 75 on November 20, 2011, at Louisville Jewish Hospital. He was preceded in death by his sons, Christopher Lyles and Michael Lyles; his mother, Alicia Lyles; and a sister, Doris Ferrell of Atlanta. Lyles was survived by his wife, the former Faith Wilson, whom he married in 1957; by another son Leonard Lyles; and by two nieces and several cousins.[17]

Lyles has been honored with a statue in the University of Louisville's Cardinal Park, which also serves as the site for the Lenny Lyles/Clark Wood Track Invitational. Louisville Central High School is host to the Lenny Lyles Invitational Track Meet.

Lyles had credited Wood, his former track coach at Louisville, for "shaping" his life. Wood pushed him to excel and he made sure Lyles got to the Penn Relays, Drake Relays and other major competitions.[18]

That Lyles was black and Wood white didn't matter to either man.

"The black-white matter shouldn't be an issue," Lyles stated. "People are people. Some act badly, others are good…. But, again, people are people."[19]

NOTES

1. "Leonard Everett 'Lenny' Lyles Obituary," *The Courier-Journal*, November 23, 2011.
2. John Steadman, "Former Colt Lyles Chooses to Give Something Back," *Baltimore Sun*, March 9, 1994.
3. Mike Rutherford, "Cardinal Football Legend Lenny Lyles Passes Away," CardChronicle.com, November 21, 2011.
4. Pro-football-reference.com.
5. *Ibid.*
6. Steadman.
7. *Ibid.*
8. Pro-football-reference.com.
9. Steadman.
10. Pro-football-reference.com.
11. *Ibid.*
12. *Ibid.*
13. Steadman.
14. "Lyles Obituary."
15. Steadman.
16. *Ibid.*
17. "Lyles Obituary."
18. Steadman.
19. *Ibid.*

Gino Marchetti

NEAL GOLDEN

Defensive end Gino Marchetti is one of six players on the 1958 Baltimore Colts who have earned election to the Pro Football Hall of Fame. He was also a member of one of the greatest college football teams that few have heard of. But before participating in football at the college level, Gino served his country with distinction.

Born the son of Italian immigrants in Smithers, West Virginia, on January 2, 1927, Marchetti enlisted in the U.S. Army after graduating from high school in Antioch California, where he earned the Most Valuable Player award as a senior.[1] He served in the army as a machine gunner in the Battle of the Bulge. The war experience changed Gino as it did so many other servicemen:

> I was what you call, maybe, a little wild.... I had gotten into a little trouble with one of the teachers. So they were going to throw me out of school. I had a choice: If I got thrown out of school, I'd have had to go home and face my father, or I could join the service.... Over there really changed me. When I heard the shells that first time, I thought about all the things in life that I did wrong to my mother.... I made a vow that if I ever got home that my life would change, which it did. I became more responsible, a better family member than I had been.[2]

Returning to California after the war, Gino wanted to continue playing football: "When I got out of the service in 1946, I still had an urge to play football, but I could not go to college to play football. I really was not good enough. Me and my buddies from Antioch High got together and formed a semi-pro team. We started playing local teams around the Bay area and Antioch, just to play. It was a lot of fun and good experience."[3]

The following year, he attended Modesto (CA) Junior College. Modesto's coaches had recruited Marchetti's brother, but told Gino he could tag along also. His play on the gridiron improved, earning him eventual induction into the MJC Hall of Fame.[4]

An immediate reward was a football scholarship to the University of San Francisco. He started at left tackle for Joe Kuharich's undefeated 1951 team on which he was one of eight who played pro football and one of five who made at least one Pro Bowl.[5] Among Gino's team-

Gino Marchetti.

mates were fellow Pro Football Hall of Famers Ollie Matson and Bob St. Clair.[6] Marchetti won All-Coast and All-Catholic honors in his senior season.[7]

The '51 Dons, ranked #14 in the Associated Press poll as the calendar turned to November, were listed among a dozen teams under consideration for the Orange Bowl.[8] But Florida law, like that of almost all other Southern states, prohibited integrated athletic contests.[9] The Dons would be invited only if the team's two African American players did not play. Marchetti and St. Clair chaired a meeting at which the players voted unanimously to reject any bowl bid that required them to leave their black players, Matson and Burt Toler, at home.[10] After that, the four Southern bowls, Gator, Orange, Sugar, and Cotton, crossed the Dons off their lists. Without the money the bowl game would have provided, the University of San Francisco administration decided to end the football program.[11] (The Orange Bowl claims that no invitation was ever sent to the University of San Francisco.)[12]

Marchetti figured that was the end of his football career. "I was not that big, really. I was 6'4" or 6'5", but I only weighed 215. What I had going for me was I had the desire, that's for damn sure. I was also fast and strong for a guy that weighed 215."[13]

The New York Yanks, picked Gino in the second round of the 1952 NFL draft. Two days after the draft, Ted Collins, the Yanks' owner, sold the franchise back to the league and the franchise and assets were granted to a Dallas group and became known as the Dallas Texans. The Texans used Gino at left defensive end. Marchetti recalled:

> I was so excited about going to play professional football. However, I went to the most disorganized camp in the world.... We didn't practice for six or seven weeks. When [head coach] Jimmy Phelan called practice, we really didn't practice. We would play volleyball—with a football—over the goal posts. Two-hand touch. We did a lot of running and fooling around, but I never saw a professional film. I am thinking, "Is this really professional football?" ... I had just gotten married and I was thinking about giving it up, because that is not what I expected.[14]

After a dismal 1–11 season, Dallas ownership returned the franchise to the league, which transferred its assets, including all the players, to a Baltimore ownership group headed by Carroll Rosenbloom.[15]

After a frustrating season at offensive left tackle for coach Keith Molesworth in the Colts' first season,[16] Marchetti blossomed when new coach Weeb Ewbank moved him to defensive end in 1954. Finally in his best position, Gino made the Pro Bowl every season from that year through 1964. He also made first team All-Pro from 1957 through 1962 and again in 1964. He admitted that he gained an edge on the blocker in front of him by anticipating the snap and beating it by a split second. "I guess about ninety or eighty-five percent of the time I played offside. I got into the neutral zone..." When asked why officials didn't penalize him, he replied: "'I got warned a lot.' 'But they never threw a flag?' 'No, because I'd get warned and I'd say, Thanks a lot. Or after a play, I'd say, How'd I look that time? I tried to be nice. But I got as much as I could get.... I wasn't way over ... but I was right on the border, just over the border.'"[17]

Gino became the captain of the defense and an undisputed leader of the entire team. Teammates admired Gino not only for his rugged play in the football trenches but also for his military service in battlefield trenches. He gladly stayed after practice to help young linemen on both sides of the ball.

Marchetti played a central role in the most controversial play of the 1958 championship game. Leading 17–14 in the fourth quarter and trying to ice the game, the Giants faced third and four at their 40. Frank Gifford took a handoff and started to his right behind two pulling guards. Marchetti tackled Frank near the 44 just before Big Daddy Lipscomb came barreling in. Everyone in the pile got up except Gino, who stayed prone with what turned out to be a broken right ankle. Marchetti recalled: "I was able to slip my blocker and get out into the flow. Gifford ran right, and I tackled him. To make sure Frank didn't go any further, Big Daddy hit the whole pile. He just wasn't going to let anybody or anything get to the 44-yard line. Daddy, not Gifford, was the one who broke my ankle."[18]

With the injured member of the Colts lying right where the play ended, referee Ron Gibbs picked up the ball and held it until Marchetti was carted off. When Gibbs put the ball back down, he put it near his back foot instead of his front foot, according to Gifford and some of his teammates. When the measurement showed the ball a foot short, New York punted. Johnny Unitas then led the most famous drive in football history to tie the game.

Marchetti told his stretcher bearers to put him down just outside the sideline so he could watch the rest of the game. "After all those years when we were so bad, I wanted at least to see the finish." When the game went into overtime, the police made Marchetti move into the locker room. "They didn't want to, but they had to. 'It could end any second now,' they said. 'If the stands empty, you'll be trampled.'" The head trainer agreed with the move. Gino was on the verge of going into shock with the pain and the cold. Gino recalled the quiet of the locker room. "We were underground, and the crowd noise was muffled. There was no radio. It was terrible." When asked how much his leg hurt, he replied, "I'd have cried if I wasn't Gino Marchetti."[19] Finally, Gino heard cleat sounds on the ramp to the door. "It burst open," recalled Gino. "And there was Buzz Nutter with the football, saying, 'We're world champions.'" Then Buzz gave the ball to his captain.[20]

Gino continued his fine play the next season at age 32 when the Colts again beat the Giants to defend their title. He stood strong against the run and rushed the passer as well as anyone. If opponents double-teamed him, they opened the door for his fellow defensive linemen to get to the quarterback.[21] Sid Gillman, coach of the Los Angeles Rams, called Marchetti "the greatest player in football. It's a waste of time to run around this guy's end. It's a lost play. You don't bother to try it."[22] Forrest Gregg, himself a Hall of Fame tackle, told an interviewer: "Gino Marchetti was the best all-around football player I played against."[23]

Marchetti explained his technique like this. "I was very, very, very quick. I loved to get my hands on a ballplayer. An offensive lineman has to set up. If I could get to him before he gets his strength, then I had an advantage. That's why I always loved bigger guys than smaller guys because bigger guys couldn't set up as quick. Or during a game they'd get lazy lifting all that weight. So my whole act was getting my hands on somebody. When I got my hands on him, he was mine."[24]

Even when the schedule expanded to 14 games in 1961, Marchetti continued his streak of consecutive games that started in 1956 and ran through the 1964 season, when he retired at age 37.

With the encouragement and financial backing of Rosenbloom, Gino started a fast food restaurant business in the Baltimore area in 1959 with teammate Alan Ameche and other partners.[25] Successful beyond their wildest expectations, the Gino's Restaurant chain expanded throughout the Northeast and needed his full attention.

However, he returned during the 1966 season at the behest of Rosenbloom after a rash of injuries hit the defensive line.[26] Gino played in only four games and functioned more as an assistant coach. He retired again at the end of that season and never looked back. Marchetti entered the Pro Football Hall of Fame six years later.

In 1982, Marchetti and his partners sold their chain of over 400 restaurants to Marriott Corporation for $48.6 million.[27] He later worked for the owner of many Wendy's Restaurants.[28]

Today, Gino lives in a suburb of Philadelphia with his second wife, Joan.[29]

NOTES

1. Don Smith, "Gino Marchetti," *The Coffin Corner* 18, no. 5 (1966).
2. William Gildea, *When the Colts Belonged to Baltimore* (Baltimore: Johns Hopkins University Press, 1994), 139–140.
3. Ken Crippen, "Where Are They Now: Gino Marchetti," Yahoo! Sports, April 15, 2014.
4. *Ibid.*; www.mjc.edu/athletics/halloffame.php.
5. Ron Fimrite, "Best Team You Never Heard Of," *Sports Illustrated*, November 12, 1990.
6. *Ibid.*
7. Smith.
8. *Arkansas Democrat*, November 8, 1951.
9. Daniel Flynn, *The War on Football: Saving America's Game* (Washington, D.C.: Regnery, 2013).
10. Alexander Wolff, "Gino Marchetti," *Sports Illustrated*, July 1, 2016.
11. Fimrite, 124.
12. www.wbur.org/onlyagame/2016/01/02/san-francisco-dons-orange-bowl-undefeated.
13. Crippen.
14. Crippen.
15. www.pressboxonline.com/story/id/3089, December 18, 2007.
16. Crippen.
17. Gildea, 143–144.
18. Tom Callahan, *Johnny U: The Life and Times of John Unitas* (New York: Crown, 2006), 162.
19. *Ibid.*, 163–165.
20. *Ibid.*, 170.
21. Smith.
22. Ron Smith, et al., *The Sporting News Selects Football's 100 Greatest Players: A Celebration of the 20th Century's Best* (NTC/Contemporary Publishing Group, 1999).
23. "Chat Transcript with Forrest Gregg," profootballhof.com, 2000.
24. Gildea,144.
25. Dave Klein, *The Game of Their Lives* (New York: Random House, 1976), 48.
26. Gildea,137.
27. *Ibid.*, 132.
28. Crippen.
29. Gildea, 146–147.

Lenny Moore

RICK SHMELTER

Hundreds of individuals have found their place among the immortals in the Professional Football Hall of Fame. Greatness at the running back position has earned many a bronze bust in the game's shrine. Some were bruising punishers that pulverized their way between the tackles, while others were fleet-footed, multi-purpose performers.

The latter category represented the talents of Leonard Edward Moore, who used deception and speed to become a scoring threat whenever his hands touched the ball. Moore stood tall not only on Baltimore's talent-laden team of the late 1950s, but throughout the entire NFL.

The incredible exploits that led Moore to the Professional Football Hall of Fame began in Reading, Pennsylvania, on November 25, 1933, as one of eight children born to a steel mill-working father. Like so many youngsters growing up in this region, the future could either be following family members into the tough, back-breaking labor of the steel mills, or dreams of pursuing other ambitions.[1]

Lenny Moore became focused on taking his talents and parlaying them into a prosperous future. His focus was not only on his personal growth, but also to assist his parents monetarily. Moore possessed extraordinary athletic skills from an early age and in addition to

Lenny Moore.

being proficient at several sports, his best attribute was speed. As an adolescent, Moore was tall with long legs, making him a lightning quick force on any playing surface.[2] Unfortunately, those athletic talents were almost lost to the times in which Moore lived. In the late 1940s while in his early teens, he felt that there would be no avenues open to him in professional sports due to the color of his skin. No African Americans were making news in America's major sports at the time, and this allowed defeatism to rear its ugly head for Moore. He loved being a part of a team, but without hope to pursue his love of football, his grades began to slip as he felt his only option was to join the army following his junior year of high school.[3]

All that changed when the Los Angeles Rams broke the unwritten NFL owners' ban against black players in 1946 by signing Kenny Washington and Woody Strode, and the Brooklyn Dodgers broke the color barrier in Major League Baseball by signing Jackie Robinson a year later. Things began to brighten up for Moore.

With renewed hope, coupled with natural abilities, and encouragement from his head coach, Moore became a local legend at Reading High School, dubbed "the Castle on the Hill." He was an excellent all-around athlete in high school, starring on the hardwood, diamond and track, but his journey to immortality started on the gridiron.[4] Moore considered Reading football coach Andy Stopper "an angel with a clipboard," and the one most responsible for putting the gifted athlete back on track toward his goal of taking the sport of football as far as he could. Stopper did not care about the color of a person's skin, only his ability. He helped foster a community not divided by race unlike a great portion of America.[5] Reading High School's motto was "Tell Me Why You Are Here?"[6] Moore's display of superior athletic skills made that an easy question to answer. He ran faster, as well as over and around, anyone wearing an opposing football uniform.

Nicknamed "the Reading Rambler" Moore scored 22 touchdowns during his high school career. He won the 1951 Astor Theater Award as the best athlete in Reading, was also recognized as the top back throughout central Pennsylvania, found a place on the Pennsylvania All-Century Team, and was enshrined into the Berks County Hall of Fame in 2012. In Moore's final game as a scholastic against Pottsville in 1951, he dazzled a crowd of 10,000 by scoring three touchdowns.[7]

Even though his high school playing days were over, Moore's devotion to his hometown never faded. He returned to the area for many events, including speaking engagements for business and youth groups. The respect he held for Coach Stopper also never waned. Even when he was an established star in the NFL, Moore would bring some of his Baltimore teammates back to Reading, much to the excitement of neighborhood children that clamored around the group and left with wide-eyed enthusiasm after obtaining autographs.[8]

Moore's incredible talent on the football field attracted attention from college programs. With the help of Coach Stopper, and assistant coach Bob Perugini, Moore decided to stay in his home state and accept a scholarship to Penn State, becoming the first in his family to attend college.[9] Perugini was a massive man and a former lineman at Penn State. His contacts at the college were still strong. In the past, Stopper and Perugini sent some of their top talent to Penn State, and once Penn State assistant coach Sever Torretti became aware of Moore, he pursued the highly gifted offensive machine.[10] Like Major League Baseball and the NFL, the college ranks became integrated in the 1940s. Penn State was no exception, and by the time Moore set foot on the campus, Penn State was only five years removed from allowing African Americans onto the football team.[11]

For many, climbing the next rung on the ladder of athletic competition can prove troublesome. Then there are those gifted athletes that never miss a beat, which was the category Moore fell into for Penn State head coach Rip Engle. During this time in college football history, freshmen were prohibited from playing on the varsity team. Moore had to wait to exhibit his skills, but when he did, he made up for lost time. In his sophomore season of 1953, Moore ran for 601 yards and scored by way of some long jaunts through the opposition.[12]

Moore emerged as one of the top running backs in the country during his junior campaign, finishing with the second highest amount of rushing yards in the nation (1,082 yards) for an eight yards per carry average and ten touchdowns. His average of eight yards a carry in 1954 remains a Penn State record. He also set a Penn State single season record as a junior with 1,486 all-purpose yards, that has since been broken.

In his senior year, Moore ran for 697 yards, five touchdowns, and averaged 5.1 yards per carry. He left Penn State as the football program's all-time leading career rusher (2,380 yards). At the time he was also first in the school's record books with 3,543 all-purpose yards, and 12 games with 100 yards rushing. In addition, when not dazzling the crowds and frustrating the opposition on offense, Moore led the Nittany Lions in interceptions twice, kickoff returns two times, and punt returns three times.[13]

Penn State head coach Rip Engle claimed that Moore was the greatest back he ever coached.[14] Joe Paterno was an assistant under Engle during Moore's career at Penn State.

Years later, as head coach of the Nittany Lions, Paterno said that Moore was possibly the best player he was ever around.[15]

By 1956, Moore's exceptional talents had conquered the high school and college ranks, and he was ready to climb the final rung of the athletic ladder, the National Football League. Weeb Ewbank was the head coach of the Baltimore Colts at the time Moore was eligible for the NFL draft. Allegedly, it was Paterno that connected Moore to the Colts after giving an incredible recommendation about the fleet-footed back to Ewbank. Paterno's praise helped convince Ewbank to select Moore with the team's first pick (ninth overall) in the 1956 NFL draft held on November 29, 1955.[16]

Long and lean at 6'1" and 175 pounds while blazing his way through opponents at Penn State, Moore's speed was never in question with pro scouts. The concern with many of the NFL organizations was if he would be durable enough for the fierce physical poundings given out in the highest level of competition. The Colts were not concerned with Moore's durability, and in time, Baltimore's decision to select "the Reading Rambler" made the Colts look like gridiron savants. Once in the pros, Moore did beef up to 190 pounds, which allowed him to have more power.[17]

When Moore arrived in Baltimore, the Colts were in the midst of transforming from a very bad team to one of relevance by the end of the Fabulous Fifties. Along with Moore at this time, names like Unitas, Berry, Donovan, Lipscomb, Marchetti and Parker became icons in Baltimore and legends of the game.

As throughout his entire sports career up to this time, Moore's amazing speed catapulted him into the Colts' starting lineup during his rookie year. In his inaugural professional season, Moore averaged 7.5 yards per carry to lead all NFL running backs in 1956. He achieved the top spot by rushing for 649 yards on a mere 86 carries.[18] Moore was selected the 1956 NFL Rookie of the Year, and earned a trip to the Pro Bowl.

Despite his stellar rookie season, Ewbank and some of Moore's teammates questioned his work ethic. They felt that Moore lacked the drive to enhance the abilities he possessed. Years after Moore hung up his cleats and moved on to the next phase of his life, he reflected back and knew of his shortcomings. He felt that extra work was not needed to reach the NFL, so why not continue relying on his natural abilities? Moore experienced a career-altering moment in his second season with the Colts that changed his perspective, and improved his work ethic.[19]

In 1957 Baltimore was a young team on the cusp of creating something special. They opened the season with three straight wins. Riding high atop of the Western Conference, the Colts charged into Detroit, also a legitimate contender. Initially, it appeared that Baltimore was sending a message to the rest of the league by jumping out to what seemed to be an insurmountable 27–3 lead over the Lions. With 55,000 Motor City faithful cheering them on, the Lions roared back to close the deficit to 27–24. As the closing minutes ticked down, Lenny Moore's professional football life took a positive upswing through a negative situation. With the ball in Baltimore's possession, the offense wanted to kill the clock and get out of Detroit with their perfect season intact. Unfortunately, Moore fumbled, the Lions recovered, and Detroit's Hall of Fame quarterback, Bobby Layne, quickly capitalized on the mishap by throwing a long touchdown pass that gave the Lions the victory, and eventually the NFL title a few months later. Baltimore's fortunes were reversed after the shocking loss as they dropped their next two games. They rebounded by winning four in a row, but ended the year with two losses to finish at 7–5, one game off the Western lead.[20]

Despite the Colts' harsh fall from the summit of the conference, Moore realized that his lackadaisical approach caused his turnover in Detroit, and he vowed to work harder during practice to improve on his talents.[21] Natural ability mixed with a strong work ethic can result in unlimited success in any athletic endeavor. Moore proved this in 1958, as he channeled both forces to create a blue and white-clad offensive juggernaut that became a scoring threat every time he touched the ball.

The road to glory for Moore during Baltimore's incredible 1958 season started with him scoring the team's first touchdown, and finishing with 36 yards on seven carries in the season opener. He also caught six passes for an additional 59 yards in a 28–15 win over Detroit. Moore suffered a non-displaced fracture of the nose, but team doctors felt the injury would not prevent him from playing.[22]

The team doctors were right in their diagnosis, as Moore's fractured nose did not hamper him the following week in a 51–38 win over the Chicago Bears. Moore set a team record with four touchdowns in one game. He evenly distributed the touchdowns, scoring two on the ground and a pair on receptions. He finished with 71 rushing yards on ten carries and caught three passes for 118 yards.[23]

Moore and the Colts continued to roll, and in a rematch with Detroit during the fourth week of the season, he ran for 136 yards and a touchdown on 12 carries, leading the Colts to a 40–14 victory and 4–0 start. In a 35–10 win over Washington the following week, Moore gained 60 yards on seven carries, and caught two passes for 62 yards. In this game, Moore banged up his knee, but like the nose injury in the opener, it would not stop him from playing.[24]

The Colts reached the halfway point of the season with a perfect 6–0 record thanks to a 56–0 mauling over the Green Bay Packers. Even though he was used sparingly in this blowout, Moore ate up 63 yards of an 83-yard second quarter drive after catching a pass from Johnny Unitas.[25]

The Colts entered the second half of the season against the New York Giants at famed Yankee Stadium. Moore was still nursing a tender knee. Used primarily as a receiver, Moore turned in a brilliant performance.[26] He caught six passes for 181 yards and a pair of touchdowns. Unfortunately, the Giants ended the Colts' unbeaten streak that day by the score of 24–21.

Baltimore got back to their winning ways by running off three straight victories. After a 17–0 win over Chicago, the Colts returned home for the first time in three weeks for a game against the Los Angeles Rams. In a 34–7 win, Moore had six receptions for 157 yards, and scored two touchdowns. His first six-pointer came after catching a Johnny Unitas pass on Baltimore's first play from scrimmage. He then raced 58 yards for the score, and followed that up with an eight-yard touchdown run in the second quarter. His time on the field was limited in the second half due to a bruised knee.[27] One week later, the San Francisco 49ers came to town for the Colts' final home game of the year. The 49ers gave the Baltimore fans little to cheer about, as they held a 27–7 lead at the half. However, in the second half, the Colts came alive and prevailed, 35–27, to not only finish the regular season with a spotless 6–0 record at home, but also clinch the franchise's first-ever championship of any kind by emerging from this comeback win with the Western Conference title firmly in their grasp. In a 21-point fourth quarter, it was a 73-yard touchdown run by Moore that put the Colts in the lead to stay. For the game, Moore led all ball carriers with 114 yards on just eight attempts.[28]

The newly crowned Western champions traveled to Los Angeles on the first weekend of December to face the 6–4 Rams. With an incredible crowd of 100,202 inside the behemoth Los Angeles Memorial Coliseum, the Colts opened up a 14–3 first quarter lead, with Moore assisting the team after scoring on a five-yard pass from Unitas. The Rams did not go quietly in front of their massive fan base, and rallied to claim a 30–28 victory.[29] The Colts finished the regular season, also on the west coast, against San Francisco. The 49ers got some revenge after blowing such a big lead two weeks earlier in Baltimore by claiming the regular season finale 21–12, as the Colts held only a brief 3–0 lead in the first quarter. Moore had a solid performance by rushing for 73 yards on seven carries, and caught three passes for 44 yards.[30]

The 1958 season not only proved to be a breakout season for the Colts as a team, but for Lenny Moore as well. He rushed for 598 yards and seven touchdowns, and led the NFL with a 7.3 yards per carry average. He also caught a career-high 50 passes for 938 yards for an 18.8 yards per carry average and seven touchdowns. In all, he compiled 1,536 total yards from scrimmage. His efforts did not go unnoticed when the NFL dished out honors. He earned his second Pro Bowl and his first All-Pro selection.[31] His great individual season was then capped by being a member of the 1958 NFL champion Colts. Baltimore and Moore achieved that immortal accolade by going into Yankee Stadium and beating the New York Giants, 23–17, in overtime to reign supreme over the league. In what was forever dubbed "the Greatest Game Ever Played," Moore hauled in six receptions for 101 yards, with the longest going for 60 yards, and he also added 23 yards rushing on eight carries.[32]

With the world championship label firmly and forever attached to the Baltimore Colts, what was left for an encore? The Colts only took a mere 364 days to answer that question. In 1959, the Colts once again ran roughshod over the NFL, and Moore, at age 26, was at the height of his individual glory. He ran for 422 yards and two touchdowns, and caught 47 passes for 846 yards and six touchdowns. He earned his second of four straight All-Pro selections, and another trip to the Pro Bowl. As a team, the Colts once again finished at 9–3, won the Western Conference, and faced the Giants in a rematch of the previous NFL title clash, held one day shy of the one-year anniversary of "the Greatest Game Ever Played." This time out, Baltimore's Memorial Stadium hosted the NFL title game, and the Colts did not allow for a nail-biting climax. After trailing 9–7 heading into the fourth quarter, Baltimore exploded for 24 points while allowing a mere seven, and easily repeated as champions by way of a 31–16 victory. Moore opened the scoring with a 60-yard reception from Unitas, and finished the game with three receptions for 126 yards.[33]

In 1960 and 1961, the Colts suffered through two disappointing seasons but Moore again made the Pro Bowl and first team All-Pro. In 1960, he rushed for 374 yards on 91 carries with four touchdowns and caught 45 passes for 936 yards and nine touchdowns. In 1961 he ran for 648 yards on 92 carries (a seven yard average) with seven touchdowns and grabbed 49 passes for 728 yards and eight touchdowns.

However, the shift to President Kennedy's "New Frontier" in the 1960s saw changes in the way Moore was used. After acquiring Jimmy Orr from the Steelers in 1961, Weeb Ewbank made the decision to use Moore strictly as a running back instead of splitting his time as a runner and receiver. Moore took the news as the majority of competitors would. Whatever was best for the team proved the standard answer, but he truly wished that he could have remained solely as a flanker.[34]

Then, during a preseason game against Pittsburgh in 1962, Moore was doing what he did best, tearing through a defense for a long gain. Unfortunately, on this occasion, he paid a serious price. After picking up 43 yards, Moore was blasted out of bounds by a pair of defenders. A sharp, shooting pain went through his knee while falling to the ground, and it immediately became apparent that something was wrong. Moore suffered a cracked kneecap that kept him off the field for five weeks, and when he did return, his trademark breakaway speed ceased to exist. It was the start of a bleak time in his professional career.[35] Moore caught only 18 passes in 1962, but he still made the Pro Bowl as he gained 470 yards on the ground.

In 1963, during the preseason, Moore's woes continued. First he suffered a hip pointer, and right before the start of the regular season, he was stricken with a severe case of appendicitis that resulted in emergency surgery. If those two problems were not enough, he was sacked yet again upon his return to the field. After playing a few weeks, Moore had his helmet knocked off and his head collided with either a foot or elbow. Regardless of the limb that struck him in the head, the effects hampered Moore's progress. Dizziness and blurred vision were the results of the blow to the head, and by this point, new head coach Don Shula decided to replace the former All-Pro standout with Tom Matte at halfback.[36]

This rash of medical problems over the previous seasons, coupled with him turning 30 years old, saw Moore's name mentioned in trade rumors. The rumors turned to apparent reality when it was reported that New York linebacker Sam Huff or Dallas running back Don Perkins might be on their way to Baltimore in exchange for Moore.[37]

The thought of being cast away after suffering through a rough patch in his career stirred up emotional disdain, but also sparked a competitive fire that had Moore on a quest to prove all detractors very wrong in their assessment of his abilities. The trade never materialized, so Moore remained with the Colts going into the 1964 season. His objective for the year was to silence the critics with a return to glory. By the end of the year, Moore backed up his words with an excellent display of renewed vigor. He ran for 584 yards, scored a league-high 16 rushing touchdowns, and 20 overall. Moore was one of the main weapons used in Baltimore's return to championship-caliber play, as the Colts captured their third conference title with Moore on the team. They finished at 12–2 for the best record in the NFL, but even though heavily favored to win the league title, they lost to Cleveland, 27–0, in a shocking upset. Moore's incredible turnaround made him an easy selection for the 1964 NFL Comeback Player of the Year Award, and he also took home the 1964 NEA NFL Most Valuable Player of the Year Award.[38]

With his quest to return to top form complete, Moore carried on with the Colts for an additional three seasons, retiring after the 1967 campaign. When the greatness of Lenny Moore reached its climax after 12 professional seasons, he left behind an illustrious body of work. He rushed for 5,174 yards, caught 363 passes for 6,039 yards, and scored 113 touchdowns, which was second only to the great Jim Brown for many years. He set an NFL record with 18 straight games of scoring at least one touchdown between 1963 and 1965. He was selected to the Pro Bowl seven times (1956, 1958–62, 1964), earned five All-Pro selections (1958–61, 1964), is a member of the NFL's 50th Anniversary Team (1969), the NFL 1950s All-Decade Team, and had his famed number 24 retired, where it resides along with other Baltimore Colts greats in M & T Bank Stadium, the home of the Baltimore Ravens. On October 8, 2013, Moore also had a road in Baltimore County named in his honor, in addition to many other accolades bestowed on him through the years.[39]

After eight years away from the game, and over a career that covered seven miles of real estate in stadiums from coast to coast, Lenny Moore took his place among the game's immortals with his induction into the Professional Football Hall of Fame on August 2, 1975, along with Roosevelt Brown, George Conner and Dante Lavelli.

Life after football saw Moore work one year with CBS as a football analyst. He later returned to the Colts doing community relations work from 1975 until they moved to Indianapolis following the 1983 season. It was then on to a career with the state of Maryland working in the Department of Juvenile Services. During his football career dating back to high school, Moore received many monikers, all of which accented his skills. His speed earned him the nicknames "the Reading Rambler" and "Lightning Lenny," "Sputnik" for the fear he instilled in defenses, and "Spats" for the way he taped his cleats. All were very creative. However, the one label to best define the pride of Reading, Pennsylvania, and the city of Baltimore, is to just call Lenny Moore a legend.[40]

NOTES

1. George Sullivan, *The Great Running Backs* (New York: Penguin, 1972), 107.
2. *Ibid.*
3. Lenny Moore with Jeffrey Jay Ellish, *All Things Being Equal* (Champaign, IL: Sports Publishing, 2005), 11.
4. Sullivan, 107.
5. Moore, 13.
6. https://en.wikipedia.org/wiki/Reading_Senior_High_School_(Reading,_Pennsylvania).
7. John A. Stopper, "Lenny Moore: Football Legend Still Feels at Home in Reading," *Reading* (PA) *Eagle*, August 8, 2010.
8. *Ibid.*
9. *Ibid.*
10. Moore, 18.
11. *Ibid.*, 29.
12. www.profootballhof.com/news/college-days-lenny-moore1.
13. *Ibid.*
14. *Ibid.*
15. Lori Shontz, "Lenny Moore: Penn State's Greatest Ever?" pennstatermag.com, September 12, 2009.
16. *Ibid.*
17. Sullivan, 107–108.
18. *Ibid.*, 108.
19. *Ibid.*
20. *Ibid.*, 108–109.
21. *Ibid.*, 109.
22. *Baltimore Sun*, September 29, 1958.
23. *Baltimore Sun*, October 5, 1958.
24. *Baltimore Sun*, October 27, 1958.
25. *Baltimore Sun*, November 3, 1958.
26. *Baltimore Sun*, November 10, 1958.
27. *Baltimore Sun*, November 24, 1958.
28. *Baltimore Sun*, December 1, 1958.
29. *Baltimore Sun*, December 7, 1958.
30. *Baltimore Sun*, December 15, 1958.
31. https://en.wikipedia.org/wiki/Lenny_Moore.
32. *Baltimore Sun*, December 29, 1958.
33. "1959 Baltimore Colts," Pro-football-reference.com.
34. Sullivan, 111.
35. *Ibid.*, 111–112.
36. *Ibid.*

37. *Ibid.*
38. *Ibid.*, 112–113.
39. https://en.wikipedia.org/wiki/Lenny_Moore.
40. *Ibid.*

Jim Mutscheller

JOSEPH WANCHO

When the discussion turns to high school football in the Keystone State, invariably the talk is about the tradition-rich schools in Western Pennsylvania. From Erie to Pittsburgh, from Meadville to Bethlehem, and all points in between and beyond, the great teams and star players of that region can keep the endless debates of various comparisons carry on for hours.

When the talk is about Beaver County, the old-timers will tell the youngsters about Joe Namath from Beaver Falls High School, who lit up the autumn sky with his golden right arm. But a decade before Joe Willie was wowing the Tiger fans, Beaver Falls had another gridiron great for whom to cheer.

Jim Mutscheller was a two-way player for Beaver Falls, at defensive end and also offensive end. Mutscheller, who was known as "Bucky" (because he was born with buck teeth), was a three-sport star (baseball, basketball, football) for the Tigers, making several all-region and all-state teams.

After a stellar career at Beaver Falls, Mutscheller enrolled at the University of Notre Dame, playing for the legendary Frank Leahy. He then carved out an eight-year career for the Baltimore Colts, proving to be a clutch receiver and a favorite target of Johnny Unitas. Mutscheller was a key part of two world championship teams in Baltimore in 1958 and 1959.

James Francis Mutscheller was born on March 31, 1930, in Beaver Falls, Pennsylvania. He was the older of two children; he had a younger sister, Mary, born to Dennis and Edna Mutscheller. Dennis worked as a laborer; his specialized work was that of a bricklayer.[1]

After Mutscheller's successful high school career, he started out as a defensive end at Notre Dame. Although a backup, he made a key interception of a Kyle Rote pass in the Cotton Bowl against Southern Methodist University in the final game of the 1949 regular season. The Irish stifled SMU late in the game to post a 27–20 victory, a perfect 10–0 season, and win the national championship. It was the fourth season in a row that Notre Dame had gone undefeated, running their record to 36–0–2 over that period.

But the Irish posted a 4–4 record in 1950 and a 7–2–1 record in 1951, and they finished both seasons unranked. That did not take anything away from Jim Mutscheller. He was moved to left offensive end, replacing Bill Wightman. Bucky responded with his best year in 1950, catching 35 passes for 426 yards and seven touchdowns. He and quarterback Bob Williams made quite a combo for a .500 team, as Mutscheller's numbers surpassed that of Leon Hart, the Irish great who had won the Heisman Trophy the year before. He was named captain of the 1951 squad, and caught another 20 passes in his final season. Mutscheller earned All- America honors. "The greatest part of Notre Dame's victories are the result of the school spirit,"[2] said Mutscheller.

After graduation, Mutscheller joined the United States Marine Corps. He served in Japan and Korea, and was elevated to the rank of Captain. Mutscheller was selected by the New York Yanks in the 12th round of the 1952 college player draft. But the Yanks folded their operation and moved to Dallas where they became the Dallas Texans in 1952. The franchise was on the move once again, becoming the Baltimore Colts for the 1953 season.

After his discharge from the U.S. Marines, Mutscheller played sparingly in his rookie season in 1954, gaining exposure by lining up on both sides of the ball.

Mutscheller shed the substitute role for good in 1955. With his big frame (6'1", 205 pounds), Bucky was a favorite target of quarterback George Shaw. Mutscheller led all receivers with 33 catches for 518 yards and seven touchdowns from his right end position.

Jim Mutscheller.

The next year started off with a bang when Mutscheller exchanged "I dos" on January 14, 1956, with the former Joan Ederer of Del Mar, California. The couple had four sons.

The Colts offense added two important components in 1956. Johnny Unitas was signed after being waived by the Pittsburgh Steelers in 1955, and Baltimore drafted running back Lenny Moore out of Penn State in the college player draft. The emergence of end Raymond Berry was also a sign that better days were ahead. All three players would end their careers with enshrinement into the Pro Football Hall of Fame in Canton, Ohio.

Perhaps one of the more thrilling games of the year was when Baltimore hosted Washington on December 23, 1956. In the season's final game, the Colts trailed the Redskins 17–6 heading into the final quarter. Moore scored on a seven-yard run to cut the deficit to 17–13. With 25 seconds left, Mutscheller snagged a deflected pass from Unitas for a 53-yard game-winning touchdown. The 32,994 fans in attendance at Memorial Stadium went into a frenzy over the Colts' 19–17 victory. For Mutscheller, he would attain career highs in receptions (44) and yards (715) for the season.

In spite of the new found offensive firepower, the Colts finished with a 5–7 record in 1956. But their offense was greatly improved, rising from 11th in the league in scoring in 1955 to fourth in the league in 1956.

Mutscheller and Berry were quite a tandem for Unitas in 1957. Mutscheller led the league with eight touchdown receptions while Berry led in receiving yards with 800.

Mutscheller scored three of those touchdowns in a game on October 13, 1957, at Green Bay in a convincing 45–17 win for the Colts. But it was more than their ability to catch the football that made them such special talents.

"One reason for the Baltimore success," said Green Bay assistant coach Ray Richards, "is that Berry and Mutscheller are the two best ends on any one team. They are by far the best blocking ends I have ever seen. Most ends these days just like to be fancy and catch the ball. But these two can block besides being able to fake, get open, turn on the speed and make remarkable catches."[3] Weeb Ewbank agreed with Richards' assessment, calling Mutscheller "the best blocking end in the pro ranks."[4]

Mutscheller, who also collected 32 catches for 558 yards, made his first and only Pro Bowl team in 1957, and was voted second team All-NFL by the UPI, NEA, and *New York Daily News*.

There may have been some doubts about Weeb Ewbank when he first took over the Colts in 1954. The results were not too flattering, as he garnered back-to-back five-win seasons in 1955 and '56. In 1958, Baltimore put it altogether, shooting to the top of the Western Conference with a 9–3 record. Their offense was number one in the league while tying Cleveland with the lowest number of turnovers with 22. For the season, Mutscheller caught 28 passes for 504 yards and seven touchdowns.

Their opponent in the NFL title game was the New York Giants on December 28, 1958, at Yankee Stadium. The game was televised nationally and to this day is considered one of the greatest games in NFL history. The teams battled to a 17–17 tie, forcing an overtime period to determine a winner. The Colts had blown a 14–3 lead, and needed to execute the two-minute drill to perfection for Unitas to lead the offense into position for a game-tying field goal. Steve Myhra obliged, connecting on a 20-yard field goal to send the game into the first sudden-death in league championship history.

The Giants won the toss, but found the Colts' defense stingy. They punted and the Colts drove 80 yards. Unitas found Mutscheller at the one-yard line on a six-yard pass. Alan Ameche dove over from the one to seal the game for Baltimore.

"John Unitas called a pass," Mutscheller recalled on the play that got the Colts to the one yard line, "60 was the formation, and the pass was a diagonal out—which meant I went diagonally straight, towards the end zone, not making any moves or anything, just going diagonally. Lenny Moore was flanked out to the right, and so John pumped a fake to Lenny and threw it to me. Fortunately, or unfortunately, I slid out on the one-yard line. The field was frozen in that corner."[5]

Baltimore posted another 9–3 record to again win the Western Conference in 1959. Mutscheller pulled in 44 catches for 699 yards and eight touchdowns. Baltimore prevailed over the Giants again in the title game, although the result was not as dramatic as the game the previous year. The Colts won 31–16.

In 1960, the Colts offensive attack was slowed by injuries. Art DeCarlo saw a lot of playing time, as Mutscheller missed suiting up for one game due to a twisted knee. When he was able to give it a go, he was less than 100 percent, playing his game on grit and guile, and catching only 18 passes for 271 yards and two touchdowns. As a result, the Colts started the season at 6–2, but lost their last four games to end the season at .500. Their two-year reign as world champions had come to an end.

Injuries took their toll on Mutscheller in 1961. Despite having knee surgery in the off season, he was still slowed by an injured leg. It was his final year in professional football, catching 20 balls for 370 yards, and accounting for two touchdowns. He retired after the season, totaling 220 catches for 3,684 yards and 40 touchdowns for his career. He averaged 16.7 yards per catch.

Since 1956 Mutscheller had been working in the insurance business. He was employed by the National Life Insurance Company of Vermont. It was a job that he enjoyed and he remained with the same firm well into the 21st century. He stayed in the Baltimore area for the remainder of his life.

Jim Mutscheller passed away on April 10, 2015, in Towson, Maryland, due to kidney failure. He was described by his teammates as steady, strong, possessing a fine sense of teamwork and always giving a high-class performance. Those were the same qualities he adhered to in his life outside the lines as well.

"You learn to make sacrifices for the good of the team. The enjoyment of football comes in the associations you make and from the satisfaction of doing a job that's assigned to you and doing it successfully,"[6] said Mutscheller.

Notes

1. 1940 United States Census.
2. *Notre Dame Football Review*, 1950, http://archives.nd.edu/Football/Football-1950s.pdf, accessed January 15, 2017.
3. John Steadman, "Glasses Make Berry Seeing-Eye Receiver," *The Sporting News*, December 10, 1958.
4. Cameron C. Snyder, "Jim Mutscheller Signs with Colts," *Baltimore Sun*, February 9, 1958.
5. "Where Are They Now: Jim Mutscheller," Baltimoreravens.com, September 24, 2009, http://www.baltimoreravens.com/news/article-1/Where-Are-They-Now-Jim- Mutscheller/0A03BF0B-12D7–40A2–92A7-CC58635CF337, accessed January 12, 2017.
6. John C. Schmidt, "Storybook Life—Jim Mutscheller's," *Baltimore Sun*, October 22, 1961.

Steve Myhra

Rick Gonsalves

The Baltimore Colts selected Steve Myhra in the 12th round of the 1956 draft as a future choice. At the University of North Dakota, Steve, at 6'1", 240 pounds, was a consensus All-America selection as an offensive guard, linebacker and placekicker in 1955–56. Myhra helped his team beat archrival North Dakota State in 1955 and 1956 by scores of 21 to 0 and 14 to 7, respectively. He was also selected as the North Central Conference MVP following his senior year.[1]

Steve was born in Wahpeton, North Dakota, on April 2, 1934, where his father owned a farm equipment business. Myhra was a carefree sort who loved the outdoors and country western music.[2]

In 1957, his first season with Baltimore, Steve made 14 extra points out of 16 attempts and four field goals out of six attempts for 26 points. Against San Francisco on November 24, Myhra kicked three extra points and two field goals to help give the Colts a 27 to 21 victory.[3] Steve also filled in for offensive guard Art Spinney and played sparingly at linebacker.[4]

By 1958, Baltimore began to gel as a contender for the NFL championship. The Colts held a 6–0 record at mid-season. The Colts got their sixth win by scoring 56 points to tie a single-game team record, in a shutout over the Green Bay Packers. That afternoon, Steve tied Tom Feamster (1956) for the team's single-game record for extra points with 8.[5]

The following week, Baltimore played the New York Giants, a team it would meet for the NFL Title, seven weeks later. John Unitas did not play in this game because of a severe rib injury. He was replaced by backup quarterback George Shaw, and the Colts lost in a close game, 24 to 21.[6]

Baltimore went on to clinch the Western Conference title with a 9–3 record. The New York Giants, however, had a 9–3 record to tie the Cleveland Browns for the Eastern Conference crown which forced a playoff game the Giants won, 10 to 0.[7]

On December 28, Baltimore again met the New York Giants at Yankee Stadium this time for the NFL championship. Now, with a healthy Unitas at quarterback, the Colts were a three-point favorite. Although the teams played a close game several weeks earlier, the 64,185 fans in attendance, along with an estimated 45 million television viewers never realized that they would be witnessing NFL history in the making.[8]

Baltimore had the opportunity to score first in the opening quarter by setting up Myhra for a 32-yard field goal attempt, just within his range. That season, Steve made 48 extra points out of 51 tries and four field goals out of ten attempts, not exactly encouraging statistics, for 60 points. The longest field goal he made in 1958 came from the 28 yard line.

This time, his 32-yard attempt just fell short of the goal posts but the Giants were called for offside. He would get another chance with this try coming from the 27, five yards closer to the uprights. Just as he made contact with the ball, middle linebacker Sam Huff broke through the Colts' line untouched to block the kick.[9] Art Donovan, Baltimore's defensive star lineman, at 6'3," 270 pounds, was also a blocker on the field goal team. Art, however, turned the wrong way, lost his balance and was knocked to the ground leaving a gaping hole for Huff to breeze through untouched. After seeing these two failed field goal attempts, Myhra's teammates had very little confidence in him for the rest of the game. Before this kick, Steve had replaced linebacker Leo Sanford, who injured his right knee and would miss the rest of the game.

Late in the fourth quarter, the Colts trailed the Giants by three points, 17 to 14. With about two

Steve Myhra.

minutes left to play in the game, New York's punter Don Chandler, one of the best in the business, unleashed a kick that Baltimore fielded at its own 14. It appeared that this punt would preserve a Giants win.

John Unitas though, thought otherwise. He drove the Colts 73 yards to the Giants' 13 yard line. With seven seconds showing on the clock, Steve entered the game to attempt a 20-yard field goal which would at least force a tie.

Players and coaches from both teams, fans in the stadium and those watching on television or listening by radio, held their collective breaths as Myhra lined up for what would be the kick of his career and one of the biggest in pro football history.

George Shaw took a knee just inside the left hash mark and scratched an X on the ground where he planned to set up the ball. Steve then took one long step behind the spot, to prepare himself for the kick. Thoughts of his two failed field goal attempts in the first quarter flashed briefly through his mind. "It was going to be a long cold winter for me back in North Dakota if I miss this field goal," he thought to himself.[10]

The ball was snapped to Shaw who gave Myhra a perfect hold. Steve hit it solidly and the ball sailed just inside of the left goal posts to create a tie. Some of the Giants' players thought that the ball drifted just outside of the left upright and began celebrating their first NFL title since 1956.[11]

"The hash marks were closer to the sidelines at that time so the angle that he had to kick from was more severe," Pat Summerall, the Giants' kicker, said. "From where I was standing, I thought he missed it at first. I turned around to somebody and began to celebrate because I thought the ball was outside the left upright."[12]

Even Lenny Moore thought that Steve's kick just missed one of the uprights:

I was on the sidelines when Myhra kicked the field goal. What was I doing? I was praying. Really. Steve hadn't been the world's greatest field goal kicker that year and in a situation like that, any kicker could feel the pressure. When he finally kicked it and there was some doubt he'd get it off at all because the clock was running, well from the trajectory I knew it was long enough. But I had no way to tell if it was true enough. We didn't know that until we looked at the official. From our angle, we couldn't really tell, it was kind of near one of the uprights, and I was just scared to death it would sail out at the last second. But he called it good, and we were tied. Then I knew we'd be in an overtime period.[13]

Raymond Berry thought that because Myhra played linebacker from the start of the game that it helped his kicking. "When you've got to play the entire game, you're doing a whole lot of things other than thinking field goal as compared to being a kicker over there waiting for your time to kick," he said.[14]

For the first time in NFL history, a championship game had ended in a tie and it would be the first ever to go into overtime. Still, many of the players from each team were not sure what would happen next. Since it was a championship game, it had to be settled by playing an overtime period called "Sudden Death."[15] It was given that name because the first team to score would win the game meaning "sudden death" for the other team.

The Giants won the coin toss and elected to receive. They could not mount a drive so they had to punt after quarterback Charlie Conerly fell a yard short of a vital first down. Don Chandler punted the ball away and the Colts fielded it at their own 19. Carl Taseff advanced the ball one yard to the 20. Unitas went to work and marched the team 80 yards in 13 plays, to set up Alan "The Horse" Ameche's one-yard scoring plunge to give the Colts their first NFL championship. In just five years, Ewbank had build the team into a winner.

After the game, coach Weeb Ewbank was asked why he did not go for the field goal, which would have been a chip shot for Myhra:

> In the game, I would have gone for a field goal and won it earlier in the overtime, but I had no confidence in my kicker, Steve Myhra. We were glad that Steve had gotten the one kick near the end of regulation time to tie it and get us into overtime. We weren't going to press our luck and ask him to make another one. Myhra was just a bad place kicker, a straight-on kicker. I had coached Lou Groza, when I was assistant coach for the Cleveland Browns. If Lou kicked ten times, his steps would leave the same marks in the dirt each time. If Myhra kicked twice, it looked like the chickens had been scratching in the dirt. He never did the same thing twice.[16]

John Unitas echoed Weeb's same words when he was asked the same question. "No offense, but I couldn't trust Myhra. We had to score a touchdown."[17]

Also, the field goal at this time in pro football was not considered to be much of a scoring weapon, so many teams did not dedicate much time during practices to perfect this vital skill. Teams would much rather go for a touchdown and if they did not make it, they would punt the ball away first before trying for the field goal.[18] Many who place-kicked in that era, also played another position. Cleveland's Lou Groza was an outstanding offensive lineman, the Packers' Paul Hornung was a running back, and Philadelphia's Bobby Walston and the 49ers' Gordie Soltau were receivers.

There was however, some speculation by a few sportswriters that Colts owner Carroll Rosenbloom, whose fondness for gambling was well known, had bet a huge sum of money along with several of his cronies on his team. He supposedly got word to Ewbank ordering him not to kick a field goal in order to beat the spread, but there was never any hardcore evidence to back this claim.[19]

What puzzled so many players on both teams was why Baltimore coach Weeb Ewbank didn't have Bert Rechichar handle the placekicking? After all, he once kicked a 56-yard field goal, which was still a league record. Plus, he still held the record for most field goals of 50 yards or more in a season with two, in 1953 and 1955. Rechichar handled kickoffs during the title game and he was much better at it than Steve. He also attempted a long field goal in the fourth quarter which came up short. Weeb had benched Bert in 1957 and 1958 because he plain did not like him since he lived a carefree life style. Ewbank, on the other hand disliked Steve less.[20]

Nonetheless, Myhra had turned a short field goal into one of the biggest kicks in pro football history. His kicking shoe is on display at the Pro Football Hall of Fame.

In 1959, the Colts and Giants met again for the NFL championship this time in Baltimore. Baltimore was behind 9–7 by the end of the third quarter. Unitas then rallied the Colts with 24 points in the fourth quarter to beat the Giants, 31 to 16 for their second straight NFL title. Steve had a much better game this time, kicking a 25-yard field goal along with four extra points.[21]

Garvin Stevens, who was a roommate of Myhra's at the University of North Dakota, introduced him to Carolyn Birkland in the late 1950s. They dated steadily and after she graduated from the University of North Dakota in 1959, they were married in Grand Forks, North Dakota, just before Baltimore's training camp began.[22]

In December of 1960, Steve was the first NFL kicker to make the cover of Life Magazine where he is shown approaching the ball on a kickoff.[23]

The 1961 season was the best in his career as a kicker and also his last with Baltimore. That year, Myhra's kicking helped the Colts to win three games with last second field goals. His 39-yard field goal gave the Colts a 27 to 24 win over the Los Angeles Rams on

September 17. He booted a 52-yard field goal, the longest of his career, to beat Minnesota, 34 to 33 on October 1. He connected on a 45-yard field goal to defeat the Detroit Lions, 17 to 14 on October 22. Steve finished that year by making 33 extra points out of 34 attempts and a league leading 21 field goals out of 39 attempts for 96 points which placed him in a third-place tie with Jim Taylor among NFL scorers. In this one season, he kicked nearly as many field goals as he did during his first four years with the team.[24]

Although he was considered to be an erratic kicker, during his tenure with the Colts, Steve set team records for most extra points, career, 180; most consecutive extra points, 42; most field goals, career, 44; most points, career, 312; most extra points, season, 50, 1959; most field goals, season, 21, 1961; most points, season, 96, 1961; most extra points, game (tied with Tom Feamster) eight vs. Green Bay, November 2, 1958; most field goals, game, three vs. St. Louis Cardinals, 36, 27, 35 yards, November 19, 1961.[25]

Steve played one more year of professional football in 1962 but this time it was for the Saskatchewan Roughriders in the Canadian Football League. He then returned to North Dakota where he and his wife Carolyn started a family. His business pursuits ran from starting an insurance company, to sportscasting, to opening a sporting goods store in Wahpeton. Over the years after Carolyn gave birth to three sons, Steve moved the family from the cold weather of North Dakota to the warm climate of Phoenix, Arizona.[26]

By 1975, Myhra began to face financial problems because too often he gave business breaks to friends. Eventually he and Carolyn were divorced. Steve then went back to North Dakota and in 1976 he was inducted into the University of North Dakota's Letter-winners Association Hall of Fame. Steve's health began to decline by the early 1990s. He had a hip replacement in 1992 and prostate surgery in 1993. In 1994, while attending a country western music festival, Myhra died of a heart attack at the age of 60.[27]

Steve traveled to Detroit Lakes, Minnesota, to attend the annual WE Fest country music show. "He was with an alumni group, talking with friends and even went out on the dance floor," said his sister Joan Holtz about that evening. "Then a short time later, he suffered a fatal heart attack."[28]

NOTES

1. *2016 University of North Dakota Media Guide.*
2. Jeff Miller, "Shaky Myhra Made the Kick That Mattered Most," December 8, 2008, http://www.espn.com/nfl/news.
3. "Steve Myhra," Pro-Football-Reference.com.
4. T.J. Troup, *The Birth of Football's 4–3 Defense* (Lanham, MD: Rowman & Littlefield, 2014), 220.
5. *2016 Baltimore Colts Media Guide.*
6. Frank Gifford with Peter Richmond, *The Glory Game* (New York: HarperCollins, 2008), 63.
7. Dave Klein, *The Game of Their Lives* (New York: Random House, 1976), 6–7.
8. Dave Goldberg, "Greatest Game: Remembering the 1958 NFL Title Game," *Savannah Morning News*, December 13, 2008.
9. Mark Bowden, *The Best Game Ever* (New York: Atlantic Monthly Press, 2008), 154–155.
10. Lou Sahadi, *One Sunday in December* (Guilford, CT: The Lyons Press, 2008), 179.
11. Miller.
12. *Ibid.*
13. Klein, 173.
14. Miller.
15. Gifford, 210–211.
16. Vince Bagli and Norman Lee Macht, *Sundays at 2:00 with the Baltimore Colts* (Centreville, MD: Tidewater, 1995), 44.

17. Raymond Berry, *All the Moves I Had* (Guilford, CT: LP, 2016), 52.

18. Rick Gonsalves, *Placekicking in the NFL: A History and Analysis* (Jefferson, NC: McFarland, 2014), 35.

19. Bowden, 203.

20. Gifford, 113–114.

21. David Neft, Richard M. Cohen, and Robert Carroll, *Pro Football: The Early Years* (Ridgefield, CT: Sports Products, 1987), 273.

22. Miller.

23. "Life Magazine 1960's," OriginalLifeMagazine.com.

24. *1962 Baltimore Colts Press Guide.*

25. *1960 Baltimore Colts Press Guide.*

26. Miller.

27. *Ibid.*

28. *Ibid.*

Andy Nelson

Joshua M. Anderson

A washing machine almost prevented Andy Nelson from playing in the NFL.

Born on May 27, 1933, in Athens, Alabama,[1] Andrew Vaughn Nelson, Sr., grew up on a 200-acre cotton farm; his father was Guy Nelson, the "Chief BBQ Man" for Limestone County.[2] A cow pasture provided a makeshift football field for Nelson and his buddies— a football is the first Christmas present that Andy remembers.[3] At Athens High School, during an era when it was a common occurrence to see the same player on offense and defense, Nelson played quarterback and defensive back. His athletic ability thrived in several sports, resulting in lettering in football, baseball, basketball, and track.[4] Though Nelson, who weighed only 160 pounds, co-captained the football team in his senior year,[5] he did not get attention from recruiters. So he spent a year working on the family farm after graduation.[6]

After a year with no football in his life, Nelson was determined to change his circumstances, leaving a note on the tractor for his father and hitchhiking to Memphis, about 200 miles away.[7] Arriving at Memphis State's practice field, he learned there were no scholarships available. However, coach Ralph Hatley gave him a tryout after hearing about the epic hitchhiking journey.[8] Nelson recalled, "I got into the running line. It so happened the guy that was tackling me was about my size. I only weighed about 160 pounds. I ran over him like a billy goat. I butted him down, kept on going. I knew I had only one shot, so I had to do it."[9]

Hatley added Nelson to the roster and got him a job working in the cafeteria, a boon because it could also help the new player put on some pounds and he enjoyed working with the food.[10] Until he noticed the grit and determination of that "little spindle-legged guy,"[11] Hatley had no specific plans for Nelson.

The pivotal year of Nelson's life, both on and off the field, proved to be 1953, when he married Bettye Bryan, as "the best play he ever made."[12] Bettye fighting through the challenges of polio provided support and motivation for her husband. While attending to her growing family she eventually recovered from her illness.[13] On the field, Nelson had two interceptions in the Tigers' loss to Bear Bryant's Kentucky Wildcats on November 14, 1953; a performance that attracted the attention of Bryant's assistant coach, Blanton Collier, who alerted Weeb Ewbank.[14]

Nelson adapted to different offensive formations and styles with ease. In 1954, he was a first-string tailback running the single wing, which has a tailback and a fullback but no quarterback. By 1955, he was a first-string quarterback running the split formation and in 1956 he led the team in touchdowns, all-purpose yards, kickoff returns, and punt returns. Nelson also contributed as a stellar defensive back throughout his collegiate career.[15]

On Thanksgiving Day, 1956, he led Memphis State to its first bowl game victory—a 32–12 win over East Tennessee in the Burley Bowl[16]; in 1957, Nelson was named a Williamson's Little All-American (1st team) as a defensive back for the 1956 season.[17] After more than 60 years, Nelson still has Memphis State's fifth highest punt return average in a single season.[18] Nelson graduated with a B.S. in health and physical education, lettering all four years.[19]

Andy Nelson.

The Colts drafted Nelson as a quarterback and a defensive back in the 11th round of the 1957 NFL draft—pick number 126, which would be the late fourth round in today's draft.[20] The *Ashville Citizen-Times* described Nelson as a "170-pound threat as a runner, passer, kicker, and receiver."[21] The *Baltimore Sun* stated, "Passes and punts. Also good defensive back."[22]

A few weeks after being drafted Nelson signed a contract with the Colts,[23] but he missed the first ten days of training camp. Don Kellett, the team's general manager, tried calling the rookie to find out why he didn't arrive as scheduled. It was to no avail—the Nelson family didn't have telephone service.[24] Nelson looked like an excellent prospect so Kellett contacted the Memphis State Coach, Tom Morris, who found Nelson and arranged a call.[25] During the conversation, Kellett learned that Nelson was mulling over an $8,000 bid to play football in Canada, while he had signed with the Colts for $6,000.

"'I'd like to play," Nelson told him, "but I just bought a washing machine for my wife and I can't leave here until it's paid for."

"How much did it cost?" asked Kellett.

"Two hundred dollars," replied Nelson.

"I'll send you the money," the GM said. "Now, get on a plane and get up here.'"[26] The "here" to which Kellett referred was Western Maryland College, where the Colts were in training.

Within days of his arrival, the press noted that Nelson, now a defensive halfback, was "impressive in the long scrimmage" and it quickly became apparent that he was a bruising tackler.[27] He earned the nickname "Bones" from Colts teammates; Art Donovan called Nelson the toughest man on the team.[28] Art DeCarlo said, "You have to like to hit people to play defense. Andy thrived on it. He loved to hit people and was as good as anybody who ever played the game in that respect."[29] During his rookie season in 1957, Nelson played in all 12 games for the Colts and grabbed five interceptions.

In 1958, after starting the season with two 13-point victories, the Colts were down 17–0 in the second quarter to an inferior Packer team. The boys from Baltimore fought back to tie the score with just a few minutes remaining in the game. Nelson explained, "I intercepted one of Bart Starr's passes and ran it back 52 yards and scored and we won in the last two minutes."[30] In Nelson's second game against the Packers, a 56–0 rout, he tallied two interceptions, including one returned for 69 yards.[31] The Colts seemed unstoppable.

Nelson was also a key factor in the team's other major comeback victory that year. In their last home game, the Colts were down 27–7 to the 49ers at halftime. Nelson and fellow safety, Ray Brown, each had two interceptions and led the Colts to score 28 unanswered points in the second half to win 35–27.[32] For the season he led the league with 199 return yards and had eight interceptions which tied for third in the league with teammate Brown. Sportswriters also took notice and Nelson was named First Team All-NFL by the *New York Daily News* and Second Team All-NFL by the UPI, AP, and the Newspaper Enterprise Association.[33]

The Colts faced the Giants in the 1958 championship game at Yankee Stadium. "It was just a feeling of playing in your first championship," remembered Nelson. "It was a good feeling. I was a big baseball fan and we were playing in Yankee Stadium. I had a lot of butterflies. It was a special place and a special time and I didn't know before the game what it would be."[34]

When Giants QB Charlie Conerly delivered to Kyle Rote on a deep pass in the third quarter, Nelson unleashed one of his trademark hits, which separated Rote from the ball at the Colts' 25 yard line. Unfortunately for Nelson and his Baltimore brethren, running back Alex Webster trailed on the play and picked up the ball, taking it all the way down to the one yard line. A few moments later the Giants scored a touchdown, but the Colts still emerged victorious, winning 23–17.[35]

The following season Nelson had six interceptions, tying for fourth in the league. It was a standout year for the Colts—40 interceptions in total, with six players having at least four. The Colts also had a reputation for extraordinary performance in the fourth quarter, regularly scoring more points in the second half of games. In the 1959 championship game's fourth quarter, both traits came to the fore thanks to Nelson. The Giants were down 14–9, but had the ball and were driving when Nelson intercepted a pass meant for Giants star receiver, Frank Gifford.[36] Nelson said, "I should have scored on that play. I ran it back 17 yards before [New York tackle] Rosey Brown ran me out of bounds [at the Giants' 14]."[37] Ewbank recognized this as the turning point in the game.[38] The Colts scored just three plays later, followed by a crescendo of two more in succession to win, 31–16.[39] Once again, Andy received honors from the press as he was named Second Team All-Pro by the UPI and First Team All-NFL by the AP and *New York Daily News*.[40]

In 1960, the Colts' coaching staff experimented with the defensive backfield, except for Andy Nelson—his job was set as left safety.[41] There was "unanimity of opinion among

Colt coaches and players that Nelson is the backbone of the world champions' secondary defense."[42] Further praise came from the fan base: "Even among the Baltimore fans, a group as perceptive as they are dedicated, the saying is that nobody can touch Andy on pass defense."[43] Assistant coach Charley Winner said, "Andy covers a lot of ground when the ball is in the air.... He has that rare knack of maintaining good position on the receiver. That's the kind of man you try to find for the safety position."[44]

Nelson continued to frustrate offenses, leading to his fourth-straight year of being in the NFL's top ten in interceptions with six picks and making the Pro Bowl. His hometown honored him with an Andy Nelson Day sponsored by the Athens Quarterback Club. Herb Bryan, president of the club, stated, "He is an inspiration to youngsters everywhere and it is only fitting that we should honor him and show him what he means to us."[45]

While Nelson was on the team for the next three seasons from 1961 to 1963, Nelson and the Colts would not make the playoffs again. The team never had a losing record, whether Weeb Ewbank or Don Shula was coach, but they could never finish better than 8–6. Nelson continued to deliver solid results, averaging two interceptions a season for the rest of his career. Even with his interceptions down, he remained a well-respected player. In 1961, his only year without interceptions, he was still being thought of as a Pro Bowl possibility as late as December of that year.[46]

On October 20, 1963, the Colts played the Detroit Lions in Detroit, storming back from a 21–10 deficit to be down just two points by the fourth quarter. Nelson intercepted Milt Plum's only pass of the day and returned it 26 yards to win the game. This made him the first and only, until Elvis Patterson joined him in 1987, defensive player with two game-winning fourth quarter touchdowns.[47] A few weeks later, Nelson bruised his kidney and missed most of the last four games of his final season with the Colts.[48] A deal with the New York Giants in 1964 sent Nelson and R.C. Owens to New York in exchange for Joe Don Looney and Lou Kirouac.[49] Giants Head Coach, Allie Sherman, explained that with the expanded roster, the team could keep six defensive backs and only had five they felt were good enough. Adding Nelson gave them more experience in the defensive lineup.[50]

The 1964 season with the Giants would be Nelson's last in the NFL. In 1966, the Atlanta Falcons expansion team gave Nelson a tryout, but ultimately cut him.[51] Between his love of the game and his need to feed a family of nine, he routinely worked two jobs. From 1967 to 1973, he spent time as a player and/or coach for some of the minor football leagues that existed at the time. During the off-season, various jobs in sales complemented the money he earned from football. He sold land in Florida, lots for $10 each, with fellow teammate Raymond Berry. He was a sales rep for a pharmaceutical company, detailing athletic tape and gauze. He even worked as a salesman for a trucking firm. "I did what I had to do to make a living with seven children,"[52] said Nelson.

In 1974, Nelson planned to work with Jack Pardee on the staff of the Washington Ambassadors of the new World Football League (WFL). However, the team moved to Orlando to became the Florida Blazers. Distance proved to be a deciding factor—and Nelson didn't want to be so far from his family. Consequently, he became the defensive backfield coach for the WFL's Philadelphia Bell as his last coaching job.[53]

Though retired from playing and coaching, football remained a large part of his life. The Memphis State Hall of Fame inducted Nelson in 1976.[54] The championship ring that Nelson received for the 1958 victory, a cherished keepsake, was stolen in 1997.[55] A few years later, his daughter Linda presented him with a replica after borrowing one from

Colts end Jim Mutscheller to have a duplicate made.[56] Nelson said, "I thought I'd never see that ring again. And when I did, it made me cry."[57] In 2003, Nelson was voted into the Limestone County Hall of Fame and named to the All-Time Baltimore Colts 50th Anniversary Team.[58] The Tennessee Hall of Fame inducted Nelson in 2008.[59]

Andy and Bettye Nelson decided to put down roots in Lutherville, Maryland, to raise their family and opened his eponymous restaurant in Cockeysville in 1981.[60] "Six days a week, he's behind the counter, dishing up everything from pulled pork 'cue to smoked catfish to Memphis ribs."[61] Through the 2010s, Nelson ran the restaurant, gave occasional interviews, and focused on family.

Family is a cornerstone for Nelson. "I've got 16 [grandchildren]," Nelson said in a 2008 interview. "I'm lucky."[62] His thoughts on football, from the same interview, underscored the devotion of many fans in the Baltimore area—once the Colts journeyed to Indianapolis in the early 1980s, they needed an outlet. "We follow the Ravens now.... These feelings when I see the uniforms. I remember the guys who wore the numbers."[63] An emotional hit more devastating than any NFL tackle struck the Nelson clan in 2010, when Bettye Nelson passed away; the Nelsons had been married for 57 years.[64]

Today, Andy Nelson's Barbeque maintains its status as a Maryland icon, offering fresh food, smoked for many hours in the family's sauce every day.[65] A picture of Nelson leaping in front of Gifford for that key interception hangs on the wall along with "Baltimore's Best BBQ" articles.[66] With numerous children and grandchildren working there, running the restaurant is a family affair.[67] "I can't stop working; I gotta keep a-goin,"[68] he says. "I just hope I leave a good name and a legacy."[69]

That's Andy Nelson—always thinking about family.

NOTES

1. http://www.pro-football-reference.com/players/N/NelsAn00.htm.
2. http://www.andynelsonsbbq.com/about-us-2/.
3. Dana Beyerle, "Brackett, Nelson Recall Playing Careers," *Gadsden Times*, December 12, 2008.
4. "Andy Nelson," http://www.lcshof.com/view.php?id=6.
5. http://tshf.net/halloffame/nelson-andy/.
6. Beyerle.
7. Michael Buckley, "Interview with Andy Nelson" in "Andy Nelson's Southern Pit Barbecue" September 2016.
8. *Ibid.*
9. *Ibid.*
10. *Ibid.*
11. "Andy Nelson Day Set Saturday at Athens," *The Tennessean*, February 14, 1960.
12. *Ibid.*
13. *Ibid.*
14. Buckley.
15. 2016_Memphis_Football_Online.pdf; "Memphis 11 Is Friday Night Foe," *Clarion Ledger*, October 21, 1955; Don Oliver, "ACC Faces MS Tonight," *Abilene Reporter-News*, October 2, 1954.
16. 2016_Memphis_Football_Online.pdf.
17. *Ibid.*
18. *Ibid.*
19. http://tshf.net/halloffame/nelson-andy/.
20. *Ibid.*
21. "Baltimore Colts Sign Andy Nelson," *Ashville Citizen-Times*, February 22, 1957.
22. "Colts' Choices in Grid Draft," *Baltimore Sun*, February 1, 1957.
23. "Colts Sign Andy Nelson," *The Tennessean*, February 22, 1957.
24. Cameron C. Snyder, "Colt Halfback Nelson Found and Will Report to Practice," *Baltimore Sun*, July 27, 1957.

25. *Ibid.*

26. Mike Klingaman, "Catching Up with BBQ Master and Former Colt Andy Nelson," *Baltimore Sun*, December 18, 2012.

27. "QBs Davidson, Unitas Sharp in Colt Drill," *Los Angeles Times*, August 4, 1957.

28. "Andy Nelson Day Set Saturday at Athens."

29. Ted Patterson, *Football in Baltimore: History and Memorabilia* (Baltimore: John Hopkins University Press, 2000), 133.

30. Beyerle.

31. "Colts Remain Only Undefeated NFL Team: 51,333 Witness 56–0 Packer Rout," *Baltimore Sun*, November 3, 1958.

32. Patterson, 143.

33. http://www.pro-football-reference.com/players/N/NelsAn00.htm.

34. Beyerle.

35. Patterson, 144.

36. Klingaman.

37. *Ibid.*

38. *Ibid.*

39. *Ibid.*

40. http://www.pro-football-reference.com/players/N/NelsAn00.htm.

41. Cooper Rollow, "Colts' Nelson Clinches Job," *Chicago Daily Tribune*, August 2, 1960.

42. *Ibid.*

43. *Ibid.*

44. *Ibid.*

45. "Andy Nelson Day Set Saturday at Athens."

46. "Ram-Colt Game Important for Pro Bowl Choices," Redlands Daily Facts, December 7, 1961.

47. http://www.footballperspective.com/which-player-has-scored-the-most-game-winning-touchdowns-part-ii/; http://www.pro-football-reference.com/players/P/PattEl21.htm; http://www.pro-football-reference.com/players/H/HarrDw00.htm; http://www.pro-football-reference.com/players/P/PetePa00.htm; http://www.pro-football-reference.com/players/H/HallDa00.htm; http://www.pro-football-reference.com/players/V/VanoTa00.htm; and http://www.pro-football-reference.com/players/B/BrowMi99.htm.

48. Pete Nevins, "Griffing, McElhenny Cut in Major Shakeup," *Bridgeport Telegram*, August 26, 1964.

49. *Ibid.*

50. Pete Nevins, "Sherman Tells Why Giants Made Moves," *Bridgeport Telegram*, August 26, 1964.

51. "Falcons Cut Andy Nelson," *The Daily Mail*, July 27, 1966.

52. Beyerle.

53. http://www.helmuthut.com/WFL/WFLBELL1.html; Len Harsh, "Clark Learning to Like Philadelphia Bell Sounds," *News–Press*, June 16, 1974.

54. http://tshf.net/halloffame/nelson-andy/.

55. Klingaman.

56. *Ibid.*

57. *Ibid.*

58. http://tshf.net/halloffame/nelson-andy/.

59. Beyerle.

60. Klingaman.

61. *Ibid.*

62. Beyerle.

63. Beyerle.

64. Klingaman.

65. http://www.andynelsonsbbq.com/about-us-2/.

66. *Ibid.*

67. Klingaman.

68. *Ibid.*

69. *Ibid.*

Buzz Nutter

Randy Snow

It is said that the quarterback is the only player who touches the ball on every play during a game, whether he is throwing to a receiver or handing the ball off to a running back. But someone has to hike the ball to the quarterback at the start of each play and the 1958 Baltimore Colts had a terrific one in Buzz Nutter.

The Colts had a pretty good quarterback too at that time, a guy named Johnny Unitas. Nutter once joked about his famous teammate by saying, "To tell you the truth, I never played with Johnny Unitas. Johnny Unitas played with me—and he had cold hands."[1]

Born on February 16, 1931, in Summersville, West Virginia, Madison Moore "Buzz" Nutter grew up more than 100 miles west, in Huntington. During his senior season in high school, Nutter practiced with the Marshall University football team for six weeks. The following year, however, he decided to attend Virginia Tech. He was six feet four and barely weighed 200 pounds.

After a standout college career, Nutter became the 12th-round selection (136th overall) of the Washington Redskins during the 1953 NFL draft. However, Nutter failed to make the Redskins team in 1953.

When he was cut by Washington, team owner George Preston Marshall offered to sign him to a contract for the following year before he left town. Nutter turned him down saying, "Mr. Marshall, I'm going to play somewhere next year, but it ain't gonna be here." Nutter spent the next year working in a West Virginia steel mill while waiting for a chance to sign with another NFL team. That chance came the following year, when he signed with the Baltimore Colts.

Nutter was not the biggest player on the offensive line, but he was one of the best centers to ever play at the position. Here is what teammate Art Donovan said about Nutter in his 1987 book, *Fatso*:

Buzz Nutter.

a scrawny little kid out of VPI [Virginia Polytechnic Institute, now known as Virginia Tech][2] who went on to be one of the best centers in the league. Buzz had the opposite problem I had with weight. He couldn't keep any on. He weighed about 230, and [head coach] Weeb [Ewbank] was always harping on him to get up to 250. I used to have to go all week without eating just to get down to 270, and wouldn't you know I'd be drooling come weigh-in day watching Buzz stick two ten-pound weights under his armpits and wearing a T-shirt on a scale to keep Weeb happy.[3]

Centers seldom get much attention during a game, unless they make a mistake on the field. Things like a bad snap on a PAT, field goal or punt, a holding penalty or a missed block will get them much unwanted attention. And you never hear of a center being drafted on a fantasy football team!

Unlike today's many specialists at key positions on the field, players in the 1950s played many positions during a game. A center not only had to be able to perform a direct snap to a quarterback, he also had to be proficient at long snapping on punts, PATs and field goals.

Nutter became the starting center for the Colts in 1956 when the incumbent starter, Dick Szymanski, left the team to join the military. Szymanski returned to the team in 1958. Just days before the start of the 1958 training camp, Nutter signed a new contract with the team.[4] That left the Colts with a tough decision to make. Who was going to be the starting center in 1958? Coaches planned to evaluate both centers for the starting job during the annual Blues vs. Whites charity intrasquad scrimmage at Memorial Stadium. Nutter (#50) was assigned to the Blue team while Szymanski (#52) was assigned to the White team.[5]

A huge crowd of 48,309 attended the scrimmage which saw the White team defeat the Blue team, 10–7.[6] Szymanski was injured during the scrimmage and was taken to the hospital, thus ending the competition at center.

As the preseason progressed, the Colts tried both Nutter and Szymanski at other positions; Nutter at offensive guard and Szymanski at linebacker. In an exhibition game played in Louisville, Kentucky, against the Giants, Szymanski intercepted a pass in the fourth quarter and returned it 26 yards for a touchdown.[7]

But when the regular season began with the home opener against the defending NFL champion Detroit Lions on September 28, Nutter was the starter at center.[8]

The week before an October game against the Washington Redskins, Nutter was speaking at a luncheon where he joked about having to hitchhike home after being cut by Washington in 1953. Redskins owner George Preston Marshall, who was in attendance at the luncheon, was not amused and said, "This young gentleman is a liar. If this is the kind of luncheon you want to have, have it for yourself…. I resent an untruth."[9]

Two days before the game against Washington, an x-ray showed that Nutter had a broken rib. In spite of the injury, he did play and got a small measure of revenge against Marshall as Baltimore won the game, 35–10.

The Colts started the season with a 6–0 record. On November 9, they travelled to Yankee Stadium to play the New York Giants. During halftime of that game, Coach Ewbank was concerned about Giants linebacker Sam Huff, who no one on the Colts offensive line could seem to handle. Ewbank asked his players what they could do about Huff. Nutter broke the silence and said, "I think we should trade for him."[10] The Colts would lose that game 24–21.

The day before the championship game against the Giants, a reporter from West Virginia asked Nutter about Sam Huff, who Nutter would be lining up against once again. Both Huff and Nutter were from West Virginia. "He's a real pro. Good player," Nutter said of Huff. When pressed further by the reporter about whether he could handle Huff during the game, all Nutter would say was, "See the game and you will get your answer."[11]

The answer came as Nutter was instrumental in protecting quarterback Johnny Unitas all game long and opening holes for running backs Alan Ameche and Lenny Moore on the way to the Colts' historic, overtime win. But his most important play may have come after the final touchdown had been scored.

After Ameche scored the game-winning touchdown in overtime, a fan on the field picked up the ball, which was lying on the ground in the end zone, and took off with it. Nutter chased the fan down, tackled him, retrieved the ball and brought it back to the locker room.

The Colts won a second consecutive NFL title in 1959, beating the Giants 31–16 and giving Nutter a second championship.

Nutter played for the Colts for one more season before a trade to Pittsburgh, where he spent four seasons.[12]

He returned to Baltimore for one final season in 1965 to end his playing career with the Colts. In all, Nutter played 12 NFL seasons and played in 153 regular season games.

After Nutter retired from playing football, he moved to La Plata, Maryland, and started a beer and soft drink distribution company. Nutter ran the aptly-named Center Distributors for more than 40 years until he passed away on April 12, 2008, at the age of 77.

Buzz was married to his wife, Carole, for 44 years until she passed away in 1997. She was Catholic, but Buzz was not. Towards the end of her life, she asked him to become a Catholic, so he did. A few months before she passed away, Buzz was baptized into the Catholic Church. They had four children together, sons David, Doug and Brian, and daughter Lisa. David runs Center Distributors to this day.

Notes

1. Tom Callahan, *Johnny U: The Life and Times of Johnny Unitas* (New York: Crown, 2006), 87.
2. "Traditions," VT.edu, http://www.vt.edu/about/traditions.html.
3. Arthur J. Donovan, Jr., and Bob Drury, *Fatso* (New York: Avon Books, 1987), 147–148.
4. "Contract Signed by Buzz Nutter," *Baltimore Sun*, July 23, 1958.
5. "Colt Whites Face Blues at Stadium," *Baltimore Sun*, August 11, 1958.
6. "48,309 Watch as Whites Nip Blues in Colt Game 10–7," *Baltimore Sun*, August 12, 1958.
7. Walter Taylor, "Colts Trample Giants 42–21 in Final Exhibition," *Baltimore Sun*, September 22, 1958.
8. Cameron Snyder, "Colts Open N.F.L. Season," *Baltimore Sun*, September 28, 1958.
9. "Buzz Nutter Obituary, WashingtonPost.com, April 18, 2008, http://www.washingtonpost.com/wp-dyn/content/article/2008/04/17/AR2008041704037.html.
10. Mark Bowden, *The Best Game Ever* (New York: Atlantic Monthly Press, 2008), 128.
11. Cameron Snyder, "Charlie's Words Put on Wall," *Baltimore Sun*, December 27, 1958.
12. Pro-Football-Reference.com, http://www.pro-football-reference.com/players/N/NuttBu00.htm.

Jim Parker

George Bozeka

Former Colts GM Ernie Accorsi once stated that Jim Parker "blocked out the sun."[1] Considered one of the best offensive linemen to ever play the game, Parker was the undisputed anchor of the Colts' championship teams of the 1950s serving as John Unitas' bodyguard.

James Thomas Parker was born on April 3, 1934, in Macon, Georgia. Growing up in East Macon, Parker's family was very poor. Jim worked on the family farm picking fruit and cotton.[2] His father, Charles Sr., a railway worker, made sure the family had a strong religious upbringing by reading the bible to his gathered children every Saturday evening. On Sundays the Parker family walked two miles to the Mt. Moriah Baptist Church for services and bible study. Wrestling and football were not allowed on the Sabbath in the Parker household.[3]

His older brother, Charles Jr., who became an All-American at Morris Brown College, a historically black college in Atlanta, was a local football star.[4] When he was growing up, Jim's heroes were Joe DiMaggio, Charley Trippi, and Vic Janowicz,

Jim Parker.

and Jim dreamed of being a gridiron hero himself.[5] He took up the game when he was a skinny 105-pound, 13-year-old[6] and languished on the high school junior varsity team at Ballard Hudson High School in Macon. After a three-month bout with appendicitis when he was 14, Parker weighed only 98 pounds and stood six feet tall.[7] His mother was scared he would get hurt playing football, but his father did not want him to be a quitter. His parents fed him oatmeal and grits three times a day and over the next four years Parker gained 100 pounds.[8]

Before his senior year of high school Parker moved to Toledo to live with his aunt and uncle and join the army.[9] While walking the halls of his new high school, Toledo Scott, head football coach Artie Brighton saw Parker, and asked him try out for the team.[10] Jim explained that he was planning to join the army and that he would need help with room and board if he were to stay in school and play football. Brighton helped Jim find a number of paper routes. In addition Parker had a job parking cars at a downtown garage.[11] Parker remembered, "I used to get up at 4:30 in the morning and go through my papers before school, then after school, I had already got me a job parkin cars, and I parked cars until 11 o'clock every night. It was hellish for that year tryin to go to school and work all these jobs. I didn't even go to prom because I couldn't afford a suit."[12]

Ohio State coach Woody Hayes heard about Parker, who made All-City and according to Jim, "only fourth team all-state," at a football banquet in Toledo, tracked him down at the garage where he was parking cars, and recruited him to play for the Buckeyes.

Despite lavish promises from other major college programs, Parker accepted a scholarship offer from Coach Hayes, who only guaranteed Jim an education.[13]

Hayes became a father figure to Jim at Ohio State, allowing Jim to stay at his home his freshmen year at a time when few blacks lived on campus.[14] Parker explained, "He told me things that I don't think he told anyone else. He told me, 'I can only play three blacks at a time.' He said he had to answer to 20,000 people downtown, that's the Quarterback Club. He locked the door in his office and told me."[15]

Parker came to Ohio State "the rawest of recruits."[16] Standing 6'2" and weighing 248 pounds, Jim was molded by Hayes and his coaching staff into one of the finest linemen in college football history combining size, strength, explosive cat-like speed, and determination.[17] Parker excelled as a guard in Hayes' run oriented, three yards and a cloud of dust offense, and on defense. Jim was a member of Ohio State's 1954 undefeated national championship team, a two time All-American, and the 1956 Outland Trophy winner, as the nation's top interior linemen.[18] Parker was inducted into the College Football Hall of Fame in 1974, and named to the College Football All-Century Team. Upon Parker's selection to the All-Century Team, Hayes stated, "Jim could block anybody. He was great on blocking, pulling, or trapping. And he gave us great protection for our passer." Woody further said that on defense, "they couldn't block Parker."[19]

Parker said of Hayes, "If he told me, 'Go out and move that stadium two inches to the right or four inches forward,' I would do it."[20]

In the 1957 NFL Draft, Parker was selected in the first round by the Baltimore Colts with the eighth overall pick of the draft. Parker was reluctant to come to Baltimore after Big Daddy Lipscomb showed him around the city. "I didn't like what I saw. I couldn't go to a movie. I couldn't go to the Hecht Company [Baltimore department store]. But I told [Colts owner Carroll] Rosenbloom, 'You find me a decent place to live in the city, and I'll come.'" Rosenbloom found him an apartment, and Baltimore became Jim's home.[21]

Jim signed a two year, no-cut contract for $12,500 a season and received a $1500 bonus, which was paid in $1 bills.[22]: "My wife and I were in G.M. Don Kellett's office negotiating.... I wouldn't sign. We broke for lunch, and he sent someone to the bank to get 1500 ones. When we came back they were all stacked on the desk. 'That's yours,' he told me. My wife [Mae] pinched the hell out of my leg. It still hurts. 'Sign it,' she said. So I signed.... When we got back to the hotel room I put all those one-dollar bills in the bathtub. 'Let's take a bath in money,' I said. Hell, that wasn't any damn money.[23]

When Parker joined the Colts, Hayes suggested to head coach Weeb Ewbank that his best chance to succeed would be on defense.[24] The Colts' coaching staff instead slotted Jim at offensive left tackle. The Colts' pass oriented attack led by quarterback Johnny Unitas was a new challenge for the now 6'3", 273-pound linemen, as he would need to learn how to pass block and protect Unitas. Ewbank, flatly told Parker, "Just remember one thing. The quickest way to make yourself unpopular is to let that guy, number 19, get hurt." That guy was John Unitas.[25]

Parker still had issues once he arrived at the Colts' Westminster training camp. After a run in with the equipment manager over his need for a custom helmet and shoulder pads, Parker left camp and headed back to Columbus. Rosenbloom stepped in and settled the dispute in Parker's favor.[26]

According to Parker, he again faced racial quotas and issues in the NFL:

The team had a quota: seven blacks. There were seven of us for eight years. At Westminster, the eighth black come, don't give a dawn how good he was, they'd ship him out at midnight … so for the eleven years I played here I had a chip on my shoulder…. I got along with my teammates because that was a close-knit family. It was outsiders. When coaches had their annual picnic at Westminster the local people didn't like mixing with us, so we had to rent the entire hall at the country club for our Colt Night. We had an amateur night and we all participated.[27]

Rosenbloom offered to move training camp for the black players, but they voted to stay to be close to their families.[28]

Matched against Gino Marchetti, one of the best pass rushers in football, in his first scrimmage, Marchetti made Parker look foolish, toying with the rookie to the delight of the squad. When the befuddled Parker exclaimed, "Wwwhat do I do now?" Art Donovan said, "If I was you Jim, I'd just applaud."[29]

After the Colts opened their 1957 exhibition season against the Bears in Cincinnati and threw the ball 47 times, Parker quipped, "We threw the ball more that day than we did all my four years at Ohio State. In the first half, I played against rookies and it wasn't so bad. Then in the second half they threw Doug Atkins at me. Man, did he give me a lesson that day."[30]

Big Daddy Lipscomb was a great mentor to Jim. "He took me under his wing from the start and taught me everything I know about offensive tackle. You wouldn't think a defense man would know as much as he did about offense."[31]

Despite the intense pressure he faced as a rookie, Parker developed quickly, and was named first team All-Conference by *The Sporting News* in 1957.

In 1958, it all came together for Parker and the Colts. The Colts defeated the Giants in the NFL championship game, and Parker was named first team All-Pro and to the Pro Bowl. Jim gave a dominating performance in the title game controlling Giants defensive end and future Hall of Famer Andy Robustelli. Paul Zimmerman wrote in *Sports Illustrated*, "His domination of Robustelli was something different, a performance so smooth, so complete, that it was used as a textbook for many years. He takes the outside rush, you run him around the corner; he goes inside, you collapse him into the pile. Parker calls it 'the most perfect game I ever played,' and even the game announcers were drawn to this unusual display of line technique that had never been seen before."[32] Robustelli simply stated that Parker was the best he ever played against.[33]

Parker was a student of the game keeping a book on opposing players, studying film, and developing and varying his technique to stay a step ahead of the defenses he faced.[34]

In 1959, the Colts repeated as NFL champions, and Parker again was named first team All-Pro and to the Pro Bowl.

Parker continued as a perennial first team All-Pro and Pro Bowl participant at tackle during the 1960, 1961 and 1962 seasons. In 1963 he was switched to left guard, and made first team All-Pro and the Pro Bowl for three more consecutive seasons at the new position as he remained Unitas' protector. Johnny U sang his praises. "He's probably the best pass blocker around. He's so damn strong and wide, you know, and he has this immense pride. You just know he's going to do the job for you."[35]

Jim's philosophy was simple. "It is better for me to get a broken arm than Unitas. I can block with one arm, he can't pass."[36]

Parker addressed the differences between the tackle and guard positions.

Guard was fun. It was trapping and pulling, decision-making on the go, seeing those defensive backs sitting out there, not being able to get out of the way. It was a train hitting a Volkswagen. You'd mow them down.

But left tackle was my home, the only job in 60 years that I really mastered. It broke up my marriage. Instead of spending time with my family, I was putting time in down in the basement, looking at films of defensive ends.[37]

But Parker enjoyed playing at the guard position. "The tackles were bigger and usually not as agile as the ends. I liked the big guys. Speed boys gave me trouble. I also noticed that the guard's blocking space was comparatively limited. The end had lots of space outside to roam."[38]

At guard, Jim also provided excellent blocking for the Colts' running backs in addition to protecting Unitas. Lenny Moore related, "I can't tell you what a comfort it has been to have his great big wide butt to hide behind. You know when you're behind him nobody is gonna run over him and grab you. And you know the man coming at you knows he's gonna be hit because Jim ain't gonna miss him. What the hell, he's got to be there for a reason. Most of the tough ones are on his side."[39]

Jim played the 1966 season at tackle and for the first time in eight seasons did not make first team All-Pro or the Pro Bowl. By the end of the 1966 season he had played in 136 consecutive games (regular and postseason combined) on the Colts' offensive line.

In 1967, Parker injured his knee in the second game of the season against the Eagles. With the Colts in the midst of a tight Western Conference Coastal Division race under coach Don Shula, Parker decided it was time to retire. "My knee has not come along the way it should. I feel I can't do it. I can't slide to my right and I can't run. This is strictly my decision and my family's. I can't help the team and I won't deprive 40 guys of their big chance."[40]

Shula stated, "it was one of the most unselfish moves ever made in sports. Jim stepped aside strictly to help the team. He will be remembered as one of the greatest offensive linemen in pro football history."[41]

Parker compared the two coaches he played for. Ewbank "was an organizer.... Weeb was the best at that, better than all of them put together. Don Shula was a kind of guy who would look you square in the eye and call you an asshole, but Weeb wasn't built that way. Whatever he was feeling, he always communicated it through somebody else. He would tell Artie Donovan or Big Daddy to tell me something." Parker simply stated that Shula was a genius who covered every phase of football.[42]

In 1973, in his first year of eligibility Parker was inducted into the Pro Football Hall of Fame, with Woody Hayes as his presenter. He was the first pure offensive linemen to be selected to the Hall. In 1994, he was named to the NFL's 75th Anniversary Team at guard.

In retirement, Parker ran a successful liquor business in the Liberty-Garrison neighborhood in Baltimore for 35 years putting in 14-hour workdays. Health issues including a stroke and diabetes forced him to close the business in 1999. "When I came back from the hospital last year, it was real hard," Parker said. "Getting in and out of the truck was hard. Waiting on the people behind the counter was tiring me out. I didn't get up and wait on them. I asked them to come behind the counter and get what they wanted and they'd bring it over to me and I'd ring it up. Most of them had gotten used to doing that. I just didn't feel up to it."[43]

On July 18, 2005, Parker died of heart failure and kidney disease in a Columbia, Missouri, nursing home.

Notes

1. Mike Klingaman, "Jim Parker, 71, Legendary Lineman of Colts Title Teams," *Baltimore Sun*, July 19.2005, http://archive.boston.com/news/globe/obituaries/articles/2005/07/19/jim_parker_71_legendary_lineman_of_colts_title_teams/, accessed December 19, 2017.

2. *Ibid.*

3. Jerry Izenberg, "Johnny Unitas's Bodyguard," *Sport Magazine*, November, 1965, 49.

4. *Ibid.,* 50.

5. Alan Natali, *Woody's Boys* (Wilmington, OH: Orange Frazier, 1995), 51.

6. Klingaman.

7. Izenberg, 50.

8. Natali, 55; Klingaman.

9. Natali, 55.

10. Donald Emmons, "A Season at Scott Launched Career," *The Toledo Blade*, July 19, 2005, http://www.toledoblade.com/High-School/2005/07/19/A-season-at-Scott-launched-career.html, accessed December 19, 2017.

11. Natali, 56.

12. *Ibid.*

13. *Ibid.*

14. Klingaman.

15. Natali, 57.

16. *Ibid.,* 52.

17. https://www.cfbhall.com, accessed August 8, 2017.

18. Jack Park, *The Official Ohio State Football Encyclopedia* (Sports Publishing LLC, 2001), 209.

19. John Steadman, "Jim Parker: Guard of the Century," *The News American*, September 26, 1969, Sports Section.

20. Natali, 59.

21. Vince Bagli and Norman C. Macht, *Sunday at 2:00 with the Baltimore Colts* (Centreville, MD: Tidewater, 1995), 19.

22. Paul Zimmerman, "Total Package," *Sports Illustrated*, September 5, 1994, 69.

23. *Ibid.*

24. Don Smith, "Jim Parker," *The Coffin Corner* 2, No. 1 (1980): 2.

25. Zimmerman, 69.

26. Bagli, 20.

27. *Ibid.*

28. *Ibid.,* 28–29.

29. Mark Bowden, *The Best Game Ever* (New York: Atlantic Monthly Press, 2008), 120–121.

30. Smith, 2.

31. Bagli, 21.

32. Zimmerman, 70.

33. Klingaman.

34. Zimmerman, 70.

35. Izenberg, 93.

36. Jim Murray, "Shadow Knows," *Los Angeles Times*, November 22, 1964, D1.

37. Zimmerman, 69.

38. Don Smith, "Jim Parker, 1973 Enshrinee," *Pro Football Hall of Fame News Release*, 1973, 2.

39. Izenberg, 51.

40. Cameron Snyder, "Jim Parker Announces Retirement," *Baltimore Sun*, December 8, 1967, C1.

41. "Jim Parker Hall of Fame Profile," *Pro! Steelers-Colts NFL Game Program*, September 23, 1979, 81.

42. Bagli, 22.

43. Laurie Willis, "Tackling His Retirement," *Baltimore Sun*, November 23, 1999, http://www.baltimoresun.com/sports/ravens/bal-parker21999-story.html, accessed December 19, 2017.

Bill Pellington

Nick Ritzmann

In 1957 the Baltimore Colts enjoyed their first winning season, but Bill Pellington missed almost all of it after breaking his arm in the first quarter of the season opener trying to clothesline tackle Detroit Lions running back Tom "The Bomb" Tracy. Teammate Art Donovan recalled, "Pellington tried to clothesline Tracy, but he missed his throat and caught him square on the helmet. He knocked Tracy down and out. And I mean out. Tracy was lying on the turf unconscious for a good fifteen minutes. The Detroit trainers and team doctors were afraid to move him off the field until they made sure all his parts were still assembled."[1]

Pellington's absence was welcome news in the other locker rooms around the league, as John Steadman reported in a wire dispatched from Green Bay in October, "Packers happy they don't have to face Pellington, whom they fear."[2] "The truth was, long after the [arm] fracture had healed, he kept his cast for knocking opposing players unconscious."[3] But he also spent over a decade as the Colts' defensive signal caller, nine years as the team captain, and served as a player-coach under Don Shula, the coach with the most victories in professional football history. The player who teammate Alex Hawkins noted "should have been thrown out of every game he ever played, and most of the practices"[4] was smart, determined and, most of all, tough.

William Alvin Pellington, Jr., was born on September 25, 1927, in the city of Paterson, New Jersey, to William A. Pellington, Sr., and Sarah (Sadie) Cross. Several years later his family moved about 15 miles north to the small town of Ramsey, where his parents operated a tavern near the New York State border. Unlike most professional football players, he did not collect awards while playing football in high school. He was a substitute football player, who did not receive a varsity letter until an honorary one was issued in 1964 when he was 36 years old, and reported "the only time I got in while I was in high school was when the score was 55–0 either for us or against us."[5] Upon graduating from high school Pellington enlisted in the U.S. Navy, where he shot up from 160 to 228 pounds in just 22 months.[6]

Bill Pellington.

After having played little high school football, and receiving zero college football scholarship offers, he began his career at tiny Defiance College in Ohio, which he attended on the G.I. Bill.[7] He played quarterback and blocking back in the single wing there, where he was one of four players from Ramsey (out of 42 players on the roster) who suited up for coach Larry "Dutch" Schultz's Yellow Jackets in 1947. He played well enough to be elected to the Defiance College Athletic Hall of Fame 30 years later. Pellington sat out the 1948 season after transferring to Rutgers University in his home state of New Jersey.

The 1949 Rutgers University Football Media Guide identifies Bill Pellington as a 21-year-old right tackle standing six feet, one inch tall, weighing 215 pounds and "showing considerable promise." He was moved up to the first string right tackle position at the conclusion of preseason training camp in September,[8] and also played some at linebacker as coach Harvey Harman's Scarlet Knights posted a 6–3 record. In 1950 he played both offensive and defensive tackle, and occasionally kicked extra points as the team finished with a 4–4 record, but did not letter in 1951. Pellington later commented, "When I went to Rutgers they looked on me as only a so-so player."[9]

The 1952 NFL draft was held on January 17 in New York City and the 12 teams selected 360 players over 30 rounds, but Bill Pellington's name was not called. However, a Rutgers assistant coach who had briefly played professional football with the Dayton Triangles in 1928 named Arthur Matsu gave a recommendation to Cleveland coach Paul Brown, and the Browns signed Pellington to a contract in April.[10] Pellington attempted to make the team as an offensive guard, but was placed on waivers in early August after "only two scrimmage plays as an offensive tackle,"[11] and afterwards turned down a chance for a tryout with the Dallas Texans. Pellington himself noted, "The Browns did not know where to play me. I was too small to play on the offensive line as I had at Rutgers and I wasn't exactly the type you'd find running the ball in the NFL."[12]

Years later, this assessment would not stop Colts head coach Weeb Ewbank (a Browns assistant coach in 1952) from reminding Pellington in a fiery pregame speech in the visiting locker room at Yankee Stadium before the 1958 NFL championship game that, "The Browns cut you after one scrimmage!"[13] Home in New Jersey, he worked some as an ironworker, helping to build the original Tappan Zee Bridge over the Hudson River in the early 1950s.[14] The Colts' *1953 Press, Radio and TV Guide* notes that after being released Pellington decided to "settle down and run his father's restaurant and night club. However, he has changed his mind and wants to take another crack at making the grade in pro ball." The list of NFL offensive players who rue the day Bill Pellington chose to "take another crack at making the grade in pro ball" runs long, as he was about to spend over a decade as "the toughest and meanest player in Colt history."[15]

As the calendar turned to 1953, Otis Douglas was hired by the new Baltimore football franchise as a "coach, trainer, and scout."[16] Douglas, who began his NFL playing career when he was 35 years old, had played football at the College of William & Mary in 1929 and 1930. The same Arthur Matsu who had earlier recommended Pellington to Paul Brown in Cleveland, had played and coached at William & Mary and gave a recommendation to Douglas, saying Pellington was "fast, smart, knew the game and should make a good pro player."[17] The Colts signed him to a contract in April. When the players began to report in July to training camp in Westminster, Maryland, Pellington wanted to get there so badly he hitchhiked all the way from northern New Jersey to compete for a slot on the active roster. Pellington "packed an overnight bag, tied his football shoes to the handle and started to hitch"[18] "Football represented such a craving that he was the only player in the thirty-five year history of the [Baltimore Colts] franchise to hitchhike to training camp, traveling from his home in Ramsey, New Jersey, to the Colts' facility at Western Maryland College in 1953."[19]

Wearing number 65 during his rookie season and initially slated to play guard, he was steered towards playing linebacker in training camp by assistant coach Nick Wasylik[20] and was also tried at fullback.[21] The Colts lacked linebackers and "Pellington was elected to give the job a try."[22] It's likely that at this point in his life, Bill Pellington had not played in 50 football games; but he would go on to start over twice that many as a linebacker for the Colts, where he was "one of the two real leaders on that unit, along with Gino Marchetti. Gino led by example, and Pellington led by verbal intimidation."[23] The Colts finished their inaugural season with a 3–9 record under head coach Keith Molesworth, but there was talent on the squad, including two future Hall of Fame players on the defensive line, Marchetti and Donovan. But Donovan noted, "[Pellington] was a tough, tough football player and no one was worried about me or Gino—it was Pellington."[24] After the season owner Carroll Rosenbloom elevated Molesworth to the front office and replaced him with former Browns assistant Weeb Ewbank. Pellington would play the remainder of his career for only two head coaches, both of whom are in the Hall of Fame.

The Colts also finished the 1954, 1955 and 1956 seasons with losing records, but Pellington was starting at linebacker and improving all the time. "If I don't see Pellington again, it will be too soon," commented ball carrier Alex Webster of the Giants. "When Pellington came into this league, he could be 'had,'" said L.A. Rams end Elroy "Crazy Legs" Hirsch, "but he's tough now, certainly one of the most underrated linebackers in the Western Division."[25] He was not just tough on the opponents: "In a Blue-White game— an intrasquad game!—[Colts center Buzz Nutter heard] Pellington shout, 'Goddamn you Sandusky, if you hold me one more time, I'm going to kill you!' The next thing you knew. Alex was standing there with his teeth in his hands." Sandusky gave Nutter a look of abject disgust and said calmly, "That son of a bitch knocked my front teeth out. In an intrasquad game."[26]

Pellington led the 1955 Colts with four fumble recoveries, and he also intercepted two passes. Coach Ewbank named Pellington (now wearing number 36) captain of the Colts prior to the 1956 regular season opener against the Chicago Bears, and he continued to call the defensive signals (along with defensive back Don Shula).[27] Despite breaking a thumb, he started all 12 games in 1956 and was also the Colts' representative at initial talks held in New York City in late December regarding the organization of a players' union and was elected to a leadership position in the nascent organization. He ended up serving as secretary-treasurer for seven years.

Even with Pellington missing almost all of the 1957 season, the Colts were a vastly improved team, and after beating the Los Angeles Rams at Memorial Stadium on December 1, they had a full game lead over San Francisco and Detroit in the West, who were deadlocked in second place. But they lost their final two games of the season, leaving them one game out of first place when the season ended.

According to Art Donovan,

when he returned in 1958, the team doctor outfitted him with a steel cast over his arm. During pregame warm-ups, [Pellington] would wrap the cast with a big, thick foam rubber tubing. The officials would check his arm-cast, tubing, and all-and tell him it was okay to play with this wrapping. But when we'd head back to the locker room for a final prayer and last-minute instructions right before kickoff, Pellington would take the thick padding off his arm and replace it with this little quarter-inch foam rubber sleeve, He'd hit somebody with that cast and it would be like hitting them with a sledgehammer. Midweek game films turned into horror movies as we'd all sit around and count how many blocks Pellington would knock off each week. I'll never forget Billy Howton, a wide receiver for the Packers, walking up to an official and telling him, "Why don't you just give the sonofabitch a gun and let him do a clean job on us."[28]

During the Colts' championship season in 1958 Pellington earned postseason honors for the first time, as he was named Second Team All-Pro by the Newspaper Enterprise Association (NEA). Pellington never received (first team) All-Pro recognition or an invitation to the Pro Bowl because "all-star voting was unrestricted by position and the three [linebackers] chosen were all middle linebackers."[29] Only in 1962 when Pellington played his first full season at middle linebacker, were two outside linebackers selected.[30]

After helping the Colts to the 1958 championship, Pellington began 1959 by breaking his right hand in an exhibition game against the Pittsburgh Steelers, then re-breaking it one week later in an exhibition game against the Chicago Cardinals. But he played on and had an outstanding season, intercepting four passes, including one thrown by Green Bay Packer quarterback Lamar McHan on October 25, which he returned 30 yards for his only NFL touchdown. Pellington played a particularly memorable game on December 5 in Kezar Stadium. The Colts traveled west with a 7–3 record to finish the season as they traditionally did, by playing their final two games in San Francisco and Los Angeles. Coach Ewbank told the team, "We beat the 49ers physically the last time and we had to go even further this time and get sadistic. Well they got so sadistic that I had to call a halt on some of them. Pellington was like a wild man. I had to take him out to cool him off. But that's the kind of play that wins games."[31] The Colts won both games and repeated as NFL champions.

The new decade began with Colts defensive assistant coach Charley Winner calling Pellington "the most underrated linebacker in the league" and another coach noted "he would be the best man on the squad in a knock down drag out fight."[32] He was 32 years old and a starting outside linebacker for a back to back world championship team. The Colts finished a disappointing 6–6, but Pellington was again named second team All-NFL by the NEA.

As the Colts assembled for their 1961 training camp, a question was posed in the Colts' press room regarding which Colts could play the most positions on a professional football team? Coach Ewbank said, "Gino Marchetti would certainly have to be considered, but don't count out Bill Pellington.... Pellington could play defensive end and even offensive tackle. He would be too light as a defensive tackle, but he would make a great offensive guard and could step in and play fullback without hurting our team a bit."[33] The 1961 season brought more of the same standout play, and he continued to call all the plays, but it also brought an important change, as Pellington was switched to middle linebacker prior to the October 22 victory over the Detroit Lions with Jackie Burkett, the Colts' 1959 first-round draft pick from Auburn University taking over one of the outside linebacker positions. Pellington intercepted two passes the following week in a tight loss at home to the Chicago Bears. The Colts ended the season with an 8–6 record.

In January of 1963 Colts owner Carroll Rosenbloom let Weeb Ewbank go and hired 33-year-old defensive assistant coach Don Shula from the Detroit Lions on the recommendation of Gino Marchetti.[34] Marchetti and Pellington had been Colts teammates with Shula, and both were older than him. After naming Charley Winner as defensive assistant coach, Shula made Marchetti and Pellington player-coaches, with Marchetti handling the defensive line and Pellington the linebackers. Despite missing some time in the pre-season with a knee injury as injuries began to take a toll, he had a fine season at the age of 36 and the Colts finished with an 8–6 record.

Pellington relinquished his coaching duties in 1964, opened Bill Pellington's Iron Horse Lounge restaurant in the spring, and announced that he would retire from playing at the end of the season. Coach Shula noted, "There might have been better football players in this league, but I've never seen a more aggressive one, or one with a greater desire."[35] The Colts lost their season opener in Minnesota, then reeled off 11 straight victories before losing at home to the Detroit Lions on December 6. Pellington and Marchetti were given a prime-time 30-minute televised tribute show on Saturday, December 12, 1964, then were given a special day of recognition before the Colts beat the Redskins the next day to finish the regular season with a 12–2 record. Pellington finished his twelve-year playing career in Cleveland, where the Browns defeated the Colts 27–0 to capture the 1964 NFL championship. Pellington was named second team All NFL by the AP and NEA for his final season efforts.

Pellington sold his restaurant in 1984, and was inducted into the inaugural class of the Rutgers University Athletics Hall of Fame in 1988.

He passed away in Baltimore on April 26, 1994, of respiratory failure associated with Alzheimer's disease. Teammate Marchetti noted, "He was a fighter and even though he wasn't a natural athlete, through hard work and determination he became one of the toughest and meanest linebackers of the game during the 1950s and 1960s."[36] Sportswriter Cameron Snyder noted, "It always surprised Bill that fans and rivals consider him a mean, vicious player: That's the game, isn't it … hit and being hit, but hit hardest."[37]

NOTES

1. Arthur J. Donovan, Jr., and Bob Drury, *Fatso: Football When Men Were Really Men* (New York: Avon Books, 1987), 172–173.

2. Cameron C. Snyder, "Colts Choice by One Point," *Baltimore Sun*, October 12, 1957.

3. Tom Callahan, *Johnny U: The Life & Times of John Unitas* (New York: Crown, 2006), 65.

4. *Ibid.*

5. George Bowen, "Pellington Puzzle to Colts 'Addicts,'" *Cumberland Evening Times*, October 7, 1964.

6. "Bill Pellington No Longer Afraid to Pack Large Bag," *Daily Times* (Salisbury, MD), August 20, 1957.

7. Dick Kelly, "Spotlight on Sports," *Hagerstown* (MD) *Daily Mail,* August 1, 1959.

8. "Harman Shifts Scarlet Lineup," *Courier News* (Bridgewater, NJ), September 13, 1949.

9. " Bill Pellington No Longer Afraid to Pack Large Bag."

10. "Sign Rutgers Ace," *Courier News* (Bridgewater, NJ), April 8, 1952.

11. Bill Pellington No Longer Afraid to Pack Large Bag."

12. Kelly.

13. Mark Bowden, *The Best Game Ever* (New York: Atlantic Monthly Press, 2009), 147.

14. Callahan, 65.

15. "25-Year Retrospective on 1958 Championship Game," *Baltimore Sun*, December 28, 1983.

16. Cameron C. Snyder, "Otis Douglas Joins Colts," *Baltimore Sun*, February 10, 1953.

17. Cameron C. Snyder, "Colts Announce Signing of Joe Campanella, Giant Defensive Tackle," *Baltimore Sun,* April 19, 1953.

18. Bill Pellington No Longer Afraid To Pack Large Bag."

19. John Steadman, "Pellington Was Intense Warrior Who Paid His Dues," *Baltimore Sun*, April 27, 1994.

20. Kelly.

21. Cameron C. Snyder, "Colts Prep for Invasion of Lions Saturday Night," *Baltimore Sun*, October 1, 1953.

22. "Bill Pellington No Longer Afraid to Pack Large Bag."

23. Frank Gifford with Peter Richmond, *The Glory Game* (New York: HarperCollins, 2008), 137.

24. DeWitt Bliss and Fred Rasmussen, "Pellington Lauded for Iron Play, Kind Heart," *Baltimore Sun*, April 27, 1994.

25. "Linebacker Is Signed by the Hosses," *Daily Times* (Salisbury, MD), July 13, 1957.

26. Callahan, 93.

27. Cameron C. Snyder, "Ewbank Names Pellington Captain of Colts for Opener," *Baltimore Sun*, September 27, 1956.

28. Donovan, 173.

29. "Pellington Puzzle to Colt 'Addicts.'"

30. Bob Maisel, "The Morning After," *Baltimore Sun*, January 20, 1963.

31. Cameron C. Snyder, "Ewbank Hits Unitas Call on Final TD," *Baltimore Sun*, December 7, 1959.

32. Cameron C. Snyder, "Pellington Underrated," Baltimore Sun, August 31, 1960.

33. Cameron C. Snyder, "Marchetti, Pellington Most Versatile Colts," *Baltimore Sun*, August 24, 1961.

34. Callahan, 198.

35. Maisel.

36. Bliss and Rasmussen.

37. Cameron C. Snyder, "Pellington, the Roughest Colt, to Quit at Year's End," *Baltimore Sun*, September 4, 1964.

Sherman Plunkett

John W. Lesko

"This guy was an ocean liner,"[1] wrote Art Donovan. "Getting past him is like taking a trip around the world,"[2] remarked Hank Stram during the 1967 AFL All-Star Game.

Although he won two league championships as a member of the Baltimore Colts and was an All-AFL performer for the New York Jets, Sherman Plunkett is best remembered for his rotundness. He was affectionately nicknamed "Big Boy" and "Tank." A quiet, modest, likeable man, he perfectly fit the stereotype of a gentle giant. Plunkett played pro football for ten years, he played in three league championship games, and he even coined a famous player's nickname.

Sherman Eugene Plunkett was born April 17, 1933, in Oklahoma City, Oklahoma. Plunkett played organized football for the first time while in the seventh grade. Two years later, he had sprouted to 6'3" and 230 pounds. He was an All-State offensive tackle at Frederick A. Douglass High School—the first black high school in Oklahoma City. Plunkett's coach, Pieya Miller, steered him into enrolling at Maryland State College where he would be a two-way tackle for the Hawks of the Central Intercollegiate Athletic Association. Located in the tiny village of Princess Anne, Maryland State College is now known as the University of Maryland Eastern Shore. Miller's connection to a college more than 1,400 miles away was his former college classmate, Vernon "Skip" McCain.

McCain coached the Hawks for 16 successful years and was later inducted into the College Football Hall of Fame. He was a great teacher-coach. In addition to coaching the football team, Coach McCain was also an assistant mathematics professor. He was a great builder of character and encouraged his players and students to do well on the field and in the classroom. McCain instilled confidence in them so that they could become successful after graduation. Star player Sylvester "Swifty" Polk stated, "Coach made it a point to come by all the players' dorm rooms. He would check your schoolwork and he would ask for input on the team as far as strategy, practice, etc. He would let us know that our opinions counted with him."[3] Based upon the way Plunkett interacted with people after he left the school, it is clear that McCain's humility and teachings rubbed off on him.

Plunkett's blocking skills were recognized and a pro football career was on the horizon. Plunkett was named to the All-CIAA team two times. In advance of the 1954 Orange Blossom Classic between the Hawks and Florida A & M, Cal Adams wrote, "Sports writers have given Plunkett top priority in the race as the man most likely to succeed as a professional player. Standing six feet, four inches tall, Sherman is said to be the most vicious tackler in the CIAA. Players on most teams met this year voted him the man who gave them the most trouble."[4]

After helping the Hawks win the CIAA title in 1955, Plunkett was drafted by the Cleveland Browns with the 71st selection in the 1956 NFL draft. Unfortunately, Plunkett did not impress the Cleveland coaching staff enough to make the team. He was released on August 4. Due to the Korean War, Plunkett was drafted into the Army a short while later.

Plunkett spent two years in the Army. He was stationed at the military base in Fort Dix, New Jersey. Roosevelt Grier, who had already established himself as a top level defensive lineman, was also stationed at Fort Dix. Grier helped Plunkett become a better football player during their time together. The service team on which they played was top notch. The squad lost only one game in two years. A highlight was travelling north to West Point and hammering Army's B team by a score of 65–0.

Sherman Plunkett.

Plunkett received first platoon All-Army honors in 1957. Joining Plunkett on the first platoon were future NFL head coach Jim Hanifan (Schweinfurt, Germany) and eventual Pro Football Hall of Famer Forrest Gregg (Fort Carson, Colorado). Grier was a second platoon selection as was future Pro Football Hall of Famer Willie Davis (Fort Carson, Colorado). Plunkett's military play caught the attention of the NFL. After his discharge from the Army, he was signed as a free agent by Baltimore Colts personnel director Keith Molesworth.

When Colts training camp opened on July 28, 1958, Plunkett's goal was just to make the team. There were no expectations that he could unseat veteran offensive tackles Jim Parker and George Preas for a starting role. Plunkett also saw time on the defensive line, but it would be even harder for him to crack the lineup on that side of the ball due to the presence of tackles Art Donovan and Eugene "Big Daddy" Lips-comb.

Plunkett played on offense and defense in the Colts' preseason opener vs. the Philadelphia Eagles in Hershey, Pennsylvania, on August 16. Colts head coach Weeb Ewbank was intrigued by Plunkett's showing. He stated to the press, "I thought Plunkett did a good job. I can't tell for sure about him or any of the players until we study the film, but my impression was he was adequate on both offense and defense."[5]

Training camp was not a walk in the park. Plunkett had to go head-to-head with All-Pros Donovan and Gino Marchetti. These master linemen gave Plunkett a good lick-ing on a daily basis. The tough treatment he received only made him a better player. He had always exhibited a great work ethic. His dedication to succeed and do right by his coaches along with his easygoing manner enabled him to withstand the punishment from the veterans. In the end, this benefited everyone on the team.

By early September, Plunkett's role on the team crystallized. Plunkett would be deployed as a reserve offensive lineman. Additionally, he would play on five special teams units. Sporting jersey number 79, Plunkett was a regular on the kickoff, kickoff return, place kicking, punt, and punt return teams. He was a nice fit for the kickoff and punt teams due to his tackling ability and speed. His blocking skills put him on the kickoff and punt return teams. His sheer size made him an ideal fit on the place kicking unit. On that particular unit Plunkett would usually align three spots to the right of the center. The goal was obstruction.

Plunkett spelled Jim Parker from time to time at offensive tackle but most of his playing time came on the special team units. After the fourth game, Ewbank was excited about the big lineman's potential. "He's learning fast. Just give him a little time, and you'll see quite a lineman one of these days. The boy has a lot of equipment. It'll take him a year to gain the necessary polish. He's eager and has a good attitude."[6] Plunkett had flashed enough potential that Ewbank would not hesitate to start him on offense if the need arose. Ewbank felt it normally takes a couple years for linemen to grasp the game from a mental standpoint. According to the coach, the mental part of the game would not hold back Plunkett.

Plunkett did not have to wait too long to receive extended playing time. Due to an injury suffered the prior week, Preas was unable to play in the November 2 game versus Green Bay. Plunkett played the whole way on offense. He did a fine job that afternoon in Baltimore's 56–0 demolition of the Packers.

A fine rookie season culminated in the title game against the New York Giants. There were many key plays made by each team in the Colts thrilling 23–17 overtime vic-tory. As big as any other play was the Colts' field goal attempt towards the end of regu-lation. Plunkett was on the field for that play. He was aligned on the right side of the line and was tasked with making sure his opponent did not squeeze by him or leap to block the kick. No problem. The youngster did all right. The opponent was stymied. The kick was good.

To this point in his football life, all Plunkett really knew was winning. He did not lose much in high school, college, or service ball. He played for a league champion in his first pro season. Then his team won the league title again the following season. When the Colts dipped to 6–6 in 1960, Plunkett finally had a taste of what it was like to play for a mediocre team.

In the 1960 training camp, Plunkett was given a strong look on defense. The defensive linemen were aging and Ewbank felt it would be easier for the team to convert Plunkett to defense than to bring in an outsider via free agency or a trade. Alas, Plunkett's demeanor was not suited for playing on the defensive side of the ball on the professional level. He did not play in an aggressive manner or embrace confrontation. The experiment ended when Ewbank determined Plunkett's size, speed and laid back personality would allow him to succeed only on offense. After another quality season as a reserve, the big guy's size spelled the end of his days with the Colts.

On September 12, 1961, Ewbank released Plunkett due to his weight. The coach had been upset with Plunkett's conditioning and wanted the lineman's weight to not exceed 300 pounds. Earlier in the summer, Plunkett was informed that he would receive an extra $500 if he reported to camp at no more than 275 pounds. That nice piece of change was not enough of an enticement to Plunkett. He showed up to camp at more than 300 pounds.

Sherman did not like telling people what he would eat and there was strong evidence that he would order food and eat alone or when he did not think others were looking. Parker was one of Plunkett's roommates and saw the struggle firsthand.

> He was the only fat man I ever saw who never ate anything. To listen to him, he never ate any breakfast, lunch or dinner, just some crackers and cheese. I remember once when Weeb sent him to Johns Hopkins Hospital to have his thyroid checked to see if anything was wrong with him. When he came back and knew he was all right he couldn't understand why he put on weight. But I knew. One night when we were rooming together he thought I was asleep. He pulled out some crackers and cheese in the middle of the night and started eating them. I told him I thought a rat was in the room when I smelled all that cheese.[7]

Another roommate was Lipscomb. Listed at 6'6" and 284 pounds, Lipscomb was known as "Big Daddy." Because they were roommates and friends, it was only natural that the other behemoth would be given a nickname that played off of Lipscomb's. It was decided that Plunkett would be "Big Boy." In the early 1960s it was important that these fellows had each other. Coaching was not anywhere near as advanced as it is today and the players tended to give pointers and tips to teammates particularly the younger ones. From a football standpoint, Lipscomb was a valuable teammate and influence on Plunkett. More importantly, their friendship extended beyond football. Baltimore was segregated at the time. The white players would go out with the white players to white establishments. "Big Daddy" and "Big Boy" would go out to the black jazz clubs together along with the other black Colts. When Lipscomb died from a heroin overdose on May 10, 1963, he was still living with Plunkett even though both were no longer with the Colts.

Sherman was signed by the San Diego Chargers on September 19, 1961. Switching to jersey number 70, Sherman filled the same role in San Diego as he had in Baltimore. The Chargers already had a young star named Ron Mix at right tackle. Plunkett did spell Mix in 1961 and performed well for AFL Western Division champions. The Chargers hosted the Houston Oilers in the league title game on Christmas Eve. Right guard Sam DeLuca was unable to play due to an injury. Chargers coach Sid Gillman moved Mix to right guard and gave the right tackle assignment to Plunkett. The Oilers were victorious but Plunkett once again found himself playing for a highly successful team.

The Chargers fell off a cliff in 1962. Their record slipped to 4–10 chiefly due to injuries. On a personal level, it was a nice season for Plunkett because he received regular playing time at right tackle. Mix was the starting right guard. DeLuca was not available due to injury. Training camp was not fun, however. Plunkett's weight was once again a major issue and his team had him checked out for a thyroid condition. He reported to camp at 320 pounds. Gillman wanted him down to 285 for the season opener in Denver on September 7. Sherman was able to get his weight down a bit and played the season with a listed figure of 290 pounds.

Ewbank was fired by the Colts after the 1962 campaign and was soon hired by the New York Jets. He hired several young assistants. Chuck Knox would be in charge of the offensive line. The roster was a motley collection of castoffs, never-weres, and youngsters. Ewbank recognized the need for a calming veteran influence like Plunkett. On August 7, Ewbank got his man. He traded the Jets' 1964 seventh-round draft choice to San Diego to bring "Big Boy" to New York. Although the weight issue was always present, Plunkett provided great value to his teams due to his superb pass blocking. With the Jets, Plunkett was finally in a spot where he could be expected to maintain a starting role for years to come.

Plunkett played for the Jets from 1963 to 1967. Sporting jersey number 79 once again, Sherman was a fixture at right tackle for the Jets. He played in every regular season game in his half decade with the team. His role became especially important when the Jets drafted a hotshot quarterback named Joe Namath before the 1965 season. Due to knee injuries, Namath was not very mobile. It was key that he receive quality blocking so that he could be kept healthy enough to play. Namath certainly got that help from Plunkett.

Paul Zimmerman wrote, "Sherm never lifted weights and seldom watched his own. God had blessed him with an unusually quick pair of feet, and he used them to keep his ample body constantly positioned in front of his man. He was effective enough to make the All-League team one year."[8] Plunkett became Namath's personal bodyguard on the field. Before road games, it was said that Namath wouldn't go on board until he knew Plunkett was already on board.

Plunkett took great pride in keeping Namath upright. Even beyond age 30, Plunkett still possessed great speed for an offensive lineman. In the 1964 training camp, Plunkett ran a 40-yard dash in 5.2 seconds. To protect Namath, he only needed to fend off opponents for a few seconds. With Namath's lightning-quick release, a few seconds was all he would need. "You get very tired protecting a scrambling quarterback but with Joe you know what to do, he goes back eight or nine yards, you get him four or five seconds."[9]

According to Zimmerman,

> In Plunkett's prime, there were few tackles better at maintaining the vacuum inside, which is the key to the passer's protective pocket, or cup. An inside rush against Plunkett was almost useless, since he could lean on a man and cave him into the logjam in the middle of the line. Plunkett knew how to practice the subtle arts, too. His hands and arms were always busy, always flirting with a 15-yard holding penalty. A quick push with both hands, a quick grab of the jersey; he knew all the tricks. But his best technique was a short, jolting punch to the midsection, not enough to cause any real injury, but sufficiently distracting to destroy timing. It used to be fun watching someone play against Big Sherm for the first time, to see the look of shock and amazement when he tasted that first solar plexus blow. It was as if a great canvas dummy had suddenly struck back, or the faithful family Labrador retriever had suddenly turned and inflicted upon its owner a deep, painful bite.[10]

Plunkett started to lose some ability in 1967. He was 34 years old and the natural aging process had taken effect. Zimmerman wrote, "When the end came for one of the big fellows, it came suddenly and without warning. During the 1967 season Plunkett started losing his quickness afoot—and this was coming off an All-Pro year in 1966. The word went out to the defensive ends, via movie projector, that Plunkett could be beaten to the outside. Moves were laid aside, and every battle became a footrace to the outside between the defensive end and Sherm, a race Sherman wound up losing too often."[11] Kansas City Chiefs defensive end Jerry Mays remarked, "Twisting him was like twisting a building. But his legs eventually went on him. Legs are so important. Even if you're properly conditioned, you usually can't get anywhere against a blocker for three quarters. Then his legs tire and he can be had."[12]

Sherman's pro football career ended when Ewbank cut him on August 7, 1968. Plunkett reported to camp at 337 pounds and considering he had already lost a step, this was not a good development. His wife, Betty, tried to help with Plunkett's weight issue. She put him on a diet each March and kept a good eye on what he would eat in their home. Plunkett still could not keep his weight down. "We just had to let him go. He got too far out of shape."[13] Only a couple days prior to the release, Ewbank stated, "If he gets down to 310, we may argue. He's supposed to report in good shape and he's not. I just told him that, with 19 games, one of these years his legs are going to give out. And he's lost speed and agility because of his excessive weight."[14] It was an unceremonious end to a career. To add insult to injury, Plunkett missed out on another championship ring when the Jets would go on to win the Super Bowl that season.

Annapolis mayor Roger W. "Pip" Moyer offered Plunkett a job in the city's recreation department. Moyer was a teammate of Sherman's on the Fort Dix team. Plunkett accepted the offer and worked with and mentored children, the majority of them from poor families, for the next 17 years.

It can be argued that Plunkett's greatest contribution to pro football was tagging Namath with a famous nickname. The July 19, 1965, issue of *Sports Illustrated* featured a cover story on the young quarterback. Namath was photographed wearing his uniform in Times Square. Each Jets player was given a copy of the magazine. When Namath entered the locker room, Plunkett in his delightful manner blurted out, "Look at him. Cat's been out on Broadway all night. You Broadway, Joe. You Broadway. Broadway Joe."[15]

Plunkett died of cancer on November 18, 1989, in Baltimore. He was survived by Betty; his mother, Dorothy Copelyn; and his brother, Charles. He was a winning football player in high school, college, service ball, and pro football. He was recognized as an All-AFL player in 1966 and was inducted into the Maryland Eastern Shore Hall of Fame in 1977. Most importantly, he was a good-natured big guy who was beloved by teammates and fans.

NOTES

1. Arthur J. Donovan, Jr., and Bob Drury, *Fatso: Football When Men Were Really Men* (New York: Avon Books, 1987), 17.

2. Paul Zimmerman, *The New Thinking Man's Guide to Pro Football* (New York: Simon & Schuster, 1984), 39–40.

3. "Vernon 'Skip' McCain: A Lost Legacy of Excellence," www.umes.edu/Football/mccain.pdf, accessed October 10, 2016.

4. Cal Adams, "Maryland State Arrives; Eyes Set on Victory Over Rattlers," *St. Petersburg Times*, December 3, 1954.

5. Cameron C. Snyder, "Billy Pricer Gets Praise," *Baltimore Sun*, August 18, 1958.

6. "Plunkett Heads for Colt Stardom," *Daily Times* (Salisbury, MD), October 25, 1958.

7. Joe Jares, "Sherman's Battle of the Bulge," *Sports Illustrated*, August 5, 1968.

8. Zimmerman, 39.

9. Robert Lipsyte, "Plunkett Has One Job," *Decatur Daily Review*, October 17, 1967.

10. Zimmerman, 40.

11. *Ibid.*

12. *Ibid.*

13. Mike Recht, "Plunkett Eats Himself Out of Job with Jets," *Daily News*, August 8, 1968.
14. Jares.
15. Mark Kriegel, *Namath: A Biography* (New York: Penguin, 2004), 155.

REFERENCES

"'All' Players Contribute to Colts' Success Story." *Afro-American*, November 15, 1958.
"Brackins, Grier. "Plunkett on All-Army Football Squad." *Washington Afro-American*, December 10, 1957.
"Chargers' Problems Big: Ladd, Plunkett." *Arizona Republic*, July 26, 1962.
Claassen, Harold. "Zaiser Gets 2nd Team 'Little Berth.'" *News Journal* (Wilmington, DE), December 1, 1955.
"Colts Tackle Faces Change." *Baltimore Sun*, July 27, 1960.
"Daily Drill of Browns Called Off by Rain." *Chicago Tribune*, August 5, 1956.
"Ex-Colt Plunkett Fastest Jet." *Afro-American*, August 8, 1964.
Hogrogian, John. "The Jets' First Training Camp." *The Coffin Corner* 17, no. 3 (1995).
"Knees Key Attack." *St. Petersburg Times*, August 28, 1968.
Land, Charles. "Work Pays Off for Tide's Ried Drinkard." *Tuscaloosa News*, September 30, 1970.
Linthicum, Jesse A. "Unitas O.K. for Giants." *Baltimore Sun*, November 3, 1958.
Maxymuk, John. *Uniform Numbers of the NFL*. Jefferson, NC: McFarland, 2005.
"Meilinger Goes to Pittsburgh with 2 Others." *The Tennessean*, September 13, 1961.
"Norwalk Athletic Association Celebrates 50 Years of Success." www.thehour.com/sports.article/Norwalk-Athletic-Association-celebrates-50-years-8247804.php, November 6, 2008, accessed October 10, 2016.
"Plunkett Must Cut His Weight." *The Morning Herald*, August 18, 1961.
"Reason for Colt Success Is Strength of Reserves," *Baltimore Sun*, November 28, 1958.
"Sherman Plunkett Dies; Played for Colts in '58–'59." *Baltimore Sun*, November 20, 1989.
"Sherman Plunkett, Former Jets Tackle, 56." *New York Times*, November 21, 1989.
www.profootballarchives.com/1958nflbal.html, accessed August 23, 2016.
"Sherman 'The Gentle Giant or Tank' Plunkett." www.umes.edu/football/selectedprohawks/selected/shermanplunkett.pdf, accessed August 23, 2016.
"Snyder, Cameron C. "Colts Begin First Drills." *Baltimore Sun*, July 29, 1958.
2014 Official NFL Record & Fact Book. New York: Time Home Entertainment, 2014.
Zimmerman, Paul. *The Last Season of Weeb Ewbank*. New York: Farrar, Straus and Giroux, 1974.

George Preas

RICK SCHABOWSKI

George Robert Preas had an 11-year career in the National Football League from 1955 to 1965. He played his entire career with the Baltimore Colts and was a very important part of the offensive line that helped them win back-to-back titles in 1958 and 1959.

Preas was born on June 25, 1933, in Roanoke, Virginia. As a youngster, he loved playing as many sports as he could at Roanoke's Fallon Park, and his activities paid off when he entered Jefferson High in Roanoke. He was selected to the All-State football team, and he also won three state wrestling championships, one at the 175-pound division, and two as a heavyweight. After high school, Preas enrolled at Virginia Tech.

The Hokies' football team had a tough season in 1950, the year before Preas arrived, going 0–10, scoring only 72 points, while surrendering a huge total of 430. Preas played a big part in the resurgence of the program. When Preas was a senior in 1954, the team went 8–0–1, and ended the season ranked 16th in the final AP poll. Preas set a record at that time, by starting in 41 consecutive games playing both offensive and defensive tackle. *The 1954 Tech Gridiron Guide* stated, "Preas can block and tackle with the best of them and his drive and experience make him one of the best players in football."[1]

He earned All-Southern Conference honors and his stellar career at Virginia Tech resulted in him being selected by the Colts in the fifth round of the NFL draft, held January 27–28, 1955, in New York City. He was the 51st overall player selected. Colts Hall of Fame receiver Raymond Berry reflected on the Preas selection. "The builders of that team selected a rock. He was a leader."[2]

When the 1955 training camp opened, the Colts moved him to offensive guard, but Preas, who was one of the quietest players on the Colts, never mouthing off or complaining, did approach Ewbank. "Coach, I want to try and make this team as a tackle and not as a guard."[3] Ewbank was very apprehensive about making the move, wondering if Preas would even make the team at that position, but Preas worked hard and ended up starting at tackle. The Colts also used Preas at defensive end. Beginning with the 1957 season, he was used strictly as an offensive tackle.

Coach Weeb Ewbank rated Colts offensive lineman Jim Parker as the league's best offensive tackle, but right behind him at number two, George Preas. Ewbank backed his high overall rating of Preas. "His techniques leave a lot to be desired, but he gets the job done. He has more second effort than is good for him sometimes. On any of our long runs, look who is downfield blocking. It is always Preas. He may not get his man but he will be down there throwing blocks and trying all the time."[4] After Don Shula replaced Ewbank as the Colts' coach, the high praises continued. Shula commented that Preas knew more about line play techniques than any other player in the NFL.

Colts center Buzz Nutter recalled when Coach Ewbank saw the Bears' lineman that Preas would be going up against, Ewbank said, "He doesn't look so tough to me."[5] Preas answered, "Yeah, Weeb, but you don't have to block him."[6]

The Colts methodically assembled a great team, and it all came together in 1958. The 4–0 Colts were playing the Washington Redskins on October 26, and Preas would have a tough assignment going against All-Pro defensive end Gene Brito. Preas noted, "They're all tough in the league. One is as bad as another, but Brito may be in a class by himself."[7] Teammate Art Spinney, a guard on the offensive line, wasn't worried. "Preas will do all right. He always does and he

George Preas.

meets top ends every Sunday. In this circuit you find no pushovers."[8] The Colts prevailed, 35–10, amassing 390 total yards, and Johnny Unitas wasn't sacked once.

Preas was one of many who played a big role in the 1958 NFL championship game victory. He played his usual good game, but he stood out in two big plays.

After the Colts stopped the Giants on the first possession of overtime, the Colts moved the ball into Giants territory, courtesy of a 21-yard pass play from Unitas to Raymond Berry. On first and ten on the Giants' 42 yard line, Unitas made a great call. Berry was having an outstanding game, having already made 11 catches, so linebacker Sam Huff was playing him close. Unitas called a trap draw up the middle with Alan Ameche carrying the ball, figuring that Huff would be out of the play. Preas didn't block Giants defensive end Jim Katcavage but instead had a different assignment. When Huff reversed direction to play defense against the run, Preas had a big block on Huff, and Ameche gained 22 yards to the Giants' 20 yard line.

The Colts scored the game-winning touchdown on a one-yard run by Ameche using a play called 16 Power. The one represented the fullback, and the six was the position in the offensive line that Ameche would run through. Colts tight end Jim Mutscheller recalled, "In the third period, we had been turned back at the goal line on four downs. The Giants assumed we were going to do the same thing in overtime and jammed the middle, but it was off-tackle instead. We blocked down to prevent penetration. Alex Sandusky and George Preas on the right side, blocked to their inside, and this provided the opening for Ameche to score."[9] Berry said the hole was so huge that anyone could've scored.

The Colts had protected Unitas from the NFL's strongest defense. Preas was the recipient of the Charles P. McCormick Unsung Hero trophy for his play in that game. He cherished the award because it was voted on by his teammates.

Preas earned his largest salary as a Colt, $15,000, in 1965, his last season in football. He would continue his success off the football field in business after retirement. He owned a Sealtest dairy franchise, the Red Lion Inn near the Virginia Tech campus, a Red Lion restaurant in Roanoke, Virginia, a number of office condominiums and a shopping center, Piccadilly Square.

Preas died on February 24, 2007, at the South Roanoke Nursing Home from complications from Parkinson's disease. He was diagnosed with the disease when he was 56. He was survived by two children and his wife, Betty Joyce, who shared George's interest in art collecting.

At the conclusion of the funeral service, Preas' children, George Jr., nicknamed Geep, and Kelly spoke about their father. Geep, a U.S. Airways pilot, said, "By all measures and standards my father was a champion. There is not one day of those 17 years [length of his illness] that he gave up the fight."[10] Kelly Preas, who lives in Oslo, Norway, where she is a director of a Montessori school, talked about how her father's illness had motivated their family to offer help to others in their coping with diseases. "We can only hope that they have the loving support from friends, family, employees, and caregivers that we've had through the years. We love you, Dad."[11]

Notes

1. "George Preas," Football Virginia Tech Virginia Sports Hall of Fame and Museum, www.vshfm/inductee_details.php?inducteesID=194.

2. Joe Kennedy, "Champion's Eulogy," *Roanoke Times*, posted March 1, 2007.

3. Cameron Snyder, "Parker Preas Gain Stature in League," *Baltimore Sun*, October 17, 1958.

4. *Ibid.*
5. Kennedy.
6. *Ibid.*
7. Cameron Snyder, "Brito, All-Pro End, Foe of Preas Sunday," *Baltimore Sun,* October 24, 1958.
8. *Ibid.*
9. John Steadman, "Colts' Preas Was a Quiet Catalyst of Victory in '58," *Tribune Digital-Baltimore Sun,* November 15, 1998.
10. Kennedy.
11. *Ibid.*

Billy Pricer

John Maxymuk

Bud Wilkinson's Oklahoma Sooners were a nearly flawless football powerhouse that peaked in the mid–1950s when the team won a record 47 straight games from 1953 to 1957, going undefeated in 1954, 1955 and 1956, and winning the national championship in the latter two seasons. Seventeen seniors in 1956 finished their college careers having never lost a game. That 17 included three-fourths of the starting backfield: quarterback Jimmy Harris, halfback Tommy McDonald and fullback Billy Pricer. All three, as well as the other starting halfback Clendon Thomas, would go on to the NFL, but only Pricer would have as much team success there as in Norman, Oklahoma, with two consecutive championships in both places—four titles in five years.

Pricer was an Oklahoma native, born in the town of Perry on September 3, 1934. He was the last of 14 children born to John and Cora Pricer and was raised with his siblings in a three-bedroom house that had just one bathroom. His father was a carpenter who worked long hours to provide for his very large family. Billy was an all-around athlete as a schoolboy and was named All-State for football and wrestling, in which he was undefeated in high school matches. He also starred at catcher in baseball.[1] He was recruited by the University of Oklahoma for both wrestling and football, but his wrestling career at OU was short-lived. The wrestling coach wanted the 5'10," 195-pound Pricer to drop to 167 pounds to compete. Wilkinson was against that, so Billy dropped wrestling and concentrated on football.[2]

Oklahoma ran the Split-T offense, a run-oriented attack in which the quarterback option play is critical. Pricer once recalled a time in practice when Wilkinson was running an option play drill where the back is supposed to keep his eyes ahead looking for the hole, not down looking for the handoff. As the runner would receive the handoff, Wilkinson would jump out from behind the blocking dummy, and the back was supposed to then hit the opposite hole. This time, though, Billy was looking down and plowed right into his coach. Pricer later told Gary King, "You could always tell when Bud was really mad at you. He'd send you down to Gomer [Jones, the line coach] and the linemen, and they'd punch the crap out of you."[3] It's useful to note here that college football was a two-way game at the time, so Pricer was both a fullback and linebacker so he was familiar with assistant coach Gomer Jones, "I loved Gomer dearly. He taught me everything I knew about being a linebacker."[4]

Pricer moved into the starting lineup as a junior in 1955 and carried the ball 69 times for 369 yards that year and 48 times for 274 yards as a senior. Primarily, he was the lead blocker, but was counted on for short yardage bursts and averaged 5.8 yards per carry in his time as a Sooner. He also averaged over 47 yards per punt in 1956.

The amiable Pricer was known for giving nicknames to his teammates and was highly respected by them. Jimmy Harris later told author Jim Dent, "Billy Pricer was probably the most underrated player and got less publicity than anybody, but he did as much or more for that '56 team as anybody."[5] During the 1956 season, eventual Maxwell Award winner McDonald told reporters, "It's Billy that does the work for me. He's terrific."[6] Wilkinson added a broader perspective on Pricer's role: "A good football team is based on defense, and it's difficult to find a boy that can back up the line and still play offense well. Pricer fits that bill. In addition to being outstanding on offense and defense, he's a fine punter and place kicker and a valuable team man. In these days of limited substitutions, he's the perfect answer."[7]

Billy Pricer.

After Pricer was drafted by the Colts in the sixth round of the 1957 NFL draft, Wilkinson told the *Baltimore Sun*, "Billy led the way and opened up the holes for such speedsters as Tommy McDonald and Clendon Thomas. Many times Pricer was able to shoulder block and then lay another player low in the secondary, and he loved to do it."[8] The Colts looked at Pricer as a possible fit in the secondary or as a linebacker, as well as being, in the words of scout Keith Molesworth, "the best blocker in the United States."[9]

Before reporting to Baltimore, though, Pricer first had to report to the Army, but was released in early August and entered Colts training camp at Western Maryland College in Westminster, Maryland, on the eighth. Weighing 205 pounds, he was tried at both fullback and linebacker, although the coaches would prefer him to weigh at least 220 to play linebacker. On offense, he competed with incumbent backup fullback Dick Young for the number two slot behind starter Alan Ameche. By September 5, Pricer had won the competition, with Young having been traded to Detroit for a draft pick.

Pricer only carried the ball twice in 1957, but played on kicking teams and won the team's respect early on when massive 280-pound defensive tackle Gene "Big Daddy" Lipscomb playfully grabbed Billy from behind one day in a bear hug. Pricer immediately reverted to his wrestling days, threw Big Daddy over his shoulder and pinned him to the ground.[10]

The championship season of 1958 began with praise from coach Weeb Ewbank following the Colts' first exhibition game against the Eagles in August, "Offensively I thought we looked pretty good. Billy Pricer really showed us something. He blocked well and ran strongly. He doesn't hit as hard as Alan Ameche but can change direction better."[11] During his second season, Pricer got a bit more playing time with ten carries from scrimmage and nine kick returns, and Ewbank considered him one of the most improved Colts. On one of those carries in week 11 against the Rams in Los Angeles on December 6, though, disaster struck.

Pricer told the *Baltimore Sun*, "I was carrying the ball when Lou Michaels grabbed me around the head. My knee was locked (like standing at attention) and someone dove into it. I could hear it snap. Boy was I scared."[12] With his leg encased in a cast for the West Coast trip, he added, "Although it is only a torn ligament, the doctors felt they should immobilize the knee for ten days. Dr. McDonnell will look at it when we get home, and I hope I will immediately be able to start therapy."[13]

Pricer was trotting and catching place kicks in practice two weeks later, as he was determined to return for the championship game against the Giants on December 28. Indeed, he was ready and in uniform for the title game. During Ewbank's famous pregame pep talk in which he went player by player saying why they weren't wanted by other teams, Weeb said of Pricer, "They said you were too small, but you have the heart and the will to win."[14] Pro Football Reference lists Pricer as playing in the game, but the *Sun* noted in an off-season piece that the Colts didn't want to risk further injury so didn't actually use Billy.[15]

When the fireplug fullback was the first of the Colts to sign his 1959 contract, Ewbank told the *Baltimore Sun*, "Having him around made life a little easier. He is invaluable as reserve strength."[16] The article assesses Pricer as "more of a control type runner who is hard to knock off balance, but he doesn't pound the line with the authority of Ameche."[17] Billy did get to carry the ball 34 times during the title defense season of 1959. His biggest day as a pro came in the finale against the Rams, when he toted the ball 17 times for 63 yards. For that year's concluding two-game West Coast trip, Pricer carried the ball 27 times for 100 yards. He also carried the ball four times and caught two passes in the championship game when the Colts defended their title by beating the Giants again.

Once again, Pricer was the first Colts veteran to sign his contract in 1960, but the team began to slip. Billy carried the ball a career-high 46 times during the year, including gaining 55 yards on 14 carries against the expansion Cowboys in Week Six. In Week Ten, Ameche severed his Achilles tendon, ending his career, but Pricer only carried the ball 12 times for 20 yards on the final West Coast pair of games.

The highlight of Billy's 1960 postseason came in a touch football game the week before the inauguration of President John Kennedy. The president's brother Ted brought Pricer in as a ringer—"Bill Evans," Kennedy campaign manager for Oklahoma—for one of the family's gridiron matches. Pricer scored six touchdowns in a family doubleheader and led his team to victory in one.[18]

With Ameche retired, the Colts traded for 13-year veteran fullback Joe "The Jet" Perry from San Francisco, and Pricer faced new competition for the backup fullback slot from rookie Mark Smolinski. Billy's case was not helped when he suffered a knee injury in the opening preseason game against the Steelers on August 12. He reinjured the knee three weeks later in another exhibition game against the Cowboys on September 1. The Colts then placed him on the taxi squad while he recovered. Once Billy was healthy, Baltimore offered him around the league but found no takers. The team activated top draft pick Tom Matte and released Pricer on November 3. Pricer joined the Dallas Texans of the American Football League for the last six weeks of the season, carrying the ball just five times for 13 yards.

For his pro career, Billy carried the ball 97 times for 316 yards and two touchdowns, while catching 15 passes for 115 yards and one touchdown. His impact on the team's success was not forgotten, though. In 1963, the *Baltimore Sun* lamented that the Colts kickoff coverage had suffered for years "ever since they let Sherman Plunkett and Billy Pricer go. These two liked nothing more than completely destroying the wedge formed by the kickoff receiving team and destroying the ball carrier as well."[19]

In retirement, Pricer had two children, operated several businesses out of Oklahoma City and was active in his church. He ballooned up to nearly 300 pounds and suffered a heart attack in 1983, necessitating a triple bypass operation. He also suffered from diabetes. He had a stroke in 1996 and then had the big toe on one foot amputated due to the diabetes in 1998. Still, he insisted on returning to Baltimore in December 1998 for the 40th anniversary of the Colts' first championship team. His wife told Gary King, "He was in really bad shape. He had just had the toe amputated, and he had to be in a wheelchair. It was a struggle getting him through the airports, but he really, really wanted to go, and we had a wonderful time."[20] Billy Pricer died on September 24, 1999, at the age of 65.

NOTES

1. Jim Dent, *The Undefeated: The Oklahoma Sooners and the Greatest Winning Streak in College Football* (New York: Thomas Dunne, 2001), 180–181.

2. Gary King, *An Autumn Remembered: Bud Wilkinson's Legendary 1956 Sooners* (Norman: University of Oklahoma Press, 1988, revised 2006), 121.

3. *Ibid.*, 118.

4. *Ibid.*

5. *Ibid.*, 117.

6. "Pricer Rated 'Dream Back' for Blocking," *Austin Statesman*, October 31, 1956.

7. *Ibid.*

8. Cameron C. Snyder, "Billy Pricer, Fullback from Oklahoma, Signs Contract with Colts," *Baltimore Sun*, February 17, 1957.

9. "Colts' Choices in Grid Draft," *Baltimore Sun*, February 1, 1957.

10. King, 122.

11. Cameron C. Snyder, "Pricer, Shaw and Plunkett Praised by Coach Ewbank," *Baltimore Sun*, August 18, 1958.

12. Cameron C. Snyder, "Fullback's Leg Encased for 10 Days," *Baltimore Sun*, December 8, 1958.

13. *Ibid.*

14. John F. Steadman, *Football's Miracle Men: The Baltimore Colts' Story* (Cleveland: Pennington Press, 1959), 170.

15. Cameron C. Snyder, "Pricer Signs Colts' Pact," *Baltimore Sun*, May 10, 1959.

16. *Ibid.*

17. *Ibid.*

18. "Billy Pricer of Colts Stars on Kennedy Team," *Washington Post*, January 31, 1961.

19. Cameron C. Snyder, "Chicago's Jones Just as Tough," *Baltimore Sun*, October 5, 1963.

20. King, 126.

Bert Rechichar

Rick Gonsalves

Albert Daniel "Bert" Rechichar was born on July 16, 1930, in Belle Vernon, Pennsylvania, a tough area known for its coal mining industry. His father was murdered by a man who took his pay envelope, and his brother Frank was killed in a mining accident. It's no wonder that Bert, the youngest of ten children, became a hard-nosed football player.[1]

Although Rechichar was born with no vision in his left eye, he starred as a 6'1," 209-pound hard-hitting halfback at Tennessee, where he played both ways during the two-platoon era. Bert was a member of the Vols' team that won back-to-back national championships in 1950–51 under coach Robert Neyland, and he earned All-SEC honors as well in 1951.[2]

The Cleveland Browns drafted Rechichar with the tenth overall pick in 1952, with a selection they had obtained from Detroit. Bert played in the defensive backfield with the Browns in 1952, and led the team with six interceptions. He also returned kick and punts for the Browns in 1952, but was sent to the Baltimore Colts for the 1953 season in a ten-for-five trade that also involved Don Shula, Carl Taseff and Art Spinney heading to Maryland These players would eventually play a major role in the Colts' transition into a championship team.[3]

Before practices, Bert would mess around by booting long field goals even though he was not the team's regular kicker. During the Baltimore Colts' home opener against the Chicago Bears, on September 27, 1953, Rechichar returned an interception 36 yards for a touchdown to tie the game at seven. It was one of seven interceptions Rechichar would make during the 1953 season. With four seconds left in the first half and the Colts in possession of the ball at midfield, Bert began to race to the locker room to use the bathroom.

Meanwhile, Buck McPhail, the regular kicker, prepared to boot a long field goal well beyond his range out of pure desperation. Otis Douglas, one of the team's assistant coaches, who had watched Bert make long field goal attempts during practice, had second thoughts and quickly called Rechichar back to try the kick. Bert turned around to yell, "What the hell do you want?"

"Get in there for McPhail. This is a long field goal attempt," Douglas said.

Bert then ran onto the field, chinstrap unbuckled, not even knowing how long the kick would be. He told holder Tom Keane, "Get the ball down because I have to go to the bathroom."[4] Keane did and Bert drove the ball through the uprights with plenty to spare from 56 yards out. The fans and even the players on both teams marveled at the kick. On his first field goal attempt as a pro, Bert set a new NFL record for the longest field goal, breaking Detroit's Glenn Presnell's mark of 54 yards set in 1934. His record would stand for 17 years until topped by Tom Dempsey's 63-yarder in 1970.[5] No one in league history has ever made such a record-setting kick on his first attempt.[6]

The kick made Bert an instant celebrity, and he made it while wearing a regular, soft-toed football shoe, not one with a square toe that kickers wore at that time. Bert's kick even made "Ripley's Believe It or Not."[7]

When the game was over and things settled down, Rechichar had more time to reflect on his record kick. "Things happened so fast. I was in such a hurry to get into the game, that I didn't even notice how far the attempt was really from. If I knew, I probably would have missed it."[8]

Bert was not done playing in that game. He made one more interception and recovered a fumble to help Baltimore secure a 13–9 win.

After the game, Rechichar was leaving the stadium when he ran into the Bears' middle linebacker Bill George. He said to Bert, "Do you know what our coach George Halas said during halftime?"

"No, I don't," Rechichar responded.

He said, "Hell of a kick, wasn't it fellas?"[9]

On October 25 of that 1953 season, Bert connected on a 52-yard field goal against the Washington Redskins to become the

Bert Rechichar.

first kicker in NFL history to make two field goals of 50 yards or more in one season.[10] He tied this record in 1955 when he kicked 50-yard field goal against the Washington Redskins on October 23 and a 52-yarder against San Francisco on November 27. In addition to this, he set another record for most field goals of 50 yards or more in a career, with 4.[11]

Bert had his best year ever as an all-around player in 1955. He made 25 extra points out of 26 attempts and ten field goals out of a league high 24 attempts to lead the team in scoring with 55 points. Bert handled kick returns for Baltimore that year, and led the NFL in number of punt returns with 30 good for 121 yards. On defense, he led the team in interceptions with six. Bert was chosen to play in his first Pro Bowl.[12]

By 1956, Bert had established himself as a hard-hitting defensive back. That season was also the first for Howard "Hopalong" Cassady, a running back out of Ohio State who won the Heisman Trophy in 1955. He was chosen by the Detroit Lions in the first round of the 1956 draft, the third player taken.

When Detroit played Baltimore for the first time that season, Bert leveled Cassady along the sidelines. Before getting off him Bert said. "Listen, Cassady, this ain't Ohio State. This is the National Football League and we tear out your eyeballs."[13]

Bert tried to intimidate receivers before they ran routes in his direction or over the middle. "You come over here," he'd shout at the Chicago Bears' Harlon Hill or the Los Angeles Rams' Bob Boyd, "and I'm going to rack you so hard you're going to think you got hit with a pickax."[14]

Alex Hawkins, later a teammate of Bert, also found him quite intimidating. "When I met him for the first time in 1959, he carried a cigar in the corner of his mouth and being blind in one eye, which remained closed as he studied me with his good eye, he gave me the feeling that if I hadn't met him in the Colts' dressing room I would have guessed his occupation as a hangman."[15]

Whether he was on the top of a pile or on the bottom, he would inflict more pain on running backs or receivers by twisting any body parts he could reach. Bert, like many other players at that time, did things like this to ensure that they would keep their jobs on teams that had limited roster spots.

Bert demonstrated one more skill that would make him a valuable asset for the team; he could punt fairly well. He led the team in 1956 by punting 33 times for 1,276 yards and a 38.7-yard average. His longest punt (in 1956 and his career) was 56 yards, the same distance as his longest field goal.[16]

For the second year in a row, Bert lead the team in interceptions in 1956 with four, and at the end of the 1957 season, he was chosen to play in the Pro Bowl for the third consecutive time. In 1957, he intercepted five passes, and kicked 22 of 25 extra points and three of 13 field goals for 31 points. In the 1957 Pro Bowl, he kicked a record four field goals of 52, 44, 42 and 41 yards to lead the East to a 19–10 victory over the West. He set two other Pro Bowl records that day as well—longest field goal (Sam Baker also made a 52-yarder in the game) and most field goals made from 40 yards or more. In recognition of his kicking heroics, he was voted the game's Most Valuable Player.[17]

Up to the 1958 season, coach Weeb Ewbank annually tried to get rid of Rechichar despite his stellar play because of his happy-go-lucky life style and gruff independent personality. Bert liked smoking cigars and going to the race track to play the horses. Some of his racetrack associates also were known gamblers. Ewbank thought that if other people saw this, it would create a bad image for the team. During the previous five years, the coach tried out every kicker he could find to see who would take Bert's job, but Rechichar always prevailed. Bert then would antagonize Ewbank each time he won his job back and warn the coach, "Don't you ever trade me."[18]

Finally, in 1958, Weeb managed to trade Rechichar to the Chicago Cardinals, but instead of reporting to the team right away, Bert went to Atlantic City to try to clear his head. He was strolling along the boardwalk when he came upon Carroll Rosenbloom, the owner of the Baltimore Colts, Don Kellett, the team's general manager and, of all people, Bert Bell, the NFL commissioner. Bell was Rosenbloom's old football coach at the University of Pennsylvania, and they both owned homes near one another on the New Jersey shore.

All three men greeted Rechichar and asked him what he was doing in Atlantic City. He told them about the trade and how he wanted to remain with the Colts. They suggested that Bert report to the Cardinals, and in the meantime, they would see what they could do to get him back with the Colts.

After reporting to the Cardinals, Rechichar was surprised to find out that the team was going to Austin, Texas, to play a preseason game with the Baltimore Colts. Bert was very familiar with the Colts' offensive plays. On one series of downs, Bert decked receiver Glenn Dillon with a vicious hit and that did not go over well with Ewbank.

When the game ended, Rechichar was told to report back to Baltimore. Rosenbloom and Kellett had kept their word. Now, Ewbank was not only furious about this deal but also about the vicious hit he put on Dillon. Upon arriving in Baltimore, Weeb told

Rechichar he expected him to conform with teams guidelines. Bert knew he could not do this so he kept a low profile. However, Weeb would never speak to Bert again.[19]

At the end of the 1958 season, on December 14 to be exact, Bert opened the scoring against the San Francisco 49ers with a 48-yard field goal in the first period. It was his only field goal of the season and his last as a Baltimore Colt.[20]

Bert played on the two Baltimore Colts championship teams of 1958–59. In the 1958 title game, the one called the "Greatest Game Ever Played." Bert handled the kickoffs, and missed one long field goal attempt in the fourth quarter. Many people wondered why Ewbank didn't use Bert in the game to kick field goals in place of the erratic Steve Myhra, especially since he held the NFL record for the longest field goal. Weeb not only didn't speak to Bert that season, he also banished him to the bench.[21]

In 1960, Ewbank finally released Rechichar. Bert had been a mystery man because during the seven seasons that he was with the Colts, no one ever knew where he lived. In fact none of his teammates knew that much about him at all off the field. On the day he was let go, he asked Alex Hawkins to give him a lift to pick up his belongings. Alex jumped at this opportunity to finally learn where Bert lived.

"Bert directed me to a half dozen back alleys and side streets where he picked up a pair of pants in this building, a jacket in that one, a couple of shirts here and a pair of shoes there. After an hour of this, Bert said, 'O.K., that's it,' Alex explained. "Bert also carried all his money with him in cash leading the other players to call him the 'First Bank of Rechichar.'"[22]

"Rechichar had an unusual way of introducing himself," Hawkins added. "The first day I reported to the Colts in 1959, he held out his hand and said, 'Hi, I'm number 44. What's your name?' He never thought of himself as Bert Rechichar. Had he been introducing himself to the President, he would have said, 'I'm number 44.'"[23]

During his seven-year stint with Baltimore, Bert scored 164 points from four touchdowns (three receiving and one interception return), 56 extra points out of 62 attempts and 28 field goals out of 81 attempts for a .346 average. At that time, he held the team record for the longest field goal, 56-yards;* most field goals in a season, ten, 1956; most field goals in a game, three, on two occasions;* most field goals, 50 yards or more, season, two times, in 1953 and 1955;* and most field goals, 50 yards or more, career, four.*[24]

In 1960, Bert was eventually signed by the Pittsburgh Steelers where he played just one season. He kicked sparingly, making just six extra points and three field goals for 15 points. The following year, Rechichar ended up with the New York Titans in the new American Football League. He played in a few games before leaving the team and ending his pro football career.

During his ten-year career, he made 62 extra points out of 68 attempts and 31 field goals out of 88 tries for a .352 average and four touchdowns for 179 points.[25] After football, he returned to his native Pennsylvania with his second wife Martha, a son Donald and a daughter Lisa and worked in construction.[26]

*NFL record as well

NOTES

1. John Steadman, "Among Tough, Talented, Rechichar Was a Natural," *Baltimore Sun,* November 16, 1997.

2. *2016 University of Tennessee Media Guide.*

3. Steadman.

4. *Ibid.*

5. William Gildea, *When the Colts Belonged to Baltimore* (Baltimore: Johns Hopkins University Press, 1996), 83–84.

6. Rick Gonsalves, *Placekicking in the NFL: A History and Analysis* (Jefferson, NC: McFarland, 2014), 50.

7. Steadman.

8. Gonsalves, 50.

9. Gildea, 89.

10. *1958 Baltimore Colts Press Guide.*

11. *Ibid.*

12. *Ibid.*

13. Norman Chad, "Giving Thanks for Some Old-School NFL True Stories," *Washington Post*, November 22, 2015.

14. Steadman.

15. Rob Fleder, ed., *Sports Illustrated, The Football Book* (New York: Sports Illustrated, 2005), 56–57.

16. "Bert Rechichar," Pro-Football-Reference.com.

17. *1959 Baltimore Colts Press Guide.*

18. Fleder, 57.

19. Gildea, 90–93.

20. *1958 National Football League Manual.*

21. Gildea, 90–93.

22. Fleder, 57.

23. *Ibid.*, 56.

24. *1960 Baltimore Colts Press Guide*; "Bert Rechichar," Pro-Football-Reference.com.

25. "Bert Rechichar," Pro-Football-Reference.com.

26. Gildea, 86–87.

Johnny Sample

GREG SELBER

To say that he was unique is to lowball it, and to say that he was influential and memorable is a vast understatement. Noting that he was one of the best all-around athletes to play in the NFL again is scratching the surface.

Johnny Sample was all of these things during a mercurial 11-year career that ended in 1968, but he was one of the original enigmatic personalities in professional sports as well, an iconoclast who became one of the forefathers of trash talk and a trailblazer concerning the exposure of racial issues in the league. Sample was quite simply a handful from start to finish.

Drafted by the Colts in 1958 after an All-America career at tiny Maryland State College, he was said to be the first player from a predominantly black college to compete in the College All-Star Game. And it was there that the controversy began for an outspoken man who never shied away from contact, on or off the field. He got into a row with coach Otto Graham in the days leading up to the game and was branded a "troublemaker" by the Hall of Fame quarterback.[1] From there, it just kept getting more interesting.

He wore out his welcome with the Colts after a 1961 preseason incident involving a fumbled kickoff and a fine he refused to pay, and thus began an odyssey that saw Sample play for two other NFL teams in five seasons.[2] With the Steelers and then the Redskins he wowed them with his performance but suffered through injuries and dust-ups for objecting to the treatment of black athletes, among other things. By the time he was blackballed by the NFL—his contention—in 1965, a once promising career seemed on the skids.[3]

But Sample resurrected himself with the New York Jets in 1966 under former Baltimore coach Weeb Ewbank and used his second chance to go in search of a revenge tour. It culminated with the veteran cornerback, now a team captain, helping defeat his old team in Super Bowl III. He'd started his tenure with a part in the Greatest Game Ever Played in 1958 and ended it with a key role in the Greatest Upset Ever a decade later, and when he dedicated the game ball for the Jets' win over the supposedly invincible Colts to the AFL—a direct slap at commissioner Pete Rozelle and the league he said had it in for him—the curtain closed on one of the most fascinating journeys a player has ever made through pro football.

Johnny Sample.

Sample was a high school standout in multiple sports while growing up in Virginia, coming of age in an era when the Civil Rights Movement was in its nascent stages. In his controversial 1970 autobiography, *Confessions of a Dirty Ballplayer*, he set down his pattern right off the bat:

> I always believed in standing up for what was right no matter what. Growing up as a child in Virginia and seeing what was done to black people had a profound effect on my life, not only as a football player, but as a husband and father as well. The agony and embarrassment that I've seen black people suffer put a hardness in me that made me what I am.... White people don't understand the feeling that swells up inside a black man who struggles to get out from under the heel. You have to use an outhouse to really know how rotten it can be. You have to be in a hurry waiting at a gas station while the attendant waits on every white man's car before he gets to yours to know how aggravating it can be. You have to be called "nigger" to know how it really feels...[4]

The young athlete showed that he would not be intimidated; as a youth he was denied service at a grocery store and a gas station, and responded by throwing a brick through the glass window at each establishment.[5]

Arriving at Maryland State in 1954, Sample quickly established himself as a major force in football, basketball, baseball, and even gymnastics. He was a running back who rushed for 2,381 yards with 37 touchdowns and was also the placekicker. Maryland State, later renamed Maryland Eastern Shore, went 27–4–3 during his tenure and Sample twice was a Little All-America selection by the *Pittsburgh Courier*. Under coach Skip McCain, the school produced a series of future professionals including Art Shell, Emerson Boozer, and Roger Brown.

Running a 9.6 second 100-yard dash at 202 pounds, Sample was selected for the College All-Star Game, a teammate of a number of Hall of Famers in the making such as Gene Hickerson, Bobby Mitchell, Ray Nitschke, and Jim Taylor. But he got little playing time after an argument with the coach, Otto Graham.

"Being the outspoken kind of guy I am frequently made me an open target," he relates in his book.[6]

Though just a seventh-round pick, Sample made the Colts' roster and was a prominent special teams contributor in 1958, and during a late-season stretch he learned what it would take to make it. In the final two games, Sample saw ample playing time at corner, and experienced what he termed a "gnawing mental fear."[7] Ironically, later he would become known as an intimidator of opposing receivers. Sample noted that if he could get into the head of a foe, he might have an advantage and this propensity for trash talking and banter became a signature element going forward.

At the time, the NFL was not a league for talkers, but Sample had never let history or convention stand in the way of his life.

"It's people like Jackie Robinson who made it possible for guys like me to be able to stand on their own two feet," he recalled in *Confessions*.[8]

In the 1958 title game, Sample found himself in the ball game in the second half following an injury to starter Milt Davis, and the next season he would build on this experience. He helped Baltimore to a repeat title, making two interceptions in the 1959 title tilt, returning one for a touchdown versus the Giants, setting a pattern for making big plays in the key junctures. That season he led the NFL in kick return average.

In 1960 he came up with four picks and three fumble recoveries for the Colts and paced the team with a 7.2 yard punt return average, also averaging 28.8 on kick returns—including a 94-yard score against the Bears—en route to second team All-Pro honors.

That was the end with the Colts as after a 1961 preseason controversy, Sample was abruptly traded to Pittsburgh. He had refused to pay a fine after fumbling a kickoff, and the Colts moved him on.

Baltimore's loss was the Steelers' gain for '61 as the new acquisition enjoyed another All-Pro campaign (first team), grabbing eight interceptions and posting 23.1 and 10.9 yard averages on kick and punt runbacks. He led the league in punt return attempts (26) and yards (283) as well as average. Sample took an interception back 39 yards for a touchdown in the opener against Dallas and claimed multiple interception games against Philadelphia (three) and Washington (two) in successive weeks.

Here his career took a nosedive as in 1962 and 1963 back and knee injuries limited Sample to a handful of games. But he came back strong for 1964. Having been dealt to the Redskins by now, he collected a revenge pick six against his former team, Pittsburgh, and for the campaign had four total picks.

Sample had another fine season in 1965 with six interceptions, including three in two games against the Cards. By now he was a veteran whose size and instincts, along with a penchant for the heavy hit, made him one of the league's most feared corners.

But again there was a snag, as contract squabbles and acrimony between Sample and management led to his exit from Washington. In his book, Sample recalled how he was signed by the Bears only to be released, and claims that he was told by a number of people that owners around the league had been instructed to steer clear. Back in the early 1960s he said he had been told by Steelers coach Buddy Parker that black players did not deserve to be paid the kind of money he was requesting (an $8,000 raise) and following his form, he argued with Parker and nearly left the team over that remark.[9]

Sample was unable to find work despite the fact that he was at the top of his game as a professional. About to retire and move on to other pursuits, Sample got a chance with the Jets of the fledgling AFL and took it.

In 1965 the team had suffered with the second worst secondary in the league, but in Sample's first season he solidified the group considerably, taking six enemy aerials. He started his Jets career with two picks against Miami to lead New York to a 19–14 opening victory. He also snared two against Houston and was a second-team All-AFL choice that season.

Elected team captain for 1967 he responded with a typical year, coming up with four interceptions, one of which he returned 41 yards for a touchdown against Buffalo. Now the stage was set for a banner year in 1968—it would prove to be his last—as Sample was to help the Jets to the Super Bowl, and a monumental upset.

It was a storybook season as the veteran collected seven interceptions for 88 return yards, terrorizing the Bills for two picks in a 25–21 victory on November 3. One went for a touchdown to give the Jets an early 10–7 lead, and it marked the Jets' only six that day: Jets kicker Jim Turner, who set a record with 34 field goals in 1968, made six that day to go with Sample's pick-six.

To cap a memorable second team All-AFL season, Sample and the Jets advanced to the Super Bowl in Miami, where he intercepted a pass at his own two yard line late in the first half, one of four picks the Jets made in their stunning 16–7 decision over the NFL Colts. Sample showed a flair for the dramatic by assisting his new team to the triumph over the buttoned-down establishment league, and as stated, followed his outlaw chops to the letter by snubbing Rozelle in the locker room afterward by awarding the game ball to the AFL.[10]

Johnny Sample was a terrific football player, as indicated by 41 career interceptions and 14 fumble recoveries. In 11 seasons he posted 2,119 return yards, averaging 26.0 yards on kickoffs and 8.2 yards on punts. A consistent All-Pro, Sample was never voted to the Pro Bowl, a roster selected by coaches and peers, showing that he was not the most popular player by any means.

But he never backed down from an opponent or a challenge from management, and later in life he would continue to be a lightning rod for both controversy and change. His 1970 book caused a major stir with its treatment with candor of issues such as racism in the NFL.

Having retired after the redemption season of 1968, by age 45 Sample had become a top-rated tennis star on the U.S. Tennis Association circuit, and was a tennis official and linesman for decades.[11] He got into community organizing, using tennis as a tool to teach inner city youth the finer points of athletic competition and discipline, and also started a career as a radio talk show host in Philadelphia.

In later years much would be made of the way Sample had been strident in speaking his mind, at a time when black athletes were still limited by quotas and expected to stay quiet on the racial issues brewing in the 1960s. He had come into the league at a time in the late 1950s when schools were still segregated and the Freedom Rides and meteoric appearances of such icons as Martin Luther King, Jr., and Malcolm X were still in the future.

By standing up for what he believed in, he generally ended up in hot water, as a peripatetic and at times traumatic football career illustrates. But he was the owner of three championship rings and some magic memories of big-time performances in the clutch, so when he died in 2005 at age 67, Sample had no regrets whatsoever. He had done it his way, with force and impact, never looking back for a second.

NOTES

1. Johnny Sample with Fred J. Hamilton and Sonny Schwartz, *Confessions of a Dirty Ballplayer* (New York: Dell, 1970, 58.
2. *Ibid.*, 76–79.
3. *Ibid.*, 110.
4. *Ibid.*, 2–3.
5. *Ibid.*, 27.
6. *Ibid.*, 8.
7. *Ibid.*, 67.
8. *Ibid.*, 26.
9. *Ibid.*, 85–86.
10. *Ibid.*, 177.
11. Jere Longman, "The First of the Big-Time Trash Talkers," *New York Times*, January 21, 2011; Delinda Lombardo, "Throwback Thursday: Johnny Sample," *The Starting Five Online*, January 2008.

Alex Sandusky

DAVID STANDISH

There's tough—and then there's Alex Sandusky.

A standout left guard for the Baltimore Colts, Sandusky only missed one game because of an injury in his career spanning from 1954 to 1966; his work ethic ignited the Colts to eight winning seasons, including championships in 1958 and 1959.

Baltimore's gridiron icons Alan Ameche and Johnny Unitas powered their way to success thanks to Sandusky's blocking; Ameche became a four-time Pro Bowl fullback and Unitas evolved into the standard by which quarterbacks were measured in the last half of the 20th century.

"Sandusky [was] as fine a guard as there is in [the NFL] and always has been," declared Detroit Lions tackle Alex Karras.[1]

Born on August 17, 1932, in McKees Rocks—a working-class steel and iron town in Allegheny County, Pennsylvania—Sandusky grew up in Stowe and played Offensive End and Defensive End for the Golden Eagles of Clarion State Teacher's College (now Clarion University) from 1950 to 1953. Sandusky chose Clarion for a geographical reason—proximity to good hunting.

After finishing 2–5 in 1950—Sandusky's freshman season—the Golden Eagles improved to 4–2–1 in 1951. Waldo Tippin took the reins of the head coach position in 1952, leading the Golden Eagles to an 8–0 regular season. An invitation emerged for the Golden Eagles to play in the Lions Bowl against East Carolina—a much bigger team, according to Sandusky,[2] who caught a 38-yard touchdown pass in the team's 13–6 win.

Sandusky emphasizes that toughness was a bedrock of success for the Golden Eagles. "We were absolutely outmatched size-wise," Sandusky said. "That was the biggest team we played, but our tenacity took over. The big thing I remember from that game was their halfback going back to the huddle and me hearing him say 'They're small, but man they hit hard.' That spoke of the character of our team."[3]

The Golden Eagles defense threw five shutouts during the eight-game 1952 regular season. In turn, the offense had some breathing room. Result: Scoring 20 or more points in six of the eight games. Sandusky was part of this offensive surge, catching five touchdown passes from quarterback David "Red" Bevevino, who set a then school record of 18 touchdowns passes. "We were a team that had a great will, a passion to win

Alex Sandusky.

and play. [Our record] was quite an achievement considering we had no scholarships or financial aid. It was a group of guys who came together there and wanted to play and wanted to win with a great passion."[4]

Clarion extended its winning streak to five additional games in the 1953 season before losing 6–0 to California (PA).

The Colts drafted Sandusky with the third pick in the 16th round of the 1954 NFL draft (184th overall).[5] and offered him a $5,000 contract contingent upon making the squad.[6] Feeling that he was in "over his head," Sandusky endured the Colts' dire training conditions: "We were packed, six to a room, in the hot attic of a dorm…. There were no air conditioners or fans. We slept on Army cots, with Army blankets. And practice was so tough you thought you were training for the Marine Corps." Coach Weeb Ewbank saw enough in Sandusky to bring him aboard and change him from a defensive end to an offensive guard.[7]

Playing through injury was a hallmark of Sandusky's era; he suffered through the 1962 season with two injured shoulders, though he wasn't aware of the infirmity at the time—he found out after he retired.[8] Karras said that Sandusky was "short and quick and [had] great agility," making him, perhaps, the most troublesome lineman that Karras played against.[9]

Sandusky credited his success to "[b]balance, technique and a little holding when the ref's not looking," in addition to playing with Colts defensive icons Gino Marchetti and Art Donovan. This mix of greatness forced Sandusky to master his position—in practice, he had to "either learn how to do it or you get killed."[10] Colts teammate Jack Call describes Sandusky succinctly: "tough guy."[11]

Protecting his colleagues was a responsibility that few NFL offensive linemen could do successfully. Lenny Moore and L.G. Dupre found daylight because of Sandusky's blocking. Further, the Colts' O-line, according to Call, "took pride in protecting [Unitas]. Everyone was focused on that…. [He] was our bread-and-butter. When he called plays in the huddle, it was like a priest talking in church."[12] Sandusky recalls that "it was almost a mortal sin to get beat by your man, if he then got to John… I remember several games when [Unitas] played hurt and we made sure that he never got his knees dirty. We took immense pride in that."[13]

Sandusky recalls the 1958 championship game between the Colts and the New York Giants as "the 'Most Meaningful Game.' After that game is when the public really caught on to the NFL. It's when the endorsements started coming in."[14] For his contributions to the Colts' eight winning seasons during his tenure and his participation in the Colts' championships in 1958 and 1959, Sandusky was named a second-team All-NFL performer in 1964 and was also an Honorable Mention All-Pro in 1958 and 1965.[15]

Colts owner Carroll Rosenbloom asked Sandusky to reconsider retiring when the emblem of Baltimore toughness ended his career in 1965 at age 33, and Sandusky agreed to play one more season; Sandusky's work ethic prompted the request.[16] After saying goodbye to the gridiron for good after the 1966 season, Sandusky began a second career— public resources management. He retired in 1989 after 24 years as director of waterway improvement for the Maryland Department of Natural Resources.[17] Sandusky and his wife, Mary, chose Florida as their new home.

Sandusky remained close with his teammates; Unitas was godfather to the Sandusky children. Likewise, Sandusky played the same role for Unitas. The quarterback and his protector had a long-lasting friendship until Unitas' death in 2002.

NOTES

1. "Alex Sandusky," Official Web Site of Clarion University, http://www.clariongoldeneagles.com/hof.aspx?hof=4, quoting 1967 *Sport Magazine*.

2. "Sandusky Headed to PA Sports Hall of Fame," Official Web Site of Clarion University, http://clariongoldeneagles.com/news/2010/8/5/featured_0805103708.aspx.

3. *Ibid.*

4. *Ibid.*

5. "1954 Baltimore Colts," http://www.databasefootball.com/teams/teamyear.htm?yr=1954&tm=BLC&lg=NFL.

6. "Sandusky Headed to PA Sports Hall of Fame," Official Web Site of Clarion University.

7. *Ibid.*

8. Mike Klingaman, "Catching Up with Former Colt Alex Sandusky," *Baltimore Sun*, November 10, 2009, http://www.baltimoresun.com/bs-mtblog-2009–11-catching_up_with_former_colt_a-story.html.

9. *Ibid.*

10. *Ibid.*

11. Jack Call, interview with author, January 9, 2017.

12. *Ibid.*

13. *Ibid.*

14. "Sandusky Headed to PA Sports Hall of Fame," Official Web Site of Clarion University.

15. *Ibid.*

16. Klingaman.

17. *Ibid.*

Leo Sanford

Joshua M. Anderson

One thousand dollars a game. This slight figure (equivalent to $8,328.35 in 2016) is the deal that Leo Sanford wanted from the Chicago Cardinals in 1958.[1] Sanford felt he was worth it after seven years of service, 84 straight games and numerous seasons as captain.[2] He had been invited to two Pro Bowls and had an excellent record: 16 career interceptions, 11 fumble recoveries, holding the Cardinals' record for longest interception return and for most return yardage in a game, and two defensive touchdowns.[3]

Ottis Leo Sanford was born on October 4, 1929, in Dallas, Texas, and grew up in Shreveport, Louisiana.[4] By 1943, he was on the Fair Park High football team, although he was one of four players to not get a uniform. He earned a uniform in 1945 when the team reached the state finals, losing to Holy Cross 31–13.[5] Stanford used an extra year of eligibility to remain with Fair Park for the 1946 season, though that team finished 6–4.[6]

In 1947, Sanford had scholarship offers from LSU, Florida, and Louisiana Tech and chose to attend nearby Louisiana Tech in Ruston, Louisiana.[7] This decision was influenced by the desire to work with Joe Aillet, who was head football coach at Louisiana Tech. Additionally, Myrna Mims, whom Sanford was wooing, was working in Shreveport. By going to a school in Ruston, he would be close to Shreveport and could visit her frequently.[8] They married June 2, 1949, in the Fairfield Avenue Presbyterian Church.[9]

At Louisiana Tech, Sanford was two-time all-conference at center and linebacker.[10] In 1948, they went 7–2–1.[11] The 1949 team's record was 7–2 and they won the Gulf States Conference championship by beating the number one small-college team in the country, Mississippi Southern, 34–13.[12] The Sanford-led defense held Mississippi Southern to -12 yards rushing.[13] In 1950, the team wasn't as strong, finishing 5–4–1, but Sanford was named to Tom Harmon's Little All-America club.[14] During Sanford's four years in college, Louisiana Tech had an overall record of 24–12–2, with Sanford starting three years, being All-GSC two years, and captaining the defense his senior year.[15]

After graduating in 1951, Leo

Leo Sanford.

and Myrna were driving to New Orleans for his job with Pan Am Southern Oil Company.[16] The couple was in an accident and for the next few days, Sanford split time between moving their belongings from Ruston and visiting Myrna in the hospital.[17] Former Tech teammate Bobby Aillet found Sanford at the hospital several days after the 1951 NFL draft and gave him the good news that he had been drafted.[18] Sanford had been selected 90th overall, in the eighth round by the Chicago Cardinals. He only made $275 a month with the oil company, so he tried pro football.[19]

Sanford experienced heavy competition for the center position with the Cardinals.[20] At six feet, one inch and 220 pounds, Sanford was a bit small for line play, but he made up for it with his speed and agility.[21] Years later, Cardinals coach Ray Richards went so far as to say, "Leo is one of the league's finest linebackers because of his speed."[22] In the summer of 1951, it wasn't so obvious, but Sanford was also a strong long-snapper. He developed this skill because Fair Park and Louisiana Tech had both used the direct center snap.[23] Sanford signed with the Cardinals on June 29 for $5,000 and played linebacker there for the next seven years.[24]

During the 1950s, the Cardinals were awful, going 24–58–2 over Sanford's career, despite his strong contributions. Sanford regularly led the Cardinals' defense and had a few spectacular games. On September 26, 1955, Leo raced for a record-breaking 92-yard interception return for a touchdown against the Steelers.[25] In 1956, Sanford called defensive signals for the Cardinals, resulting in their only winning season that decade, including a game against the Eagles where he had two interceptions and a fumble recovery.[26]

On his record, Sanford was confident negotiating his contract with the Cardinals' owner Walt Wolfner in 1958.[27] However, the contract talks broke down over Sanford demanding $1,000 a game, so he returned home without signing a deal.[28] The Baltimore Colts called to speak with Sanford about changing teams, and they were able to negotiate contract terms agreeable to both parties.[29] Sanford had no idea what the Cardinals had gotten for him in trade and even joked that maybe the team received so little that they didn't want to embarrass him by publicly releasing the information, speculating, "Maybe a few pairs of worn-out socks or something like that."[30] The Cardinals finalized the deal and Sanford was traded to the Baltimore Colts in 1958. In fact, the trade was for linebacker Dale Meinert, who had played three years for the Edmonton Eskimos, but the Baltimore Colts owned his playing rights.[31] Meinert lasted a decade with the Cardinals.

Sanford had never missed a game since the draft and two weeks into the 1958 season explained to the press his secret to staying healthy. He never permitted himself to go over his playing weight of 230 pounds by sticking to a strict diet that avoided salt, sugar, starches, and alcohol. This, coupled with plenty of hard work, generally in the Louisiana oil fields during the off-season, helped to keep him in football-playing shape.[32] Unfortunately, his robust health built on discipline would not last.

With the addition of Sanford, the Colts' defense found its fighting form. Sanford was frequently complimented on his play by both management and players.[33] This was in spite of his missing the second half of the game against the Washington Redskins because of an ankle injury.[34] This injury also kept him out of the second Green Bay game; a 56–0 shellacking where the Colts were up by 28 at halftime.[35]

In the seventh game of the 1958 season, a key match-up with the Giants, Sanford was back to his usual spot as starting right linebacker.[36] He started the following game as well, when the Colts held the Bears to season lows in passing yards, total yards, and points, in a 17–0 win. Unfortunately, Leo's return to health was short-lived.

In the Colts first game against the Rams on November 23, Sanford suffered a badly wrenched knee.[37] Head Coach, Weeb Ewbank, seriously considered placing him on injured reserve but Sanford, with the help of two trainers, convinced him he could be ready for the postseason.[38] For the first couple of weeks, Leo spent four to five hours every day getting passive and resistive physical therapy exercise and then, while the Colts were on the West Coast, was given the assignment of running up and down steps at the team practice facilities in Brookside Park.[39]

Sanford was indeed ready to go for the title game and started on defense for the Colts that day. He described the feeling of running onto the field, "I guess if a guy is in athletics, that has to be the top thing he'll ever do: playing in Yankee Stadium in a championship game—with so much background, thinking of the number of great athletes who'd been there before…. It was just an outstanding feeling."[40]

Unfortunately, that outstanding feeling would soon change to one of pain and agony. "My right knee had gone out earlier that year. They go after a guy if they think he has a weakness. They ran an off-tackle play, and Roosevelt Brown went out on me. I was fighting that off, and the thing just went out" resulting in a torn knee ligament.[41] That collision with All-Pro tackle Roosevelt Brown, on a clean play, kept him mostly off the field, "But I still limped on the field to perform long snaps," Sanford said proudly.[42]

Over 30,000 fans met the Colts at Friendship Airport outside Baltimore on their return from the game.[43] Youngsters climbed on and around the buses. Johnny Unitas and Leo Sanford got off the buses and shook hands with the people.[44] It was the excitement of the fans that so impressed Sanford when he said, "My mouth was open when we got back to the Baltimore airport after the championship game. I knew those people were rabid, but I had never in my life seen a turnout like that."[45] Sanford was philosophical about the injury, saying, "How can I holler? This [is] the first time since I went up to Chicago that I've had an injury that kept me out for even one whole game."[46] He was able to rehabilitate the injury by using the "iron boot" to strengthen the knee over the off-season.[47]

Sanford thought his knee was fully rehabilitated from the wintertime workouts, but after jumping for a pass, it went out again. The Colts had him travel to Baltimore for ligament repair surgery.[48] "The inside cartilage, medial cartilage, was bad, but the outside cartilage was good and there was no damage to the joint."[49] By late March, he had "only the tiniest hobble to show for the experience."[50] In June, Sanford was viewed as a backup offensive lineman as well as a defensive starter by some, but personally he didn't feel his knee was back in playing shape.[51]

In the off-season, the Colts traded for Marv Matuszak, whom they had hoped to sign the previous year. Leo's response was "It's not the kind of trade I like, but he's a good man and I'll just have to put out that much more to stay with the club."[52] Unfortunately, a couple of days later, Sanford injured his knee again, collapsing to the ground in agony.[53] On August 6, Dr. E. J. McDonnell of Union Memorial Hospital pronounced Sanford "satisfactory" after removing lateral cartilage.[54] Leo was held out of the College All-Star Game and reporters were beginning to wonder about the Colts linebackers, citing Sanford's two knee operations.[55] In late September, Sanford was placed on the inactive list by his request and the team reported that Sanford "may take a while" before playing again.[56] By late October, Sanford was reported as having retired.[57] Sanford spent the entire 1959 season scouting opponents from the press box.[58]

In early 1960, Sanford still expected to return to the Colts. Jack Fiser, who regularly reported on Sanford's activities for Leo's hometown paper, speculated, "Sanford is thinking of the new American Football League as a sort of hole-card...."[59] However, in July of 1960, Baltimore traded him to the Dallas Cowboys.[60] Sanford had good contract negotiations with Tex Schramm, remarking that "they surprised me, they went more than half way."[61] His knee was medically cleared, though not as sound as before the injuries, so Leo thought he might play center. He felt it would increase his longevity since "playing offensive center you generally get hit from only one direction," and "Backing-up the line you get hit from all directions."[62] Sanford joined the team on July 16, but after a week of training with the team, Sanford walked into Tom Landry's office and told him he was giving up the game.[63] Sadly, his knee "wasn't bearing up under the training grind."[64]

When Sanford retired, he returned to his off-season job of selling sporting goods for Harbuck's.[65] Sanford soon left sporting goods and got into the class ring business, which has carried on in his family for three generations.[66] In 1969, he was named to the all-time Louisiana Sports Writers Association collegiate teams First 100 Years of Football team as a center.[67] In 1983, Leo won the Distinguished America Award from the National Football Foundation and Hall of Fame in conjunction with the Independence Bowl for a "former football player who becomes successful in other endeavors later in life."[68]

The Louisiana Tech Hall of Fame, in only its second year of existence, inducted Sanford in 1985.[69] He became the first center ever inducted into the Louisiana Sports Hall of Fame in 1990.[70] In 1997, he was an honorary captain in Tech's first game against the Pac 10.[71] Leo was honored on the field as a Louisiana "Legend of Football" and is still sometimes asked by reporters about how the team and its coaches are doing.[72] In 1999 Leo and Myrna Sanford celebrated their 50th wedding anniversary with their four children and ten grandchildren.[73] Sadly, Myrna passed away on March 31, 2018. Sanford still lives in the home on the southern shore of Cross Lake, Louisiana, that he bought with his share of the winnings from the championship game, and he is still happy to reminisce about "the greatest game ever played."[74]

Though Sanford did not get his $1,000 a game from the Cardinals, it is clear he got a great deal and so did everyone else. The Baltimore Colts got the help they needed at the positions of linebacker and long-snapper. The city of Baltimore got a championship. The Chicago Cardinals did well, with Dale Meinert becoming a three-time Pro Bowler himself.[75] Sanford got an NFL championship, a long career after football, a wonderful marriage and many friends and family; yes, he got a very good deal and he knows it.[76]

Notes

1. Leo Sanford, interview with author, August 18, 2016; http://www.dollartimes.com/inflation/inflation.php?amount=1000&year=1958.

2. Leo Sanford, interview with author, August 18, 2016.

3. http://www.pro-football-reference.com/players/S/SanfLe00.htm; "Wilson's Performance Doesn't Help Cards," *Alton* (IL) *Evening Telegraph*, December 24, 1965; "Cardinals Host Weak Redskins This Weekend," *Daily Standard* (Sikeston, MO), November 30, 1961.

4. http://www.pro-football-reference.com/players/S/SanfLe00.htm; http://www.latechsports.com/hallfame/leo_sanford.html.

5. http://www.lasportsshall.com/inductees/football/leo-sanford and www.14–0productions.com/football-champions.html.

6. "Season's Records," *Shreveport Times*, November 28, 1946; "Montgomery, Hedges Toss for Tallies," *Shreveport Times*, November 28, 1946.

7. http://www.fairparkalumni.com/id1_leo_sanford.htm; http://www.lasportsshall.com/inductess/football/leo-sanford/

8. http://www.lasportshall.com/inductees/football/leo-sanford/.

9. "Sanford," *Shreveport Times*, May 30, 1999.

10. http://www.latechsports.com/hallfame/leo_sanford.html.

11. http://www.winsipedia.com/games/louisiana-tech.

12. http://www.lasportshall.com/inductees/football/leo-sanford/.

13. *Ibid.*

14. http://www.latechsports.com/hallfame/leo_sanford.html; "Joe Murry Is New Mentor at Bastrop," *Shreveport Times*, June 5, 1963.

15. http://www.shreveporttimes.com/story/sports/2015/07/24/leo-sanford-kicks-time-top-list/30646739/.

16. http://www.lasportshall.com/inductees/football/leo-sanford/.

17. *Ibid.*

18. *Ibid.*

19. *Ibid.*

20. http://www.lasportshall.com/inductees/football/leo-sanford/; Edward Prell, "Groom, Irish Star, Signed by Cardinals," *Chicago Daily Tribune*, May 15, 1951.

21. http://www.lasportshall.com/inductees/football/leo-sanford/.

22. *Ibid.*

23. *Ibid.*

24. http://www.lasportshall.com/inductees/football/leo-sanford/; "Cards Sign Sanford," *Akron Beacon Journal*, June 29, 1951.

25. "Wilson's Performance Doesn't Help Cards"; http://www.lasportshall.com/inductees/football/leo-sanford/.

26. http://www.lasportshall.com/inductees/football/leo-sanford/.

27. Jack Fiser, "Case of the Stray Linebacker," *Shreveport Times*, July 17, 1958.

28. Leo Sanford, interview with author, August 18, 2016.

29. *Ibid.*

30. "Case of the Stray Linebacker."

31. "Ex-CFL Player Dale Meinert," www.cbc.ca/m/sports/football/ex-cfl-player-dale-meinert-dies-1.513765.

32. "Leo Sanford Lays 'Em Low," *The Daily Times* (Salisbury, MD), October 11, 1958.

33. "Rookies, Maturity Help Colts' Rise," *The Morning News* (Wilmington, DE), November 4, 1958; Leo Sanford, interview with author, August 18, 2016.

34. "Sanford Expected to Play Sunday," *Shreveport Times*, October 30, 1958.

35. Cameron C. Snyder, "Shaw Replaces Hurt Unitas, Guides Team to Five Touchdowns," *Baltimore Sun*, November 3, 1958.

36. "Colts-Giants Line-Up," *Baltimore Sun*, November 9, 1958.

37. "Leo Sanford Back with Colts; Giants May Lose Rosey Grier," *Baltimore Sun*, December 24, 1958.

38. *Ibid.*

39. *Ibid.*

40. Frank Gifford with Peter Richmond, *The Glory Game* (New York: HarperCollins, 2008), 86.

41. Jimmy Watson, "Local Man Attends 'Greatest Game' Event," *Shreveport Times*, December 28, 2008; Jack Fiser, "Sanford's Pot of Gold," *Shreveport Times*, January 11, 1959.

42. http://www.fairparkalumni.com/id1_leo_sanford.htm; Gifford, 215.

43. Ted Patterson, *Football in Baltimore: History and Memorabilia* (Baltimore: John Hopkins University Press, 2000), 148.

44. *Ibid.*, 148.

45. "Sanford's Pot of Gold."

46. *Ibid.*

47. *Ibid.*

48. Jack Fiser, "Good for Ten More," *Shreveport Times*, March 24, 1959.

49. "Good for Ten More"; "Colts' Sanford Has Surgery on Knee," *Troy* (NY) *Record*, August 7, 1959.

50. "Good for Ten More."

51. "World Pro Football Champions: Awesome Offense Returns Intact To Baltimore Colts for

1959 Action," *Evening Sun* (Hanover, PA), June 2, 1959; "Early Pigskinning," *Shreveport Times*, June 16, 1959.

52. Bill Baker, "Shreveport's Leo Sanford Set for Ninth NFL Season," *Shreveport Times*, July 26, 1959; Cameron C. Snyder, "Former Set for Action on Sunday," *Baltimore Sun*, November 18, 1958; "Marv Matuszak Signs Pact with Packers," *Baltimore Sun*, November 18, 1958.

53. Cameron C. Snyder, "Shaw Sticks by Decision," *Baltimore Sun*, July 26, 1959.

54. "Colts' Sanford Has Surgery on Knee."

55. George Bowen, "Complacency Biggest Baltimore Bugaboo," *North Adams* (MA) *Transcript*, August 10, 1959; "Sports Section" *Daily Mail* (Hagerstown, MD), August 12, 1959.

56. Jack Russell, "It's Tough to Repeat in NFL," *The Times* (San Mateo, CA), September 23, 1959; "The Week in Sports," *Baltimore Sun*, September 20, 1959.

57. "Gifford Latest Addition to NFL Injured Ranks," *Santa Cruz* (CA) *Sentinel*, October 29, 1959.

58. http://www.lasportshall.com/inductees/football/leo-sanford/.

59. Jack Fiser, "No Obits for Sanford," *Shreveport Times*, February 3, 1960.

60. Jack Fiser, "Leo Gets the Green Light," *Shreveport Times*, July 15, 1960.

61. *Ibid.*

62. *Ibid.*

63. http://www.lasportshall.com/inductees/football/leo-sanford/; Jack Fiser, "Football Through a Lorgnette," *Shreveport Times*, July 22, 1960; *The Eagle* (Bryan, TX), July 15, 1960.

64. "Injured Knee Blamed: Cowboys Lose Services of Veteran Leo Sanford," *Lubbock Avalanche-Journal*, July 22, 1960.

65. http://www.lasportshall.com/inductees/football/leo-sanford/; "Leo Sanford Joins Harbuck Sales Staff," *Shreveport Times*, January 22, 1959.

66. Gifford, 257; Leo Sanford, interview with author, August 18, 2016.

67. http://www.lasportshall.com/inductees/football/leo-sanford/; http://www.shreveporttimes.com/story/sports/2015/07/24/leo-sanford-kicks-time-top-list/30646739/.

68. http://www.latechsports.com/hallfame/leo_sanford.html; "Sanford, Hedges Will be Honored," *Shreveport Times*, December 9, 1983.

69. https://www.latechsports.com/hallfame/latc-hallfame.html; https://www.latechsports.com/hallfame/leo_sanford.html.

70. http://www.lasportshall.com/inductees/football/leo-sanford/.

71. "Louisiana Tech," *Shreveport Times*, October 3, 1997.

72. Jimmy Watson, "Louisiana Tech Honors 1959 Bulldogs Team," *Shreveport Times*, October 1, 2009; Kelly Morris, "Fans Have Positive Reaction to Dykes," *Shreveport Times*, January 21, 2010; Jimmy Watson, "Terry Bradshaw Says Local Bowl Game Is Critical," *Shreveport Times*, April 10, 2015.

73. "Sanford."

74. http://www.fairparkalumni.com/id1_leo_sanford.htm; "Leo Sanford Joins Harbuck Sales Staff"; Gifford, 257.

75. http://www.pro-football-reference.com/players/M/MeinDa00.htm.

76. Leo Sanford, interview with author, August 18, 2016.

George Shaw

Jay Zahn

George Shaw once said, "I was born in the Depression in 1933, and my dad had been a successful operator of four or five grocery stores, but he lost those. Then he went to work in the fruit produce business. He'd always encourage me, but he'd remind me, 'You might be in a good period now, but you will go through cycles when things won't be so pleasant.'"[1] The words of his father would prove prophetic for George's football career.

George Howard Shaw was born July 25, 1933, in Portland, Oregon, the youngest of four brothers. All four brothers would go on to play college football. George followed his brothers to Portland's Grant High; he quarterbacked the Grant Generals to two consecutive Oregon state football championships and received national prep All-America recognition. Shaw was considered the best recruit in the Northwest. George dickered until mid–August 1951 before deciding to attend the University of Oregon. Oregon's Eugene campus was just a couple of hours from Portland, and the Ducks played some games at Portland's Multnomah Stadium, site of George's high school football triumphs.

George Shaw.

Due to the Korean War, freshmen were eligible for varsity play in 1951. Seen as having "great poise for a rookie,"[2] George worked his way up to backup quarterback on the offense. He was more prominent on defense. Starting at safety, George intercepted 13 passes over a ten-game schedule, setting an NCAA record that would stand for 17 years. The next year, starting at quarterback, George set conference records for pass completions and attempts in a game against Cal.

In 1953 the NCAA re-instituted limited substitution in football. The new rules were a perfect fit for all-around athlete Shaw, as a game against Southern Cal demonstrated. In a 13–7 upset win, George ran for 70 yards, passed for 45, and caught three passes for 44 yards and a touchdown when split out as an end. He also got off a 51-yard punt, kicked an extra point, and made several key tackles as a defensive back.

In that same game, George also proved his sportsmanship. The Trojans' George Timberlake roughed Shaw up after a tackle. As an official seemed about to penalize Timberlake, the usually quiet and unassuming Shaw stepped in. "Let it go," he said to the official. Then Shaw stared at his tormenter. "Timberlake, you're too good a ballplayer to be pulling that kind of stuff. Let's just play the game, shall we?"[3]

In Shaw's senior season of 1954, he led the Ducks to their first winning season since 1948. He also battled all year for the nationwide lead in all-purpose yardage, a battle he would win with 1,536 yards. George received All-America mentions and Heisman votes, but placed third among quarterbacks in both to Notre Dame's Ralph Guglielmi and Cal's Paul Larson.

His college football career complete, George awaited interest from pro football. At the time, the first pick in the collegiate draft was a "bonus choice" that rotated among all teams. In 1955, the Colts held the bonus choice, as well as the second pick in the first round. The Colts staff decided to focus on improving the league's worst offense in points scored and yardage. Alabama quarterback Bobby Freeman, the Colts' preferred bonus choice, signed with the Canadian League before the draft. The choice then came down to Wisconsin fullback Alan Ameche or either Shaw or Ralph Guglielmi.

The Colts wound up choosing Shaw with the bonus choice, then also landed Ameche with their regular first round pick two picks later. Coach Weeb Ewbank later explained the choice. He said, "It was tough to pick the best one, but I'm sure we did…. They raved about Ralph Guglielmi. He is a good quarterback, but Shaw is the best thing to come along for many years. He isn't just a passer. He can do everything…. I rate him a more versatile performer than Otto Graham of the Cleveland Browns."[4]

Shaw still had unfinished business left at Oregon. In addition to his economics degree, George had a senior season of baseball with the Ducks to complete. A center fielder, Shaw was as big a star on the diamond as the gridiron; he'd led the Ducks to their first, and so far only, appearance in the College World Series.

He waited until June of 1955 before finally turning his back on a baseball career and signing with the Colts for a $17,500 bonus. George explained his choice:

> It never really came out at the time, but I always wanted to be a professional baseball player. But you have to consider the time. There was Korea. Our whole class was in ROTC, and we were all scheduled for two years of service. But with the war winding down they postponed our enlistment for two years. I had to make a decision. The Yankees and Red Sox both wanted me, but if I had signed to play baseball I figured I would have to spend two years in the minors and then go into the service. That happened to a lot of guys at that time and the years away ruined their careers. So I thought if I play football, I can play two years for the Colts right away.[5]

The College All-Star Game delayed Shaw's reporting date to the Colts. At quarterback, the Colts had lost last year's number one draft choice, Cotton Davidson, to the service. But incumbent Gary Kerkorian remained, and the team had also picked up Jack Scarbath from the Redskins. Shaw wasted no time making a good impression, leading three touchdown drives against the Redskins in his first exhibition game, and ripping off a 62-yard touchdown run against the Giants the next week. By the end of camp, Scarbath had been returned to the Redskins and Kerkorian was on the bench.

Shaw earned the start at home against the Chicago Bears in his first NFL regular season game. He wasn't the only member of the Colts starting his first game; six rookies in all broke into the Colts' starting offensive lineup. Hosting the Bears in the first game of 1955, the new lineup was an immediate smash as Alan Ameche took off for a 79-yard touchdown run on the game's first play. Featuring a run heavy approach emphasizing Ameche and the speedy Shaw, the Colts won the Bears game, and the next two as well, as Shaw threw for two touchdowns apiece against the Lions and Packers. The young team was off to a 3–0 start, a first for any Baltimore Colts team.

The winning streak was broken in a return match with the Bears in Chicago. Also broken were Shaw's faceguard and four of his teeth. With Bear Ed Sprinkle holding Shaw by the legs, George Connor sent a shoulder into Shaw's face. "We won't be seeing him anymore today,"[6] commented teammate Art Donovan, as Shaw left the field spurting blood. But Colts trainer Eddie Block fashioned a wad of gum into a crude mouthpiece, and Shaw went back into the game, earning Donovan's respect.

Shaw and the Colts earned the respect of Baltimore fans as well; despite the loss to Chicago, 6,000 turned out to greet the team at the airport. More went through the turnstiles of Memorial Stadium, as a record of 51,587 attended the next week's game against Washington. For the season home attendance would be up 57 percent over 1954.

The young team leveled off, but stayed in the Western Conference race until a late season loss against the Rams. Shaw's passing numbers were around the middle of the pack, but he supplemented his passing with 301 yards rushing, second among NFL quarterbacks to Green Bay's Tobin Rote. Most impressive was that he started all 12 games at quarterback, the first rookie to do that since Rote pulled it off in 1950. Shaw finished second in Rookie of the Year voting to teammate Ameche.

Shaw came back to Baltimore in 1956 hoping to build on his rookie success. One change in the team occurred when backup Kerkorian retired to practice law; minor league free agent John Unitas would take his place.

Shaw started 1956 the same way as 1955, with an opening day home victory over the Bears, hitting on 19 of 25 passes for 253 yards and two touchdowns. Again, the return engagement with the Bears came three weeks hence, and again Shaw met with mayhem from the Midway monsters. In the second quarter 275-pound tackle Fred Williams crashed into Shaw's left knee in a pileup. Shaw's knee ligaments were torn. When the injury didn't respond to treatment, Shaw was put on the inactive list. On came Unitas.

While Shaw was healing, the rookie Unitas was making just as good an impression as Shaw had in 1955. Unitas wasn't the runner Shaw was, but he was a better passer. When Shaw was finally ready to go in the last game of 1956, it was only because of Unitas' own rib injury that Shaw got the start. Shaw lasted until the second quarter until the knee gave way again after a quarterback sack. Back came Unitas.

Off season knee surgery followed for Shaw. So did a call from Uncle Sam. Shaw only served six months at Fort Benning, Ga., but still missed the first month of the Colts' 1957 training camp. If Shaw had ideas of getting his job back, he wouldn't get much of a chance. His knee still wasn't right. He'd play only three regular season games and attempt just nine passes, mostly in mop-up duty. Meanwhile, Unitas won the league MVP award.

George was healthy for 1958, but his mop-up role continued until Johnny Unitas suffered several fractured ribs when the Colts hosted Green Bay in Week Six. Shaw entered, and was merciless against a hapless Packer squad missing a couple of defensive backs. Despite liberal substitution, he and the Colts poured it on in a driving rainstorm. Shaw threw for three touchdowns while completing ten of 13 attempts, and ran for another, turning a 21–0 lead into a 56–0 rout. Coach Ewbank said after the game, "I could not hold 'em down … that crowd just keeps pushing us along, asking for more. And Shaw was anxious; he hadn't played in so long."[7]

The next week Shaw would face his first full game in over two years, and a tougher challenge, the Giants in Yankee Stadium. A record crowd for a Giants game turned out to see a rusty Shaw hit on only 11 of 29 passes. But three went for scores, and a fourth was dropped in the end zone by Lenny Lyles in the fourth quarter. It wouldn't be enough, as a late field goal by Pat Summerall lifted the Giants to a 24–21 win, giving the Colts their first loss.

Shaw took the loss hard on the train ride back to Baltimore. "The last couple years sitting on the bench haven't been easy," he said. "You watch the rest of the players wanting so much to win. You sit there and hope when your chance does come that you will be able to make a contribution. We are close to a championship now, the first one for most of the veterans. If my efforts could have helped us win today and get closer to the title I would have been happy. That's all I wanted—just to make a contribution to a victory."[8]

The next week figured to be a tough test as well, as the Colts played the Bears in Chicago, site of past calamity for Shaw. But George rode a hot streak of nine straight completed passes to 14 second quarter points, more than enough in a 17–0 victory. By the next week Unitas had healed, and George went back to his understudy role. After the Colts had clinched the West, he did start the final game of the season in San Francisco, a game the Colts lost 21 to 12.

George didn't see action under center in the 1958 NFL championship game, but he did play a role in the victory. During the season, he had taken over the role of holder on place kicks. Late in the game, George rushed on to the field to hold for Steve Myhra's 20-yard field goal attempt that would send the game into sudden death overtime. Recalling the moment, George said, "The field was frozen and it was cold. We didn't have hand warmers or heaters to keep us warm. We just put our hands between our legs and tried to keep them from freezing. I've woken up since then in the middle of the night thinking, 'What if I dropped the ball?' I got the snap from center, spun the ball to put the laces in front and Steve kicked it through. When the ball reached my hands it felt like a heavy hunk of ice."[9]

In February of 1959 George asked Colts management to trade him. General manager Don Kellett said, "George came to us in 1958 and said he had no future. He wanted to be traded. I told him there was no assurance he wouldn't find the same difficulty with another club. Besides that, I didn't want to let him go. He was too fine a ball player. But he was insistent."[10] It took until July and a training camp walkout by Shaw to force the deal. On July 29, 1959, the Colts traded Shaw to the Giants for two draft choices.

The Giants starting job was not open, but regular Charlie Conerly was at least a dozen years older than Unitas. Shaw beat out long time backup Don Heinrich and others for the backup job. When Conerly went out with an ankle injury, Shaw got his first start in midseason. He was playing well when he severely sprained his right thumb, and was done for the season.

Shaw was healthy again in 1960. When the aging Conerly went out again with elbow and dental woes, George got regular playing time for the first time since 1956. He started fast, with four touchdown passes against the Cardinals, but his fortunes faded with those of the team. Consecutive losses to the Eagles knocked the Giants out of the championship picture for the year.

After the 1960 season, the Giants decided to move on from George Shaw. The expansion Minnesota Vikings traded a number one draft choice for George. He was given the number one quarterback job in training camp, but brash rookie Fran Tarkenton outplayed him in preseason games. But Tarkenton cooled off, and George would get another chance.

In Week 3 of the 1961 season, Shaw and the Vikings travelled to Baltimore to face the Colts and Johnny Unitas. Jim Klobuchar wrote, "Shaw … played the entire game at quarterback with a grim gallantry that made this one of his finest hours. It came before Baltimore partisans who once cheered his quarterbacking as a Colt."[11] Shaw survived eight sacks and rallied the Vikings to take the lead four separate times, only to be bested by Unitas as Steve Myhra kicked a 52-yard field goal as time ran out to give the Colts a 34–33 victory. Shaw continued sharing the quarterback job until his knee again gave out in a game at Green Bay; he was out for the season.

By 1962 Shaw competed with younger quarterbacks for a backup job to Tarkenton. Still battling the knee, he lost the competition after a poor performance in a preseason game played at Portland's Multnomah Stadium, site of high school and college triumphs for Shaw. "I never in my life wanted to play a good football game as much as that day," he said. "My family was there, and my friends. My five-year-old son saw me play for the first time."[12]

Shaw was released by the Vikings after that game, but the Denver Broncos signed George shortly thereafter. He played extensively as a backup, yet recorded the poorest statistics of his career. The Broncos would release Shaw to the taxi squad in 1963 training camp, and he retired a short time later, returning to Portland. George hosted a local NFL pre-game show for a few years, but his primary job was as an investment counselor.

George Shaw had physically escaped the shadow of Johnny Unitas, but he could not escape the effect on his own psyche. Latter-day teammates complained that his leadership lacked force and flair. His quotes became excessively deferential. George himself described his condition as "second-stringitis." Jim Klobuchar described it thusly: "George Shaw was an experienced quarterback, technically hale as a player, a man of intelligence and decency. But injuries and blighted hopes had beaten him down. He had lost the edge of assertiveness."[13] George's knee injuries didn't help his career either; once a speedy runner, he rushed for only 67 yards the last six seasons of his career as compared to 364 in his first two.

Shaw died January 3, 1998, in Portland after a long battle with bone marrow cancer. He was survived by his wife Patricia, five children, and 12 grandchildren. Earlier Jim Klobuchar reflected on Shaw's football career. He wrote, "He was the toast of Baltimore, the rookie quarterback from Oregon who rescued the then-new Colts from futility … [1955] was the turning point season for a young team that later was to become one of pro football's finest. Shaw had that one season in the sun. He was the man in command, a gifted passer and a player potentially headed for greatness."[14] Then the sun set, and his football luck ran out.

NOTES

1. Nick Bertram, "Ex-UO All-America Shaw Credits Era for His Success," *The Oregonian*, July 18, 1978.

2. Don McLeod, "New Coach, New Men Tell Story at Oregon," *The Oregonian*, September 9, 1951.

3. Frank Litsky, "George Shaw, 64, Backup to Great N.F.L. Quarterbacks," *New York Times*, January 12, 1998.

4. Sid Hartman, "Ewbank: Guessed Right on Shaw," *Minneapolis Star Tribune*, September 8, 1955

5. Bertram.

6. Arthur J. Donovan, Jr., and Bob Drury, *Fatso* (New York: Avon Books, 1987), 179.

7. Art Daley, "'Got Two Nice Breaks Right Away,' Ewbank," *Green Bay Press-Gazette*, November 3, 1958.

8. John F. Steadman, *From Colts to Ravens* (Centreville, MD: Tidewater, 1997), 138.

9. *Ibid.*, 144.

10. Jim Klobuchar, "Vikings vs. Colts—Familiar Role for Shaw," *Minneapolis Star Tribune*, August 18, 1961.

11. Jim Klobuchar, "Colts Stun Vikings 34–33 on Last-Second Field Goal," *Minneapolis Star Tribune*, October 2, 1961.

12. Jim Klobuchar, "Shaw Swan Song: 'Wanted to Play; It Didn't Work Out,'" *Minneapolis Star Tribune*, August 29, 1962.

13. Jim Klobuchar and Fran Tarkenton, *Tarkenton* (New York: Harper & Row, 1976).

14. "Vikings vs. Colts—Familiar Role for Shaw."

Don Shinnick

NICK RITZMANN

Deep inside Yankee Stadium before the scheduled 2:05 afternoon kickoff of the 1958 National Football League championship game, Colts head coach Weeb Ewbank "pulled out some handwritten notes from his pocket ... loosened his vocal cords ... and gave the motivational speech of his life."[1] One theme of the speech was how many of the Colts had been considered "a bunch of rejects, retreads and new recruits."[2] Linebacker Don Shinnick was only in his second year in the NFL, but no one would have considered him a reject or retread. The "jovial extrovert"[3] who was "one of the boys"[4] was a strongly devout Christian who after leading the Colts in prayer before every game, played a rugged brand of football, holding down one of their linebacker positions for over a decade. Shinnick would play in four NFL championship games and win three (1958, 1959, 1968), retiring with 37 career pass interceptions, a record for linebackers that stands today. Then, after his playing career ended, he had a notable career as an assistant coach.

Donald Dee Shinnick was born on May 15, 1935, at St. Luke's Hospital in Kansas City, Missouri, to Matthew and Viola Cope Shinnick. He joined two siblings, a sister Shirley and a brother Dick. Following a divorce, his mother relocated the family to San Pedro, California, in the early 1940s. San Pedro is a community in Los Angeles, located on the southern end of the Palos Verdes Peninsula, and its main asset remains its proximity to Los Angeles Harbor. The fathers of most of Don Shinnick's boyhood friends were "fishermen or longshoremen, while his stepfather ran a hamburger business."[5]

Don Shinnick.

In the fall of 1950 he was introduced to Southern California football fans as "Big Don Shinnick, [an] 180-pound 10th grader"[6] for the San Pedro High School Pirates, then started at fullback for the Pirates in 1951 as an 190-pound junior. During his senior football season in 1952, he played well enough that The Helms Athletic Foundation in Los Angeles named the now-six-foot-two, 200-pounder as the "blocking back" on their All-Los Angeles City High School football team, and co-player of the year in the Marine League.

After graduation, he enrolled at Valley Junior College in Los

Angeles, where he would play fullback and handle punting chores for the Monarchs. He missed games in the Fall of 1953 with injuries, but was named the best Junior College player in the Los Angeles area, then followed his brother Richard and enrolled at UCLA in early 1954. Although he could not practice during Spring football because of a Pacific Coast Conference rule, he played some rugby, then was described as a "tank-type fullback" when he first suited up for coach Henry "Red" Sanders' very formidable team.[7] In 1953 the 8–2 Bruins had allowed only 76 points all season and won the Pacific Coast Conference championship. The 1954 Bruins finished 9–0 and were named UPI national champions. They surrendered only 40 points all season and scored 367, and their new fullback from San Pedro gained 210 yards on only 28 carries, scoring a touchdown in a 61–0 rout at Oregon State.

In 1955, due to depth at fullback, Shinnick, the heaviest player on the squad at 231 pounds, was moved to guard and played 183.5 minutes at that position during the season. Sanders took advantage of December practice sessions for the 1956 Rose Bowl against Michigan State and switched Shinnick to blocking back on offense and linebacker on defense.

Shinnick's senior season at UCLA was impacted by the Pacific Coast Conference's decision in the Spring of 1956 to level sanctions against the Bruins. Each Bruin senior was allowed to play in only five successive games, and Shinnick chose games 6–10. In early November UCLA hosted a Stanford team that was favored by two touchdowns. Shinnick led the way in the 14–13 upset, terrorizing Stanford quarterback John Brodie by keying off of how he positioned his feet to discern if Stanford was planning to run or pass, then kicking the game-winning extra point and blocking a Stanford extra point. Coach Sanders called it "the most deserved victory I've ever seen a bunch of players earn," and "all things considered … the finest win I have ever enjoyed."[8] Shinnick was selected the AP Back Of The Week, and when the season ended he was selected honorable mention All-America by the UPI and was given the Bruin Bench Award by UCLA as the outstanding senior. In late December at San Francisco's Kezar Stadium he was awarded the Spaulding Trophy for his play as the outstanding lineman in the 1956 East-West Shrine Game.

Although he had a great career at UCLA, the two most noteworthy things happened off the field. First, he met the woman (Marsha Tatlow) he would be married to for the rest of his life, and second, he committed his life to Christ. The Campus Crusade for Christ organization was founded in 1951 at UCLA, and prominent Bruin football players became involved, including Donn Moomaw, Bob Davenport, and Shinnick. In addition to attending seminary school in the off-season during his career, he spent decades afterwards crisscrossing the United States attending and speaking at more than one thousand Christian gatherings of all sizes and types, from large meetings of the Fellowship of Christian Athletes to small youth groups in rural towns. Only two days after the Colts lost in Super Bowl III, he was in Salisbury on Maryland's rural Eastern Shore addressing a Crusade for Christ group, where it was noted that "he speaks almost four days a week in a different region in the United States."[9]

Four days after Thanksgiving 1956 representatives of the 12 teams in the National Football League gathered at the Warwick Hotel in Philadelphia and selected 49 players (over four rounds) in what *Baltimore Sun* writer Cameron Snyder termed an "abbreviated draft meeting. The other twenty-six rounds of the draft were held in January [1957] along with the annual league meeting."[10] "The first four rounds were held … almost two months earlier than previous years to beat Canadian teams to the Nation's top 1957 intercollegiate graduates."[11]

With their second-round selection (20th overall) the Colts chose Shinnick. It was reported that "the Baltimore Colts were hesitant about drafting Don Shinnick because they'd heard about his religious activities on campus and feared it might keep him from playing football on Sunday, like another UCLA All-America[n] Bob Davenport."[12] Coach Sid Gillman wanted to draft Shinnick for his hometown Los Angeles Rams, but "decided not to because he refuses to play Sunday ball"[13] In January 1953 The Rams had used their first-round pick on UCLA's Donn Moomaw, another Southern California native who had earned consensus All-America honors in 1952. Moomaw was reluctant to play football on Sunday and went to play in Canada. So, when Shinnick told Gillman the same, the Rams coach decided to pass him up, However, Don Kellett, Colts general manager hustled out to California for a visit with the young collegian and convinced him that playing football on Sunday would not lead to perdition.

Finally Shinnick agreed. "I guess if it's all right for the farmer to milk cows on Sunday, it'll be all right for me."[14]

Shinnick was offered a contract by Toronto of the Canadian Big Four League but signed with the Colts late in January 1957, played in the College All-Star Game on August 9 in Chicago, and then was in Baltimore for the annual intrasquad scrimmage at Memorial Stadium three nights later. Playing a big role as a rookie, Shinnick started every game at linebacker and recorded his first interception in the fourth quarter of the season's second game against quarterback Ed Brown and the Chicago Bears. The interception was important at the time because it stopped a Bears drive in Colts territory aiding the Colts' 29–14 victory.

Teammates praised Shinnick's play. Andy Nelson felt "Don never played the play the way it was drawn up … he played his own defense."[15] Raymond Berry called Shinnick a "natural instinctive defensive player … who [studied film and] inspired other Colt players to start studying film too, because they saw how he knew what other teams were going to do on various downs and distances, what quarterback's tendencies were, and so on … he studied more film than all the rest of the defensive players put together."[16] Berry notes,

> One of the famous jokes about Shinnick stems from a game we played against, I think, the Packers. The ball was snapped and the Packers started to run a play, and Shinnick hollered out, "They don't have that play! They don't have that play!" One time we played the Rams in the Coliseum in Los Angeles. We were on defense and one of our defensive guys hit the quarterback. The ball went up in the air and Shinnick, who had taken on a blocker, had gone down. He was on the ground when the fumble or interception return began by Dick Szymanski. The camera caught Shinnick as he sat there watching a 30- or 40-yard run back, and he was clapping, giving Szymanski an ovation while he was running. That was Shinnick—always doing something unique…. He was such a positive guy who loved people, and he played his guts out.[17]

The Colts' linebacker corps underwent some changes in 1958. First, Bill Pellington returned from missing almost all of the 1957 season with a broken arm. Second, in July the Colts sent Dale Meinert to the Chicago Cardinals in exchange for Leo Sanford, who was selected to the 1956 and 1957 Pro Bowl games. Shinnick remained a starter, but shifted to middle linebacker with Pellington and Sanford flanking him. He sat out the penultimate regular season game in Los Angeles with a leg injury but played the next week in San Francisco as the Colts dropped their final two games on the West Coast, then flew home to prepare for the championship game on December 28 in Yankee Stadium. In the championship, it was Shinnick's tackle of Giants quarterback Charlie Conerly on third down early in overtime that forced a Giants punt and got the ball back for the Colts.

In 1959 Don Shinnick was returned to an outside linebacker position, where he would play for the rest of his NFL career. He was named to UPI's All-NFL team (second team), and intercepted seven passes to tie for the league high. The Colts again played the Giants for the NFL championship, this time in Baltimore, and again they won, breaking a close game open in the second half.

The Colts ran out to a 6–2 start in 1960, but lost their final four games after a 24–20 victory over the Bears in a "bloody gang fight in Chicago"[18] as Shinnick intercepted five passes for the season. In 1961 the regular season expanded to 14 games. The Colts posted an 8–6 record as Shinnick swiped two passes. He intercepted five more passes in 1962, but after the Colts finished the season with a 7–7 record, owner Carroll Rosenbloom let Weeb Ewbank go and replaced him with Don Shula. Shula posted an 8–6 record in his first year, with Shinnick intercepting a pair of passes. He had three interceptions in 1964 as the Colts won the Western Conference with a 12–2 record, losing the championship game in Cleveland to the Browns.

The Colts finished the 1965 regular season with a record of 10–3–1, losing an iconic playoff game at Green Bay. Don Shinnick had only one interception on the year, but it was an important one as it helped preserve a 26–21 victory over the Chicago Bears at Wrigley Field in November in what one writer termed a "hitters game, where the faint of heart had to hide their eyes at the brutal play."[19] Shinnick broke his forearm in the game, and returned to action in a 42–27 loss to the Green Bay Packers on December 12 in a foggy Memorial Stadium. The Colts had to travel to Green Bay to playoff for the Western Conference Title on the day after Christmas. The game could not have started better for the Colts as on the first play from scrimmage defensive back Lenny Lyles forced a fumble by the Packers Bill Anderson, which Shinnick scooped off the turf and returned for a 25-yard touchdown. Green Bay quarterback Bart Starr injured his ribs on the play trying to tackle Shinnick and would have to leave the game (except to hold on field goal attempts). Shinnick missed his defensive signal on the play. Otherwise he would not have been near the ball.[20] After falling behind 10–0, the Packers eventually tied the score with a controversial field goal by Don Chandler. Then in the overtime period, Chandler kicked the winning field goal.

In 1966, the Colts finished with a 9–5 record. Although Shinnick missed time in the preseason with a hyperextended elbow, he recovered and notched three interceptions, including two in a victory over the Atlanta Falcons on November 13. Late in the season the Colts began quite a run, as author Tom Callahan notes, "For a remarkable stretch that almost no one remembers-starting on December 18, 1966 and ending on January 12, 1969-Shula's Colts played a total of thirty football games and lost two."[21]

The Colts had an outstanding season in 1967, finishing with a record of 11–1–2, and "were the first team since the 1934 Chicago Bears to play 13 games without losing."[22] Shinnick missed some time in the preseason with a broken hand, but picked off three passes, including two in a victory over the Philadelphia Eagles in the second game of the season for which he was named NFL Defensive Player of the Week.

The Colts were even better in 1968, finishing the regular season with a 13–1 record and recording postseason victories over the Minnesota Vikings and Cleveland Browns to capture the NFL championship. It was Don Shinnick's 12th year playing professional football, and he reported to camp at a lighter weight than in the previous years. He missed some time in the preseason after fracturing a cheekbone in a scrimmage, and missed one month in the early season with a pulled hamstring muscle. After asking to be traded in the middle of the season, he intercepted the final pass of his career on November 24 in a victory over the visiting Minnesota Vikings, then recovered a fumble in the NFL championship game against the Cleveland Browns.

In early January the Colts traveled to Miami to play coach Weeb Ewbank's New York Jets, the champions of the American Football League, in Super Bowl III. When Don Shinnick stepped onto the field in Miami, he became the first player from UCLA to play in a Super Bowl. Despite being labeled an 18-point underdog by the odds makers, the Jets won 16–7, and Jets running back Matt Snell had 121 rushing yards. Many of these runs were aimed at the right side of the Colts defense, which featured 36-year-old end Ordell Braase, 33-year-old Shinnick, and 32-year-old defensive back Lenny Lyles, who were all nursing minor injuries. Their side had a difficult day in Miami, but Shinnick still started on opening day 1969 in a 27–20 loss to the Los Angeles Rams at Memorial Stadium. He pulled a leg muscle at practice before a home game against the San Francisco 49ers on October 26, and after attempting to play in the game, he was replaced in the second half by rookie linebacker Ted Hendricks. Shinnick was placed on the waived/injured list on October 30, asked for a trade, and then asked for his release, which was granted by the Colts in early December.

Although his playing career was over, his time in pro football was not. In 1970, Shinnick began a long coaching career, spending time as a defensive assistant with the Bears (1970–71), Cardinals (1972), Raiders (1973–77) and Patriots (1985–89). He also coached at the high school and small college level from 1978 to 1981 and in 1994.

Don and his wife Marsha had five sons, four of whom played Division I college football. In the late 1990s Don Shinnick began showing the effects of Frontal Lobe Dementia, a degenerative brain disease, and passed away at the age of 68 in a Modesto, California, rest home on January 20, 2004.

NOTES

1. Mark Bowden, *The Best Game Ever* (New York: Atlantic Monthly Press, 2008), 147.

2. Don Shinnick as told to James C. Hefley, *Always A Winner* (Grand Rapids: Zondervan, 1969).

3. Cameron C. Snyder, "Shinnick Fractures Cheek, Undergoes Surgery Here," *Baltimore Sun*, July 22, 1968.

4. "Colt Shinnick Is Anxious to Get Back in Action," *The Daily Times* (Salisbury, MD), October 20, 1968.

5. Shinnick.

6. John De La Vega, "Pirate Prep Team Laden with Talent," *Los Angeles Times*, September 27, 1950.

7. Dick Hyland, "Bruins Dig in Immediately on Basic Football," *Los Angeles Times*, September 2, 1954.

8. Paul Zimmerman, "Should Have Carried Team—Red," *Los Angeles Times*, November 4, 1956.

9. Rick Cullen, "Staying on Christian Team Hard, Colt Says," *The Daily Times* (Salisbury, MD), January 15, 1969.

10. Cameron C. Snyder, "Parker, 262-Pound Ohio State Lineman, First Colt Pick," *Baltimore Sun*, November 27, 1956.

11. John Dell, "Peaks, McDonald Drawn by Eagles in NFL Draft," *Philadelphia Inquirer*, November 27, 1956.

12. "Shinnick Will Not Play on Sunday, Said the L.A. Rams," *The Daily Times* (Salisbury, MD), November 19, 1957.

13. *Ibid.*

14. "Sports Briefs," *Los Angeles Times*, January 25, 1957.

15. Frank Gifford with Peter Richmond, *The Glory Game* (New York: HarperCollins, 2008), 218.

16. Raymond Berry with Wayne Stewart, *All the Moves I Had: A Football Life* (Guilford, CT: LP, 2016), 105.

17. *Ibid.*

18. Tom Callahan, *Johnny U: The Life & Times of John Unitas* (New York: Crown, 2006), 191.

19. Cameron C. Snyder, "Colts Nip Bears To Gain Lead," *Baltimore Sun*, November 8, 1965.

20. Cameron C. Snyder, "Colts 1-Point Choice Over Packers," *Baltimore Sun*, September 8, 1966.

21. Callahan, 202.

22. "Next Game Is On Colts Mind," *The Capital* (Annapolis, MD), December 11, 1967.

Jackie Simpson

JOHN MAXYMUK

Given the telephone number of former Colts teammate Buzz Nutter in the mid–1990s, Jackie Simpson gave Buzz a call one night and both two-time champions received a shock. Nutter told Simpson that he thought Jackie was dead and had been so for a decade; in fact, when the Colts would get together for reunions, they would recall their fallen comrade.[1]

However, there were two pro football Jackie Simpsons whose careers ran concurrently. Both played in the Southeastern Conference in the mid–1950s and subsequently professionally in both the U.S. and Canada. The other Jackie Simpson was two years younger than the Colts' Simpson and from Mississippi. He was a 6,' 225-pound guard/linebacker who spent four years playing in Canada, then four in the American Football League before finishing his playing career back in Canada, where he was known as "Jacki." He coached in the AFL and NFL from 1967 until his sudden death from natural causes in June 1983. That death notice was misreported to the 1958 Colts' alumni.

Our Jackie Simpson was born in Miami, Florida, to Ruby Simpson and grew up playing pee-wee football with future coach and broadcaster Lee Corso. At Miami Edison High School, Simpson competed against both Corso (at Miami Jackson High School) and future actor Burt Reynolds (at Palm Beach High).[2] Jackie scored 20 touchdowns in his senior year and was named All-State, All-South and All-America.

The 5'10," 170-pound Simpson was a speedy, elusive halfback on both sides of the ball and matriculated at the University of Florida in 1953. Both Corso and Reynolds attended Florida State, but the two Sunshine State schools did not play against each other in that era. The star of the 3–5–2 Gators that year was fullback Rick Casares, but Simpson got on the field for 152 minutes as a freshman, gained 193 yards rushing on 24 carries and scored his first three college touchdowns.

As a sophomore in 1954, Simpson was joined in the backfield by future pros Mal Hammack and Don Chandler, and the Gators pushed their record to 5–5. Jackie gained 215 yards on 49 carries and scored three touchdowns rushing and one receiving, as well as returning punts for a 6.3 yard average and kickoff for 24.9 yards each. He also recovered a fumble and intercepted a pass and was named third team All-SEC.

In 1955, Florida slipped to 4–6, but Simpson had his biggest season. The junior led the team with 422 yards rushing on 65 carries for two touchdowns, returned 17 punts for 267 yards and a touchdown, caught four passes for 52 yards and intercepted a pass that he returned 100 yards for a touchdown. The 100-yard interception return is still a Florida record and occurred in the season opener against Mississippi State. Jackie also ripped off a 46-yard touchdown run in that 20–14 victory, and a punt return touchdown against LSU that covered 62 yards. Again, he was named third team All-SEC.

Finally, as a senior, Simpson moved up to second team All-SEC, despite having less impressive statistics. He rushed for just 191 yards on 34 carries and two touchdowns and caught just three passes for 42 yards. The team rose to a 6–3–1 record, though, buoyed by the addition of new backs Bernie Parrish and Johnny Symank. Altogether, Simpson gained 1,021 yards on 172 carries (5.9 average) and nine touchdowns in four years at Florida. He also caught 20 passes for 250 yards, returned punts for at least 305 yards and kicks for at least 358 yards.

In the 1957 NFL draft the Colts nabbed Simpson in the fourth round. Now up to 185 pounds, Simpson was the first pick signed by Colts GM Don Kellett on December 27, for $7,800 and a $1,000 bonus following the North-South Shrine Game in Miami. Kellett told the *Baltimore Sun*, "I am very pleased with his defensive halfback play, but we expected him to be good defensively. He surprised me on the offense, however. Jackie runs real good, is quick and very fast. The times he carried the ball on quick openers, he showed good form, and on punt returns, he is exceptional. Besides all this, he is a nice kid who loves to play football."[3]

Jackie Simpson.

Before reporting to the Colts, however, he was drafted by Uncle Sam and spent 21 months with the 82nd Airborne paratroopers stationed at Fort Bragg, North Carolina, while also playing service ball. After his discharge late in 1958, Simpson joined the Colts' practice sessions and was activated by the team on December 5 for the last two games of the season, replacing third string quarterback Gary Kerkorian on the roster. It was the last roster move the Colts would be permitted before the championship game at the end of the month.

In his first NFL game against the Rams in Los Angeles on December 6, Simpson unfortunately foreshadowed his championship game performance to come. In the second quarter, Jackie received a Rams kickoff and fumbled when hit by Jimmy Jones, with the ball being recovered by the Rams' John Houser at the 20 yard line. Fortunately, an interception by Carl Taseff a few plays later ended the scoring threat, as Baltimore went on to win 30–28.

Taseff would play a key role in Simpson's championship game bobble on December 28 as well. In the second quarter of the title game with the Colts leading the Giants 7–3, Don Chandler boomed a punt from midfield. Simpson and Taseff waited for the kick around their own 20 yard line. The veteran Taseff had the responsibility to holler if Simpson should fair catch the punt, but Jackie couldn't hear his teammate above the din of the crowd noise. As he caught the punt, Simpson was hit nearly instantaneously by Giants cover men Billy Lott and Buzz Guy. The ball went flying, only to be recovered around the eight by tackle Roosevelt Brown who raced into the end zone with an apparent touchdown. Simpson later said, "Going back to the Colts bench to see Ewbank was the toughest walk I ever took."[4]

However the officials, who had originally signaled a Colts recovery, ruled that the punt was a muff and gave the Giants the ball on the 10. On the next play, Frank Gifford fumbled for the second time in the quarter, and Don Joyce recovered for Baltimore. In the locker room after the game, Giants coach Jim Lee Howell drew attention to the play, "I thought the Colt back had possession of the ball and then fumbled, which would have made Roosevelt Brown's recovery and run into the end zone a touchdown. If he [Jackie Simpson] muffed the kick, then it's a dead ball at the point it is recovered. To me it appeared the receiver took a couple of steps before fumbling."[5] Viewing the game film 60 years later, it's clearly a bang-bang play. Simpson does appear to shuffle his feet as if trying to run, but is hit so quickly that the call could have gone either way.

The following July, two veterans of the 1958 championship team reported to training camp with the rookies: Simpson and guard Fred Thurston. Both had joined the team late the previous year and thus missed Weeb Ewbank's full indoctrination. Three days later, Thurston was traded to Green Bay. Simpson found himself in a three-way fight for backup defensive back role with veteran Art DeCarlo and rookie Jimmy Carr. Carr, who would have the longest and most successful career of the threesome, was traded to the Eagles for a draft pick at the end of August, and both Simpson and DeCarlo returned for the defending champions in 1959. Simpson appeared in ten games but left no statistical mark—no interceptions, punt returns or kick returns. The 1960 season was a similar story. Jackie played in all 12 games but left no statistical record.

In December 1960, though, reports indicated that Steelers coach Buddy Parker had offered fullback Charley Scales to Baltimore for either Jackie Simpson or Milt Davis.[6] Instead Ewbank obtained Joe "The Jet" Perry from San Francisco to replace retiring fullback Alan Ameche. Both Simpson and DeCarlo were on the list of eight players to be made available for the expansion Minnesota Vikings to draft from in late January 1961 when Parker came calling again. On January 25, the Colts sent Simpson to Pittsburgh for defensive tackle Billy Ray Smith who would be a solid starter for the Colts for nearly a decade.

Parker commented on the trade at the time, "Simpson probably will be a starting defensive back for us. He better be."[7] Unfortunately, it never worked out that way for Jackie despite the Steelers replacing all four defensive backfield starters in 1961. Early in training camp he was hampered by a severe charley horse and then came down with strep throat before the start of the season. He did find playing time in eight games, though, and picked the first and only two passes of his NFL career in the two games against the Redskins that season. Simpson, however, tore ligaments in his ankle tackling

Jim Brown in Week Eight and saw limited action after that. He appeared in 13 games in 1962, but mostly as a nickelback defender. Returning to training camp in 1963, Simpson had one more return disaster in a preseason game against the Packers in Miami when his fumble on the opening kickoff in his hometown led to the Packers' first score.

After being cut by the Steelers, Simpson went north to Canada and hooked up with Toronto on the recommendation of his former Gator teammate Jim Rountree. In eight games with the Argos, he picked off three passes, ran the ball ten times and returned 20 punts. He spent 1964 with Hamilton, picking off five passes, and then landed in Montreal as part of an eight-man trade for a two-year stint starting in 1965. Montreal coach Jim Trimble noted, "I shift Simpson between offense and defense. He works his tail off and keeps his mouth shut. I don't have to go looking for him either. He's always standing right beside me."[8]

Simpson retired following the 1966 season, having played four years in the CFL and five in the NFL. Canada was where he played his best ball, recording 14 interceptions, three fumble recoveries, 14 rushes, 26 kick returns and 41 punt returns. He later owned a lounge in Miami and worked in the parking and roofing industries before eventually retiring to Pensacola. He was elected to the University of Florida Athletic Hall of Fame in 2001. In a 2015 interview, he said, "I had several injuries from my football career and was knocked out cold in a game against Detroit. In recent years, I have had knee, hip and back surgeries. I petitioned the NFL to help me with the medical expenses, but because NFL teams did not keep records of player injuries back then, they denied my request for assistance."[9] Simpson died in Pensacola on December 20, 2017.

Reminiscing about the Colts years, he summed up his time in Baltimore: "I've always had a nagging regret I could never crack Baltimore's starting lineup. But it was quite a club, and the overtime championship game in New York was certainly one of the greatest of all time. I'll never forget that march with Johnny Unitas passing to Raymond Berry to set up Steve Myhra's field goal for the tie."[10]

Notes

1. John Steadman, "Ex-Colt Simpson Glad Obit Was Dead Wrong," *Baltimore Sun*, February 1, 1995.

2. The People of Pensacola, September 5, 2015, www.facebook.com/Humans of Pensacola/posts/696251883839408:0, accessed March 15, 2017.

3. Cameron C. Snyder, "Simpson Signs with the Colts," *Baltimore Sun*, December 28, 1956.

4. John Steadman, *From Colts to Ravens* (Centreville, MD: Tidewater, 1997), 142.

5. Cameron C. Snyder, "Colts Game to Live Long in Memories," *Baltimore Sun*, December 30, 1958.

6. Jimmy Miller, "Parker, Aides Tracking Latest Draft Choices," *Pittsburgh Post-Gazette*, December 30, 1960.

7. Cameron C. Snyder, "Colts Trade Simpson for Steelers' Billy Ray Smith," *Baltimore Sun*, January 26, 1961.

8. Seymour S. Smith, "Ex-Colt Simpson Fills Hero Role in Canadian Football," *Baltimore Sun*, September 23, 1965.

9. People of Pensacola.

10. Smith.

Art Spinney

BILL LAMBERT

Ed King, one-time governor of Massachusetts, said of Art Spinney, his teammate from both Boston College and the Baltimore Colts, "He was the toughest single person I ever encountered, he handed out punishment with clean, hard-hitting, but he'd play himself into total fatigue. As an individual, he was one good, solid American man."[1]

Arthur F. Spinney was born on November 8, 1927, in Saugus, Massachusetts. Saugus is still a small town in Massachusetts, notable for having nearly 100 Revolutionary War veterans among its ancestors. It's also known as the town that started the 19th-century ice industry when Frederic Tudor cut ice from a family farm and shipped it to Martinique.[2]

Art played football at Saugus High School where he was named captain of the team in 1944. That team was undefeated in ten games. From Saugus High, he spent a year at Manlius, a military prep school, on the arrangement of Cornell coach Ed McKeever. After McKeever resigned as coach, Spinney was left without a future path until his high school coach Dave Lucey brought Art to Boston College, where Lucey worked as an assistant coach. The Episcopalian Spinney was a rarity at the Jesuit school, and his college career was threatened also by a rheumatic heart condition.[3]

Boston College had a number of tough World War II veterans on its football squad. Coach Denny Myers was returning from a three-year hitch in the Navy himself. Art was elected captain of the 1949 squad over future Hall of Famers Ernie Stautner and Art Donovan. Donovan would play with Spinney in the NFL as well. Head coach Myers called the Spinney appointment "a splendid choice." At that point in his career, Art was the only BC player who had started every game in the prior two years.[4]

At Boston College, Art was a four-year starter at end and twice earned All-New England honors for his spirited play as a blocker and pass receiver. His 24 pass receptions in 1948 established a Boston College season record at the time. Two decades later, he was inducted into the Boston College Varsity Club Athletic Hall of Fame in 1972.[5]

Art was drafted by the Balti-

Art Spinney.

more Colts in the 15th round of the 1950 NFL draft. The 1950 Colts finished an abysmal 1–11. Despite having notable players on the team such as Y.A. Tittle and Hardy Brown, coach Clem Crowe's team had one of the worst offenses and defenses in the league. Art was converted to guard and played in two games while starting one. He did manage to garner two receptions for 19 yards.[6]

Many athletes during the 1950s were called to serve in the armed forces. Art spent the 1951 and 1952 NFL seasons serving his country during the Korean War. In that time, the original Colts disbanded and Spinney was re-drafted by the Packers who dealt him to the Browns. Once released from the military, Spinney was traded to the new Baltimore Colts franchise risen out of the ashes of the failed Dallas Texans. On March 25, 1953, the Colts acquired ten players from Cleveland, including Spinney, Don Shula, Carl Taseff and Bert Rechichar for five players including future Hall of Famer Mike McCormack and Don Colo.[7]

The 1953 Colts fared slightly better than the 1950 version winning three games. Spinney played in all 12 games that year and recovered one fumble while playing defensive end.

Spinney was switched to offensive guard in 1954,[8] and again Art played in all 12 games.[9] Over the next three seasons, Spinney developed into one of the best offensive guards in the league. In 1957, he was named second team All-NFL by the *New York Daily News*.[10]

Art played in 12 games during the 1958 season and started in the celebrated NFL championship sudden death overtime win against the New York Giants (23–17). He was named second team All-NFL by the Associated Press, NEA, and UPI.[11]

Spinney successfully negated the size and strength of the Giants' talented defensive tackle, Roosevelt Grier, during the title game. Grier's teammates accused him of catching a case of "Spinneyitis." John Unitas recalled Spinney's dominant play. "Grier complained of being held. On the next play, Art drove Rosey off the line with a tremendous block, then looked at the official and said, 'How was that, Mr. Official?' The official smiled and answered, 'A great block, son, a great block.'"[12]

1959 was another championship year for Weeb Ewbank's Colts. Art Spinney started the NFL championship game and played in 12 games. He also made the Pro Bowl for the first time and was named second team All–NFL by the Associated Press and first team by the *New York Daily News* and UPI.[13]

Art Spinney's last season was 1960. Art played in ten games that year and repeated as a Pro Bowl guard, while being named second team All-NFL by the NEA.[14]

Teammates had high praise for Art. Art Donovan, a teammate of Spinney's at Boston College and the Colts said, "What a tough guy and competitor. He never took a cheap shot. He gave the game everything and never let up. I loved him like a brother."[15]

Former Colts end Jim Mutscheller, said of Art, "He was held in the highest esteem as a player and gentlemen, A lot of times players on the line would forget their assignments on a play but Art would tell them as they headed to the line of scrimmage. He could have played on any team in any era of football."[16]

During Spinney's playing career, 12 Colts players were hired by Bethlehem Steel for an off-season management training program. Steve Eusted, a Bethlehem official, singled out Spinney for high praise. "All players performed well, but it's our opinion the standout is Spinney, who has exceptional leadership qualities. I believe he could go to the top in our company if that's what he wants to do."[17]

Instead, Art opted to marry Mary Pappas, a hometown girl, and go into coaching initially after retirement. He coached the line at Boston College and for the Boston/New England Patriots. Former teammate Don Shula asked him to be an assistant with the Miami Dolphins, but Art declined.[18]

Later, he spent two decades with the Massachusetts Port Authority and the State Department of Transportation in public relations roles. He also worked at the American Biltrite Rubber Company of Cambridge, Massachusetts, as a consultant to its Sports Surfaces Division. He was awarded a patent in 1972 along with Lawrence J. Warnalis of Medford, Massachusetts, for an artificial grass product Poly-Turf, as well as its associated layers applied on top of asphalt, as the proper way to construct a football or soccer field with artificial turf.[19]

Art passed away at the age of 66 on May 27, 1994, in Lynn, Massachusetts.[20] Upon his death *Baltimore Sun* reporter John Steadman put his career in perspective: "Art Spinney was tough, tenacious, and talented. He possessed well-developed techniques that made him one of the most skillful guards in an era when salaries were modest and pro football players were a select fraternity- only 12 teams with 34 players on a roster, which tells you much about the quality of the game and the men on the field."[21]

Notes

1. John Steadman, "Spinney Was Block of Intensity Colts Came to Admire," *Baltimore Sun*, May 6, 1994.
2. "Saugus, Massachusetts," Wikipedia.
3. "Art Spinney Selected as Captain of '49 Eagle Football Squad," *Heights*, December 10, 1948.
4. "1946, 1947, 1948, 1949, 1950 Boston College Eagles Stats," College Football at Sports-Reference.com.
5. "Boston College Athletics," RSS.
6. "1950 Baltimore Colts Statistics & Players," Pro-Football-Reference.com.
7. "Coach Don Shula's Career Highlights," News RSS.
8. "1953 Baltimore Colts Statistics & Players," Pro-Football-Reference.com.
9. "1954 Baltimore Colts Statistics & Players," Pro-Football-Reference.com.
10. "1957 Baltimore Colts Statistics & Players," Pro-Football-Reference.com.
11. "1958 Baltimore Colts Statistics & Players," Pro-Football-Reference.com.
12. Steadman.
13. "1959 Baltimore Colts Statistics & Players," Pro-Football-Reference.com.
14. "1960 Baltimore Colts Statistics & Players," Pro-Football-Reference.com.
15. Steadman.
16. *Ibid.*
17. *Ibid.*
18. *Ibid.*
19. "Art Spinney," Wikipedia.
20. "Art Spinney (1927–1994)—Find a Grave Memorial."
21. Steadman.

Dick Szymanski

David Standish

Dick ("Syzzie," "Syzmo," or "Peaches") Szymanki[1] enjoyed a long and varied NFL career over 26 years and four separate decades as a lineman and later as a scout, coach, and executive vice president/general manager. He was selected to the Pro Bowl three times and helped the Colts win three NFL championships in 1958, 1959 and 1968. He will always be remembered as a tough and gritty competitor and "Johnny Unitas' Center."

Dick Szymanski was born on October 7, 1932, in Toledo, Ohio. He excelled in athletics early. He was an All-American in football for the Libbey High School Cowboys in Toledo. He was also All-City in baseball and basketball. He later started and lettered for the Notre Dame Fighting Irish from 1951 to 1954, while earning a degree in business administration before entering the NFL draft in 1955.

At Notre Dame, Szymanski played under coaches Frank Leahy and Terry Brennan. Leahy himself had a notable college football career, playing for legendary coach Knute Rockne as a tackle from 1928 to 1930. Leahy was notorious for demanding toughness from his players, and was well-known for grueling conditioning, drilling and practicing with full-hitting and even making his quarterbacks take snaps until their fingers bled.[2] One can easily see how this legacy of toughness would later carry over into Szymanski's NFL years.

Szymanski's Notre Dame years were a fruitful time for the Irish. From 1951 to 1954, Notre Dame complied a 32–5–3 record. In 1952, the Irish went 4–1 against top 10 teams.[3] In 1953, the Irish defeated Oklahoma, which was the Sooners' only loss that season. They also snapped Georgia Tech's 31-game unbeaten streak. Szymanski was part of the College All-Star team that upset the Cleveland Browns 30–27 on August 12, 1955, along with Notre Dame teammate, Ralph Guglielmi and future Colts teammate L.G. Dupre.[4]

Dick Szymanski.

Szymanski entered the NFL draft in 1955. He was drafted by the Baltimore Colts in the second round with the 16th overall pick.[5] Szymanski attributes the Colts' interest in him to the fact that he could play both offense and defense.[6] He began his Colts career at center in 1955 and was selected to the Pro Bowl in his rookie season.[7] In 1956 he was drafted into the Army and served in the Special Services in Germany.[8] While serving his country in Germany he found some time to keep in football shape, playing for the Army's 13th Regiment football team in Ulm, Germany.[9] He returned to the Colts in 1957 and moved to linebacker. He injured his knee in the eighth game of the 1958 season against the Bears and was unable to play in the 1958 championship game.

Teammate Art Donovan recalled the injury and Szymanski's toughness.

We were coming out of the locker room at Wrigley to get on the team bus and I offered him a hand. I think I asked him if I could carry his shoulder bag or something innocuous like that. At any rate, he got all indignant, yelling at me, "Don't you worry about me, Fatso, I'm just fine! I'll be seeing you in practice Tuesday and I'll be kicking your ass!" Yet whenever that bus hit a bump on the way to the airport, I noticed old Syzzie was squirming in pain. In those days, you just didn't want to show it … when I called his apartment the next morning to check up on him, his landlady told me he had checked into Union Memorial Hospital. I found out he was being operated on, so I stopped by that afternoon just in time to see him being wheeled back into his room on a gurney.

He was in pain, yelling for more shots. But as soon as he saw me standing at his bedside, suddenly there was nothing wrong with him. I told him to take the shots while he could get them. But suddenly he didn't need shots anymore. I figured I better get the hell out of the hospital before Syzzie went into shock from refusing painkillers in front of a teammate. And I was the guy's best friend. Imagine if a coach or an owner had walked in. He probably would have been doing jumping jacks.[10]

Szymanski led all NFL middle linebackers with five interceptions in 1959, including one for a touchdown.[11] Szymanski caught the wrath of coach Ewbank during the 1959 season after getting called for unnecessary roughness against the 49ers. Dick shot back at his coach replying, "Why, Coach, it says right in our [playbook], made up by you, that one of the unpardonable sins is to hit no one."[12] As part of the linebacking corps of Szymanski, Don Shinnick and Bill Pellington, the formidable defense helped the Colts repeat as world champs in 1959.

In 1961 Szymanski moved back to the offensive line at center and in 1962 he was selected to his second Pro Bowl.[13] He would spend the rest of his career known as "Johnny Unitas' Center" and would protect Unitas until his retirement in 1969 after the Colts loss to the New York Jets in Super Bowl III.[14] He was selected to the Pro Bowl for the third and final time in his career in 1964.[15]

Szymanski would go on to serve the Baltimore Colts after his retirement in the front office as a scout, assistant personnel director, offensive line coach, director of player personnel, and executive vice president and general manager.[16] In 1977, his first season as general manager, Szymanski's Colts finished first in the AFC East with a 10–4 record, but would eventually lose at home to the defending Super Bowl champion Oakland Raiders in the AFC divisional playoffs on Christmas Eve.[17] Szymanski would serve as general manager and executive vice president until 1981.[18] In 1982 he went on to join the Atlanta Falcons as a scout until 1984.[19] He later joined the NFL Alumni Network, eventually becoming executive director in 1991–92.[20]

In 2016, Szymanski reminisced about his time with the Colts and his teammates. "How many broken bones have I had? Don't ask. Despite all of the football injuries, I can walk. Must be my genes. What depresses me more than anything is when I get a phone call, or read in the paper that one of my teammates has passed away. You'd think you'd get over it, but you don't. There aren't many left, but I'll tell you what—they were tough guys. I know I wouldn't want to have played against us."[21]

NOTES

1. Jack Call, interview with author, January 9, 2017.
2. https://en.wikipedia.org/wiki/Frank_Leahy.
3. https://notredame.rivals.com/news/notre-dame-s-top-classes-no-6.
4. *Eugene Register-Guard*, Associated Press. August 13, 1955.
5. http://www.pro-football-reference.com/years/1955/draft.htm.
6. http://www.baltimoresun.com/sports/bs-sp-catching-up-szymanski-20161229-story.html.

7. http://www.pro-football-reference.com/players/S/SzymDi00.htm.
8. http://www.polishsportshof.com/?page_id=1017.
9. *Delaware County Daily Times* from Chester, Pennsylvania, March 30, 1968.
10. Arthur J, Donovan Jr., and Bob Drury, *Fatso* (New York: Avon Books, 1987), 166–167.
11. http://www.pro-football-reference.com/players/S/SzymDi00.htm.
12. Mike Klingaman, "Catching up with Former Colt Player, Scout, Coach, and General Manager Dick Szymanski," *Baltimore Sun*, December 20, 2016.
13. http://www.pro-football-reference.com/players/S/SzymDi00.htm.
14. http://www.polishsportshof.com/?page_id=1017.
15. http://www.pro-football-reference.com/players/S/SzymDi00.htm.
16. http://www.polishsportshof.com/?page_id=1017.
17. http://www.pro-football-reference.com/boxscores/197712240clt.htm.
18. https://www.washingtonpost.com/archive/sports/1982/05/08/szymanski-quits-colts-after-six-years-as-gm/5e443302–1ff4–49b6–9887-d35315fbce38/?utm_term=.202746c43082.
19. http://www.polishsportshof.com/?page_id=1017.
20. *Ibid.*
21. Klingaman.

Carl Taseff

Joseph Wancho

Carl Taseff may not be the best-known member of the 1958 Baltimore Colts, but his long and successful career in the game merits accolades. A star in high school and college football, he played professionally for 11 years, coached for 27 more and was a part of four world championship teams.

Carl Taseff was one of three sons (brothers Edward and George) born to Nick and Slavka Taseff on September 28, 1928, in Parma, Ohio. But he was raised on the lower east side of Cleveland on East 34th Street. Nick Taseff was the proprietor of Rose Lunch, a café located at East 37th and Woodland Avenue in Cleveland. Taseff was a star quarterback and fullback for East High School. Noted for his ability as a "T quarterback," Taseff also gave the Blue Bombers' opponents a headache with his running ability. Switched to fullback for his senior season, he was considered a bruiser for that position at five feet, 11 inches and 175 pounds.

After graduating from East High, Taseff enrolled at John Carroll University, a private Jesuit college on a sprawling campus in University Heights, Ohio. There he met another incoming freshman from Painesville, Ohio, Don Shula. Thus began a friendship that lasted more than 50 years. John Carroll was a member of the Big Four Conference, which also included Case Tech, Baldwin-Wallace, and Western Reserve University.

Perhaps the biggest game of Taseff's career and in John Carroll history occurred on November 10, 1950, at Cleveland Stadium against eastern power Syracuse. JCU played host to Syracuse, a power from the football-rich east. A crowd of 16,724 made their way into the stadium on the shores of Lake Erie. A bigger throng was anticipated, but no doubt the 27-degree temperature may have given some fans second thoughts about attending the game.

Trailing 16–7 at halftime, the Blue Streaks rallied for two touchdowns in the fourth quarter to pull off the upset, 21–16. Taseff figured in all three touchdowns for the Streaks, running for two and throwing to end Joe Minor for the other. Taseff's one-yard plunge with one just under one minute to play was the difference.

During his collegiate career, Taseff rushed for 3,829 yards and scored 60 touchdowns for the Blue Streaks. He was named to the All-Big Four team (1947–50), AP All-Ohio team (1947–50), AP Little All-American team (1950) and All-Ohio Conference team (1947–48). Taseff played in the North-South Shrine Bowl game in Miami in 1951 and won the Cleveland Touchdown Club's Outstanding Player Award in 1950. Taseff was the second highest scorer in the nation in 1950 for all colleges and ranked third in rushing for small colleges that same season.[1]

After graduation from college, Taseff was selected by the Cleveland Browns in the 22nd round of the 1951 NFL Draft. Taseff had

Carl Taseff.

familiar company as Shula was also taken by the Browns in the ninth round. "Both Shula and Taseff are sound in fundamentals," said Cleveland coach Paul Brown. "Taseff looks like a terrific runner and has a lot of the same ability that made Edgar Jones so important to us for four years."[2]

But Taseff was cut by the Browns at the end of training camp. He cleared waivers and was declared a free agent. However, a knee injury to halfback Dopey Phelps in October gave Taseff the opportunity to be placed back on Cleveland's active roster. "We miss Dopey's speed on kickoff and punt returns," said Brown, "but Carl is more suitable for some of our other units. After considering all angles and discussing it with the boys, we decided it would be to our advantage to keep Taseff."[3]

His best game for the Browns was on December 16 against the Eagles. He ran seven times for 32 yards and scored a touchdown. The Browns went on to win the American Conference. They would face the Los Angeles Rams in the 1951 NFL title game. Cleveland had upset the Rams in the 1950 title game, 30–28 on a last-minute field goal by Lou Groza. The Rams exacted some revenge on Cleveland in 1951, winning 24–17.

Taseff's 1952 season ended before it began as he and Shula, both members of the Ohio National Guard's 27th Infantry Division, were called into duty at Camp Polk in Louisiana." This is taking us away from a good job," said Taseff. "But it has to be done and we might as well do it with a smile."[4] Both players were transferred to special services and were placed in charge of the Camp Polk touch football league.

Taseff and Shula became part of NFL history on March 25, 1953, when they were part of a 15-player trade that saw ten players go from Cleveland to Baltimore. For Taseff, it meant leaving a perennial first place organization in the Eastern Conference for one that was not yet competitive in the Western Conference, as well as a position change. The Colts would use him primarily on the defensive side of the ball, employing him in the secondary.

The move by Colts head coach Keith Molesworth looked like a brilliant maneuver. In an exhibition game against the Chicago Cardinals in Lubbock, Texas, Taseff totaled three interceptions and ran one back 41 yards for a touchdown in a 10–7 Baltimore victory.

The three interceptions equaled his regular season total. But the Colts found another use for Taseff. On October 31 against Green Bay, he returned his only punt of the year 71 yards to pay dirt for one of the few highlights in a 3–9 season. For Taseff, the season was even darker as his father Slavka passed away during the campaign.

Baltimore replaced Molesworth with Weeb Ewbank. The new head man already had plans for Taseff. "I would like to use him as a runner," said Ewbank. "If any of our draft hopes come through as defensive halfback, Carl will be carrying the ball for us next season."[5] Due to injuries, Taseff was pressed into duty in the offensive backfield. In a game against Green Bay, he carried the ball 15 times for 122 yards, and caught three passes for 15 yards. On the season, Taseff ran for 228 yards and added another 159 yards through the air. He also continued his regular duties as a defensive halfback and return man. But the change of coaches did not immediately change the Colts fortunes, which again showed only three victories in 1954.

But there was little doubt that Ewbank was the right man to lead the team to new heights. Some rookies and first year players started to mature under his direction. On offense, Raymond Berry, Jim Mutscheller, Alan Ameche and L.G. Dupre were bringing new skill sets to the Colts. Dick Szymanski and Dick Chorovich were also rookies who were plugged into the offensive line. Linebacker Joe Campanella and defensive back Bert Rechichar, who came over from Cleveland with Taseff, were mixed in with veteran linemen Gino Marchetti and Art Donovan. The foundation was being laid for a successful future.

Taseff continued to play his usual consistent game. He maintained his duties as the starting defensive left halfback and punt returner, and led the league in 1956 in both punt returns (27) and yardage (233) On October 14, at Milwaukee County Stadium, Taseff returned a punt 90 yards for a touchdown. He also had a 58-yard return to set up the Colts' first score in what turned out to be a 38–33 loss to the Packers.

The 1956 season also brought two key pieces that legitimatized the Colts into a football power for years to come. Baltimore acquired Johnny Unitas and drafted Lenny Moore out of Penn State with the ninth overall pick in the draft. Both Unitas and Moore, whose careers would end with enshrinement in Canton, Ohio, were cornerstones of some great Colts teams in the future.

The Colts upped their victory total to five wins in 1956. In 1957, their record climbed to seven wins and a third-place finish in the Western Conference. But their ascent in the standings was made without Taseff. In the fourth game of the season in Detroit, a blow from the elbow of John Henry Johnson broke Taseff's nose. Though doctors reset Taseff's nose that evening, the bleeding would not stop and he was lost for the season.

It all came together for the Colts in 1958, as they won the Western Conference with a 9–3 record and faced the New York Giants in what would become one of the most famous games in league history. The two teams battled to a 17–17 tie after regulation before fullback Alan Ameche's one yard run in overtime gave Baltimore its first world championship. It was Taseff's most productive pro season, as he led the league in punt returns with 29, intercepted a career-high seven passes and was named Second Team All-Pro by both the AP and UPI. The 1959 season was a carbon copy of the previous year for Baltimore, as they finished 9–3 again and won the Western Conference, then repeated as NFL champions with a 31–16 win over the New York Giants. Taseff played in all 12 games as a defensive halfback and a punt returner. In 1960, he was used primarily as a kick returner, handling 14 chances for 291 yards with an average of 20.8 per return.

Baltimore waived Taseff in the middle of the 1961 season to make room for the return of top draft pick Tom Matte from the injured list. The Colts held a "Carl Taseff Night" to honor his contributions to the team's success. "I've known him only a short time, but I will remember him for a long time,"[6] said defensive Billy Ray Smith. "I've never seen a finer tackler,"[7] added Jim Mutscheller.

Taseff signed with the Philadelphia Eagles for the remainder of the 1961 season, then served as a player-coach with the American Football League's Buffalo Bills in 1962. His career totals show 117 punt returns for an average of 7.3 yards per return and 21 pass interceptions.

In retirement, Taseff and Colts teammate Bill Pellington were partners in the liquid tile business. He also kept his hand in football, working as a defensive backfield coach with the Boston Patriots (1964) and the Detroit Lions (1965–66).

When the Miami Dolphins hired Don Shula as head coach in 1970, Shula hired his old friend Taseff to be his running backs coach. Taseff held that position for 23 years, then retired after serving as an offensive assistant in 1994. Under his tutelage, the Dolphins had the first two running backs (Larry Csonka and Mercury Morris) to each run for more than 1,000 yards in the same season in 1972.

After retirement, Taseff resided in Weston, Florida. He and his wife Sandy had two daughters, Cindy and Susan.

Carl Taseff passed away as a result of pneumonia on February, 27, 2005 at the age of 76. "I always had great respect for Carl as a player and a coach and the special relationship with him as a friend," Shula said at the time. "He was a very dedicated and goal-oriented person. He only knew one way to play and one way to coach. And that was to win."[8]

NOTES

1. "John Carroll University Athletic Hall of Fame," John Carroll University website, accessed December 12, 2016.

2. Harold Sauerbrei, "Both Taseff and Shula Make Strong Bids," *Cleveland Plain Dealer*, August 2, 1951.

3. Harold Sauerbrei, "Taseff to Retain Job with Browns," *Cleveland Plain Dealer*, December 8, 1951.

4. John G. Blair, "Summer Greets Last Units of 37th Arriving at Camp," *Cleveland Plain Dealer*, January 26, 1952.

5. Cameron C. Snyder, "Taseff Signs with Colts," *Baltimore Sun*, April 4, 1954.

6. Edward C. Atwater, "Colt Corral Honors Taseff with Trophy," *Baltimore Sun*, November, 7, 1961.

7. *Ibid.*

8. Joe Schad, "Former Dolphin Assistant Dies of Pneumonia," *Palm Beach Post*, February 28, 2005.

Fuzzy Thurston

RICK SCHABOWSKI

Although best known as the left guard on Vince Lombardi's five championship teams in the 1960s, Frederick Charles Thurston was actually a member of six championship teams, and his first was in Baltimore.

Fred was born to Charles and Marie Thurston at Luther Hospital in Altoona, Wisconsin, a small town near Eau Claire, on December 29, 1933. He was the youngest of eight children, the only one born in a hospital, and was probably the biggest, ten pounds and 22 inches. One of his sisters, Dorothy, nicknamed him "Fuzzy" because when he was a baby he had dark, curly locks. When Fuzzy was four, his father died from a heart attack. Thurston recalled, "I had a loving mother and great brothers and sisters. From my perspective at an early age, I had everything I needed in life. Looking back, I realize that I really didn't have much."[1]

He attended Altoona High School and was the family's only child to graduate. Thurston explained, "they quit school and went to work because our mother needed their help and because they wanted to give me a chance to earn a high school diploma, go to college, and have a better life. They loved me, and I loved them. They sacrificed a lot for me. The fact that they didn't graduate from high school didn't embarrass me. It motivated me. I didn't want to let them down."[2]

He had a supportive high school coach, Einar Pedersen, who was an excellent coach and motivator. Thurston played basketball four years at Altoona and earned a basketball scholarship to Valparaiso University in Indiana. At Valparaiso, Thurston's Physical Education professor, Walt Reiner, told Fuzzy that he was very impressed with Thurston's play on the basketball court and that he thought he'd be an excellent football player because of his strength and agility. Thurston took Reiner's offer and participated in spring football practice.

Fuzzy Thurston.

Head coach Emery Bauer used Thurston at defensive end during the spring drills, but moved him to the offensive line when the regular season began. Thurston was named to the all-conference team two times and also was named the most valuable player of the conference, a rare distinction for an offensive lineman. Pro scouts took notice of his abilities, and he was chosen in the fifth round of the 1956 draft by the Philadelphia Eagles. "They tried me at tackle, and I thought I was going to make the team," Thurston said. "Hughie Devore was the coach. Then a week before the season started, Frank Wydo came back from retirement, and I got my Army draft notice. The Eagles let me go, and two weeks later I was in the Army."[3]

During the summer of 1956, before going

to the Eagles' camp, Thurston met Susan Eggleston on a beach where Thurston was working out. They started dating and communicated by mail while he was at the Eagles camp and on the Army base. On October 3, 1956, they were married at the First Lutheran Church in Eau Claire.

While serving in the U.S. Army, Thurston spoke with Wayne Robinson, a teammate when Thurston was with the Eagles who was now coaching with the Winnipeg Blue Bombers, and Robinson invited Thurston to tryout when he was discharged. Also in Thurston's army unit was Harlon Hill of the Chicago Bears. Hill told George Halas about Thurston, and the Bears signed him in July 1958 but cut him September 1, because they had a surplus of guards. The Eagles reclaimed him.

Thurston recalled, "The day before the season opened, the Eagles cut me again. I headed for Winnipeg. The Colts tried to get in touch with me, but I was already on my way to Canada. The Colts finally got the license number of my car and tried to have me intercepted at the border, but I got to Winnipeg and spent the night in the hotel. The Colts reached me there by phone the next morning. I went to Robinson and talked it over. He said he thought I ought to join the Colts because he was sure I was good enough to play in the NFL."[4]

Winnipeg's head coach, Bud Grant, strongly urged Thurston to accept the Colts' contract offer. Grant regretted losing the services of Thurston, but he thought that Thurston should give the NFL another try.

Thurston made the Colts' roster at guard, backing up Art Spinney and Alex Sandusky. Thurston was very happy when he was activated from the taxi squad: "I practiced with the team, made friends and waited for my chance to play. It came after six weeks when the Colts activated me for the Green Bay game. As a Wisconsin native, I was excited to be playing against the Green Bay Packers. I still loved the Packers, even when I was playing against them. I couldn't help but think to myself, 'Thank God I play for the Colts.' The Packers were not very good at that time."[5]

The Colts ended up winning 56–0, and Thurston played left guard for the last two series of the game. He then started the last two games of the regular season when Sandusky was out due to injury. Thurston and the Colts won the NFL championship that season.

Thurston enjoyed playing special teams, the coaches loved his hustle and attitude, and with Art Spinney aging, it seemed possible that he would move into a starting role the following season. After the birth of his son Griff, on July 17, 1959, he drove all the way to Baltimore the following day, and was feeling great. When he arrived at the training camp, he found a note on his door to see Coach Ewbank in the morning.

Recalling the meeting Thurston remembered:

> I woke up around six o'clock, and after a shower and a bite to eat, I went straight to Coach Ewbank's office. I walked in, sat down, and could tell immediately that something was up. He told me I was a good football player, and that I would become a really, really good one before I was through. But … Coach Ewbank said that the Colts needed a linebacker in the worst way and that he had no choice but to trade me to the Green Bay Packers. Coach Ewbank informed me that, while he liked my potential, he needed another linebacker, so the Colts traded me to Green Bay for Marv Matuszak.[6]

At first, Thurston was very upset, especially with Colts coach Weeb Ewbank. "I didn't understand why he couldn't have told me this before I got in the car and drove eighteen hours. I was pissed off."[7] During the long ride back home his emotions settled down.

I was going home. I was a Wisconsin native, born and bred in Altoona, home of the Railroaders. I was going to be playing for the Green Bay Packers, the team I idolized and dreamed about growing up in that tiny town in northeast Wisconsin. All I ever wanted when I was a kid was maybe, just maybe a chance to watch a Packers game at City Stadium. How faraway it seemed. How wonderful it would be. I was going to be playing for the team I loved while I was growing up. I wasn't going to be a loser. I was coming home. It was just a matter of rearranging my attitude and my expectations, and it was going to be all right. In fact, it was going to be fantastic.[8]

Thurston made the 1959 Packers and started as one of the guards, the other being Jerry Kramer. Lombardi liked the deal for Thurston because he thought bringing in a player from a championship team would give the Packers a boost, and he was also a vocal, enthusiastic player who got the team psyched up and ready to play.

Thurston was amazed that Lombardi's teaching was passionate and enthusiastic, "He could romance a block to the point where the guy who was going to do it really thought he enjoyed this thing."[9]

Lombardi assessed Fuzzy in *Run to Daylight*, "He made it big with us. When we traded for him we'd seen just enough of him in the movies to know he could handle the pass block, but we didn't know if he had the speed to pull and we knew nothing of his personality. He's not quite as good as a pulling guard as Jerry Kramer, but he's a good short-trap blocker and he's got enough quickness, size, strength and determination so that, when he and Jerry come swinging around the corner together like a pair of matched Percherons, you can see that defensive man's eye-balls pop."[10]

Kramer had high esteem for his blocking partner: "Fuzzy was very smart, the guards are always pulling in Lombardi's offense. A lot of trapping, a lot of sweeps and a lot of pull plays. Fuzzy never pulled the wrong way. Not even once. And I never pulled the wrong way. The two of us together always knew what the hell we were doing. We did that as good as we possibly could. I had a faith and a trust that Fuzzy would do the right thing. He was very consistent. I don't remember a mistake Fuzzy ever made."[11]

Gale Gillingham replaced Thurston in the Packers' starting lineup in 1967, with Thurston going to play on the special teams. Thurston's career had gone full-circle. "I remember, as a rookie with the Colts, receiving compliments from some of the veterans because I played so hard on special teams and never complained. I also received letters of admiration from Packers fans when I played so hard on special teams and never complained at the end of my career."[12] Super Bowl II proved to be the final game in Thurston's career, and also the last game for Lombardi as the Packers' head coach. They were together from Lombardi's first game in 1959 until the end in 1968. During that time, the Packers won five championships and Fuzzy was named first or second team All-Pro five times.

On July 4, 1968, Thurston followed teammate and business partner Max McGee in retirement. Thurston was leaving with a business already in place. Along with McGee and Appleton businessman Bill Martine, the group had a number of steakhouses operating in Wisconsin. They were planning to expand, but retirement didn't go smoothly for Thurston. The restaurants he owned collapsed, and in the late 1970s he was forced to file for bankruptcy.

Health issues also plagued Thurston. In 1979 he was diagnosed with cancer of the larynx, and after radiation treatment failed, one of his vocal cords was removed in 1981. The other cord was removed in January 1982, and an artificial vocal box was made from his diaphragm. The only way he could communicate was by whispering through the hole in his throat while holding a hand to his chest.

Thurston resurrected the restaurant/bar business and gave credit to Lombardi: "I played for a guy [Lombardi] who never thought to fail was the end of the world, but he thought never to come back is the biggest sin in the world, and I want to make it back."[13] Indeed, Fuzzy's #63 Bar & Grill is still a thriving establishment in Green Bay.

After a long, courageous bout with not only cancer but also Alzheimer's Disease, Fuzzy passed away on December 14, 2014, leaving behind his children, Mark, Griff and Tori, and his grandchildren, Olivia and Fred Thurston and Joey Kluck. His wife had passed away on October 23, 2012.

At the funeral, longtime teammate and friend Jerry Kramer summed up Thurston's spirit: "Well, I love Fuzzy, first of all, and I admire his attitude and spirit. He's always been to me like a five-year-old boy on Christmas morning, and he got a bucket of horse-shit for Christmas and shouted, 'Yippee!' When everyone asked why he was so happy, he'd say, 'With all this horseshit, there's got to be a pony around here somewhere.' He will find the good and right in everything."[14]

Notes

1. Bill Wenzel, *What a Wonderful World: Fuzzy Thurston, A Story of Personal Triumph* (Example Product Manufacturer, 2006), 28.

2. *Ibid.,*33.

3. Chuck Johnson, *Greatest Packers of Them All* (New York: G. P. Putnam's Sons, 1968), 117.

4. *Ibid.*

5. Wenzel, 54–55.

6. *Ibid.*, 57–58.

7. *Ibid.*, 58.

8. *Ibid.*, 60–61.

9. Donald Phillips, *Run to Win* (New York: St. Martin's Griffin, 2001), 91.

10. Vince Lombardi with W. C. Heinz, *Run to Daylight* (Englewood Cliffs, NJ: Prentice-Hall, 1963), 56.

11. Bob Fox, "Green Bay Packers: Remembering Fuzzy Thurston," *The Bleacher Report*, December 15, 2014.

12. Wenzel, 90.

13. Avrum D. Lank, "Fuzzy Thurston Guarding Against Bad Luck This Time," *Milwaukee Sentinel*, June 3, 1983.

14. Wenzel, 103.

Johnny Unitas

George Bozeka

Arguably the greatest quarterback of his or any generation, Johnny Unitas was also the quintessential embodiment of his era of professional football. As *Sports Illustrated* reporter Frank Deford eloquently wrote after Unitas' death,

> They didn't have coaches with headphones and Polaroids and fax machines then, sitting on high, telling quarterbacks what plays to call. In those halcyon days, quarterbacks were field generals, not field lieutenants. And there was Unitas after he called a play (and probably checked off and called another play when he saw what the ruffians across the line were up to), shuffling back into the pocket, standing there in his hightops, waiting, looking, poised. I never saw war, so that is still my vision of manhood. Unitas standing courageously in the pocket, his left arm

flung out diagonal to the upper deck, his right cocked for the business, down among the mortals. Lock and load…. Yes, I know there have been wonderful quarterbacks since Unitas hung up his hightops, I admit I'm prejudiced. But the best quarterback ever? The best player? Let me put it this way: If there was one game scheduled, Earth versus the Klingons, with the fate of the universe on the line, any person with his wits about him would have Johnny U calling the signals in the huddle, up under center, back in the pocket.[1]

John Constantine Unitas was born in Pittsburgh on May 7, 1933, the third child (of four) of Francis Joseph and Helen (Superfisky) Unitas who were both of Lithuanian descent. Francis and Helen worked in the coal industry, eventually raising enough money to own their own coal delivery business. Francis was a tall, powerful man who excelled at athletics, including boxing, baseball, and the shot put, and Helen was the self-taught organist for Sunday Mass at the local Catholic church. They lived in a small and overflowing one bedroom home in the Brookline section of Pittsburgh with several members of Helen's extended family including her parents, cousins, and a great uncle.[2]

When John was five years old, his father Francis suddenly died at the age of 37. Francis caught a cold while working in the rain delivering coal. The cold developed into pneumonia, which caused renal failure, uremic poisoning, and death.[3]

After Francis' death, John's mother moved the family to a modest two-bedroom home in the Mount Washington neighborhood. She continued to supervise the coal business, worked for a bakery, sold insurance, cleaned office buildings, and studied bookkeeping, eventually getting a job with the city of Pittsburgh. John remembered proudly, "Just watching my mother, how hard she had to work for everything we had, was the greatest thing I ever saw."[4]

John's mother stressed education. Every day and in all kinds of weather, John would walk to St. Justin's school, nearly a mile away, with his younger sister Shirley. Shirley recalled,

John wasn't much of a talker, and there were days when he never said a word. Mom worked hard, and every day she had a list of chores we all had to do. You always got them done. She had it so hard you would never think of causing her trouble. We were poor and went to school in washed-out clothes, while other kids had blouses and

Johnny Unitas.

skirts. No one really associated with us. Times were tough. My mother raised four kids by herself. She had a saying: "If it's a need, we can talk about it, but if it's a want, don't bring it up." One time the nuns from school called the house wondering if John and I were malnourished. That's how bad it was. My mother really got mad about that. There was always food on the table. We were just built that way.[5]

John was a good kid who did what he was told, but he did have some childhood moments that could have cost him his football career. Once, a friend of his older brother Leonard whose father was a policeman gave Leonard a .38 bullet fragment. Leonard shot at it with his bb gun, and the casing hit John in the leg. He was rushed to the hospital, and doctors removed most of the casing fragments, but some stayed in John's leg for the rest of his life. Later, during John's teen years, his mother bought a revolver for protection. John was cleaning the gun. The gun accidentally discharged and a bullet went clean through his right index finger. They saved the finger but John could never properly bend the first joint of the finger again.[6]

Young John loved football, particularly Notre Dame football. He wasn't an avid reader or distinguished student, but every book he took out of the library was about football or quarterbacks like Sid Luckman. He borrowed a book about Knute Rockne from the library so many times that the librarian finally gave him the book. Because Rockne based his backfield shifts on the dancing moves of chorus girls John started to realize that football was a game of precision and timing.[7]

The first sport Unitas played at St Justin's High School was baseball. Nobody took him seriously on the football field because he was a skinny, gangling kid. His sophomore year, he was eligible to play on the varsity football team. The coach was playing him at halfback and end until the week before the first game of the season. The starting quarterback broke his ankle, and after trying a number of players out at the position, the coach decided to give Unitas the job. Unitas performed well enough in the first game to keep the job for good.[8]

James "Max" Carey became head football coach at St Justin's for John's junior season. He would have a huge influence on Unitas. A low-key businesslike coach who never raised his voice, Carey mentored Unitas on the offense and quarterback position. He told John it was his job to call the plays, but that he would have to defend and be responsible for his decisions. Unitas explained that "Max Carey was the person who taught me that a quarterback can't be just one of the boys. You really have to be a little aloof from everyone else even though you want to be friends with them and join in all the different things they want to do. You just don't do it. You can sit with them. You can have a joke. You can have a drink. But you always have to keep a certain distance."[9]

His senior season, Unitas was named quarterback on the Pittsburgh All-Catholic High School team, and honorable mention on one All-America High School team. With the help of Coach Carey, St. Justin's Father Thomas McCarthy, and some alumni, Unitas got a tryout at his beloved Notre Dame. Irish coach Frank Leahy was out of town, but assistant coach Bernie Crimmins kept Unitas in South Bend for a week, before finally deciding that John was too small for the Irish.[10]

Unitas had tryouts at both Indiana and Pitt. Indiana did not show an interest in John. Pitt offered a scholarship, but John failed the entrance exam. Discouraged, Coach Carey came through for Unitas in a huge fashion. Carey met John Dromo, a Louisville assistant, at a clinic run by Paul Brown. Dromo mentioned that they needed a good passer. Carey recommended Unitas. Head coach Frank Camp invited John for a tryout.

Camp liked what he saw and offered Unitas a scholarship. Unitas took the entrance exam and failed, but the entrance board agreed to admit him for the first semester on probation.[11]

Unitas began his 1951 freshmen season as the third string quarterback on the varsity. After losing three of their first four games, Camp decided to give Unitas his first start against St. Bonaventure. Down 19–0, Unitas completed 11 consecutive passes, including three for touchdowns, to give the Cardinals a 21–19 lead. St Bonaventure kicked a late field goal to win 22–21, but Unitas had earned the starting quarterback job. Unitas went on to lead the Cardinals to four consecutive victories to finish 5–4.[12] For the season Unitas completed 46 of 99 passes for 602 yards and nine touchdowns.[13]

In addition to his success on the field, Unitas was doing well in the classroom and his academic probation was lifted, but off field events during the spring of 1952 would doom the remainder of Unitas' college career at Louisville.[14]

After a long night of drinking, three Louisville football players and two female companions stole a case of beer and were involved in a police chase. Traveling at an estimated 80 mph, they lost control and hit two trees. Two of the players were killed, and the driver, Jack Browning, the quarterback Unitas replaced, was charged with two counts of manslaughter and drunken and reckless driving. Browning took a plea deal that required immediate enlistment in the army. In the aftermath, Louisville deemphasized sports by cutting scholarships and implementing tougher academic standards. Louisville would not have another winning season during Unitas' college career.[15]

Over the next three seasons from 1952 to 1954, Unitas courageously and industriously led an undermanned Louisville football team. In 1952, Unitas completed 104 of 197 passes for 1540 yards and 12 touchdowns as the Cardinals finished 3–5. During a Week Two 41–14 victory over Florida State, John completed 17 of 22 passes for 198 yards and three touchdowns. At one point he got desperate and threw a left-handed shovel pass between his legs for a 15-yard gain against the Seminoles. In 1953, The Cardinals finished 1–7 as Unitas completed 49 of 95 passes for 470 yards and three touchdowns. A week before the 1954 season opener Unitas suffered a hairline fracture of his ankle during practice. He missed the opener and then played the remainder of the season against the recommendation of team doctors. The Cardinals finished 3–6 as Unitas passed for 527 yards and three touchdowns.[16]

Assistant coach Clark Wood best characterized Unitas' time at Louisville during the 1953 season:

> The schedule kept getting tougher and tougher, and we kept getting worse and worse. We couldn't bring in anyone at all. There was nothing we could do except our best. John took it like any intelligent person would. He was realistic. He understood the game of football, and got pleasure in just doing the right things. Of course, he didn't give a damn about statistics, especially his own. Despite everything, someone came in one day and said, "Do you know, you're the third-rated small-college passer in the nation?" John laughed and said, "Big deal." Our blockers gave him so little time to throw that he was often forced to run to sort of drop the ball over the defensive line to the receiver. It didn't even look like a pass. "Looks don't count," he said.
>
> Losing didn't kill his self-confidence, I can tell you that. He was the most confident person—confident in his own ability—that I ever met. Maybe going through all of this was what made him what he was in years to come. Did you ever think of that? Unless something really tries to destroy you, how can you know you're indestructible? John knew he was indestructible. All I can tell you is that we lost to Tennessee that year fifty-nine to six. Yet, everyone knew that John was the best football player on the field. When he left, it was to a standing ovation. I don't expect anyone to believe that who didn't see it.[17]

John celebrated the end of the 1954 college season by marrying his girlfriend Dorothy Hoelle who he had begun to date when he was a junior in high school.

Unitas was selected by Pittsburgh in the ninth round of the 1955 NFL draft with the 102nd pick. Steelers training camp was a nightmare for John. Unitas was razzed by veteran teammates who nicknamed him "Clem," after Clem Kadiddlehopper, the dimwitted country bumpkin played by comic Red Skelton, and he was astonished by the total lack of professionalism in the Steelers organization. With four quarterbacks in camp, coach Walt Kiesling ignored Unitas considering him too dense to understand the Steelers' playbook. On September 5, Kiesling cut an angry Unitas, who felt he wasn't given a fair opportunity.[18]

The Rooney family believed that Kiesling had made a mistake, but they could not change his mind. Coach Carey suggested that John send a telegram to Paul Brown, and Art Rooney reached out to Brown on Unitas' behalf. Unfortunately for Unitas, Otto Graham had agreed to play for Cleveland for one more season. Brown contacted Unitas with the discouraging news, but did invite John to come to Browns training camp the following July.[19]

Unitas kept busy by doing construction work earning an average of $125 a week, and playing semipro football for the Bloomfield Rams for $6 a game. John and Dorothy now had one child and another on the way, and they were living with her parents. John considered semipro ball a way to stay in shape until he could get another crack at the big leagues. That chance came when Don Kellett, the Colts' general manager, placed a call to Unitas. Kellett recalled, "One afternoon I was going over some old draft lists. This was in February of 1956. I noticed Unitas' name on one of them. He had been high up on the Pittsburgh list when he was a senior at Louisville. And I had heard from someplace about his sand-lot playing. So I called him."[20]

Legend was that Kellett and the Colts got Unitas after a mere 80-cent phone call. According to Michael MacCambridge it actually it took "two 84-cent long-distance calls, one in the afternoon, when Dorothy Unitas told Kellett her husband wasn't home from work yet, and another later in the evening, when Unitas answered the phone." MacCambridge continued, "Kellett invited Unitas to come workout for [Weeb] Ewbank the following week, with the understanding that if he passed muster then, he'd be invited to training camp and offered a $7000 contract if he made the team."[21] Ewbank was impressed, and Unitas became a Colt.

Unitas remembered that from the beginning Ewbank "spent time with me, talked with me, watched me, criticized me, offered suggestions to me, and in every way acted as though he considered me a part of his football team. After my experience with the Steelers, it was a brand new world, and the best part of it was that I was made to feel that I belonged in it."[22]

Ewbank immediately recognized he had something special in Unitas:

> We took pictures of John under center, and when he set up, and right at the last, when he followed through. The thing that we noticed right away was the way that he followed through. It was exceptional. His arm went through so far that he turned his hand over like a pitcher. It was like throwing a screwball. I often wondered how he kept from injuring his arm. When he followed through, you could see the back of his hand. I worried he might get what they call a tennis elbow. But, boy, I saw the way he could throw and I never bothered him about it. You knew right away. We knew that as soon as he learned the offense he would be our quarterback.[23]

John survived training camp in 1956 and was slotted as the second team quarterback behind starter George Shaw. In Week Four Shaw went down with a knee injury against the Bears. Unitas came in and proceeded to have his first pass attempt intercepted and returned for a touchdown by J.C. Caroline. Unitas persevered and finished the game with nine completions in 19 attempts for 131 yards and a touchdown.[24]

For the 1956 season John completed 110 of 198 passes for 1498 yards and nine touchdowns. His completion percentage of 55.6 was a rookie record. Unitas also threw touchdown passes in the final three games of the season starting a record 47-game streak where he threw at least one touchdown pass (Unitas broke Cecil Isbell's record 23-game streak set in 1942. Unitas' record was surpassed by Drew Brees in 2012 at 54 games).

Unitas continued his amazing ascent from obscurity in 1957. The Colts finished the season with a 7–5 record as John completed 172 of 301 passes for 2550 yards and 24 touchdowns. He was named league MVP and first team All-Pro by the Newspaper Enterprise Association (NEA).

In 1958, Unitas would become "The Golden Arm." The Colts won the Western Conference crown with a 9–3 record. Unitas led the Colts to six consecutive victories to open the season, but he was injured in a Week Six win over Green Bay, breaking three ribs and puncturing a lung. He missed the next two games but came back in Week Nine to complete the season. In the nine games Unitas started the Colts went 8–1. He finished the season with 136 completions out of 263 attempts for 2007 yards and 19 touchdowns.

This set the stage for the 1958 NFL championship game at Yankee Stadium in New York against the Eastern Conference champion Giants. As Deford wrote, "With each passing game … Unitas elevated above the others until, on December 28, 1958, he entered the pantheon of gods."[25]

The Colts defeated the Giants in the first sudden death NFL championship game 23–17 to win the title. Unitas was other worldly in the game, completing 26 of 40 passes for 349 yards (breaking Sammy Baugh's title game record from 1937) and a touchdown. Statistics aside he is best remembered for his leadership and performance during two methodical Colts drives that he engineered-one for a field goal to tie the game 17–17 in regulation and the other for a touchdown to win the game in overtime.

The Giants were haunted by and in awe of Unitas' performance. Giants linebacker Sam Huff recalled, "He was the master. Several times we thought we had him. But he always came up with the big play. On that field-goal drive, I think he hit Berry nine straight times. We couldn't stop him. He always did the unexpected. And, for this reason, you could never get a pattern on him no matter how many computers you may have. He had it all."[26] Unitas was named the MVP of the championship game, and consensus first team All-Pro.

The Colts repeated as NFL champs in 1959, defeating the Giants 31–16 in Baltimore in another come from behind victory. Unitas had another stellar performance in the title game completing 18 of 29 passes for 264 yards and two touchdowns. For the season he completed 193 of 367 passes for 2899 yards and a league record 32 touchdowns. He was named title game MVP, league MVP by the UPI, AP and Maxwell Club, and consensus first team All-Pro.

Legendary *New York Journal American* columnist Jimmy Cannon captured the essence of the 1959 title game.

> They chased [Giants quarterback Charlie] Conerly to the frontier of panic. Even when he had loose receivers, he seemed to feel the Colts pressing him. Meanwhile, like a pacifist ignoring a

gang rumble, Johnny U stood there, insolent in his deliberation. If he were about to introduce a long pass, he would fake with an elaborate deceit, turning in rapid body feints. The passes for distance were meant for Lenny Moore, who fled as if he knew a secret shortcut through the forest of Giants pass defense patterns. The short flips, Johnny U jerked with a wrist-flicked quickness to either Raymond Berry or Jim Mutscheller. Unitas suggested a man trying to complete a dart game before the bartender put out the lights.[27]

In 1960, Baltimore seemed on their way to another title game appearance, opening 6–2, but the bottom fell out as the Colts lost their last four games to finish 6–6. Unitas had another good season completing 190 of 378 passes for 3099 yards and 25 touchdowns and earning a Pro Bowl nod. His 47 game touchdown streak ended in a Week 11 loss to the Rams.

The 1961 and 1962 seasons were more of the same as the Colts finished 8–6 and 7–7, respectively. Unitas made the Pro Bowl squad both seasons completing 229 of 420 passes for 2990 yards and 16 touchdowns in 1961 and completing 222 of 389 passes for 2967 yards and 23 touchdowns in 1962, but over the three-season span since the 1959 championship John had thrown more interceptions (71) than touchdowns (64). Unitas was at odds with Ewbank's conservatism on offense, thriving when he had a chance to gamble and improvise.[28]

The Colts were a team in flux. After the 1962 season Ewbank was fired and replaced by Don Shula, at age 33, the youngest coach in the NFL. In 1963, Shula's first season, the Colts were 3–5 after eight weeks, but finished with a flourish winning five of their last six games to go 8–6. With a more open offensive scheme, Unitas passed for a career and league best 3481 yards, completing 237 of 410 passes for 20 touchdowns.

In 1964, Shula and the Colts finished atop the Western Conference with an outstanding record of 12–2. The Colts were heavily favored in the NFL championship game against Jim Brown and the Cleveland Browns who finished atop the Eastern Conference with a 10–3–1 record. On a cold, windy day in Cleveland, the Colts were upset by the Browns 27–0, as Unitas was a dismal 12 for 20 for 95 yards with two interceptions. For the season, Unitas completed 158 of 305 passes for 2824 yards and 19 touchdowns. Unitas was named the league MVP by the AP, UPI, and Maxwell Club. He was also consensus first team All-Pro.

From 1965 to 1967, the Colts faced the buzz saw that was Vince Lombardi's Green Bay dynasty. Despite a combined 30–10–3 regular season record they were unable to overcome the Packers.

In 1965, Unitas suffered a knee injury and played only 11 games as Baltimore ended the regular season tied with Green Bay atop the Western Conference with a 10–3–1 record, setting up a playoff game to decide the Conference. Unitas missed the playoff game as Green Bay won 13–10. In games Unitas started, the Colts finished 8–2–1 as he completed 164 of 282 passes for 2530 yards and 23 touchdowns.

The Colts finished 9–5 in 1966 as Unitas completed 195 of 348 passes for 2748 yards and 22 touchdowns. In 1965 he made most first team All-Pro teams, and in 1966 he was named to the Pro Bowl.

In 1967, Unitas had a great year, completing 255 of 436 passes (both career highs) for 3428 yards and 20 touchdowns. The Colts finished tied with the Rams atop the new Coastal Division of the Western Conference with an 11–1–2 record, but lost out on the playoffs because of a tiebreaker. Unitas was named league MVP for a fourth time and consensus first team All-Pro.

Nineteen sixty-eight would be a nightmarish season for Unitas. Raymond Berry and Lenny Moore had both retired. Throughout training camp Unitas suffered with swelling and pain in his throwing arm plus a lack of arm strength. With a high pain threshold and warrior's attitude, he had dealt with similar issues over the last few seasons, but this was different. The throwing motion that had so impressed Ewbank in 1956 was taking its toll.

It was estimated that Unitas had thrown over 8,000 passes during his career. During the final exhibition game against Dallas the pain became unbearable. Team doctors concluded that he had a torn muscle aggravated by chronic tendonitis. Rest was the only remedy.[29] Unitas himself stated, "With this arm, I couldn't knock a sick cat off a flower pot."[30]

Unitas saw very limited action during the regular season. When he did play he could not throw deep. Earl Morrall took over and had a career season as the Colts finished 13–1, and defeated the Browns 34–0 in the NFL championship game to avenge their only regular season loss. This set up the historic Super Bowl III matchup with Weeb Ewbank, Joe Namath and the New York Jets. The Colts were heavily favored to destroy the Jets. With the Colts down 13–0 in the third quarter, Shula inserted Unitas. Former teammate Johnny Sample, now with the Jets, was concerned. "I told my teammates about what Unitas could do, especially under fire. I knew we'd be in trouble if he started."[31] Unitas battled valiantly, but he could not overturn the inevitable 16–7 victory by the Jets.

Unitas' arm showed improvement in 1969. The Colts finished second in the Coastal Division with an 8–5–1 record as John completed 178 of 327 passes for 2342 yards and 12 touchdowns. After the season, Shula left to take the head coaching position in Miami. The low key Don McCafferty became the new Baltimore head coach. Tensions had been running high between Shula and Unitas, so a new, more patient coach was a welcome change.[32]

In 1970, the Colts became a member of the American Football Conference Eastern Division in the newly merged and aligned NFL. Physically aging, Unitas pieced together a masterful season, leading the Colts to a first place finish in the Eastern Division with an 11–2–1 record. The Colts then defeated the Bengals and Raiders in the post season to earn a berth in Super Bowl V against the Cowboys. Statistically, Unitas was not remarkable, completing 166 of 321 passes for 2213 yards and 14 touchdowns but he led the Colts with a chess-like precision. Unitas started the Super Bowl game and completed a 75-yard touchdown pass to John Mackey in the second quarter, but he was knocked out of the game, and Earl Morrall came in to lead the Colts to a 16–13 victory. Unitas was named NFL Man of the Year.

The 1970 Super Bowl season would be Unitas' last hurrah. The highlight of his final three seasons from 1971 to 1973 was a memorable Week 2 duel with Joe Namath in 1972. The Jets defeated the Colts 44–34, but the two quarterbacks combined for 872 passing yards with Unitas completing 26 of 45 passes for 376 yards and two touchdowns and Namath completing 15 of 28 passes for 496 yards and six touchdowns.

It was painful to watch Unitas complete his career in 1973 in the powder blue and lightning bolt uniforms of the San Diego Chargers. As Tom Callahan stated in his book *Johnny U*, "In the mind's eye, nobody pictures Babe Ruth as a Boston Brave, or Joe Namath as a Los Angeles Ram, or Bob Cousy and Walt Frazier as Cincinnati Royals and Cleveland Cavaliers. But the sights of Unitas in Charger livery isn't an easy image to shake. It's like watching Willie Mays stumbling in the outfield as a New York Met."[33]

During the summer of 1974, Johnny U retired. At the time of his retirement, he had NFL career records for passing yards—40,239 and touchdown passes—290. Over 18 NFL seasons he played in 211 games, attempted 5186 passes and completed 2830 for a completion percentage of 54.6. Unitas also ran for 1777 yards on 450 carries for an additional 13 touchdowns. He was elected to the Pro Football Hall of Fame in his first year of eligibility in 1979. He was also named to the NFL's 1960s All-Decade Team and 75th Anniversary Team. His number 19 was retired by the Colts.

After retiring Unitas spent some time in the 1970s as a color commentator on CBS. He was angered by the Colts move to Indianapolis in 1984, cutting ties to the relocated team, and declaring himself strictly a member of the *Baltimore* Colts for the rest of his life, although he did embrace the Baltimore Ravens franchise.

Unitas suffered in later years from the battering he took on the football field. He had two knee replacements and experienced difficulty with the use of his hands and fingers. In 2001, Unitas related, "I have no strength in the fingers. I can't use a hammer or saw around the house. I can't button buttons. I can't use zippers. Very difficult to tie shoes. I can't brush my teeth with it, because I can't hold a brush. I can't hold a fork with the right hand. I can't pick this phone up…. You give me a full cup of coffee, and I can't hold it. I can't comb my hair."[34]

Unitas was divorced from his first wife Dorothy in 1972. They had five children. He was married a second time to Sandra Lemon. They had three children.

Unitas died of a sudden heart attack while working out on September 11, 2002. According to Callahan, when the news reached Colts teammate Jim Parker, Parker drove into the country, pulled off to the side of an empty road and wept. Parker stated, "It was the first time that I wasn't there to protect him."[35]

Mickey Herskowitz put Unitas and his era into perspective: "Remember the fifties? Ike was just what the country needed, a president who didn't meddle in the affairs of government. We escaped our problems by plunging into sports, and some guys would have played football for an ice cream cone. Unitas, the son of Lithuanian immigrants who became the most admired quarterback of his time, was part of that era. There may not be another folk hero like him; it just doesn't happen that way anymore."[36]

But perhaps fellow teammate and Hall of Famer John Mackey said it best: "Playing with Johnny Unitas was like being in the huddle with God."[37]

NOTES

1. Frank Deford, "The Best There Ever Was," *Sports Illustrated*, September 23, 2002, 64.
2. Tom Callahan, *Johnny U: The Life and Times of John Unitas* (New York: Crown, 2006), 7–9.
3. Dave Klein, *The Game of Their Lives* (New York: Random House, 2006), 196–197.
4. Callahan, 11–12.
5. Lou Sahadi, *Johnny Unitas: America's Quarterback* (Chicago: Triumph Books, 2004), 29.
6. Sahadi, 29–30; John C. Unitas, Jr., with Edward L. Brown, *Johnny U and Me: The Man Behind the Golden Arm* (Chicago: Triumph Books, 2014), 19–20.
7. Callahan, 17; Sahadi, 29.
8. Sahadi 31; John Unitas with Ed Fitzgerald, *Pro Quarterback: My Own Story* (New York: Simon & Schuster, 1965), 26–27.
9. Callahan, 22.
10. Unitas, 27–28.
11. *Ibid.*, 28–32.
12. *Ibid.*, 32–33.
13. *The 2016 University of Louisville Football Media Guide*, http://gocards.com/sports/2016/7/20/2016-football-media-guide.aspx, accessed December 18, 2017.

14. Callahan, 33.

15. Callahan, 33.

16. Sahadi, 35–38; *The 2016 University of Louisville Football Media Guide*; Johnnyunitas.com, http://www.johnnyunitas.com/about-unitas/bio, accessed December 18, 2017.

17. Callahan, 37–38.

18. Michael MacCambridge, *America's Game: The Epic Story of How Pro Football Captured A Nation* (New York: Random House, 2004), 90.

19. MacCambridge, 91; Unitas, 42.

20. Jimmy Breslin, "The Passer Nobody Wanted," *The Saturday Evening Post*, November 1, 1958, 105.

21. MacCambridge, 92.

22. Unitas, 46.

23. Sahadi, 50.

24. Chris Willis, "The Bodyguard and Johnny U," *The Coffin Corner* 20, no. 3 (1998): 5.

25. Deford, 63.

26. Sahadi, 195–196.

27. Callahan, 186–187.

28. Sahadi, 84.

29. Sahadi, 89; Roger Kahn, "The Longest Year of John Unitas," *Sport Magazine*, April 1969, 34.

30. Kahn, 83.

31. MacCambridge, 255.

32. Sahadi, 123.

33. Callahan, 239.

34. William Nack, "The Wrecking Yard," *Sports Illustrated*, May 7, 2001, 66.

35. Callahan, 269.

36. Mickey Herskowitz, "Goodbye Johnny U," in *The NFL Literary Companion: A Game of Passion*, John Wiebusch and Brian Silverman, ed. (Atlanta: Turner, 1994), 380.

37. Callahan, 220.

REFERENCE

"Johnny Unitas." profootballreference.com. https://www.pro-football-reference.com/players/U/Unit Jo00.htm.

PART 4

The Stadium

Memorial Stadium

Matthew Keddie

The venue located at 900 East 33rd Street in downtown Baltimore, better known as Memorial Stadium, served as the home of Baltimore sports teams from 1944 to 1997.[1] The site on which Memorial Stadium was situated, Venable Park, was home to sports activities as far back as the 1920s. An original stadium was built on the site in 1922.[2] It was a horseshoe-shaped venue with seating for 40,000, mostly constructed of dirt and wood.[3] The dedicated stadium contrasted with the prosperous aspiration for a fine, Olympic quality venue. Its location sprung about as a result of a football game on December 3, 1921, between two military teams, on the campus of Johns Hopkins University. The Quantico Marines squared off against the Army's Third Area Corp squad, as Quantico emerged with a 22–0 shutout.[4] With the mayor of Baltimore, Joseph Broening, in attendance, the fan experience offered the necessity for a permanent sports venue in the city. The result: Venable Stadium. The significance was, this site would be the building block for an awe-inspiring stadium in the decades to come that would house Baltimore sports for more than 50 years.

Throughout its history, Venable Stadium was also referred to as Municipal Stadium, Baltimore Stadium, and even Babe Ruth Stadium, for a time.[5] In its early years, Venable Stadium hosted high school and college football games.[6] Local college teams such as the University of Maryland Terrapins and Naval Academy Midshipmen hosted contests there. Typically, these games drew throngs of fans to the stadium. In the 1940s, the venue extended its bounds to host Baltimore's baseball Orioles of the International League. The O's called the stadium home for nine seasons, 1944 thru 1953, after their former home, Oriole Park, was victim of a catastrophic fire midway through the 1944 season.[7] Part of the reason also concerned finances. Venable Stadium was not a profitable operation, but with the Orioles' use, the building had to be altered for baseball. The decision proved intelligent because the Orioles experienced high levels of success in the International League.[8] The team won IL championships in 1944 and again in 1950. Meanwhile, the city explored plans to rebuild the stadium into a high caliber venue for baseball with the hope of also maintaining an NFL franchise.[9] The rebuild began in 1950, and was completed in several phases at a cost of $6.5 million.[10] The horseshoe-shaped scheme carried over as the new venue also featured an open end facing the north, a seating capacity of 31,000 and the multi-purpose utilization for both baseball and football.[11] The design teams selected reinforced concrete as the building material and eliminated bleachers for real seats.[12] An upper deck was installed by 1954, and on April 15, 1954, the new American League Orioles played their home opening game.[13] The name Memorial Stadium was chosen to honor Maryland residents who dedicated themselves in the service, particularly

Memorial Stadium (courtesy Mark Palczewski).

World War II and the Korean War.[14] The building was often also dubbed "The Old Gray Lady of 33rd Street."[15] The thought of naming the venue after baseball legend and Baltimore native Babe Ruth was experimented with, but was eventually nixed.[16]

Both the Orioles and Colts enjoyed success at Memorial Stadium. The O's drew more than million fans in 1954, and the Colts routinely sold out home games.[17] Further upgrades and improvements were made over the coming years, including luxury boxes and increasing the seating capacity.[18] For baseball games, the capacity rose to over 52,000 by 1965, and topped out at 53,371 in its final season in 1991.[19] For football, seating served 60,000 by 1963, and was upped to 65,000 in its final two seasons.[20]

Memorial Stadium had its share of setbacks. Tragedy struck the venue on two separate occasions. On May 2, 1964, a tragic accident involving the jamming of an escalator caused one death, while injuring 46.[21] On December 19, 1976, a small private airplane flying in the area smashed into the bleachers in the open end of the stadium.[22] Luckily, nobody was injured, as the crash occurred during the waning minutes of a playoff game between the Steelers and Colts.

In the early 1970s, Colts ownership changed hands affecting the team's play on the field. Performance declined which directly correlated to a drop in attendance. Memorial Stadium was nearing 30 years old. Its aging infrastructure, coupled with the desperate need for upgrades to keep the venue current, had become high priorities. The new owners decided not to address the needs, and the decision silently sealed the fate of the stadium, which created tension with the city.[23] The Colts had explored relocation, and by 1984, the team moved to Indianapolis. The plan for a new baseball stadium proceeded forward, and the Orioles moved out of Memorial Stadium in 1991. Thus, the future of the building was uncertain. There were valiant attempts to utilize the stadium for other events, such as rock concerts. However, strong opposition existed from neighborhood residents.[24] The Cleveland Browns moved to Baltimore following the 1995 season, and became the Baltimore Ravens. The team played the 1996 and 1997 seasons in Memorial Stadium, but built their own stadium, originally known as Ravens Stadium at Camden Yards, now M & T Bank Stadium.[25] In 2001, Memorial Stadium was demolished, despite strong opposition from residents and sports fans in the area. The fate of the venue laid in the hands of the state government. Governor Martin O'Malley favored the complete razing of the stadium and site, despite numerous proposals to save and preserve the area.[26]

Despite the downturn of events that led to the stadium's demolition, Memorial Stadium was a site of many iconic memories in Baltimore sports. Its most celebrated tenant, the Baltimore Colts, leveraged the stadium's intricacies to create a powerful home field advantage from 1953 to 1983. Locals believed Baltimore had one of the great fan bases and stadiums in all of sports. David Spranger, a fan who attended hundreds of games at Memorial Stadium believes so, "Going to games at Memorial Stadium was some kind of experience. Most NFL fans look at Baltimore as one of the best home-field advantages, but not many realize where it all started. It started at 33rd street."[27] The Colts' late kickoff times (2 p.m.), combined with the fog coming in from the Chesapeake Bay, gave the second halves of their home games an eerie, noirish quality.

In their 30 years of occupancy, the Colts compiled a 118–89–5 regular season record for a .557 win percentage. The Colts posted a 4–2 playoff record there, too. Further, Baltimore produced undefeated home records on two separate occasions. First, in 1958 the Colts won all six home games for a perfect 6–0 mark. Later in 1967, the Colts went unbeaten at 6–0–1. The home dominance propelled Baltimore to their NFL title victory in 1958. All the success and winning drew the attention of external media. *Chicago Tribune* writer Cooper Rollow labeled the Colts' venue "The World's Largest Outdoor Insane Asylum" in 1959. Its location, environment, and base of passionate fans reinforced the name.

In the 15 years from 1957 to 1971, the Colts did not suffer a single losing season, and the results were largely from defending the turf at Memorial Stadium. The table below lists the Colts' record at Memorial Stadium during this time. The Colts only had one losing home record in 1962. Discounting that year, Baltimore won at least four contests per season. By 1963, the Colts had transformed Memorial Stadium into a house of horrors for opponents. From 1963 to 1971, Baltimore went a stunning 47–14–3 (0.734 win percentage) at home.

Colts Win–Loss–Tie Record at Memorial Stadium from 1957 to 1971

Season	Wins	Losses	Ties
1957	4	2	
1958	6	0	
1959	4	2	
1960	4	2	
1961	5	2	
1962	3	4	
1963	4	3	
1964	6	1	
1965	5	2	

Season	Wins	Losses	Ties
1966	5	2	
1967	6	0	1
1968	6	1	
1969	4	2	1
1970	5	1	1
1971	5	2	
	72	26	3

In 1958, Memorial Stadium served as a tremendous home-field advantage for the Colts. They stormed the competition, outscoring their six opponents by a whopping 142 points, 239 points for versus 97 points against. Baltimore averaged approximately 40 points per game, while only yielding roughly 16. The Colts manufactured 34 total touchdowns at home, compared to just 19 on the road.[28] Scoring does not tell the whole story. The Colts capitalized on the turnover margin as well. Baltimore won the turnover battle against each opponent to visit Memorial Stadium. In fact, the team carried a +23 turnover difference at home. This output included +9 against the Los Angeles Rams in a 34–7 shellacking on November 23.[29] That season, the Colts placed noteworthy beatdowns on opposing foes. On November 2, 1958, the Colts handed the Packers their worst defeat in the franchise's 40 years of existence, 56–0.[30]

Memorial Stadium hosted a number of thumping, heart-pounding Colts football games. One of the most entertaining contests ever played at Memorial Stadium was the 1959 NFL championship game, a rematch of the 1958 title game, on December 27, 1959.

The Colts leveraged a 24-point fourth quarter output to take control of the game and seal the victory, 31–16.[31] The game exemplified a battle between two superpowers, as it pitted the top-ranked offense in the Colts against the league's top ranked defense in the Giants.[32] Baltimore scored first on a 60-yard pass from Johnny Unitas to Lenny Moore for a 7–0 advantage. The Giants answered with three Pat Summerall field goals in the first, second, and third quarters to take a 9–7 lead. In the fourth quarter, New York chose to go for a first down on fourth and one at the Baltimore 27 yard line. New York ran the ball up the middle with Alex Webster, who was met ferociously by Colts tackle Ray Krouse for a loss of one on the play. The stand propelled Baltimore, "the ballgame began to explode in the Giants' collective face," and became the call which cost New York the game.[33] Baltimore took the ball, and embarked on a long drive capped by a four-yard rushing score by Unitas, to take back the lead, 14–9, and never looked back.[34] After trading three and outs, the Giants faced a critical third down on their own nine. As quarterback Charlie Conerly dropped back, he fired the ball down field, and it was intercepted by Andy Nelson at the Giants 31, who returned it to the 15. Baltimore scored another touchdown on a pass to Jerry Richardson, extending their advantage to 21–9. Conerly tossed another interception on New York's ensuing possession, and Baltimore capitalized yet again. Johnny Sample snatched the ball out of the air and ran it back into the end zone for a score. The extra point made it 28–9 Colts, who added a Steve Myhra field goal to net 31 points. The Giants added a touchdown late on a pass from Conerly to Bob Schnelker making the final, 31–16 Colts. After the final gun, the stadium erupted in complete euphoria. A large portion of the 57,545 in attendance stormed the field, grabbing any and everything they could, to turn into memorabilia; "they stole the helmet right off my head" said Gino Marchetti of the Colts.[35] Fans tore down the goal posts, too, and carried them out of the stadium, into the streets. Amidst the pandemonium, Johnny Unitas was named the game's MVP for the second consecutive year. Richard Nixon made a surprise appearance in the Colts' locker room, saying, "the best I have ever seen."[36]

A memorable upset in Colts history took place on December 9, 1973, when the Miami Dolphins came into town for a late season showdown. The Dolphins were the reigning Super Bowl champions, and on a roll, having won 28 of its previous 29 contests heading into the game. Contrastingly, the Colts were moving in the opposite direction, limping in at 2–10, mired in a 6-game losing streak. To make matters worse, Miami dominated Baltimore in the team's previous three regular season encounters, outscoring the Colts, 83–0, all Dolphins wins. The news outlets reported Miami opted to rest several of its key starters, including quarterback Bob Griese.[37] The Colts' head coach, Howard Schellenberger viewed it as a sign of disrespect. He uttered to his team, "Miami's going to play some back-up players because they don't respect you! If you guys don't play a lot better, many of you won't be playing pro football next year!"[38] The statements were awe inspiring because the Colts did not look like a 2–10 team on the field. They played a near flawless game. The defense held the Dolphins to 228 total yards, recorded two sacks, and held Miami to as many points as turnovers, 3, in the 16–3 win. The key was Baltimore's defense holding the Miami offense in check: Larry Csonka and Mercury Morris were limited to 77 yards on the ground. Following the game, the Baltimore faithful stormed the field in glee. Several ran over to Colts defensive end Roy Hilton, rose him off the ground, and carried him off the field as a salute to the team's miraculous effort.[39]

Notes

1. "Memorial Stadium," *Ballparks of Baseball—The Fields of Major League Baseball*, http://www.ballparksofbaseball.com/ballparks/memorial-stadium, accessed December 26, 2016.

2. Tom Flynn, "Venable Park," *Baltimore Post Examiner*, August 1, 2005.

3. *Ibid.*

4. *Ibid.*

5. *Ibid.*

6. Bill Glauber, "Poly, City Usher Out Glorious Era at Memorial Stadium in Last Thanksgiving Game," *Baltimore Sun*, November 26, 1992.

7. "The World's Largest Outdoor Insane Asylum: Memorial Stadium, Part I," Maryland Historical Society, http://www.mdhs.org/underbelly/2014/12/11/the-worlds-largest-outdoor-insane-asylum-memorial-stadium-part-i, accessed December 26, 2016; "The World's Largest Outdoor Insane Asylum: Memorial Stadium, Part II," Maryland Historical Society, http://www.mdhs.org/underbelly/2015/01/22/the-worlds-largest-outdoor-insane-asylum-memorial-stadium-part-ii, accessed December 26, 2016.

8. *Ibid.*

9. *Ibid.*

10. *Ibid.*

11. *Ibid.*

12. *Ibid.*

13. "Memorial Stadium."

14. *Ibid.*

15. Byron Bennett, "Memorial Stadium—Time Will Not Dim the Glory of Their Deeds," *Deadball Baseball*, last modified February 12, 2012, http://deadballbaseball.com/?p=1225.

16. *Ibid.*

17. "The World's Largest Outdoor Insane Asylum: Memorial Stadium, Part II."

18. *Ibid.*

19. "Memorial Stadium," Ballparks.com, last modified February 2005, .http://www.ballparks.com/baseball/american/memori.htm.

20. *Ibid.*

21. "46 Hurt, 1 Dead in Escalator Jam Saturday," *Gettysburg Times* (Gettysburg, PA), May 4, 1964.

22. "Becoming a Part of the Game," CheckSix.com, last modified November 22, 2014, http://www.check-six.com/Crash_Sites/N6276J-Kroner.htm.

23. "Life Before Indianapolis: A History of the Baltimore Colts," History of the Baltimore Colts, 2016, http://bonesaw.tripod.com/Baltimore.htm.

24. "The World's Largest Outdoor Insane Asylum: Memorial Stadium, Part II."

25. *Ibid.*

26. *Ibid.*

27. Peter J. DiLutis, "Memorial Stadium Memories," Maryland Sports Landmarks, https://marylandsportslandmarks.wordpress.com/memorial-stadium-memories-live-on-in-baltimore, accessed December 26, 2016.

28. "1958 Baltimore Colts Statistics & Players," Pro-Football-Reference.com.

29. DiLutis.

30. Art Daley, "Colts Deal Pack Worst Defeat in History, 56–0," *Green Bay Press Gazette*, November 3, 1958.

31. George Strickler, "Colts Retain Title; Beat Giants, 31–16, Break Game Wide Open with 24-Point Fourth Period," *Chicago Tribune*, December 28, 1959.

32. Mike Klingaman, "The Greatest Game Nobody Remembers," *Baltimore Sun*, December 20, 2009.

33. *Ibid.*

34. *Ibid.*

35. *Ibid.*

36. *Ibid.*

37. Randy Campbell, "Following Perfection: The 1973 Miami Dolphins," Finsmob Unleashed.

38. *Ibid.*

39. Joe Zagorski, *The NFL in the 1970s: Pro Football's Most Important Decade* (Jefferson, NC: McFarland, 2016), 133.

The Baltimore Colts Marching Band

RANDY SNOW

On a gloomy night in March of 1984, several Mayflower moving trucks departed Baltimore in a snowstorm for Indianapolis. The trucks did not just carry the team's equipment and office furniture, but the heart and soul of the city. Overnight, the team was gone, never to return.

But, as luck would have it, there was one thing that the movers did not take with them; the uniforms of the team's marching band. This fortuitous event would play a monumental role in healing the city in the aftermath of the team's untimely departure, as well as for the next 12 years, until a new NFL team would come to town.

The band was originally formed on September 7, 1947, when the first incarnation of the Baltimore Colts came to town. This was a team, not in the NFL, but in a rival pro football league known as the All-America Football Conference. The Colts were actually a relocated AAFC team that played in Florida in 1946 called the Miami Seahawks. The Colts' team colors at the time were green and silver.

After the 1949 season, the AAFC folded and the Colts joined the NFL along with

The Baltimore Colts' Marching Band

The Leader of The Band, Bob Cissin

Colts Marching Band.

two other AAFC teams, the Cleveland Browns and the San Francisco 49ers. That particular Colts team played just one season in the NFL and then folded as well.

In 1951 and 1952, the band continued to play and make local appearances until another new Baltimore Colts team came to town, once again in the form of a relocated franchise. This time it was an NFL team called the Dallas Texans. The Texans played just one season in Dallas (1952) before relocating to Baltimore. The Texans' colors were blue and white and the new Colts team kept the colors, which became the iconic look of the Baltimore Colts beginning in 1953.

The band was as much a part of the team as any player or coach. It was there and performed at the 1958 championship game at Yankee Stadium in New York. In fact, after the field goal that tied the game, a member of the color guard retrieved the ball and held it for posterity. But other fans who were there also wanted the ball. It was passed off to Danny O'Toole, a drummer in the band. In order to make sure that the ball made its way back to Baltimore, O'Toole placed it in his drum case. But fearing that it still might be discovered and taken, he took the head off his drum and placed it inside the drum for the trip home.[1]

It seemed that the band was everywhere in those days, playing in parades and other events, not only to promote the team, but the city of Baltimore as well. In 1962, the Colts Marching Band even played at the Maryland Democratic Convention for John F. Kennedy.[2]

When the team departed Baltimore in 1984, a strange series of events occurred that could have been taken right out of a spy novel. While the rest of the team's equipment was being trucked out of town, no one knew that a big part of the team was not actually at the team facilities like they normally would have been.

On the night of the midnight move, the band uniforms were actually off site at the local Kirsh Cleaners being cleaned and repaired when the moving vans unexpectedly arrived to take the Colts' equipment to Indianapolis.

The following day, an employee at the cleaners called the band's president, John Ziemann to tell him that he had the uniforms at the store. Not sure what to do, Ziemann retrieved the uniforms and tried to find a place to hide them. He thought about hiding them at his house, but did not want to get caught with them in his possession. Another member of the band suggested a different hiding place. His family had access to a mausoleum in a local cemetery and that is where the uniforms were eventually hidden.

For the next 12 years, (1984–95) the band continued to perform without an NFL team to support.

The first year the band played at various events in and around Baltimore, including the annual Preakness horse race. But in 1985 they were invited to play at an NFL game in Cleveland by none other than team owner Art Modell. At first, the crowd did not know how to react to a band representing an NFL team that did not even exist anymore, but as their halftime performance came to an end, the fans gave them a rousing ovation. The band was invited back to Cleveland every year after that.

The Colts' biggest fan in those days was Hurst "Loudy" Loudenslager. He was at the Colts' first home game in 1947 and even worked for the club for several years. In all the years the Colts were in town, he only missed one home game. He loved the team and its players. He would make birthday cakes for players and coaches and he would meet the team at the airport when they returned from away games, greeting them and playing the Colts' fight song on a record player.

Loudy took the departure of the Colts' team as hard as anyone in the city. On the night when the moving vans took his team away, he was there, standing with other fans by the fence in the rain and snow, watching the trucks drive off into the night.

In September 1984, on the day when the Colts should have been kicking off a new season in Baltimore, Loudy went to Memorial Stadium, went to his regular seat and sat alone, staring out into an empty stadium.

When he passed away in April of 1989 from a heart attack at the age of 74, his family buried him in a Colts uniform. Several former Colts players, including Johnny Unitas, Lenny Moore and Art Donovan, were pallbearers at his funeral. Members of band were there at the cemetery, in uniform, and played a slow, somber version of the fight song.[3]

In March of 1987, the Maryland State Legislature was debating whether or not to fund two new stadiums, one for Major League Baseball's Baltimore Orioles and another for a possible new NFL franchise. Opposition to the plan was growing. So the band went and performed on the steps of the Maryland State House prior to an evening session. The Governor of Maryland, William Donald Schaefer, was there as well to support the band and the stadium initiative. Shortly after that, the legislation passed.

The band continued to perform around the country at events and parades. They even played during halftime at the Pro Football Hall of Fame game on July 27, 1991, which featured the Detroit Lions and the Denver Broncos.[4] They received a standing ovation. Not only did they perform at halftime of the game but they were in the Hall of Fame parade as well.

In 1994, a new pro football team did come to town, but it was not an NFL team, it was a team in the Canadian Football League. The Colts Marching Band, of course, played at their home games. Originally the team was called the Baltimore CFL Colts. The CFL team's colors were also blue and white and it had a horse head on the helmet that was somewhat similar to today's Denver Broncos logo.

Since the NFL owned the Colts nickname, a lawsuit was filed by the NFL to stop the CFL team from using the Colts' nickname. But the team found a way around it anyway. Whenever the team scored, or made a first down, the public address announcer at Memorial Stadium would say, "Your Baltimore CFL…" and would leave it to the crowd to yell, "Colts."

The 1994 team was actually a good one and played in the CFL championship game called the Grey Cup. They lost to the British Columbia Lions 26–23 in Vancouver, Canada on a last second field goal. Baltimore led the CFL in attendance in 1994, averaging 37,000 fans per game.[5] The following year, the team officially became known as the Baltimore Stallions.

In 1995, average attendance dropped to 30,000 per game, but it still ranked second among all CFL teams. In their second year, the Stallions posted a 15–3 regular season record. On November 6, 1995, during the time when the Stallions were taking part in the CFL playoffs, the official announcement was made that Art Modell was moving the Browns to Baltimore. The team would eventually be renamed the Ravens.

The Stallions would go on to win the Grey Cup on November 19, 1995, beating the Calgary Stampeders 37–20 in Saskatchewan. The Stampeders were led by quarterback Doug Flutie. The Stallions will forever be known as the first (and probably only) U.S. team to ever win the Grey Cup. The CFL also folded all its other U.S. teams following the 1995 season after a three-season expansion experiment.

The band played at a total of 23 CFL games, but did not travel to Canada to play at either of the two Grey Cup games that the Stallions participated in.

Following the 1995 season, knowing that the NFL Cleveland franchise was coming to town, the Stallions were relocated to Canada where they became the Montreal Alouettes of today. Montreal had been without its CFL team for nine years after the former Alouettes team folded in 1987.

While the band, and the city, waited for another NFL team to arrive, the Colts Marching Band would travel and play at 30 other NFL games. They were warmly greeted by the fans of the other NFL teams and appreciated for what they continued to do even though their team was no longer there.

There were mixed emotions for Baltimore fans when the announcement was made that the Browns were coming to town. They were happy to be getting a new NFL team in town, but they also empathized with the fans in Cleveland because they remembered just how much it hurt to lose a beloved franchise with a deep history.

During the first two years that the Ravens played in Baltimore, the band continued to be known as the Colts Marching Band. It was a way of bridging the football past of the city with the future.

On September 7, 1997, the Colts Marching Band celebrated its 50th anniversary during a halftime performance of the game between the Ravens and the Cincinnati Bengals.

The Baltimore Colts Marching Band performed for the final time on July 11, 1998, in a parade marking the opening of the ESPN Zone at the Baltimore Inner Harbor. The next time they appeared in public was one month later, on August 8, 1998, at a preseason game between the Ravens and the Chicago Bears. This time they were known as Baltimore's Marching Ravens and sported their new purple uniforms to match the Ravens team colors. Today, the band consists of 150 band members and equipment personnel.

And what ever became of John Ziemann, the man who hid the band uniforms in a cemetery mausoleum in 1986 in order to keep them from going to Indianapolis? He is still the band's president today. He joined the Colts Marching Band in 1962 in the percussion section and is married to Charlene Wills, who is a former Baltimore Colts Cheerleader. She is also the director of the Ravens' flag line.

If there was one thing that held fans together during the lean years without an NFL team it was the Colts' fight song. For many fans, seeing the band perform was special, but when they played the fight song, everyone sang along. It was ingrained into their minds like the Pledge of Allegiance or the National Anthem, and they could sing it at the drop of a hat. Written by Jo Lombardi and Benjamin Klasmer in 1947, the song held a special place in the hearts of Colts fans when all they had was a band, and a song.[6]

The Baltimore Colts Fight Song

Let's go, you Baltimore Colts,
And put that ball across the line.
So drive on, you Baltimore Colts,
Go in and strike like lightning bolts.
FIGHT! FIGHT! FIGHT!
Rear up, you Colts, and let's fight;
Crash through and show them your might,
For Baltimore and Maryland,
You will march on to victory!

So it is safe to say that the Baltimore Colts Marching Band is responsible for maintaining the football hopes of a city during the intervening years between teams, not once, but twice. (1951–52 and 1984–95). It has been performing continuously for over 70 years now, in one form or another, and shows no signs of slowing down. While the current trend in the NFL is to offer little or no entertainment during halftime at many of its games, Baltimore continues to entertain its fans with music and a visual spectacle that harkens back to a simpler time when a song was a powerful anthem that stirred the spirits of thousands of fans, cheering on their beloved team. *For Baltimore and Maryland, you will march on to victory!*

NOTES

1. *The Band That Wouldn't Die*, ESPN 30 for 30 Documentary, directed by Barry Levinson, 2009.

2. "Marching Band History," BaltimoreRavens.com, http://www.baltimoreravens.com/raven-stown/marching-ravens/history.html.

3. William Gildea, "The Loss of a Legend," WashingtonPost.com, April 28, 1989, https://www.washingtonpost.com/archive/sports/1989/04/28/the-loss-of-a-legend/93759b37-ac55–4e05–9c34–700fc26f84da/.

4. "Pro Football Hall of Fame games," ProFootball.com, https://web.archive.org/web/20060719203242/http://profootballhof.com/enshrinement/series2.jsp.

5. Ben Jacobs, "Baltimore's Greatest Canadian Sports Team," TheClassical.org, December 15, 2011, http://theclassical.org/articles/baltimores-greatest-canadian-sports-team-a-brief-history-of-the-cfl-colts.

6. "Colts Fight Song," ColtsHeritage.com, http://www.coltsheritage.com/fight.php.

PART 5

The Press

Joe Croghan
and Ernie Harwell

JOE MARREN

Time is not on anyone's side. It just flies in this petty pace from day to day. Consider this: There was a misty, quaint time before "The Greatest Game Ever Played," and then there were the changes that came with the sport after TGGEP (Baltimore's 23–17 overtime win over the New York Giants in 1958—the first overtime championship game in NFL history). WBAL (as in BALtimore) broadcasters Ernie Harwell and Joe Croghan lived, saw and broadcast through those changes and some of their own as time passed.

So let's talk about the changes time hath wrought with those two sportscasters in their respective careers. To do so let's start with a moment in time that defines this book: NBC carried the title game that was played on December 28, 1958, in Yankee Stadium. What's different? Plenty.

The first noticed change is that the NFL's title game has since been christened with a name. It's now called the Super Bowl. Although originally played between teams from the NFL and AFL, it's now a contest between the winner of the AFC vs. the NFC. But everyone knows that, so what other changes are out there to discuss?

Well, let's go to the networks. NBC has broadcast some Super Bowls in the past and will carry the game again in the future. So did, and so could, CBS. Or ABC. Or the Fox Network. Or maybe even the NFL's own network (that's a huge change in and of itself). Or … well, who knows what the future will bring as we continue to pull signals down from the ether that we now pack into cables that snake across the nation.

Late December playoff games? Oh man, fuhgeddaboutit. The 16-game regular season is just wrapping up by then. After the regular season ends there's still a month of playoff games to slog through in January.

Yankee Stadium? Well, the new one is still in the Bronx, just across from what's left of the ol' House that Ruth Built. But championship games are played in neutral cities now, unless by some quirk of fate a mostly warm-weather city, or one with a domed stadium, makes it to the title game in its home town (and none has as of Super Bowl 52). But there's something else: Yankee Stadium was built for baseball and adapted for football. Time has changed things. Now there are stadiums built just for football and adapted for soccer, or track, or mega rock concerts, or usually anything but baseball. And the Major League Baseball owners worried about that as far back as the 1944 winter meetings when they passed the Barrow Regulation that prohibited a MLB club from renting its ballpark to a football team, or anyone else, as long as the baseball team had a shot at the World

Series. Remember that this was at a time when there were no baseball playoffs unless there was a tie in the final standings.

But let's leave all that talk about baseball for another publication. We're talking football here, and this chapter is about football broadcasters and how things change. Although changes would come to the press box, Croghan and Harwell were old school but they still had to change in the way it was expected those in the sports broadcast biz would change. In other words, they began in radio by covering baseball (and Harwell had some print experience). That was the routine back then but it's not exactly the career path followed by today's football broadcasters, as the top six paragraphs note.

Croghan's career went through changes in various cities but he ended up back in the Baltimore area where he was born in 1921. He graduated from Loyola College in 1943 and began his broadcasting career by default rather than design. It all started on a troop ship returning home from Europe at the end of World War II. One of his jobs was to make announcements on the ship's internal communication system. Some of the soldiers on the ship going home with him told him that he should consider a career in broadcasting. By 1947 that idea turned into reality when he was hired by WANN radio in Annapolis to broadcast Navy football games, among other events.

Annapolis was just one of the stops along his 38-year career path in radio and television. In the 1950s and '60s he did the play-by-play on either WBAL-TV or WBAL radio of, at various times, baseball's Baltimore Orioles and Washington Senators, as well as for the football Colts. He was WBAL's first sports director and a member of the Orioles' broadcast team at the start of the 1960s.

In the mid–1960s he began a series of moves between Baltimore and Miami to work in the broadcast booth covering either the Colts or the Dolphins on either television or radio. The first move in '66 took him to WCKT-TV in Miami where he worked as an announcer on Dolphins games. He was back in Baltimore in '69 and on the broadcast team covering the Colts on WCBM radio. Then it was back to Miami to host *The Don Shula Show* on WPLG-TV, channel 10, until 1974. The show was usually on the air at 8:30 p.m. on Mondays and one of the memorable shows was the January 1973 broadcast after the Dolphins' perfect 17–0 season in 1972. Shula pulled out the Vince Lombardi trophy from underneath a coffee table on the set. Croghan, as usual, seemed nonplussed as he helped make sure it didn't fall off the table in front of him, Shula, defensive tackle Manny Fernandez and quarterback Bob Griese. Unbridled emotions were not a hallmark of the show as Croghan, in his understated way, dissected the game with the coach and players, talked about coaching changes, and wondered aloud which players would be back in '73. Occasionally Croghan would push up his black-rim glasses with a finger, but the delivery was professional, cool and calm. And that's the way that Shula apparently liked it.

"I enjoyed my relationship with him," Shula said of Croghan. "I always thought he was one of the top people in the profession."[1]

Joe Croghan.

Perhaps he was cool and efficient at covering championship teams because he was in the midst of an animated mob that was overcome with sheer and unbridled joy after the Colts beat the Giants in 1958.

In the 1950s Baltimore was looked upon as just an inconvenient but necessary train stop to drop off or take on passengers coming from or going to Washington or Philly and other points. It was another blue-collar town with factories, plants and a port, nothing special to it and it certainly wasn't a New York. And that's precisely what made winning a championship football game in a baseball palace in New York so special. A few sentences of history for context are necessary here: Baltimore had a woeful team in the old All-America Football Conference that struggled to a dismal 10–29–1 record in three seasons from 1947 to 1949. That team lasted one year in the NFL in 1950, going 1–11. The city didn't have an NFL team in 1951 or '52. In the four seasons from 1953 to 1957 the best the Colts could do was a 7–5 record in '57. Then came 1958 and talk about changes! A title was the team's Christmas present to the city.

After the championship game many of the players and coaches flew back that night to what was then called Friendship Field in Baltimore. They were met at the airport by about 30,000 raucous, boisterous, riotous, noisy fans. The crowd danced on the roof of the team bus and crushed a police car. The fans clogged not only the airport, but the roads for miles leading to the airport and radio stations had to ask people to stay away for safety's sake, regardless of whether they intended to be naughty or nice.

Let Croghan set the stage: "If you were at the airport, as I was, you could never forget it. All the folks in the crowd wanted was to see the players, to make them realize how happy they had made them feel. I came close to getting trampled in the process because of the way the waiting crowd surged back and forth. I could have been crushed by the rush. Instead of doing a broadcast and interviewing the team members, I had to cut my broadcast cord and stand on top of a mobile unit truck."[2]

So Croghan could afford to seem a little blasé when Shula pulled out the Lombardi Trophy on the set in '73. After surviving the '58 celebration he could rightfully have said, "Ummm, yeah. Been there, done that."

Croghan retired in 1985 and moved to Towson, Maryland, just a handful of miles north of Baltimore on Route 45. He died of cancer in November 1995 at age 74.

Although he had hundreds, more likely thousands, of friends who were listeners and fellow broadcasters, it was a newspaper journalist who really summed up his life. John Steadman, the legendary Baltimore sportswriter, said of Croghan: "He was easy to listen to, and he dropped stories right into your lap with as comfortable a fit as wearing an old pair of slippers."[3]

Harwell also went through the same changes as many broadcasters did, starting with one sport and one medium and then moving to another sport (baseball to football) or medium (radio to television) as the needs of the job changed. But Harwell added another change that not all of the sportscasters of his generation had (he was born in 1918 in the small town of Washington, Georgia, but grew up in Atlanta): He had print experience.

The print side started with a regular column in his high school newspaper, the *Tattler*, and he won the top prize in a 1936 national journalism contest for students. His next step was even bigger. In 1934, when he was 16, he wrote to *The Sporting News* and asked to be their correspondent for the Atlanta Crackers, at the time a Class A team in baseball's Southern Association. Wanting to sound older and more experienced, he signed the letter as W. Earnest Harwell. It worked and Harwell went on to have a 31-year run with the paper in one capacity or another.

In the long run, however, Harwell's legacy wasn't cemented as a *Sporting News* columnist but as a broadcaster for 55 years, 42 of them (1960–91 and 1993–2002) calling Detroit Tigers games on either PASS Sports TV, WKBD-TV, WJR radio or WXYT radio.

"I think I've done more games than anybody. Seven decades and 55 years. Even the old-timers came a little bit after I did," Harwell once said.[4]

At one time or another he also was in the booth announcing baseball games for the Brooklyn Dodgers (1948–49), New York Giants (1950–53), Baltimore Orioles (1954–59) and the California Angels (1992). And in football he was the announcer for New York Giants in 1952 and was the Colts' play-by-play announcer on WBAL from 1956 to 1958.

Those who knew Harwell as a boy in Atlanta might not have thought the youngster with the speech impediment would one day make a living as a sportscaster. Yet in the cash-starved days of the Depression his father worked out a deal with a local elocution teacher and gradually young Ernie improved. He later won a local debating contest, which decades later the elocution teacher reminded Harwell about when she wrote to him: "I shall never forget the day you won the medal. Your dad stood there with tears streaming down his face and said. 'This is the happiest day of my life.'"[5]

Harwell himself had many happy days and probably among them is the day in 1940, during his senior year at Emory University, when he became sports director at WSB radio in Atlanta where he hosted a 15-minute program twice a week.

He continued with the genesis of his broadcast career and here's where the print legacy returns (although he had worked for the *Emory Wheel* student newspaper in college and also did some work for the *Atlanta Constitution*) because after he enlisted in the Marines in 1942 he became a correspondent for the Corps' *Leatherneck* newspaper. But remember, he was also still involved in broadcasting. In 1943 he started doing Atlanta Crackers baseball games back on WSB. Unfortunately, people complained that someone in military service shouldn't be announcing baseball so Harwell had to quit. Luckily for him and all his eventual listeners down the decades the Crackers wanted him back when the war ended and he returned to the broadcast booth (though now with WATL radio) in 1946.

But his big break came in an unprecedented trade with baseball's Dodgers in 1948. Harwell had already been asked to fill in for Dodgers play-by-play announcer Red Barber when the sportscaster was set to go to London to cover the Olympics for CBS radio from July 29 to August 14. But Barber suffered a bleeding ulcer attack in July and the Dodgers needed an immediate replacement. So Harwell, a radio announcer, was traded by the minor league Crackers, a team unaffiliated at the time with a major league franchise, to the major league Dodgers for catcher Cliff Dapper. (Dapper's only season in the big leagues was in 1942 with the Dodgers; he caught eight games and in 17 at-bats had eight hits, including a double and a home run. Dapper would become Atlanta's manager for the 1949 season. The Crackers would finish with a 71–82 record in '49, finishing fifth in the eight-team league.) And here comes the cliché: The rest was history as Harwell began his announcing duties on August 4 and only signed off the air decades later.

"He [Barber] was still weak and he couldn't do a whole lot, so Connie [Desmond] and I did pretty much the bulk of the work the rest of the season. The first game he came back to was when Rex Barney pitched a no-hitter at the Polo Grounds. And that was the first game I ever worked with Red," Harwell recalled.[6] The Dodgers won 2–0 in the game on September 9.

In 1949 home games were broadcast on television and Harwell, Barber and Desmond rotated the televised games with one of them on TV and the other two in the radio booth. It wasn't as easy as some may think it seems because each medium had approaches to covering events that are quite different.

"I realized that you had to keep your mouth shut a lot more on TV than you did on radio," Harwell explained.[7]

Maybe so, but it was the smooth, low-keyed voice (one biographer likened it to a "dripping Georgia peach cobbler") that attracted fans. As the *New York Times* once noted, "His honeyed Georgia voice and easy, colorful descriptions lulled many a schoolchild awake at night listening to games."[8]

Changes. By the time the 1950 season rolled around Harwell was still in New York City, though in a different borough and announcing a different team as he moved from Flatbush to Coogan's Bluff, from the Dodgers to the Giants. It all came to a boil in the third game of a National League playoff series on October 3, 1951, between the Dodgers and the Giants. In the ninth inning that afternoon at the Polo Grounds Brooklyn's right-handed pitcher Ralph Branca threw a fastball to the Giants' Bobby Thomson, also a rightie, for a game- and series-ending three-run homer to win the game, 5–4, for the Giants (who would later lose to the Yankees in the World Series, four games to two).

It was the first nationally televised baseball game and Harwell would work it for WPIX-TV with NBC picking up the broadcast feed for a national audience.

"I would be on NBC-TV coast-to-coast on the biggest game in baseball history. [Russ] Hodges, my partner, would have to settle for radio," Harwell later wrote.[9]

When Thomson hit the homer Harwell said he kept it low-key and said something like "It's gone" and let the pictures take over. Hodges, though, would go into baseball lore by yelling, "The Giants win the pennant!" Shout that in amazement four or five times and you'll get an idea of what it was like in the radio booth. Ah, but then let's remember that Harwell was in the TV booth. As Harwell related when he accepted the Ford Frick Award and was inducted into the broadcasters' wing of the Baseball Hall of Fame in 1981: "Russ Hodges was on the radio, and that's the guy you hear all the time [on replays]. Television had no instant replay, no recording in those days. Only Mrs. Harwell knows that I did the telecast of Bobby Thomson's home run."[10]

Changes are what it's all about, as Harwell noted. At the end of the 1953 season the St. Louis Browns moved to Baltimore and were renamed the Orioles. Harwell also moved to Baltimore and became the first announcer for the American League team on WBAL in '54. The other change was taking up duties calling the Colts' games for the station in 1956. A Baltimore Sun article from 2009 said that Harwell had fond memories of Baltimore and Memorial Stadium. However, even though he liked Baltimore, he couldn't pass up a chance to move to Detroit and broadcast Tigers games on WJR (or, as Harwell pronounced the team nickname in his Southern style, "Ti-guhs"), and broadcasting baseball was probably playing to his strengths.

According to Harwell, "I probably fit it [baseball] better than I did with football. There were some people in my early days who thought I was a better football than baseball broadcaster. I think, in football, it moves along, and if you have an authoritative voice, and don't correct yourself and can call the play quickly, and beat the crowd noise, you can be a great football announcer. Nowadays they have a lot more advantages. They can look at videos, at replays. I enjoyed football, but baseball is a better game for radio than any other sport."[11]

So then, what to concentrate on when calling a game?

"The game has got to be paramount. People are going to listen to the game no matter who's announcing it, they want to find out who's winning and what the score is and everything else is pretty much secondary," Harwell advised.[12]

Harwell retired in 2002, at age 84. In September 2009 he announced that he had inoperable bile duct cancer and had just months to live. The end came on May 4, 2010, in his home in Novi, Michigan. He was 92.

The National Sportscasters and Sportswriters Association named him Michigan Sportscaster of the Year 19 times. Among the many other honors he received, besides the Frick Award, was that in 1991 he was inducted into the American Sportscasters Hall of Fame; in 1992 he was inducted into the National Radio Hall of Fame; and in 2002 a statue of him was erected at Detroit's Comerica Park.

NOTES

1. Fred Rasmussen, "Joe Croghan Had a 38-Year Broadcasting Career in Radio and Television," *Baltimore Sun*, November 3, 1995.

2. John Steadman, "Some Games Are Worth Remembering," *Baltimore Evening Sun*, December 24, 1988, http://articles.latimes.com/1988–12-24/sports/sp-374_1_worth-remembering, accessed November 16, 2016.

3. Rasmussen.

4. "Ernie Harwell Biography—A Life in Baseball, Moves Up to the Majors, 'Thank You,' Not 'Goodbye,'" http://sports.jrank.org/pages/1968/Harwell-Ernie.html, accessed November 16, 2016.

5. "When Ernie Harwell Met Babe Ruth," http://www.npr.org/programs/morning/features/2002/aug/ernieharwell/excerpt.html, Accessed November 16, 2016.

6. Matt Bohn, "Ernie Harwell," http://sabr.org/bioproj/person/3aee1452, accessed October 31, 2016.

7. *Ibid.*

8. Frederick N. Rasmussen, "Tigers' Broadcaster Gave Voice to the Early Orioles," *Baltimore Sun*, September 13, 2009, 5A.

9. Bohn.

10. *Ibid.*; David Panian, "Meeting Ernie Harwell a Joy No Matter the Situation," http://www.lenconnect.com/article/20100508/NEWS/305089954, accessed Oct. 31, 2016.

11. Bohn.

12. *Ibid.*

Cameron Snyder and John Steadman

JOE MARREN

Baltimore in the late 1950s would never be confused with a Paris on the Chesapeake. Don't be confused, it was in the top ten in U.S. population but the economy depended more on manufacturing and shipping than chic. Blue-collar workers MADE things in Baltimore, like a lot of steel at the Bethlehem plant in Sparrows Point, and 75 percent of the region's manufacturing might centered around jobs in the city.

Gino Marchetti, a defensive end with the Colts from 1953 to 1966, knew about the city's work ethic. Although he made it to the Hall of Fame in Canton in 1972, he only made $8,500 from his day job playing football in 1958. To put it in context, it was about $3,000 more than an average worker got paid. In other words, it was enough to be somewhat comfortable but not comfortable enough even by 1950s standards when a steak dinner cost about a dollar. So Marchetti put in his time at the steel plant in the offseason.

"We were working-class people," he said. "Autographs weren't much in demand. When people recognized players, they'd just slap you on the back."[1]

That camaraderie, that attitude of being "one of us" meant that the beat reporters who covered the Colts also had to be regular folks to connect the team with the fans. In other words, the reporters couldn't be impressed by chichi and had to have a built-in BS detector, like the city itself; they had to be folks like Cameron Snyder of the *Baltimore Sun*, who would sometimes practice with the players, or John Steadman who was with the *Baltimore News-Post* at the time and who would one day turn down a World Series assignment to keep his streak of reporting on consecutive pro football games alive.

Although born in West Virginia, Snyder went to high school in the Baltimore area and played football, lacrosse and wrestled at Calvert Hall College, a college-prep school. He then went on to North Carolina State and Drexel University, where he played offensive and defensive tackle before graduating in 1941.

Snyder was good enough to be offered a tryout with the Chicago Bears but World War II and the Army changed those plans. He was drafted and served in an infantry unit in the China-Burma-India Theater of Operations, rising from private to captain before his discharge in 1946.

There was no doubt that Snyder was tough because he was one of the few—perhaps the only—writer who could get away with ribbing legendary quarterback Johnny Unitas, as a story from Tom Callahan's book *The Life and Times of Johnny Unitas* attests:

> Cameron Snyder of *The Baltimore Sun* noticed how reminiscent many of the passages [in a book ghost-written for Unitas] were of newspaper stories Snyder had written or read. Whole columns by John Steadman of the *News-Post* and *Sunday American* appeared to have been redrawn in the first person and incorporated into the narrative....
>
> When next he saw Unitas, Snyder asked dryly, "I got your book and I have only one question. Did you write it?"
>
> "Hell," Unitas said, "I didn't even read it."[2]

Someone who could get away with razzing Unitas could also suit up if the opportunity presented itself, as Hall of Fame defensive lineman Art Donovan tells it: "He [Snyder] was a great fellow. He knew football because he played in college. Sometimes at Colts practice the coaches let 'Toughie' fill in at offensive guard."[3]

But if Snyder was tough, he was also fair and helpful. Susan Reimer remembered a time

Cameron Snyder (courtesy Pro Football Hall of Fame).

when she was assigned to write feature stories for the *Sun* about the Colts: "The great beat writer [Snyder], with the straw hat and his deep growl, his goatee and his twitchy eyebrows, let every player know he was to treat me decently. It was his way of letting me know I had his support in the man's world of the NFL. It is a kindness I will never forget."[4]

Snyder covered the Colts for the *Sun* for parts of four decades before retiring in 1986. In 1982 he joined Steadman (1975) as a recipient of the Dick McCann Memorial Award at the Professional Football Hall of Fame for long and distinguished reporting on professional football for a career that included Super Bowl III and the 1958 championship game. His account of that first overtime title game in the December 29 edition of the paper wasn't poetry, but it included almost all of the journalistic five Ws and an H in addition to capturing the changing mood of the game and the times for the Colts and their fans:

> Six years of sweat and frustration bore fruit today as the Colts stormed 80 yards in thirteen plays to win the National Football League championship, 23 to 17, in a sudden-death playoff with the New York Giants at Yankee Stadium.
> Propelled by John Unitas's passes and Raymond Berry's catches, the Colts forced the game into the first sudden-death extra period in pro history when Steve Myhra place kicked a 20-yard field goal with [seven] seconds left in the regulation time.[5]

Snyder died of lung cancer in January 2010. He was 93. The pallbearers carried his body out of the church to the strains of the Colts fight song.

That's just how Snyder rolled because even at away games he was all about the Colts. Sometimes, when he went to dinner with other beat writers such as Steadman, they'd stop and press the flesh with any fans they might meet along the route from the hotel to the restaurant. And that was fine, up to a point: "He [Steadman] would stop and talk to them for an hour," Snyder recalled. "I'd say, 'Come on, John, let's eat'—but he wouldn't leave until he knew every one of those fans by name."[6]

The connection between team and fans was important for people like Snyder and Steadman because the Colts were the city's link to nascent glamour. People in Baltimore drank beer, as did millions of others in bigger cities; Baltimoreans were proud and so were fans of more successful teams; and the city was mostly blue-collar at a time when the Rust Belt was still shiny. It was way before television made Fell's Point famous for life on the streets and before the Inner Harbor was re-imagined, renewed and revitalized into an urban jewel. The players sported assorted bumps from busted noses and had missing teeth and some wouldn't think twice about tackling any crazy fan who dared to run onto the field where they clearly didn't belong. Star players still had crew-cuts and wore black high-tops even when both were oh-so-out-of-date. It was writers like Snyder and Steadman who spoke to those fans and players and gave the rest of us a peek into their world.

Steadman was born in Baltimore on Valentine's Day in 1927. His father, John Francis Steadman, was Baltimore's deputy fire chief and died of a heart attack at age 49 when his oldest son was 13. Besides his son, John, also surviving was John's mother, Mary, and two siblings, Thomas and Betty. The younger John Steadman lettered in football, basketball and baseball in high school and went on to be a catcher in the Pittsburgh Pirates' system for a year, batting .125.

Although he was a good athlete, Steadman was better at writing about sports and his career spanned more than 50 years, which included every All-America Football Conference and National Football League game involving a Baltimore team from 1947 to December 2000. That love of Charm City football translated to reporting on 719 consecutive games played by the Baltimore Colts and Ravens (except for 1951–52 and 1984–95 when Baltimore didn't have an NFL team). He was so intent on keeping the streak alive that he passed on a World Series game in 1966 to cover a Colts-Bears game October 9 in Wrigley Field. (The Colts lost, 27–17, giving both teams a 2–2 record; meanwhile, the Orioles beat the Los Angeles Dodgers, 1–0, in Memorial Stadium to sweep the series). Ernie Accorsi, former *Baltimore Sun* reporter, public relations manager for the Colts and GM of the Giants remembers that Orioles GM Frank Cashen said, "He's [Steadman] my best friend and he went to the Colts-Bears game!"[7]

John Steadman (courtesy Pro Football Hall of Fame).

Steadman also covered all of the first 34 Super Bowls (always in a suit and tie), up until his death on January 1, 2001. And he did it while also undergoing chemotherapy and radiation treatments for cancer.

"He was Ripken before Ripken," said noted sportswriter Frank Deford, who grew up in Baltimore.[8]

Steadman began at the *Baltimore News-Post* and worked there from 1945 to 1954, then he took some years off to be a front-office guy for the Colts from '55 to '57 (as an assistant GM and publicity director) and he returned to journalism as sports editor of the *News American* in January '58. Steadman was only 30 at the time and was then the youngest sports editor at a big-city newspaper.

"Once you've worked on a newspaper, it's like a man who goes to sea and eternally loves the roll of a ship and where it's going," Deford explained about why Steadman possibly returned to the daily grind of newspapers.[9]

But the work didn't scare Steadman because he wrote six columns a week in the controlled chaos of the third-floor sports office and did two daily radio sports shows on WBAL (at 7:15 a.m. and 6:05 p.m.). The paper folded in 1986 and he moved his beat to *The Baltimore Evening Sun* until 1995 when it shut down. Papers were closed out from underneath him but Steadman survived and worked at the *Sun* until his death in 2001.

What was in those columns and stories he conscientiously churned out? Let Accorsi sum it up: He was "the heart and soul of Baltimore professional football."[10]

Steadman himself said it was always more about the people than the games, and that's why he was a voice for the underdog.

"He knew what to write, and how and when to write it. John was an outstanding journalist, a credit to the profession," said Sam Lacy at the time of Steadman's death. Lacy was then the sports editor of the *Baltimore Afro-American* newspaper.[11]

Steadman had the gift that he could remind people of our shared foibles and grace. He once stood and applauded his priest at Mass for a homily that urged parishioners to live one's faith as an example to others. After the assassination of the Rev. Dr. Martin

Luther King in 1968 Steadman wrote that all of us must look after each other and be our brother's keeper.

Unitas said that Steadman could be counted on to take up any cause that was just. For sports fans there were many. For example, he criticized Colts owner Carroll Rosenbloom ("an evil man") for charging full price for preseason games; he defended a fan for blowing a bugle at the stadium; and he lambasted Robert Irsay—whom Steadman labeled "a drunk who was not responsible for himself"[12]—for taking the Colts to Indianapolis in the early morning hours of March 29, 1984.

And as much as he grieved that the citizens of Baltimore lost its team to Indy, he also grieved that the good people of Cleveland lost their team to Baltimore. It just wasn't ethical for an owner to do such a thing, Steadman believed. So he welcomed the newly named Ravens to town with mixed feelings because he wanted an expansion franchise not an existing one. (It should be noted that when it was announced in 1952 that Baltimore would get a new NFL team Steadman was the first reporter to break the story. He got a $25 bonus and used the money to buy beer and shrimp for the sports staff.)

Where there was logos there was also pathos because Steadman had a devilish sense of humor. On April 6, 1992, when Camden Yards opened, Steadman hired a man to fly a plane over the ballpark with a banner saying "The Babe Says Hi" since Babe Ruth grew up on a street about where center field now sits. But the Secret Service nixed the idea because President Bush 41 would be at the game. Steadman also covered a Colts game from a seat on the bench for a different perspective. He somehow convinced halfback Buddy Young to race against a real colt. And he once came to the paper dressed as a bird watcher because he said he was searching for the real Baltimore Oriole. In 1965 Steadman said he'd eat his column if the Orioles didn't win the American League pennant. They finished 94–68, eight games behind the AL-winning Minnesota Twins, who lost the World Series to the Los Angeles Dodgers, four games to three. So, on October 1, Steadman kept his promise and did indeed eat his words cooked into a steak at the Chesapeake Restaurant.

But maybe one of his most talked-about pieces was when he wrote the game story of the '58 championship game BEFORE the game. "John Steadman has given himself the green light to write the game details even before the kickoff," wrote Bob Wolff in a 1988 *New York Times* article. "This is spooky. John's writing who boots the ball, who returns it, who makes the tackle and where the ball is spotted. The whole game in advance. How can anybody, especially a man of John's reputation, put his neck on the line like that?"[13]

The thing is, Steadman was eerily right about a lot of it: the tying field goal, Alan Ameche's winning touchdown and even the score, 23–17. What he didn't predict but what also happened was that the telecast changed the sport and television forever in America. Football and televised games became an integral part of American life after that game that December day.

He knew so much—apparently even before it happened—that in 1998, when the Colts had a 40th reunion of the '58 title team, Steadman was asked to be master of ceremonies.

"There was an encyclopedia of historical records wrapped up in his brain," said receiver and Hall of Famer Raymond Berry. "His interest was so deep you had to love the guy."[14]

The players as well as the fans just about always appreciated Steadman. Art Donovan recalled the day he met Steadman at training camp at Western Maryland College in 1950:

"It must have been 100 degrees. John came by the bench and put wet towels on my head. I thought, 'Who is this guy? He doesn't know us.' But he did it like he was one of our friends. I'll remember that to the day I die."[15]

Not all good things last forever. Steadman told the world about his cancer in 1999 but put off many treatments so that he could keep The Streak alive. The Streak ended before the man, on December 10, 2000, when he wrote about a 24–3 Ravens win against the visiting Chargers. Steadman passed away on January 1, 2001. He was 73.

It was reported that more than 400 people attended his funeral at St. Jude Shrine in downtown Baltimore.

"All the people of Baltimore loved the man. He stood up for everybody," explained Unitas.[16]

Just two more thoughts, from different fields but focusing on the same profession, sum up what Steadman meant to his craft and his city.

"Despite all his pain and suffering [because of his cancer], John walked away a winner. He lived life on his own terms. He believed in his religion, his family and the newspaper business and never deviated from it," said former Orioles GM Cashen.[17]

And this from former colleague John Eisenberg: "Seldom does a newspaperman rise above the daily muddle and become a landmark, but Steadman did. No business was done, no issue settled, no image finalized until he had weighed in. For 40 years, what he thought about sports in Baltimore mattered more than what anyone else thought.... John Steadman made you proud to be in the newspaper business. If only the rest of us could handle the job so deftly."[18]

NOTES

1. Mike Klingaman, "Save the Date: 1958," *Baltimore Sun*, December 21, 2008.
2. Tom Callahan, *Johnny U: The Life and Times of Johnny Unitas* (New York: Crown, 2006), 7.
3. Mike Klingaman, "Former Sun Sportswriter Cameron Snyder Dies at 93," *Baltimore Sun*, January 30, 2010.
4. Susan Reimer, "A Great Beat Writer Who Also Had a Great Heart," *Baltimore Sun*, February 3, 2010.
5. Cameron Snyder, "Colts Win Championship," *Baltimore Sun*, December 29, 1958.
6. Mike Klingaman, "Steadman's Passion Captured City's Heart," *Baltimore Sun*, January 2, 2001.
7. Harvey Araton, "Accorsi Fashions Salute to Steadman Amid Glory," *Baltimore Sun*, January 17, 2001.
8. Mike Klingaman, "A Baltimore Legend, Champion of Underdogs," *Baltimore Sun*, January 2, 2001.
9. *Ibid.*
10. Ken Rosenthal, "Always on Sunday, Steadman Endures; Even Cancer Fight Hasn't Stopped Streak from '50," *Baltimore Sun*, December 26, 1999.
11. Klingaman, "A Baltimore Legend."
12. Rosenthal.
13. Bob Wolff, "Views of Sport; There Are No Great Teams Anymore ... and No Games to Rival the 'Greatest Ever,'" *New York Times*, December 25, 1988, http://www.nytimes.com/1988/12/25/sports/views-sport-there-are-no-great-teams-anymore, accessed October 31, 2016.
14. Klingaman, "Steadman's Passion Captured City's Heart."
15. *Ibid.*
16. Jay Apperson, "A Monumental Farewell," *Baltimore Sun*, January 6, 2001.
17. Klingaman, "Steadman's Passion Captured City's Heart."
18. John Eisenberg, "A Trusted Conscience Passes, Leaving a Void No One Can Fill," *Baltimore Sun*, January 2, 2001.

Chuck Thompson and Bailey Goss

JOE MARREN

Holy cow! Baseball has compiled Ruthian numbers in any tally of its contributions to American culture, ranging from idioms to songs and comedy routines (*Who, after all, IS on first?*), as well as bloopers and blunders, saints and sinners. It has both stood against and acquiesced to racism, and it has also baffled professors with its infield pop fly rule. (James Joyce supposedly said of his masterpiece, *Ulysses*, that he put so many puzzles into it that it would keep the professors guessing for centuries about what he really meant. The infield pop fly rule has bedeviled umpires and fans since at least 1901; so one century down, numerous ones to come.) Well, let's "go to war, Miss Agnes!"

And then there are people, legends, really, who transcend sports. This story is about that feel-good vibe as one city identified with one announcer who told the fans how the home-town teams were doing in good times and bad. The story begins with baseball and an announcer with bona fides that stretch to the Hall of Fame in Cooperstown. And it includes football and an epic game and how a coin flip determined that Chuck Thompson would call the overtime period of the 1958 NFL title game between his Baltimore Colts and the New York Giants.

There is a parallel here because no announcer is an island. So this chapter is also about the relatively short but still distinguished career of Baltimore's Bailey Goss.

To be honest, it's also partly about beer. So grab a cold one, sit back, and, as Thompson would say, "ain't the beer cold!" in the telling of their stories.

Thompson spent almost six decades broadcasting sports, most of it in Baltimore calling Orioles baseball games (of the International and American League variety), the football Colts (of the ol' All-America Football Conference and then the NFL), baseball's Washington Senators, Baltimore Bullets of the NBA, and Navy football. But he also spent three years in Philadelphia where he was announcing games for the Phillies (National League), Athletics (American League before they moved to Kansas City), Warriors of the NBA (before the move to the Bay Area in '62), and Temple University men's hoops. Along the way he also did NBC's baseball Game of the Week in 1959 and '60. He was chiefly known for his work broadcasting baseball, but he was even better known as the signature voice of much of Baltimore sports.

Fellow sportscaster Ted Patterson called him "the voice of God in Baltimore."[1]

Such a distinguished career led to some pretty heavy-duty accolades, perhaps none better than winning the 17th Ford Frick Award in 1993 and earning a place in the broadcasting wing of the Baseball Hall of Fame.

As Vince Bagli, one of his broadcasting partners for Colts games, said about the honor: "He was a joy to work with. He was the best who ever worked in this area. Other than Brooks Robinson, the best ovation [at an Orioles game] was when they said that Chuck Thompson was going to Cooperstown."[2]

Thompson was born June 10, 1921, in Palmer, Massachusetts. The family lived in Springfield, Massachusetts, until 1927 when they all moved to Reading, Pennsylvania. And although the family domicile in Pennsylvania was about 290 or so miles away from the familiar haunts of Palmer, Thompson was able to go back there to spend summers with an aunt. It was on summer ball fields in New England, and on occasional jaunts 75 or so miles east to the lyric little bandbox of Fenway Park in Boston, that Thompson fell in love with the game.

In junior high and high school when he was back in Reading Thompson did the expected jock things like play on the school basketball, soccer and football teams as well as sandlot baseball. But he also had an artistic side and in 1938, just after his junior year in high school, he started singing with the Joe Lombardo Band, earning $1 a night for singing eight songs and $5 for a New Year's Eve celebration.[3]

Although the job didn't pay much it was an entrée to the rest of his life because on a continuous dare from a local woman he auditioned with WRAW in Reading in 1939. As Thompson explains: "She kept daring me to go to the program director ... for a singing audition and finally I did. But when I did, mainly because I had played ball in high school, the audition developed into a sports broadcast. I'm sure it turned out the right way because this gave me my start."[4]

Working at WRAW was not only the start of Thompson's career—he was in the right place at the right time for some professional breaks that came his way there and elsewhere—but it also played a part in his life and subsequent career. We'll take the second-most influential first: It was at the Reading station that Thompson met Bailey Goss, who would share an announcer's booth with him at WBAL in Baltimore; Thompson would call the games and Goss would chatter and do the beer ads (remember, this story is also about beer, but more on that later). And it was while working in Reading that Thompson married his high school girlfriend, Rose Heffner, on November 15, 1941. They raised three children together until her death from cancer in 1985.

Now about that big break that came his way hinted at the paragraph above: Thompson called a college football game between Reading's own Albright College (by the way, Goss graduated from Albright in 1935) and Carnegie Tech (today's Carnegie Mellon University) that was broadcast on a feed back to Pittsburgh, the home of Carnegie Tech. His work on the game caught the attention of the N.W. Ayer Advertising Agency in Philadelphia, which controlled high school and college broadcasts along the Eastern Seaboard. Thompson credits one of execs there, Les Quailey, with teaching him how to do play-by-play.

No one should believe that things last forever and Thompson left WRAW and its sister station WEEU in early 1942 in a disagreement over his pay, which means that not only wasn't he paid enough but that he was also ready for bigger challenges in a bigger market. And that's exactly what happened because after bouncing around a few weeks Thompson signed on with WIBG in Philadelphia to do staff announcing and twice daily sports programs as well as some college football games. But what man proposes, the Army disposes and Thompson was drafted in October 1943. He served in the 30th Division in Europe and returned home in 1945.

WIBG was waiting for him when he got back home and fate intervened in the person—or, to be more precise, a missing person, specifically the elevator operator at Philly's Shibe Park—during a late season doubleheader in 1946. The regular Phillies announcers, Byrum Saam and Claude Haring, were on the field between games against the New York Giants for "Radio Appreciation Day." When the hoopla ended they headed back to the announcing booth (or so they thought, but without the elevator operator and his key, well ... c'est la vie).

"The only way to the booth was by elevator and the operator wasn't there when the activity on the field was over," Thompson recalled. "The next thing I knew … I just started talking."[5]

"With Saam and Haring still absent, I tried to describe the game—without a score-card, lineup, or anything," Thompson said.[6] By the time the regulars got back to the booth it was the bottom of the first inning.

Quailey redux: Good ol' friend Quailey was also in the booth and persuaded the vets to work with Thompson. As he put it much later: "This impromptu audition led to me being added to the broadcast team in 1947 for the Phillies' and A's home games. I've wondered many times over the years what would have happened had the elevator man been on hand to bring Saam and Haring back on time. Would I have wound up in play-by-play? Would I have wound up in baseball?"[7] It's a moot point because "the audition" worked and Thompson did two innings of play-by-play for Phillies and A's home games in the 1947 and '48 seasons.

It also directly led to 47 years calling sporting events, all but the first three in Baltimore, which is where the next twist in the Thompson story comes in. Simply put, Saam was the announcer in Philly and wasn't going anywhere. Enter Quailey. Again. Quailey arranged an audition for Thompson in Baltimore in 1949 and the rest is history, except for the part about the beer.

OK now, for the thirsty readers who have patiently waited this long, here is where the beer comes into the story. The Gunther Brewing Co. owned the rights to broadcast the IL Orioles and Thompson was hired to call the Orioles' home games, recreate the away games for the radio audience, and also do the announcing for the AAFC Colts. But in 1954, when the St. Louis Browns moved to Baltimore and were re-christened the AL's Orioles, another brewery—the National Bohemian Brewing Co. ("Natty Boh")—owned the rights and Thompson would soon be out of a job because of his previous connections with Gunther. Although Thompson was able to work games in 1955 with broadcaster Ernie Harwell on WCBM-AM and WMAR-TV, the deal didn't last long because of the competing breweries.

"It was made more frustrating because the ballclub and the fans wanted me to do the games and so did Bailey Goss, who was the color man," Thompson wrote in his book, *Ain't the Beer Cold*.[8]

So Thompson just drove 40 miles down the road to broadcast the Washington Senators from 1957 to '60 on WWDC-AM and WTOP-TV. He also did the NFL's Saturday night game on the old DuMont TV network. Baltimore came to its senses and Thompson finally got to broadcast Orioles games on WBAL-AM and WJZ-TV in 1962, which is where he stayed until he retired (in 1987 for the first time before coming back in 1991 to work part-time on Orioles broadcasts; after the 2000 season he no longer did play-by-play due to failing eyesight but instead did occasional commentary).

One of his trademark phrases at Orioles games when the hits and runs were piling up for the good guys was "Ain't the beer cold!" He borrowed the phrase from an enthusiastic spotter who worked Colts games with him, but he stopped using the phrase in the 1970s out of respect for the views of listeners who were teetotalers and objected to it.

Another phrase, "Go to war, Miss Agnes!" was also retired as the Vietnam War dragged on before the last American combat soldier was brought home in 1973.

"It was something I could no longer justify because of the mounting American casualties," Thompson wrote in *Ain't the Beer Cold*.[9] According to U.S. government data there were 58,220 American troops who died in Indochina (including Vietnam, Laos and Cambodia), and 1,014 of them were from Maryland.

Thompson's life was more than buzzwords, beer and baseball. (But even so, what a legacy!) And this is a book about football, after all. He called Colts games on CBS-TV in the 1950s and '60s, and also alongside Vince Bagli on WCBM Radio from 1973 until the Colts left town under cover of darkness in 1984.

NBC broadcast the NFL's championship game on December 28, 1958. Thompson worked the game with Chris Schenkel. Broadcasts then weren't as formatted or marketed as they are today and so Thompson and Schenkel flipped a coin to see who would do the play-by-play in which half. Schenkel won the toss and said he would call the second half, leaving the first—and any overtime—to Thompson.

"The sudden-death game, witnessed by some 50 million people on television, probably did more to establish the NFL as a TV property than any other game previously played," Thompson wrote in *Ain't the Beer Cold.*[10]

As fulfilling as life was for Thompson in the booth, the breaks didn't always come his way outside the booth. His wife, Rose, died in 1985. But Thompson eventually met and married (in 1988) his second wife, a widow named Betty Kaplan. Thompson wrote that it was Betty who got him back into church where he used that professional and pol-

From left: Chuck Thompson, Bailey Goss, Ernie Harwell, unknown (courtesy Ernie Harwell Sports Collection, Detroit Public Library).

ished voice that called so many balls, strikes and touchdowns to call out numbers at St. Leo's Roman Catholic Church bingo games.

Thompson died after a stroke on March 6, 2005. He was 83.

The National Sportscasters and Sportswriters Association named Thompson its Maryland Sportscaster of the Year every year from 1959 to 1966. In January 2009 the American Sportscasters Association ranked him 34th on its list of the Top 50 Sportscasters of All Time.

As was already pointed out a lot of career points intersected between Thompson and Bailey Goss. Their careers were parallel, not perpendicular, but some further mention of Goss here will give context to both their lives. And be warned: There's beer involved.

Goss was born in Sunbury, Pennsylvania, on the banks of the Susquehanna River practically in the middle of the state. He was an outstanding athlete in high school and college. After getting his start in radio in Reading, Pennsylvania, he replaced Garry Moore (who had a television show on CBS in the 1950s and '60s) on WBAL in Baltimore. Goss also appeared with Baltimore's Jim McKay on sports programs before McKay went on to the network.

All those brushes with noted people aside, let's assume that the intersections between Thompson and Goss can be drawn out. With all due respect to Pythagoras we don't care about the hypotenuse or the sides of any triangles that correspond to the area of an adjoining square. No, we care about social interactions and the ol' tried and tested a-squared plus b-squared equals c-squared will work its inherent magic and logic with sports broadcasters because accomplishments-squared plus broadcasting-squared equals career-squared. Thompson's and Goss' accomplishments and careers spent broadcasting ball games from a booth fits Pythagoras' formula. And, to be honest, the beer probably helped.

Why? Here's why: It has already been mentioned that the two announcers worked together at WRAW in Reading and that Goss was an alum of Albright College (Class of 1935), and broadcasting a college football game from Albright was one of several lucky breaks for Thompson. When Goss got to Baltimore in 1942 he worked athletic contests sponsored by National Bohemian Brewing, which would include baseball, football, bowling, wrestling and golf. "Mr. Boh" (a one-eyed character that was the trademark of the brewery) was a fixture on the afternoon "Bailey Goss Show" on Channel 2 in town.

Goss' life ended in May 1962 due to injuries sustained in a car accident. He was 49.

NOTES

1. Matt Bohn, "Chuck Thompson," http://sabr.org/bioproj/person/5e29b015, accessed May 3, 2017.
2. Ed Waldman, "Chuck Thompson, Voice of the Baltimore Orioles, Dies," http://www.americansportscastersonline.com/thompsonmemoriam.html, accessed May 3, 2017.
3. *Ibid.*
4. Bohn.
5. Jim Henneman, "Two for the Hall: Chuck Thompson Joins Broadcast Legends After Having a Ball for Many Ears," http://www.baltimoresun.com/sports/bal-thompson080193-story.html, accessed May 3, 2017.
6. Bohn.
7. *Ibid.*
8. *Ibid.*
9. *Ibid.*
10. Bohn.

Sam Lacy

ED GRUVER

He was small and wiry, but in many respects Sam Lacy was as much a giant of a man in the worlds of sports and civil rights as the icons he covered during his nine decades as a sportswriter, columnist, reporter, editor and radio/television commentator.

Through his work Lacy provided a voice for black athletes and fans across the country. He grew to become a persuasive figure for civil rights and in the movement to racially integrate sports. In 1948 he was the first black member of the Baseball Writers Association of America (BBWAA) and in 1997 the BBWAA honored him with the J.G. Taylor Spink Award for outstanding writing. One year later he was inducted in the writers' and broadcasters' wing of the Baseball Hall of Fame.[1]

Lacy helped influence generations of sportswriters, serving as a role model for contemporaries Roger Kahn and Shirley Povich and writers who followed, like William Rhoden. He was also a great role model for his family; his son, Tim, who followed in his father's footsteps and became a columnist for the *Afro-American* newspapers, a group of weeklies based in Baltimore.

Tim told writer Alex Holt in a 2015 interview that he keeps a picture of his father nearby when he's writing and will recall his dad telling him as he often did when their desks were just a few feet apart in the *Afro-American* offices, "Uh-uh-uh, no, no, no, you don't want to go that way, take [the story] in another direction."

"The best part of it is we were always good friends," Tim told Holt. "He was my best bud."

Tim said that while writing about sports was his father's job, the part he liked least about it was the traveling that took him away from his home and family. What his father did enjoy, Tim said, was seeing his work come to fruition. "He enjoyed seeing barriers broken down."[2]

Lacy also served as a father figure for many of the black athletes he covered. Baltimore Colts Hall of Fame offensive tackle Jim Parker, who starred for the Colts in their 1958 and '59 championship seasons, told Sam's son Tim Lacy in 2005 that Sam was the "saving grace for a lot of black ballplayers. We needed somebody to be a father figure or mother figure to kind of give us a little guidance under the surface because it was a rough life for that."[3]

Lenny Moore, a star running

Sam Lacy (courtesy National Baseball Hall of Fame and Museum).

back for the Colts' title teams in 1958 and '59, said, "Every African-American athlete owes Sam Lacy a debt of gratitude."[4]

Rhoden, a *New York Times* sportswriter, said Lacy's mission was "breaking down those hardcore barriers of segregation."[5] In his football coverage, that meant fighting for the end of segregation on the "lily white" Redskins and pushing Colts management on such issues as unequal accommodations on the road and the lack of black coaches.

As early as 1949 Lacy was telling his readers he wouldn't let them forget "for one moment during the coming fall that every other club in the All-America Conference [other than the Colts] has at least one colored player on its roster." As late as 1972 he was chiding Baltimore's pro sports franchises for a lack of blacks in front offices.

Moore said he knew Lacy faced death threats for his bold stance on race relations, he knew that Lacy confronted the Ku Klux Klan in person, had a cross burned on his lawn and faced segregation in the press box, hotels and restaurants.

"His life was on the line just by being visible," the Colts' Hall of Famer told writer Mike Klingaman. "Guys like Sam banged on doors and fought the fight that made it possible for guys like me to play for the Colts—and with each generation, that door cracked a little more."

Samuel Harold "Sam" Lacy was born October 23, 1903, in Mystic, Connecticut, to law firm researcher Samuel Erskine Lacy and Rose Lacy, a full-blooded Shinnecock Native American. Small in stature, he had the sharp, distinctive facial features of his mother. Lacy's paternal grandfather, Henry Erskine Lacy, was the first black detective in the Washington, D.C., police department.[6]

The Lacy family moved to Washington, D.C., when Sam was young and his father became a fan of the Washington Senators baseball team. Young Sam likewise developed an interest in baseball and because his family home was located at 13th and U streets just five blocks from the Senators' Griffith Stadium, he began spending much of his spare time at the ballpark. A precocious youth, Sam soon began running errands for ballplayers and shagged fly balls during batting practice at Griffith Stadium for the Senators and their co-tenant and Negro League counterpart, the Homestead Grays.

As a youth Lacy saw firsthand how pervasive racism was when he witnessed his father being spat upon by a ballplayer during the annual Opening Day parade of players. He recalled how his father, who was then 79 years old, had lined up for hours along with other fans to await the arrival of the athletes. As he watched his aging father cheering on the players, Lacy said one of the white athletes spit in his father's face. Lacy's father was so hurt by the insult he vowed to never again attend a game and for the remaining years of his life never did.[7]

Young Sam continued to work at Griffith Stadium as a food vendor, selling peanuts and popcorn in the Jim Crow segregated seating section in right field. He was a golf caddy and caddied for Britain's "Long" Jim Barnes at the 1921 United States Open held at the nearby Columbia Country Club. Barnes went on to win the Open. Lacy also did odd jobs, including operating an elevator and working as a chauffeur, although he had never before driven a car.

Lacy was athletic, competing in football, baseball and basketball at Armstrong Technical School in Washington. Following graduation he enrolled at Howard University and earned a bachelor's degree in education. While at Howard University, Lacy began covering sports on a part-time basis for the *Washington Tribune*, an African American newspaper. He worked under the tutelage of editor Lewis Lautier.

with a great deal of racism, Robinson was named Major League Baseball Rookie of the Year in '47 and National League MVP in 1949.

Lacy was among those who covered Robinson's rocky road to success in the major leagues. He was with Robinson in Cuba for winter baseball, and in Daytona Beach, Florida, for Dodgers spring training games. Lacy saw firsthand the racism Robinson endured and was subjected to it as well. He and Robinson dined at segregated restaurants and slept in "blacks only" boarding houses. Lacy himself was barred from press boxes in major league ballparks. White sportswriters like New York's Dick Young stood up for him, they joined Lacy in reporting from a press box roof in New Orleans during a minor league game, and their actions helped force the integration of big league press boxes. Rickey would tell Lacy he could report from the Dodgers' dugout. Lacy was also denied rooms in white-only hotels and had a cross burned by the Ku Klux Klan on the lawn of his rooming house down South.

Tim Lacy told the *Baltimore Sun* in 2013 he was angered over the lack of inclusion of his father's role in the movie *42* that was released that year and told the story of Robinson breaking baseball's color barrier.

"I think it's a travesty," Tim Lacy told the *Sun*. "Because if you know the story [Sam Lacy] was instrumental in the effort to get that done."[15]

Lacy was indeed instrumental in Robinson's integrating major league baseball in 1947 and two years later Lacy was there for the first interracial college football game ever played in Maryland when all-white Trenton (NJ) College visited a black college, Maryland State.

Lacy pushed for more color barriers to be broken down. He sought equal pay for black athletes and the end of segregated accommodations on team road trips; the inclusion of blacks in the Baseball Hall of Fame; more black broadcasters and umpires; and, in the NFL, black coaches. He also spurred Washington Redskins owner George Preston Marshall to end the quota limiting black players on the NFL club's roster.

Fellow Baltimore sports writer John Steadman of the *Sun* noted in a 1999 article that Lacy took up the issue of why there were few black quarterbacks and coaches in the NFL. By the turn of the century Lacy was elated the number of black players had increased from 18.8 percent of the rosters in 1962 to 70 percent. Pro football, Steadman noted, was a far cry from 1946, when the only blacks were Woody Strode and Kenny Washington with the Los Angeles Rams and Marion Motley and Bill Willis with the Cleveland Browns.

In 1968, Lacy joined WBAL-TV as a sports commentator, a position he held for the next eight years. He remained with the *Afro-American* almost 60 years. In 1999 Lacy collaborated with colleague Moses Newsom on an autobiography titled *Fighting for Fairness: The Life Story of Hall of Fame Sportswriter Sam Lacy*. In it he detailed his relations with the Colts and Redskins regarding the lack of black athletes, coaches and front office personnel in pro football. While Lacy said he questioned the leadership of the Redskins he had nothing but admiration for the Colts when Carroll Rosenbloom was the owner and Don Kellett the general manager. He rated Rosenbloom's Colts as being among the NFL's best in race relations.

Lacy said it was no surprise when Rosenbloom announced in 1963 the Colts would not be returning to Western Maryland College for preseason practice if "racial bars which exist in the town of Westminster and the adjacent community have not been completely eliminated." Rosenbloom said the Colts could no longer condone the indignities suffered by black athletes Moore, Parker, et al., their families and friends. Lacy said in his autobiography he wrote about the Colts "as much with my heart as with my typewriter." In 1973 he underwent ulcer surgery but continued to keep Colts management on its collective toes, questioning in print their decision to keep players like Lydell Mitchell and Roy Hilton on the bench while playing what Lacy declared was "inferior white players."[16]

Lacy died of heart and kidney failure at age 99 on May 8, 2003, just days after writing his final column for the *Afro-American*. He had spurned more lucrative offers to stay at the black newspaper and in 1998 he explained his reason why: "No other paper in the country would have given me the kind of license. I've made my own decisions. I cover everything that I want to. I sacrificed a few dollars, true, but I lived a comfortable life. I get paid enough to be satisfied. I don't expect to die rich."[17]

Lacy died at Washington Hospital Center in Washington, D.C. He had checked in a week earlier due to a loss of appetite. His survivors included a son, Samuel (Tim) Lacy and a daughter, Michaelyn Lacy, four grandchildren and five great-grandchildren.[18]

Lacy's career achievements and awards were extensive. Yet as Moore noted following Lacy's passing, "Every other African-American athlete needs to pay homage to this man here, but many don't even know who he is. Fighting for fairness, that's what Sam was about. Sam was in the trench, in the trenches with Jackie Robinson."[19]

In the trenches with Jackie and with black athletes ranging from neighborhood, high school and college kids to professional superstars Jesse Owens, Josh Gibson and Tiger Woods; Joe Louis, Arthur Ashe, Wilma Rudolph and many others.

"When I came to Baltimore in 1956 from Penn State University, there were a lot of things going on in the sports world that people knew about," Moore said at Lacy's memorial service. "There are plenty of athletes that need to stand in honor of this man. There are no words to describe the inner pain that one goes through when you are segregated, when you are chastised. This man here, over the periods of time, made it possible for a guy like me to be presented to the Pro Football Hall of Fame."

Looking down upon the casket from the podium at Mount Zion Baptist Church, Moore spoke for himself and many others when he said simply, "Thank you, Sam."[20]

They were just three words, but they spoke volumes.

Notes

1. Galus Chamberlain, greatblackheroes.com, December 23, 2013.
2. Alex, Holt, *Still No Cheering in the Press Box*, 2015.
3. Derrill Holly, *Midland Daily News*, May 15, 2003.
4. *Ibid.*
5. *Ibid.*
6. Tom Prendergast and Michael Watkins, "Sam Lacy," *Contemporary Black Biography* 54 (2006).
7. Chamberlain.
8. "African-American Registry," aaregistry.org.
9. Frank Litsky, "Sam Lacy, 99, Fought Racism as Sportswriter," *New York Times*, May 12, 2003.
10. Prendergast and Watkins.
11. *Ibid.*
12. Holt.
13. Chamberlain.
14. *Ibid.*
15. Kevin Cowherd, "Sam Lacy's Son Upset by Snub of Dad in '42,'" *Baltimore Sun*, April 15, 2013.
16. Sam Lacy with Moses J. Newson, *Fighting For Fairness: The Life Story of Hall of Fame Sportswriter Sam Lacy* (Centreville, MD: Tidewater, 2009), 114.

17. Prendergast and Watkins.

18. Litsky.

19. Mike Preston, "Lacy Was a Grand Champion for Biggest of Sports' Causes," *Baltimore Sun*, May 17, 2003.

20. *Ibid.*

Bob Wolff

John Vorperian

In 2012, Bob Wolff was listed by the Guinness Book of World Records in two prime categories: longest career as a broadcaster and as the longest-running sportscaster. Enshrined in the National Baseball Hall of Fame, the National Basketball Hall of Fame, the National Sportscasters and Sportswriters Hall of Fame, the Madison Square Garden Walk of Fame and the Long Island Journalism Hall of Fame, he won countless Emmy Awards and the TV Ace Award.

Wolff earned the distinction of being the only person to call the play-by-play of all four major pro sports championships, a World Series, an NBA final, a Stanley Cup final and a Super Bowl. Over the course of a nine decade career, mostly at Madison Square Garden, Wolff called the New York Knicks for 27 years, the New York Rangers for 20 years, the Holiday Festival for 29 years, and the National Invitational Basketball Tournament (NIT) for 25 years.

The Sigma Nu fraternity member broadcast credits also include the Millrose Games for 32 years, the National Horse Show for 32 years, the Westminster Kennel Club Dog Show for 33 years, plus Virginia Slims tennis, Golden Gloves, gymnastics, surfing, college hockey, golf, Rose Bowls, Gator Bowls, Sugar Bowls and college basketball tournaments. He once said, "If you added all the time up, I've spent about seven days of my life standing for the national anthem."[1] As the Baltimore Colts' radio voice he was there for "The Greatest Game Ever Played" the 1958 NFL championship overtime win against the New York Giants.

Robert Alfred Wolff was born on November 29, 1920, in New York, New York, to Richard and Estelle (nee Cohn) Wolff. Richard was a mechanical engineer and Estelle, a homemaker. The family resided in Woodmere, New York. Wolff attended Woodmere Academy where the thin-framed, speedy, quick-handed youngster displayed solid athletic talent on the school football, basketball and baseball teams.

His academy football exploits made news-

Bob Wolff (courtesy National Baseball Hall of Fame and Museum).

paper headlines. In his senior year he was named All-State, but baseball was his true passion. Wolff credited his high school baseball coach "Pop" LaRue for taking personal time hitting fly balls and throwing extra batting practice to him which helped bolster his playing skills. The *New York World-Telegram and Sun* assessed the suburban New York teenager as a top baseball prospect. Why not? In his final year he had a .583 batting average and possessed speed, range and a strong throwing arm.

In 1939, the 150-pound athlete arrived at Duke University. He selected Duke because at the time the school had sent more players to the pros than any other college. Also managing the Blue Devils was Jack Coombs a former Philadelphia Athletic pitcher. In order to pay for college, Wolff worked a number of on-campus jobs. He juggled those chores along with attending classes and baseball practice. But the jobs were dull. This was the era of the Big Bands and radio was king.

Wolff approached WDNC a CBS radio station in Durham with a proposal. Duke had no radio department or campus radio station. Guided by the notion "selling an idea you control," a principle he repeatedly employed throughout his lengthy broadcasting career, the 19-year-old offered the following arrangement to WDNC management. He would write, produce, and announce a sports program that would appeal to the Duke University community. He'd also secure sponsors that wanted to sell products and services to Duke students. Immediately getting a yes from WDNC brass he then went to Duke's PR department. There he confirmed his suspicions that their press releases got newspaper but not radio coverage. Wolff guaranteed Blue Devil flacks he could get their news releases onto the airwaves. They agreed. Wolff now had a radio deal and content for broadcast.

During his freshman baseball season, he broke an ankle in a rundown play during a ball game. His athletic career had been halted. Wolff had his sports radio program, but with the additional time and diamond game background, he was now asked by WDNC to announce the remainder of the Duke's baseball games, which he did. Furthermore he executed another media arrangement with a 50–50 profit split with a local theater owner. Wolff would broadcast a live music show entitled *Duke Parade* from the Durham movie house venue.

Upon graduation in 1942, the Phi Beta Kappa alum successfully applied for a commission in the Naval reserves as a supply officer. Accepted as an Ensign, he passed the physical and was sent to Harvard Business School to be trained in accounting and logistics. He worked hard to achieve the top mark of A in all his courses. Dispatched to Camp Peary, in Virginia, he was assigned with the 11th Special Seabees Battalion. There he encountered a Navy nurse. Wolff said, "The big news ... was the arrival of a large group of Navy nurses.... As I looked around, my eyes spotted a beautiful brunette—Jane Louise Hoy—and I was instantly spellbound.... At that moment I knew she was the one."[2] He called upon her and they dated steadily. Unfortunately, he got orders to be sent overseas but Jane agreed she would wait for him to return stateside.

The 11th Special Battalion was assigned to the Solomon Islands in the Pacific. Deposited on an isle named Banika they were given the mission of building a complete base with a landing strip, commissary, ship's store, and medical facilities.

As a result of his experience in the Solomons, Wolff was ordered back to Washington, D.C., to revamp Navy supply regulations to incorporate advance base procedures. Lieutenant Wolff's new assignment included writing new training materials and instructional movies.

On May 5, 1945, Wolff and Jane Louise Hoy were married at the Navy Hospital

Chapel in Bethesda, MD. In 1946 he returned to the civilian work force and became the sports director for Washington, D.C.'s WINX radio.

Also in '46, the 26-year-old racked up a number of District of Columbia media firsts. Wolff became the first television sportscaster in the Nation's capital for WTTG-TV. He was the Washington Capitols' first telecaster for their inaugural 1946–47 season in the Basketball Association of America. The team was coached by Red Auerbach. The professional league later altered its name to the National Basketball Association (today's NBA).

In 1947, Wolff was hired as the Washington Senators first TV play-by-play announcer. Television sets in the District numbered less than a thousand and the Wolffs did not own one. Jane had to go to an appliance store to watch Bob's telecasts. The Senators originated in 1901. Four years later in 1905, it became vogue to use "Nationals" as the major league club's nickname. Either moniker was correct. Wolff kept such in mind with his announcing and emphasized the appropriate nickname when either Senate Beer or National Brewing Company was the corporate sponsor for the ball club.

Lowly Washington was clearly a second division team. Wolff added a sports TV program *The Washington Nationals Show* using players, the coaches or manager as guests and ran films of old-time stars like Hall-of-Famer Walter Johnson. The front-office loved the program—as it helped boost the team's ticket sales. With Wolff on ukulele, he organized some players into a singing group called the *Singing Senators*. He had them perform on-camera during rain delays. They even appeared nationally on NBC-TV's morning show hosted by Dave Garroway.

"The team may be losing but the broadcast should be winning."[3] Wolff wrote that principle in his 2011 *Guide to Sportscasting*. He came to the ballpark each day "prepared to tell updated human-interest player stories, discuss baseball topics, render opinions, and intersperse some humorous anecdotes so that the audience and I could share some entertaining moments together regardless who won or lost."[4] He received a mountain of fan letters. One follower wrote, "I want to commend you for the excellent manner … you broadcast Senators baseball games. You have the faculty of effectively describing the various plays … which enables the listener to clearly understand what is going on in the field of play."[5] The missive was signed "J. Edgar Hoover, Director, Federal Bureau of Investigation."

Wolff signed with New York's WPIX-TV to do Madison Square Garden sporting events for the 1954–55 season. From October into December he would handle three events a week, and then from January 1 to mid–March the number would be bumped up to four weekly happenings. Also he would continue his WWDC radio nightly commentary. He was also in the booth for pro football telecasts of the Washington Redskins over the ABC-TV network. His relationship with MSG lasted into 2016.

In 1956 Wolff was selected to be a World Series radio broadcaster for the Mutual Broadcast System and Armed Forces radio. He was heard nationwide and around the globe broadcasting Yankee Don Larsen's perfect game, the first in Series history. Wolff also was on NBC radio for play-by-play for the 1958 and 1961 World Series.

On Memorial Day 1957 between games of a double-header against the Yankees at Griffith Stadium (Washington, D.C.) Wolff selected a seemingly average fan out of the stands to interview for WWDC-radio. He recalled the exchange in his 1996 memoir *It's Not Who Won or Lost the Game—It's How You Sold the Beer:*

"Are you originally from Washington, sir?"

"No, I'm a Californian. I was and still am."

"Have you done much traveling around the country?"

"I've been in most of the 48 states at one time Or another. And I've also traveled a bit abroad in the last few years."

"What sort of work do you do, sir?"

"I work for the government."

"Oh?"

"My boss is President Eisenhower. I'm the vice president."

"Ladies and gentlemen, our guest has been Vice President Richard Nixon."[6]

The creative segment received warm and favorable press coverage.

In addition to Larsen's Perfect Game, Wolff's other historic call at Yankee Stadium was on December 28, 1958. Calling the NFL Title contest for the Colts, Wolff in his usual comprehensive preparation mode came across a startling piece of information as he was going over his last minute notes. On the journey up to New York Wolff came across an item for his notes and commented to his statistician, then college-age assistant Maury Povich, now famed TV personality, that "the whole game in advance? How can anybody, especially a man of John's reputation, put his neck on the line like that?"[7] *Baltimore News-Post* reporter John Steadman had written the game's play-by-play 24 hours before kickoff.

A total of 64,185 football fanatics were in attendance as the Colts knotted the score in the fourth quarter and took the game onto overtime and won 23–17. Wolff recalled, "I was limp at the end of the broadcast. The emotion was overwhelming."[8] The game's importance propelled the NFL onto a higher ranking. As Wolff noted, "Televised NFL football moved from being a game in America to a way of life."[9]

In Baltimore the city showed overwhelming love for the Colts. Thirty thousand fans were on hand to greet them at the airport. Wolff's broadcast sponsor National Brewing Company put out a highlight record as a promotion that aired on the radio waves every hour. Ten thousand discs were gone in a single day. As Wolff remembered, "Every jukebox in town had my call blaring. 'The Colts are the World Champions—Ameche scores!'"[10]

Wolff posed in his memoir that John Steadman had the vision of the game correctly assessed, including the Colts tying in the fourth quarter, Ameche scoring for the win and the final totals 23–17.

Wolff stayed with the Washington baseball franchise into the 1961 season, the Senators first year in Minnesota as the newly christened Twins.

Some other professional teams for which Wolff was the regional voice for were the Baltimore Colts, Cleveland Browns, and Washington Redskins of the NFL, the Detroit Pistons, and New York Knickerbockers of the NBA, and the Tampa Bay Rowdies of the initial NASL. For many years, the roving sportscaster averaged over 250 play-by-plays plus pre and post-game shows as well as nightly commentaries per year.

In the early 1960s he was the play-by-play announcer for NBC's *Game of the Week* teaming up with former St. Louis Cardinal and Pittsburgh Pirate catcher Joe Garagiola.

Over the course of time Wolff lessened his DC ties and firmed up his New York presence. In 1986 he became News 12 Long Island's inaugural sports director and sports anchor. He also ventured back to college. He taught communications studies as a professor at both Pace University and St. John's University.

In April 2013 he donated some 1,400 video and audio recordings representing more than 70 years of his broadcasts and interviews to the Library of Congress. That content included talks with legends like Babe Ruth, Ty Cobb, Ted Williams, Jackie Robinson, Joe DiMaggio, Joe Louis and Jim Thorpe.

Curt Smith, a historian of broadcasting commented Wolff had a voice that was "erudite but not unapproachable."[11] Smith further noted, Wolff had "a sense of humor—and he was always honest. There was no phony baloney with Bob Wolff."[12]

Wolff once said of his career, "I felt the one thing that gave me longevity was coming up with angles, creative points, story lines. I approached every sport with the soul of a sportswriter."[13]

Wolff died on July 15, 2017, at his home in South Nyack, New York, at the age of 96. He was survived by his wife, Jane, sons Dr. Rob Wolff; Rick Wolff; daughter Margy Jane Clark; nine grandchildren; and 11 great-grandchildren.

NOTES

1. "Bob Wolff, Sports Broadcaster, Dies at 96; 78-Year Career Included '56 Perfect Game," *New York Times,* July 17, 2017.
2. Bob Wolff, *Bob Wolff's Complete Guide To Sportscasting* (New York: Skyhorse, 2011), 46.
3. *Ibid.,* 298.
4. *Ibid.*
5. *Ibid.,* 300.
6. Bob Wolff, *It's Not Who Won or Lost the Game: It's How You Sold the Beer* (South Bend, IL: Diamond Communications, 1996), 51–54; "Bob Wolff, Sports Broadcaster, Dies at 96; 78-Year Career Included '56 Perfect Game."
7. *Ibid.,* 16.
8. *Ibid.,* 19.
9. *Ibid.*
10. *Ibid.*
11. "Bob Wolff, Sports Broadcaster, Dies at 96; 78-Year Career Included '56 Perfect Game."
12. *Ibid.*
13. *Ibid.*

REFERENCES

Bowden, Mark. *The Best Game Ever.* New York: Atlantic Monthly Press, 2008.
"50-yard Line." *1952 Maryland Media Guide.*
Gifford, Frank, with Peter Richmond. *The Glory Game.* New York: HarperCollins, 2008.
http://baseballhall.org/discover/awards/ford-c-frick/bob-wolff.
http://en.wikipedia.org/wiki/Bob_Wolff.
http://lipulse.com/2014/07/22/legendary-sportscaster-bob-wolff-makes-guinness-book-of-world-records/.
http://longisland.news.12.com/news-team/bob-wolff-1.4084431.
http://usatoday30.usatoday.com/sports/baseball/2011–06-23-bob-wolff-don-larsen_n.htm.
http://www.foxsports.com/mlb/story/vin-scully-bob-wolff-remain-voices-for-the-ages-091916.
http://www.nytimes.com/2010/11/30/sports/30sandomir.htm?_r=0.
http://www.rocklandtimes.com/2016/11/08celebrities-of-rockland-a-perfect-day-with-hall-of-famer-bob-wolff/.
Wolff, Bob. Telephone interview with author. December 13, 2016.
www.americansportcastersonline.com/bob_wolff_birthday.html.
www.baseballbytheletters.com/2010/07/12/broadcaster-bob-wolff-senators-bp-pitcher-2/.
www.latinosports.com/broadcaster-bob-wolff-honored-yankee-stadium/.
www.newsday.com/sports/media/for-announcer-bob-wolff-it-s-perfect
www.staatalent.com/Headlines/09/06/04wolff.htm.
www.theinfolist.com/php/SummaryGet.php?FindGo=Bob%20Wolff.

About the Contributors

Joshua M. **Anderson** is the president of the Chess Journalists of America. He has written articles for both chess and football publications and is working on a biography of the Byrne brothers, chess players who were contemporaries of Bobby Fischer's.

George **Bozeka** is a retired attorney living in Akron, Ohio. He edited *The 1966 Green Bay Packers* (2016), the first book in the Professional Football Researchers Association's (PFRA) Great Teams in Pro Football History series published by McFarland. He is the author of a number of articles published in the PFRA's *The Coffin Corner*.

Denis M. **Crawford** of Boardman, Ohio, is a freelance writer who has written articles for Bucpower.com and *The Coffin Corner*. He is the author of three books: *McKay's Men: The Story of the 1979 Tampa Bay Buccaneers*, *Hugh Culverhouse and the Tampa Bay Buccaneers*, and *All the Fun Life Would Allow: The Life of Johnny F. Bassett*.

Lee **Elder** is the secretary and media coordinator for the PFRA and has written several articles for *The Coffin Corner*. A former sportswriter and broadcaster, he is a member of the Imperial Valley High School Football Coaches Association Hall of Fame. He lives in Tallmadge, Ohio, where he is a public relations representative.

Ron **Fitch** is an e-learning and instructional technology professional at the University of Minnesota–Twin Cities. He has been a member of the PFRA since 2014.

Mark L. **Ford** is the executive director of the PFRA and the author of *A History of NFL Preseason and Exhibition Games*, a two-volume set covering the years 1960 to 2013. He is a lawyer in Harlan, Kentucky.

Michael **Frank** is a pension actuary and longtime member of PFRA who has seen NFL games in every stadium and visited Johnny Unitas' grave.

Patrick **Gallivan** is a freelance writer living in San Antonio. He is the author of numerous articles in *The Coffin Corner* and is working on a book covering the significant historical changes in the country and professional football during the 1960s.

Bert **Gambini** is a news content manager for the University at Buffalo. He worked for more than two decades in Buffalo radio, including 18 years as a program host on NPR member station WBFO. He is a frequent contributor to *The Coffin Corner*.

Neal **Golden**, a high school teacher of mathematics and computer science since 1963, wrote the first high school computer programming textbook published in the United States (1975). He publishes a football e-zine on his website, goldenrankings.com, from his home in New Orleans.

Rick **Gonsalves** is a retired high school teacher and community service director. He runs the Cape Ann Kicking Academy in Gloucester, Massachusetts, where he has been coaching placekickers and punters since 1970, and is the author of the books *Specialty Teams* and *Placekicking in the NFL: A History and Analysis*.

Ed **Gruver** is an award-winning writer and researcher living in Lancaster, Pennsylvania. He is the author of six books, four on football, including *The Ice Bowl, From Baltimore to Broadway,* and *The American Football League.* He was also a contributing writer to *Total Football I* and *Total Football II.* He has been a member of the PFRA since 1992.

Simon **Herrera** is a researcher, freelance writer and organizer specializing in early 1900s pro football. He maintains a website on the Rock Island, Illinois, Independents (NFL, 1920–25), and in 2015 he co-organized an annual living-history football game in Rock Island featuring replica equipment and a mix of 1920s and modern flag football rules.

Matthew **Keddie** joined the PFRA in 2015. He serves on the Hall of Very Good Committee and has contributed relevant works.

David **Krell** is a television news producer, attorney, and author. His 2015 book *Our Bums: The Brooklyn Dodgers in History, Memory and Popular Culture* received an honorable mention in the Society for American Baseball Research's Ron Gabriel Award contest.

Bill **Lambert** lives in the Detroit area and has been interested in the 1958 Baltimore Colts championship team since meeting Raymond Berry at a local church event as a child. He is a longtime member of the PFRA and fan of the Lions and Steelers.

John W. **Lesko** works for the New Jersey Department of Labor. He has written an article for *The Coffin Corner* on all the games in major pro football history that did not feature a touchdown.

Joe **Marren** is a professor and the chair of the communication department at SUNY–Buffalo State. Before entering academia, he was an award-winning newspaper reporter and editor for various publications in western New York. He is the author of numerous essays and articles on subjects ranging from sports to media theory.

John **Maxymuk** of Cherry Hill, New Jersey, is a reference librarian at Rutgers University. He has written 11 books on professional football and four on libraries and computers. His most recent book is a second edition of *Eagle Facts and Trivia,* and he is currently working on a second book on NFL coaches.

Rupert **Patrick** is a pro football historian and writer whose work has appeared in the PFRA's *Coffin Corner* and the *Wall Street Journal.* He lives in Greenville, South Carolina.

Nick **Ritzmann** is a lifelong football fan and has been a member of the PFRA since 2009. He resides in northern New Jersey.

Rick **Schabowski** is a retired machinist who teaches for the Wisconsin Regional Training Partnership. He is also president of the Wisconsin Old Time Ballplayers Association, president of the Ken Keltner Badger State Chapter of SABR, and a member of the Hoop Historians. He has contributed to a number of SABR book projects and to the PFRA book on the Packers.

Greg **Selber** is a professor of communication at the University of Texas–Rio Grande Valley and the author of books on high school football and college basketball. A 30-year veteran sports reporter, he was the 2011 Putt Powell Award winner as Texas state sportswriter of the year.

Rich **Shmelter** is a writer and researcher specializing in sports history, American crime history, and Hollywood's Golden Age (1920–59). He is the author of several books, including team encyclopedias on the Oakland/Los Angeles Raiders and USC Trojans football.

Randy **Snow** lives in Kalamazoo, Michigan, and has been a member of the PFRA since 2011. He has written more than 350 football-related articles for various newspapers and web sites. He also lectures on football history and runs his own website, the World of Football.

David **Standish** is a lawyer and life-long New York Giants fan, although he still has a soft spot in his heart for the old Houston Oilers. This is his first time writing for the PFRA. He lives in Bayonne, New Jersey.

Kenn **Tomasch** is a writer, editor and sports historian living in Phoenix. In 2017, he won the PFRA's Bob Carroll Memorial Writing Award.

John **Vorperian** is host and executive producer of *Beyond the Game*, a nationally syndicated sports cable television program. A member of the PFRA since 2000, he teaches sports law and sports history seminars at several colleges and law schools. He is also a lawyer and lives in White Plains, New York.

Joseph **Wancho** resides in Westlake, Ohio, and is a lifelong Cleveland Browns fan. He serves on the SABR Minor League Research Committee and was editor of SABR's *Pitching to the Pennant: The 1954 Cleveland Indians*.

Jay **Zahn** contributed biographies on Donny Anderson, Marv Fleming, and Ron Kostelnik to the PFRA book on the 1966 Green Bay Packers. He has also had articles published in the PFRA's *Coffin Corner*. A computer programmer and data analyst, he lives in Madison, Wisconsin.

Index